HOOVER INSTITUTION
BIBLIOGRAPHICAL SERIES XI

THE CHINESE COMMUNIST MOVEMENT 1937-1949

An Annotated Bibliography of Selected Materials in the Chinese Collection of the Hoover Institution on War, Revolution, and Peace

By

Chün-tu Hsüeh

THE HOOVER INSTITUTION
ON WAR, REVOLUTION, AND PEACE
STANFORD UNIVERSITY
1962

HOOVER INSTITUTION
BIBLIOGRAPHICAL SERIES XI

THE CHINESE COMMUNIST MOVEMENT 1937-1949

An Annotated Bibliography of Selected Materials in the Chinese Collection of the Hoover Institution on War, Revolution, and Peace

By

Chün-tu Hsüeh

THE HOOVER INSTITUTION
ON WAR, REVOLUTION, AND PEACE
STANFORD UNIVERSITY
1962

The views expressed herein are entirely those of the author; hence statements of interpretation do not necessarily reflect the views of the Hoover Institution.

© 1962 by the Board of Trustees of
the Leland Stanford Junior University

All rights reserved

Library of Congress Catalog Card Number: 62-20987
Printed in the United States of America

FOREWORD

Since 1926, the Hoover Institution has been engaged in making known to scholars and research institutions the scope and character of its collections. With the publication in 1960 of Dr. Chün-tu Hsüeh's The Chinese Communist Movement, 1921-1937, another volume was added to the growing list of the Hoover Institution's collection of surveys and bibliographies.

We now take pleasure in presenting a second volume by Dr. Hsüeh, which brings up to 1949 the survey of primary and secondary Chinese materials on the history of Chinese Communism available in the Hoover Institution. Subsequent compilations will carry this work forward into the post-1949 period.

Dr. Hsüeh, by virtue of his education in both China and the United States, his own research and publications in the field, and his familiarity with the holdings of the Hoover Institution, was well equipped for the preparation of this bibliography. The completed work should be of great value to scholars interested in China and in the holdings of the Hoover Institution.

We wish to thank the Provost's Special Committee on East Asian Studies of Stanford University for making funds available for Dr. Hsüeh to undertake the compilation of this bibliography and for the Committee's partial financial assistance in the publication of this work.

W. Glenn Campbell
Director

The Hoover Institution
August 1, 1962

PREFACE

This bibliography has been compiled along lines similar to those followed in its predecessor, <u>The Chinese Communist Movement, 1921-1937</u> (Stanford, Hoover Institution, 1960). It contains some 863 titles selected from the extensive holdings of books, pamphlets, periodicals, newspapers, and manuscripts in the East Asian Collection of the Hoover Institution. Chinese translations of works in other languages have been excluded, as have literary publications by Communists and Communist front organizations; all articles except those reprinted in pamphlet form have also been omitted.

The first volume listed materials dating from 1919 to the outbreak of the Sino-Japanese War in July 1937, so organized as to document various stages of the tumultuous history of the Chinese Communist Party: the embryonic period (1919-21), the founding of the Chinese Communist Party (CCP), Kuomintang and CCP relations (1923-27), the period of reorientation (1927-31), the Kiangsi Soviet (1931-34), the Long March (1934-35), and the early Yenan period (1935-37).

The present volume lists the holdings of the Hoover Institution that bear on the crucial twelve-year period after 1937. Its contents fall into three main sections: Part I lists general works, biographies, and items pertaining to Mao Tse-tung; Part II deals with the period of the Sino-Japanese War (1937-45); and Part III is concerned with the postwar years (1945-49). Within each Part, the main divisions (which are based on the sources available) are topical and are arranged in rough chronological order.

Within each division, entries are arranged alphabetically by author, or by title when the author is unknown (as is the usual case with periodicals and newspapers). Edited or compiled works of well-known authors are listed by author rather than by editor or compiler. Works by authors who have used various names are listed under the name appearing on the title page of the work in question. Although a single entry may bear on a number of topics, all entries have been listed only once; since the location of many entries is therefore necessarily arbitrary, the reader should consult related sections of the bibliography, as well as the Contents and the Index.

Each entry is preceded by a number. Immediately following it are: the name of the author, editor, or compiler, romanized and then in

Chinese characters; the romanized title followed by Chinese characters; the English translation of the title in parentheses; the place of publication, publisher, and date of publication; and the Hoover Library call number in parentheses. In the case of newspapers and periodicals, the issue or volume numbers supplied refer to the holdings available in the Hoover Institution for the period 1937-49. As a rule, no pagination is given for periodicals and newspapers, or for books where pagination is not continuous. The English translations of certain titles undoubtedly leave much to be desired; indeed, some titles were found to be virtually untranslatable. "Official" or "standard" translations have been used when known to the compiler.

The names of publishers are abbreviated throughout; their full names, romanized and in Chinese characters, are given in Appendix II. Chinese characters are provided in Appendix I for obscure places of publication. Chinese characters for titles of publications and for personal, geographical, and institutional names (whether romanized or in English translations) appearing in an annotation are given in Appendix I, rather than in the body of the annotation itself (as was done in the previous volume).

The romanization follows the Wade-Giles system, except for some well-known geographical and personal names (e. g. , Chu Teh and Ch'en Yi, instead of Chu Te and Ch'en I). Except for the apostrophe and umlaut, no diacritical marks are used; and in geographical names all diacritical marks are omitted. A few simplified Chinese characters appear in the titles of recent publications, but for the sake of convenience, they are written in the conventional form. Both "Peiping" and "Peking" are used as they appear in the Chinese text or according to usage at the time of publication.

This bibliography does not list titles annotated in the previous volume. A number of works listed in the previous volume (particularly those in the first two sections) also relate to the Chinese Communist movement of 1937-49.

The Addendum to this volume lists some rare periodicals dating from the early phases of the Chinese Communist movement acquired after the publication of the first volume. This compilation is the work of Mr. Eugene Wu, Curator of the East Asian Collection at the Hoover Institution. Mr. Wu also read the entire manuscript and made valuable comments and suggestions.

My thanks are due to Mrs. Isabel MacKenzie and Mrs. Joan Sterling for typing the manuscript; and to Mr. Dennis J. Doolin for his preparation of the Index. I wish also to express my thanks to the staff of the Hoover Institution, and especially to Mr. Karol Maichel, Curator of the East European Collection, who, in my absence, handled the final phases of preparing the manuscript for publication. My thanks are also due to Dr. W. Glenn Campbell, Director of the Hoover Institution, for making possible the publication of the volume.

The compilation of this bibliography, as with the previous volume, was made possible by funds provided by the Provost's Special Committee on East Asian Studies of Stanford University. Once again I wish to express my gratitude to Dean Albert H. Bowker (Chairman of the Committee), Professor Thomas C. Smith, Professor Robert C. North, and the other members of the Committee for their support of the project.

January 28, 1962

HSÜEH Chün-tu
Research Associate
Department of Political Science
Stanford University

CONTENTS

	Page
FOREWORD	iii
PREFACE	iv
ABBREVIATIONS	x

PART ONE: GENERAL WORKS

		Page
I.	GENERAL	3
II.	BIOGRAPHY	12
III.	MAO TSE-TUNG	16

PART TWO: THE WAR PERIOD, 1937-45

			Page
IV.	GENERAL		23
V.	THE PARTY		31
VI.	THE UNITED FRONT		44
	A.	GENERAL	44
	B.	CH'EN TU-HSIU	56
	C.	KMT-CCP RELATIONS	59
VII.	THE NEW FOURTH ARMY INCIDENT		65
VIII.	THE ARMY		70
	A.	GENERAL	70
	B.	WAR EFFORT	76
	C.	THE MILITIA	82
IX.	THE BORDER REGIONS		84
	A.	THE SHENSI-KANSU-NINGSIA BORDER REGION	85
		1. General	85
		2. Yenan	87
		3. Political Systems	91

		a.	The Assembly	91
		b.	Others	94

        4. Land and Social Reforms   96
        5. Production Drives   97
        6. Garrison Troops   103
        7. Education   107

    B. THE SHANSI-CHAHAR-HOPEH BORDER REGION   112
    C. THE SHANSI-HOPEH-SHANTUNG-HONAN BORDER REGION   116
    D. THE SHANTUNG BASE AREA   121

        1. General   122
        2. Chiaotung   125
        3. Other Areas   129

    E. THE KWANGTUNG BASE AREA   130
    F. OTHER REGIONS   132

PART THREE: THE POSTWAR PERIOD, 1945-49

X. GENERAL WORKS   139

    A. GENERAL   139
    B. NEWSPAPERS   142

XI. MANCHURIA   153

XII. THE PARTY   160

XIII. KUOMINTANG-COMMUNIST RELATIONS   166

    A. GENERAL   166
    B. THE POLITICAL CONSULTATIVE CONFERENCE   178
    C. THE MARSHALL MEDIATION   181

XIV. THE CIVIL WAR   187

XV. THE DEMOCRATIC AND LIBERAL GROUPS   195

    A. GENERAL SURVEY   195
    B. THE DEMOCRATIC LEAGUE   199
    C. THE DEMOCRATIC-SOCIALIST PARTY   204

	D.	THE YOUTH PARTY	206
	E.	OTHER GROUPS AND INDIVIDUALISTS	207
XVI.	STUDENT DEMONSTRATIONS		219
XVII.	THE NEW DEMOCRATIC YOUTH LEAGUE		221
XVIII.	LAND REFORM		226
XIX.	THE LABOR MOVEMENT		233
XX.	THE WOMEN'S MOVEMENT		238
XXI.	INDUSTRIAL AND TRADE POLICIES		239
XXII.	THE COMMUNIST RULE		242
XXIII.	THE YEAR OF TRIUMPH		249

APPENDIX

	I.	A List of Personal, Corporate, and Geographical Names Appearing in the Annotations	258
	II.	List of Publishers	268

ADDENDUM 273

INDEX 282

ABBREVIATIONS

CC	Central Committee
CCP	Chinese Communist Party
CEC	Central Executive Committee
CI	Communist International (Comintern)
CPSU	Communist Party of the Soviet Union
ECCI	Executive Committee of the Communist International
KMT	Kuomintang (The Nationalist Party of China)

PART ONE

GENERAL WORKS

I. GENERAL

General reference works, such as dictionaries, bibliographies, and indexes, have been listed in the previous volume (The Chinese Communist Movement, 1921-1937). The works listed below relate more to the whole period covered by this bibliography than to any one period covered in Part Two or Part Three.

1. Chiang Kai-shek (Chiang Chung-cheng 蔣中正). Su-O tsai Chung-kuo 蘇俄在中國 (Soviet Russia in China). Taipei, Chung-yang wen-wu, 1957. 444 pp. (2495/4431)

   A summing up of thirty years of Sino-Soviet relations. For an official English translation of this book, see Soviet Russia in China: A Summing Up at Seventy (New York: Farrar, Strauss, and Cudahy, 1957; 392 pp.).

2. Ch'ün-chung 羣眾 (alt. 群眾) (The Masses). Vol. I, No. 13; Vol. II, Nos. 11, 12, 14; Vol. III, Nos. 1-3, 6/7-11, 20-23, 25; Vol. IV, Nos. 1-6, 14, 18; Vol. V, Nos. 6, 7, 9/10, 11; Vol. VIII, Nos. 1/2-5, 8-18; Vol. IX, Nos. 13, 14; Vol. X, Nos. 1-24; Vol. XI, Nos. 1-12; Vol. XII, Nos. 1-12; Vol. XIII, Nos. 1-11/12; Vol. XIV, Nos. 1-8. Hankow, Chungking, and Shanghai. March 12, 1938 - February 23, 1947. (4292.01/1563)

   This leading CCP weekly began publication in Hankow on December 11, 1937. However, from issue Vol. II, No. 12 (December 25, 1938) it was published (at intervals ranging from ten days to three weeks) in Chungking; but it appeared regularly again in Shanghai from issue Vol. XI, No. 5 (June 3, 1946). Its contents fall into these categories: (1) CCP policy and resolutions; (2) the writings of CCP leaders; (3) analyses of current domestic and foreign affairs; (4) reports of the Sino-Japanese War and of Communist activities behind the enemy lines; (5) scholarly articles in the field of politics, economics, history, philosophy, and literature; and (6) documents on current affairs. When the New China Daily ceased publication in May 1939 after the

Japanese bombing of Chungking, the Ch'ün-chung also served as a newspaper (from Vol. II, No. 24/25) by publishing news dispatches until the New China Daily resumed publication on August 13 of the same year.

CCP statements, resolutions, and documents appear in the following issues: Vol. II, No. 12 (December 25, 1938; regarding the Sixth Congress of the CCP); Vol. III, Nos. 1 (May 21, 1939) and 8/9 (July 16, 1939); Vol. VIII, No. 9 (June 1, 1943; regarding the dissolution of the Comintern, followed by several articles on the subject in issue No. 10); Vol. X, Nos. 17 and 20 (September - November 1945); Vol. XIII, Nos. 2 (October 27, 1946) and 5 (November 18, 1946); and Vol. XIV, No. 6 (February 10, 1947).

Mao Tse-tung's writings, speeches, and interviews with reporters may be found in Vol. III, Nos. 3 (June 1939), 8/9 and 10 (July 23, 1939); Vol. X, Nos. 2 (February 10, 1945), 5/6 (April 5, 1945), and 16 (August 25, 1945; regarding an exchange of telegrams with the American Communist leaders); Vol. XI, Nos. 9/10 (June 30, 1946); Vol. XII, No. 12 (October 13, 1946); and Vol. XIV, No. 2 (January 13, 1947).

As to the writings, speeches, or interviews of other Communist leaders, the following may be mentioned:

Ch'en Chia-k'ang: A number of articles on Chinese philosophy appear in Vol. VIII, and again in Vols. XIII and XIV, those in the latter being concerned with domestic and foreign affairs. His article on the Democratic League in Vol. XIV, No. 3 (January 20, 1947) is of special interest.

Ch'en Po-ta: Vol. IV, No. 14 (May 20, 1940); Vol. X, No. 21/22 (November 25, 1945; a criticism of Yen Hsi-shan); Vol. X, No. 23 (December 15, 1945; entitled "Yüan Shih-k'ai the Traitor") and No. 24 (December 25, 1945; refuting the Ta Kung Pao's editorial of July 20, 1945. This issue has a cumulative subject index of the magazine for the year 1945).

Chou En-lai: Vol. III, No. 8/9; Vol. XII, Nos. 6-12 (August 31 - October 13, 1946); Vol. VIII, Nos. 6 (November 25, 1946) and 10 (December 22, 1946); Vol. XIV, Nos. 1 and 3 (January 7-20, 1947). Most of Chou's documents are related to the Marshall mediation.

Feng Chung-yün: Vol. XII, No. 10 (September 29, 1946; regarding the Manchurian activities of Lo Teng-hsien, then known as Ta-p'ing, who was the chief Communist leader there in 1931).

Hua Kang: Vol. VIII, Nos. 3 (February 1, 1943), 11 and 15; Vol. XI, Nos. 2, 5 and 6 (January 31 - June 10, 1946); Vol. XIII, Nos. 6 (November 25, 1946), 10 and 11/12; and Vol. XIV, Nos. 3 and 4/5.

K'ai Feng: Vol. III, No. 6/7.

Li Fu-ch'un: Vol. X, No. 5/6.

Li Wei-han: Vol. XIV, No. 3.

Lin Tsu-han: Vol. IX, No. 13 (July 15, 1944).

Liu Ning-i: Vol. XII, No. 6 (August 31, 1946) and frequently in Vols. XIII and XIV.

Liu Shao-ch'i: Vol. III, No. 8/9.

Lo Fu: Vol. III, No. 8/9 and Vol. V, No. 7 (October 5, 1940).

Lo Mai: Vol. X, No. 2 and Vol. XII, No. 1 (July 28, 1946).

Lu Ting-i: Vol. XIV, Nos. 3 and 4/5.

P'an Tzu-nien: frequently in the first four volumes (to May 1940) and again from Vol. XI, No. 9/10 (June 30, 1946). His article on "cultural work behind the enemy lines" (Vol. II, No. 14) is useful.

Po Ku: Vol. III, No. 8/9; and Vol. IV, No. 6 (February 29, 1940).

Madame Sun Yat-sen: Vol. XII, No. 1 (July 28, 1946; a statement on the current situation).

Teng Fa: Vol. III, No. 8/9.

Teng Hsiao-p'ing: Vol. III, No. 8/9.

Teng Ying-ch'ao (Madame Chou En-lai): Vol. XI, No. 8; Vol. XII, Nos. 7 and 12.

Tung Pi-wu: Vol. III, No. 10 (July 23, 1939); Vol. IX, No. 13 (July 15, 1944); and Vol. XII, No. 9 (September 22, 1946).

Wang Ming (Ch'en Shao-yü): Vol. III, No. 8/9 and Vol. IV, No. 5 (February 20, 1940).

Wu Yü-chang: Vol. III, No. 6/7.

The article by Ch'en Yi, dated June 21, 1939, in Vol. III, No. 22 (November 30, 1939) is an excellent summary of the activities of his forces for the year May 1938 to June 1939. Other writings and discussions on military affairs include:

Chu Teh: Vol. II, No. 14 (February 14, 1939); Vol. XII, No. 2 (August 3, 1946); and Vol. XIII, No. 8 (December 9, 1946; regarding Chu's birthday, with a chronological biography of him).

Lin Piao: Vol. XI, No. 8.

Liu Po-ch'eng: Vol. III, Nos. 6/7 (July 2, 1939); and Vol. VIII, No. 15 (September 16, 1943).

Lü Cheng-ts'ao: Vol. VIII, No. 15 and Vol. XIII, No. 10 (December 22, 1946).

Nieh Jung-chen: Vol. VIII, No. 17 (October 16, 1940).

P'eng Te-huai: Vol. III, No. 8/9; Vol. IV, No. 1 (January 10, 1940); Vol. V, No. 9/10 (October 30, 1940); and Vol. VIII, No. 13/14 (August 31, 1943).

T'an Cheng: Vol. IV, No. 5 (February 20, 1940).

Tso Ch'üan: Vol. IV, No. 1.

Yeh Chien-ying: Vol. III, Nos. 10 (July 23, 1939) and 11 (August 13, 1939; regarding the death of Huang Wen-chieh, former secretary of the Central Bureau of the CC of the CCP in Shanghai).

A frequent contributor on international affairs was [Chang] Han-fu: in the first four volumes and again from Vol. XI, No. 1 (January 15, 1946), after almost six years of silence. Another frequent contributor was Yü Huai (Vol. VIII, Nos. 17-18, October 16 - November 1, 1943), whose style is so similar to that of Ch'iao Mu that Yü Huai was probably another pseudonym of Ch'iao Kuan-hua. A number of articles criticizing the China policy of the United States appear in the postwar issues, which also include discussions of such current events as the Political Consultative Conference, the activities of the "democratic and liberal groups," war criminals, and the San Francisco Conference of the United Nations.

With respect to the Communist bases, see Vol. III, Nos. 1 (May 21, 1939), 2, and 21 (November 30, 1939) for information on the Shansi-Hopeh-Honan Border Region; see Vol. IX, No. 13 (July 15, 1944) for the political system and Vol. X, No. 10 (June 1, 1945) for the land policy of the Shansi-Chahar-Hopeh Border Region; Vol. IV, No. 1 (January 1940), Vol. V, No. 6 (September 25, 1940), and Vol. VIII, No. 8 (May 1, 1943) deal respectively with the political system, the general economic condition, and handicrafts in the Shensi-Kansu-Ningsia Border Region. A general description of elections in the "liberated areas" can be found in issue Vol. X, No. 17.

As to the wartime movement for party rectification, special sections were devoted to the discussion of Sinicized Marxism in Vol. VIII, Nos. 11 and 12 (July 16-31, 1943). Regarding the Communist Parties of other countries, a letter from the secretary-general of the Communist Party of the Philippines to the Philippine and Chinese people, dated January 28, 1939, appears in Vol. III, No. 3. A letter from the Japanese Communist leader Okano Susuma (Nosaka Sanzo) to the Japanese people is in Vol. VIII, No. 16 (September 30, 1943); his lengthy address at the CCP Seventh Congress in May 1945, and also a brief history of the Japanese Communist Party, are available in Vol. X, No. 15 (August 5, 1945). Vol. X, Nos. 16-18 (August 25 - October 1, 1945) include several articles and translations concerning the reorganization of the American Communist Party.

3.   Ch'ün-chung 群眾 . Vol. I, No. 1 - Vol. III, No. 42/43. Hong Kong, January 30, 1947 - October 20, 1949. (4292.01/1563.1)

This is a complete set (totaling 143 issues) of the Hong Kong edition of a leading CCP weekly published for South China and overseas readers. Its contents are not identical with the Shanghai edition of the magazine, although some of its articles are reprints from the Shanghai edition. The writings may be classified into several categories, such as current political events, peace negotiations, civil war, conditions in the "liberated areas," Manchuria, land law, student riots, the labor movement, activities of the "liberal and democratic groups," party documents, and editorials of the New China News Agency.

Among the frequent contributors are: Ch'iao Mu, Fang Fang, Lu Ting-i, Li Wei-han, Liu Ning-i, Chang Han-fu, Ch'en Po-ta, Kuo Mo-jo and P'eng Chen.

For important comments by the CCP or its leaders on foreign affairs, consult the following issues: Vol. I, Nos. 7, 19, and 29; Vol. II, No. 7; and Vol. III, Nos. 30-39. The resolutions of the CC of the CCP, July 10, 1948, on the Tito problem are found in Vol. II, No. 27. Documents relating to the New Democratic Youth League appear in Vol. III, Nos. 3, 17-21; and documents pertaining to the founding of the People's Republic of China are included in Vol. III, Nos. 40 and 41.

Mao Tse-tung's interviews, speeches, writings, and statements appear in the following issues: Vol. I, Nos. 19 and 49; Vol. II, No. 44; and Vol. III, No. 4. His "On People's Democratic Dictatorship" appears in Vol. III, No. 28. Two articles by Fang Fang discussing his military views are found in Vol. II, Nos. 3 and 29.

Other material of interest includes Li Li-san's two speeches at the All-China Labor Congress at Harbin in 1948 (Vol. II, Nos. 31 and 36), Liu Shao-ch'i's "On Nationalism and Internationalism" (Vol. II, No. 45), and Kao Kang's "Mongolia and the Party Policy Toward Nationalities" (Vol. II, No. 48).

The contents of the magazine generally reflect the important political developments of any given time, a fact which it is well to keep in mind.

4. Chung-kuo kung-ch'an tang chi ch'i yü kuo-chi chih kuan-hsi kang-yao 中國共產黨及其與國際之關係綱要 (A Compendium of the Relations Between the Chinese Communist Party and International Communism). n.p., n. pub., n.d. mimeo. [34] pages. (4292.2/5640.14)

This book covers important Party events from 1921 through 1950, but devotes little attention to the relations indicated by the title.

5. Hsüeh Mu-ch'iao 薛暮橋. Chung-kuo ko-ming chi-pen wen-t'i 中國革命基本問題 (The fundamental Problem

of the Chinese Revolution). Revised enlarged ed. Hong Kong, Nan-hai, 1948. 122 pp. (4292.1/4444)

This book consists of five chapters, dealing with various classes in, and developments of, the Chinese revolution. It was originally one of the Social Science Series--nine lectures of the Anti-Japanese Military and Political Academy in Yenan, published in 1938 under the title She-hui k'o-hsüeh chi-ch'u chiao-ch'eng. The revisions for the present edition were made while the author was in the "liberated areas," and without previous consultations with him. The additional materials are discussions of the country under the system of New Democracy.

6. Hu Ch'iu-yüan 胡秋原. Chung-kuo chih pei-chi 中國之悲劇 (The Chinese Tragedy). Hong Kong, Chung-kuo wen-t'i, 1950. 76 pp. (4292.08/4227)

This book, written by a well-known political commentator, attempts to explain the fall of China to Communism. The author was a "liberal Marxist" before the early 1930's, traveled to England and Russia in 1934, and had "completely abandoned Marxism" by the time he left the Soviet Union in the summer of 1936; but he did not take an open anti-Russian stand until 1945. In his opinion the cultural and philosophical vacuum in modern China, the KMT imitation of the CPSU (including the cult of Sun Yat-sen), and the one-party and one-leader doctrines paved the way for Chinese acceptance of Communism and the final victory of the CCP.

7. [Kuo-min cheng-fu.]. Nei-cheng pu. Tiao-ch'a chü 國民政府內政部調查局. Kung-ch'an tang ti chieh-p'ou 共產黨的解剖 (An Analysis of the Communist Party). [Taipei], same, 1951. 86 pp. (4292.1/6710)

Published by the Bureau of Investigation of the Ministry of the Interior of the National Government, this pamphlet examines not only the theory and practice of the CCP but also the Communist Party as a whole. It is divided into four chapters: (1) introduction; (2) the basic reasons for not understanding the nature of the Communist Party; (3) a key to the understanding of the Communist Party; and (4) the Communist Party's characteristics.

8. Li Shih-han 李石涵 . Ts'ung ch'i-ch'i tao pa-i-wu 從七七到八一五 (From July 7 to August 15). 3rd ed. Huachung, Hsin-hua, 1949. 129 pp. (2991/4413a)

   A chronology of important political events in China from the outbreak of the Sino-Japanese War in 1937 to the Japanese surrender in 1945, compiled from the Chinese Communist viewpoint. It includes a number of wartime financial statistical tables of the National Government as well as a list of the important KMT collaborators with the Japanese.

9. Liao Kai-lung 廖蓋隆 . Hsin Chung-kuo shih tsen-yang tan-sheng ti 新中國是怎樣誕生的 (How the New China Was Born). 2nd ed. revised and enlarged. Shanghai, Hai-yen, 1951. 271 pp. (2992.7/0247.2)

   This book had eight printings within a year after its first publication in 1950. It gives a clear and concise account of the Communist success from the founding of the CCP to the establishment of the People's Republic of China. A chapter on the post-1949 era through July 1951 is added at the end of the book. The writings are based on the Communist sources that are generally known. A short version of this book was published in 1952 by the People's Publishing House of Peking (Jen-min ch'u-pan she) as a text for high school students, under the title <u>Chung-kuo jen-min chieh-fang chan-cheng ho hsin Chung-kuo wu-nien chien-shih</u>.

10. Sun Pao-i 孫寶毅 . Chung-kung ho-i hsing-ch'i yü pi-k'ua 中共何以興起與必垮 (Reasons for the Chinese Communists' Rise and Their Inevitable Fall). Hong Kong, Tzu-yu, 1952. 71 pp. (4292.2/1930)

    This book opens with discussions of the Western impact on China in the nineteenth century. According to the author, who is a leading member of the Democratic Socialist Party, the victory of the Communists was due to the KMT's failure to fulfill its "historical mission." He asserts that because the CCP "does not meet the fundamental demands of historical development" it will therefore eventually fail.

11. T'ang Tsung 唐縱. Fei-tang ti tou-cheng ts'e-lüeh 匪黨的鬥爭策略 (The Strategy of the Bandit Party). Taipei, Yang-ming, 1951. 28 pp. (4292.2/0628)

   Written by a leading KMT member, this pamphlet is divided into six chapters analyzing the CCP strategy for seizing power in terms of theories, principles, and practices.

12. Teng Ch'u-min 鄧初民. Chung-kuo cheng-chih wen-t'i chiang-hua 中國政治問題講話 (Chinese Political Problems). 2nd ed. Hong Kong, Wen-hua, 1950. 198 pp. (4292.12/1237a)

   A presentation of Chinese politics, economics, culture, and revolution from the viewpoint of New Democracy. There is an appendix of documents relating to the New Political Consultative Conference. (The 1949 edition, however, does not include the appendix.)

13. Ts'ui Kao-chün 崔高俊. Chung-kuo hung-huo ssu-shih nien 中國紅禍四十年 (Forty Years' Red Catastrophe in China). Taipei, Cheng-kung, 1959. 230 pp. (4292.2/2102)

   A critical account of CCP history (1918-58), written by a young instructor of the Cadre School for Political Workers and published by the same school in Taiwan.

14. Yeh Hu-sheng 葉蠖生. Jen-min ti sheng-li 人民的勝利 (People's Victory). Peking, Kung-jen, 1956. 116 pp. (2991.2/4952)

   A brief account of the establishment of Communist bases during the Sino-Japanese War, with eulogies to the Communist record against Japan.

15. Yü Chen-pang 余振邦. Kung-ch'an tang p'ou-hsi 共產黨剖析 (An Analysis of the Chinese Communist Party). Taipei, Hua-ch'iang, 1955. 36 pp. (4292.1/8955)

A critical analysis of CCP theory and strategy, based on secondary sources.

II. BIOGRAPHY

None of the works included in this section are full-length biographies. Although marred by inaccurate details, the following biographical sketches nevertheless furnish useful general information on the persons concerned.

16. Chang Ta-chün 張大軍 (ed.). Chung-kung jen-ming tien 中共人名典 (Who's Who in Communist China). Hong Kong, Tzu-yu, 1956. 224 pp. (4292.31/1343)

   A biographical dictionary of Communist China, giving brief biographical data on a number of persons.

17. Chao Kuan-i 趙貫一 and Wei Tan-po 韋丹柏. Chung-kung jen-wu su-miao 中共人物素描 (Biographical Sketches of Chinese Communists). Kowloon, Tzu-yu, 1951. 106 pp. (4292.31/4871)

   Twenty-two biographical sketches of Communist leaders, written in bitter and vulgar language by two anti-Communist writers, who seem to have firsthand knowledge of some of the leaders they describe.

18. Chin-Ch'a-Chi pien-ch'ü chi Chang-shih ko-chieh chui-tao "ssu-pa" yü-nan lieh-shih ch'ou-wei-hui 晉察冀邊區暨張市各界追悼"四八"遇難烈士籌委會 (ed.). Chui-tao "ssu-pa" yü-nan lieh-shih chi-nien ts'e 追悼"四八"遇難烈士紀念冊 (A Special Publication in Commemoration of the Victims Who Died in the "April 8 Accident"). [Kalgan], [same] 1946. 292 pp. (4292.31/3968)

   On April 8, 1946, an airplane carrying Ch'in Pang-hsien, Yeh T'ing (with his wife and daughter), Wang Jo-fei, Teng fa, and their entourage crashed enroute from Chungking to Yenan. Edited by the Preparatory Committee of Kalgan and the Shansi-Chahar-Hopeh Border Region in commemoration of the victims who died in the "April 8 Accident," this publication includes a brief account of the accident, biographical sketches of the dead, journalists' reports of commemoration meetings held in various cities of China, and other related records.

19. Chin-Chi-Lu-Yü pien-ch'ü ko-chieh chui-tao ta-hui ch'ou-wei-hui 晉冀魯豫邊區各界追悼大會籌委會 (ed.). "Ssu-pa" hsün-kuo chu lieh-shih chi-nien ts'e "四八"殉國烈士紀念冊 (A Special Publication in Commemoration of the Victims Who Died for the Country in the "April 8 Accident"). n.p., same, 1946. 159 pp. (4292.31/3968.12)

Edited and published by the Preparatory Committee of the Commemoration Meeting of the Shansi-Hopeh-Shantung-Honan Border Region, this volume contains more memorial articles by Communist leaders than any other volume on the same subject listed in this section.

20. Chou-mo pao-she 週末報社 (comp.). Hsin Chung-kuo jen-wu chih 新中國人物誌 (Biographical Dictionary of New China). Hong Kong, Chou-mo pao-she, 1950. 268 pp. (4292.31/3543.1)

Biographical sketches of 208 Communist and non-Communist leaders active in the first year of the new Communist regime. Sources of information are well-known Chinese newspapers and journals, as well as the compiler's own knowledge.

21. Chung-kung jen-wu 中共人物 (Chinese Communist Leaders). Shanghai, She-hui, 1949. 60 pp. (4292.31/5482)

Forty-two biographical sketches written in simple language, and not of a high standard.

22. Chung-kuo kung-ch'an tang. Hu-nan sheng wei-yüan hui. Hsüan-ch'uan pu 中國共產黨湖南省委員會宣傳部 (ed.).

Hu-nan ko-ming lieh-shih chuan 湖南革命烈士傳 (Biographies of Hunanese Revolutionary Martyrs). Changsha, T'ung-su, 1952. 117 pp. (4292.31/5640)

    Edited by the Propaganda Department of the Hunan Provincial Committee of the CCP in commemoration of the 30th anniversary of the founding of the party, this book consists of 27 biographical sketches of Hunanese Communists, many of them not very well known. Some of the sketches are very brief.

23. Chung [kuo] kung-[ch'an tang] tai-piao t'uan 中國共產黨代表團 (ed.). "Ssu-pa" pei-nan lieh-shih chi-nien ts'e "四八"被難烈士紀念冊 (A Special Publication in Commemoration of the "April 8 Accident" Victims). [Chungking], same, 1946. 624 pp. (4292.31/3968.1)

    Edited and published by the CCP delegation to Chungking, the contents of this book are essentially the same as in other volumes of the same nature listed in this section. This publication, however, contains many more memorial articles, not only by Communist but non-Communist leaders as well.

24. Hai-yün 海雲 (comp.). Jen-min chiang-ling ch'ün-hsiang 人民將領群像 (Portraits of Communist Generals). Macao, Ch'un-ch'iu, 1947. 74 pp. (4292.31/3513)

    Favorable biographical sketches of eleven Communist military leaders, with the original authors identified.

25. Hsin-hua shih-shih ts'ung-k'an she 新華時事叢刊社 (ed.). Chung-kuo jen-min cheng-chih hsieh-shang hui-i ti-i chieh ch'üan-ti hui-i tai-piao fang-wen chi 中國人民政治協商會議第一屆全體會議代表訪問記 (Interviews with Delegates to the First Plenum of the Chinese People's Political Consultative Conference). Shanghai, Hsin-hua, 1950. 170 pp. (4292.31/0465)

    Most of the 62 persons interviewed were non-Communist delegates to the People's Political Consultative Conference held in Peiping in September 1949. The articles are selected from major newspapers of the new regime.

26. Hua Ying-shen 華應申 (ed.). Chung-kuo kung-ch'an tang lieh-shih chuan 中國共產黨烈士傳 (Biographies of Chinese Communist Martyrs). Peking, Ch'ing-nien, 1951. 260 pp. (4292.3/4505a)

   A collection of biographical sketches of 23 Communists, with articles written in commemoration of them. Those particularly related to the period covered by this bibliography are Jen Pi-shih, Kuan Hsiang-ying, Tso Ch'üan, Lo Ping-hui, Wang Jo-fei, Ch'in Pang-hsien, Yeh T'ing, Teng Fa, Yang Ching-yü, and Li Chao-lin. Among the writers of the articles are K'ang Sheng, Ch'en Yi, Hsiao San, Jao Sou-shih, Ts'ai Ch'ang, Liao Ch'eng-chih, and Feng Chung-yün.

27. Kan Yu-lan 甘友蘭. Mao Tse-tung chi-ch'i chi-t'uan 毛澤東及其集團 (Mao Tse-tung and His Clique). Kowloon, Tzu-yu, 1954. 250 pp. (4292.31/4744)

   An anti-Communist publication, written in a lucid style, which presents a plausible story of Mao, his close associates, and the relations in the power struggle within the Party. It is an interesting account, but the accuracy of the facts, and thus of the interpretation, is difficult to verify.

28. Sheng-li ch'u-pan she wen-hua tzu-liao shih 勝利出版社文化資料室 (comp.). Chung-kung nei-mu 中共內幕 (Inside the Communist Party of China). Shanghai, same, 1946. 24 pp. (4292.31/7222)

   Useful biographical sketches of 92 Communist leaders.

III. MAO TSE-TUNG

Aside from Mao's <u>Selected Works</u>, this section is comprised chiefly of critiques of Mao and his works. Many of the articles and speeches contained in the <u>Selected Works</u> have been published or reprinted in pamphlet form at various times; more than 80 items are available in the Hoover Library, and "On New Democracy" alone exists in at least 14 editions. None of these pamphlets are listed here because they can be found in the <u>Selected Works</u>.

29. Chang Ju-hsin 張如心 . Mao Tse-tung lun 毛澤東論 (On Mao Tse-tung). Hong Kong, Hsin min-chu, 1946. 112 pp. (4736.26/2135.75)

    This is not a systematic study, but a fragmentary examination of Mao's ideas on life, on "scientific method," on "style of work," and the "New Democracy." Some of the writings were originally published in the <u>Pei-fang wen-hua</u> monthly from speeches Mao delivered at the United North China University in Kalgan. An appendix contains excerpts of writings by Liu Shao-ch'i, Chu Teh, and other Communist leaders on various aspects of Mao's thought.

30. _____. Mao Tse-tung ti ssu-hsiang chi tso-feng 毛澤東的思想及作風 (Mao Tse-tung's Thought and Style of Work). Chiamussu, Tung-pei shu-tien, 1946. 106 pp. (4292.3/2135.25)

    The contents of this book are identical with those of the one listed above except that the appendix is omitted and a report on the youth-study problems is added. Various editions of these two books have been published under different titles.

31. Chang Ti-fei 張滌非 . Yü Mao Tse-tung lun Chung-kuo ko-ming 與毛澤東論中國革命 (Discussion with Mao Tse-tung on Chinese Revolution). Chuchiang, Sheng-li, 1941. 68 pp. (4292.121/1331)

    A critical review of "On New Democracy." The author appears to have known Mao Tse-tung in the 1920's. The book contains an advertisement for nine books published by the same company relating to the Chinese Communist movement, books that are rarely seen nowadays.

32. Ch'en Po-ta 陳伯達 and others. "Chung-kuo chih ming-yun" p'i-p'an 中國之命運批判 (A Critique of "China's Destiny"). n.p., Chieh-fang, [1943]. 172 pp. (2985/4451.3)

   In addition to three editorials from the Liberation Daily, this volume includes seven articles on Chiang Kai-shek's China's Destiny by Ch'en Po-ta, Fan Wen-lan, and others. These "book reviews" represent probably the first of three severe personal attacks on Chiang Kai-shek made by the Communists from 1937 to 1946. (The other two were Mao Tse-tung's telegram, issued in the name of Chu Teh, refusing to accept Chiang Kai-shek's order in regard to the Japanese surrender, and the editorial in the Liberation Daily of April 6, 1946, entitled "In Refutation of Chiang Kai-shek.") With one exception, all the editorials and articles were written in August 1943. Of various editions of this book, this is probably the best one.

33. Chung-hsin ch'u-pan she 中心出版社 (ed.). Mao Tse-tung t'an-hua ti chien-t'ao 毛澤東談話的檢討 (An Examination of Mao Tse-tung's Talk). [Kwangtung], same, n.d. 34 pp. (4292.121/5322)

   A refutation of Mao Tse-tung's statements in a talk with a reporter of the Central News Agency, September 11, 1939. In that interview Mao discussed democracy, KMT-CCP relations, border governments, and other problems. This pamphlet appears to be a reprint, but often in China, articles are reproduced without the original authors' names.

34. Jen Cho-hsüan 任卓宣. Mao Tse-tung p'i-p'an 毛澤東批判 (A Critique of Mao Tse-tung). n.p., Ta-kung, 1942. 100 pp. (4292.3/2135.27)

   An ex-Communist KMT theorist's criticism of Mao Tse-tung's "On New Democracy" and Sinicized Marxism.

35. Li Mien 李勉. Jen-min min-chu chuan-cheng ti li-lun yü shih-chien 人民民主專政的理論與實踐 (The Theory and Practice of the People's Democratic Dictatorship). 2nd ed. Kowloon, T'uan-chieh, 1949. 129 pp. (4292.121/4421)

Reprints of newspaper and periodical articles selected by a study group for a study of Mao Tse-tung's "On the People's Democratic Dictatorship." An appendix contains documents on the People's Political Consultative Conference.

36. Mao Tse-tung 毛澤東. Mao Tse-tung hsüan-chi 毛澤東選集 (Selected Works of Mao Tse-tung). Vols. II-IV. Peking, Jen-min ch'u-pan, 1952-60. 299-805, 809-1144, and 1123 (sic.)-1520 pp. (4292.11/2135c)

These three volumes cover the period from 1937 to 1949: Vols. II (March 1952) and III (February 1953) cover the period of the Sino-Japanese War, 1937-45; Vol. IV (September 1960) covers the period from the Japanese surrender in 1945 to the Communist victory in 1949.

For an English translation of Vol. II, which includes "On New Democracy" and discussions of the military strategy in the war against Japan and the political problems in KMT-CCP relations, see Mao Tse-tung, Selected Works, Vols. II-III (New York: International Publishers, 1954).

For an English translation of Vol. III, which contains Mao's writings from 1941-45, including "On Coalition Government," see Mao Tse-tung, Selected Works, Vol. IV (New York: International Publishers, 1956). Because Volume II had been translated into two volumes in English by the International Publishers, Volume III in Chinese became Vol. IV in English. However, Vol. IV in Chinese has now been published as Vol. IV of Selected Works in English by the Foreign Languages Press, Peking, in 1961. It has created some confusion about the contents of the English volumes.

The first three volumes of Mao's Selected Works in Chinese were published within a year of each other. Volume IV was released in 1960, more than seven and a half years after Volume III; many of the 72 documents collected in it had never been published before, and some had been issued before but not under Mao's name.

37. Mao Tse-tung ssu-hsiang shih Chung-kuo jen-min ta ko-ming sheng-li ti ch'i-chih 毛澤東思想是中國人民大革命勝利的旗幟 (Mao Tse-tung's Thought Is a Key to the Victory of the Great Chinese People's Revolution). Peking, Chung-kuo

ch'ing-nien, 1960. 128 pp. (4292.11/2135.35)

Reprints of six articles commenting on Volume IV of Mao Tse-tung's Selected Works, including Lin Piao's article in the Red Flag (Hung-ch'i, issue No. 19 of 1960), an editorial from the same issue of that magazine, and an editorial from the Peking People's Daily for September 30, 1960. Lin's article, which praises Mao's military strategy, is of particular significance.

38. Mao Tse-tung ti chün-shih lu-hsien chi chung-kung ti wu ta cheng-ts'e 毛澤東的軍事路綫及中共的五大政策 (Mao Tse-tung's Military Line and the Five Policies of the Chinese Communist Party). n.p., n. pub., n.d. 16 pp. (4292.7/2352)

A hostile analysis of Mao's military strategy and a sketchy narrative of the so-called five policies of the CCP: party expansion, land reform, destruction of family ethics, development of the militia, and economic and social control. This was apparently published between 1945 and 1949.

39. Ta-chung jih-pao she 大眾日報社 (ed.). K'ang-chan wu chou-nien t'e-chi 抗戰五週年特輯 (A Special Publication in Commemoration of the Fifth Anniversary of the Outbreak of the Sino-Japanese War). n.p., same, 1942. 144 pp. (2991.03/4664)

Statements and articles by Chiang Kai-shek, Lin Po-ch'ü, the Liberation Daily, and others in commemoration of the fifth anniversary of the beginning of the Sino-Japanese War.

40. Wang Ssu-ch'eng 王思誠. Mao Tse-tung yü hung-huo 毛澤東與紅禍 (Mao Tse-tung and the Red Catastrophe). Taipei, Chung-kuo kuo-min tang ti-liu tsu, 1959. 586 pp. (4292.3/2135.191)

Published by the Sixth Section of the Central Committee of the Kuomintang, this study provides a chronological account of the Chinese Communist movement from the beginning through September 1959, with its focus on the personality and activities of Mao Tse-tung. The first five chapters of the book are a biography of Mao Tse-tung to 1922, based on such general and well-known sources as the writings of Edgar Snow. Chapters VI-IX cover the years 1922 to 1937 and Chapters X and XI the years 1937 to 1949. The last three chapters deal with the post-1949 era. The materials have been well organized by the author; with a few exceptions, however, no sources are given.

41. Yeh Ch'ing 葉青 (pseud. of Jen Cho-hsüan 任卓宣). Po Mao Tse-tung ti "Lun jen-min min-chu chuan-cheng" 駁毛澤東的"論人民民主專政" (In Refutation of Mao Tse-tung's "On People's Democratic Dictatorship"). Taipei, Chung-yang wen-wu, 1952. 58 pp. (4292.11/2123.081)

   A critical and fragmentary review written by an ex-Communist KMT theorist in September 1949.

42. Yin Keng-nan 尹耕南. Lun Chung-kuo cheng-chih yü Chung-kuo wen-hua ti tung-hsiang 論中國政治與中國文化的動向 (The Development of Chinese Politics and Civilization). Chungking, Kuo-min, 1943. 86 pp. (4292.12/1554)

   A critique of Mao Tse-tung's "On New Democracy" in terms of the character of Chinese politics and civilization.

PART TWO

THE WAR PERIOD, 1937-45

IV. GENERAL

The works listed below are not necessarily of a general nature, but they cannot be classified under any one section in Part Two, for they cover the years 1937-45 and are not confined to one particular area. For example, surveys of affairs in the border regions, and discussions of political, economic, cultural, and educational policies during the war are listed under this section.

43. Chieh-fang 解放 (The Liberation). Nos. 3-5, 9, 11-23, 28-60/61, 63/64, 66-68, 70-72, 74-82, 85-98/99, 101, 102, 105, 106/107, 127, 128, 130, 131/132, and 133. Yenan, 1937 - 1941. Partly microfilm. (4292.01/2204)

   An official organ of the CCP, carrying at first writings in the following four categories: comments on current affairs, articles, reports, and literature. Later, literary contributions were kept to a minimum. The contents of the available issues of this weekly fall into these main areas: party documents, writings and speeches of Communist leaders, comments on current national and international affairs, conditions in the Border Regions, the Sino-Japanese War, the United Front, the organization of the masses, and news on the Soviet Union and international communism.

   Party documents and statements are available in Nos. 19, 28, 31 (February 25, 1938; containing the decision to expel Chang Kuo-t'ao from the Party); No. 43/44 (special issue in commemoration of the 17th anniversary of the founding of the Party); and No. 57 (November 25, 1938; a special issue for the Enlarged Plenum of the CC of the CCP).

   Listed here are writings, speeches, and statements by Communist leaders that may be found in various issues:

   Ch'en Po-ta: Nos. 40, 46, 50, 55, 58, 70, 85, 87/88, 89, and 102

   Ch'en Shao-yü (Wang Ming): Nos. 30, 36, 70, 75/76, 82, 89, 91/92, 93, 98/99, and 100

Ch'en Yün: No. 72

Chou En-lai: Nos. 36, 48, 55, 81, and 133

Chu Teh: Nos. 29, 43/44, 53, 58, 75/76, 96, and 131/132

Feng Wen-pin: Nos. 67 and 106/107

Ho Lung: No. 79

Hsiao K'o: No. 51

Jen Pi-shih: No. 29

K'ai Feng: Nos. 4, 50, 56, and 133

K'ang Sheng: Nos. 29, 30, and 98/99

Kao Kang: No. 131/132

Li Fu-ch'un: Nos. 17, 19, 85, 89, and 106/107

Liao Ch'eng-chih: No. 18

Lin Piao: No. 43/44

Lin Po-ch'ü: Nos. 5, 49, 55, and 96

Liu Shao-ch'i: Nos. 43/44, 75/76, 77, and 81

Lo Fu: Nos. 3, 17, 22, 29, 37, 39, and 90

Lo Jui-ch'ing: Nos. 30, 34, 35, 42, 46-48, and 75/76

Lo Mai: Nos. 54, 79, 86, 105, and 106/107

Mao Tse-tung: Nos. 4, 18, 23, 32, 33, 40, 43/44, 45, 47, 57, 70, 71, 75/76, 81, 85, 86, 96, and 98/99

P'eng Chen: Nos. 55 and 96

P'eng Te-huai: No. 87/88

Po Ku: Nos. 30, 36, 45, 56, and 75/76

Teng Fa: Nos. 75/76, 102, 105, and 127

Teng Hsiao-p'ing: No. 72

Wang Chia-hsiang: Nos. 75/76 and 86

Wang Jo-fei: No. 35

Wang Shou-tao: Nos. 17 and 96

Wu Yü-chang: Nos. 52 and 97

Some of the issues are devoted to a particular subject. Among these are No. 66, a special issue on the women's movement; No. 68, on the First Assembly of the Shensi-Kansu-Ningsia Border Region; No. 78, on international communism; No. 87/88, on a Communist conference in the Shansi-Chahar-Hopeh Border Region; No. 95, on a Communist conference in the Shensi-Kansu-Ningsia Border Region; and No. 100, on the Association for Promoting Constitutional Government, Yenan. Other issues contain news about other publications: No. 30 contains an article introducing the publication of the New China Daily in Hankow, and No. 98/99 advertises a long list of books published by the China Publishing House (Chung-kuo ch'u-pan she) of Hong Kong, an authorized publishing house for the CCP.

44. Chieh-fang jih-pao 解放日報 (Liberation Daily). Yenan, May 16, 1941 - February 1947. (almost complete). (newspaper)

A rare set of editions of the most important CCP newspaper published in Yenan. It was first published on May 16, 1941, and ceased publication on March 27, 1947. The last few issues (not available) were published at Wayaopao after Yenan had been captured by KMT forces on March 19, 1947. See also item no. 433.

45. _____. (ed.). Chiang Chieh-shih ti no-yen yü tzu-pai 蔣介石的諾言與自白 (Chiang Kai-shek's Promises and Admissions). n.p., Ta-chung shu-tien, 1945. 199 pp. (2985/2064)

The first two sections of this book, edited by the Liberation Daily, are quotations of Chiang Kai-shek's statements and self-criticisms dating from the 1920's, compiled for the purpose of showing that he had not fulfilled his political promises and commitments. The third part is a chronology of important political events in China from September 18, 1931, to July 7, 1937. The last section is a record of the alleged KMT attempts at compromise with the Japanese government since the outbreak of the Sino-Japanese War.

46. Chiu-i pa i-lai 九一八以來 (Since September 18, 1931). n.p., n. pub., 1944. 121 pp. (2988/2064c)

    A chronology of important political events in China from the Japanese invasion of Manchuria on September 18, 1931, to the autumn of 1943, compiled from articles and reports in the Chinese Communist press.

47. Chün-ta tsung-hsiao cheng-chih pu 軍大總校政治部 (ed.). Chung-kuo chin-tai cheng-chih chien-shih 中國近代政治簡史 (A Brief Political History of Modern China). Huachung, Hsin-hua, 1949. 264 pp. (2970/3424)

    Edited by the Political Department of the Anti-Japanese Military and Political Academy, this is a Communist view of Chinese political history from the Opium War to 1946; more than one-third of the book deals with the 1937-46 period.

48. Chung-kuo chieh-fang ch'ü jen-min tai-piao hui-i ch'ou-pei wei-yüan hui mi-shu ch'u 中國解放區人民代表會議籌備委員會秘書處 (ed.). Chen-chih kang-ling ts'an-k'ao tzu-liao 政治綱領參考資料 (Source Book for Political Programs). n.p., same, 1945. [112] pp. (4737/5620)

    Edited and published by the Secretariat of the Preparatory Committee of the People's Congress in the Liberated Areas, this book is divided into two parts. Part I contains selected political programs of the KMT, the Democratic League, and the political parties of several European countries. Part II consists of the political programs of various Communist wartime "border regions" and "liberated areas."

49. Chung-kuo kung-ch'an tang tui chung-hua min-tsu ti kung-hsien 中國共產黨對中華民族的貢獻 (Contributions of the Chinese Communist Party to China). Shantung, Hsin-hua, [1944?]. 109 pp. microfilm. (2991/5640)

   A general survey of the Communist areas and bases other than the Shensi-Kansu-Ningsia Border Region.

50. Chung-kuo ti-hou k'ang-Jih min-chu ken-chü ti kai-k'uang 中國敵後抗日民主根據地的概況 (General Conditions of the Anti-Japanese and Democratic Bases Behind the Enemy Lines in China). [Yenan, Hsin-hua?], 1944. 59 pp. (4292.24/5602)

   A CCP companion volume to an atlas (not available) of the Communist bases behind the Japanese lines during World War II. It is a summary report of the political, economic, and especially, military affairs of the fourteen bases (excluding the Shensi-Kansu-Ningsia Border Region): four in North China, eight in Central China, and two in South China. See also item no. 52.

51. Fan-kung 反攻 (Counterattack). Vol. I, No. 2; Vol. XIII, Nos. 1/2-3; Vol. XIV, Nos. 2/3; and Vol. XVII, No. 1. Wuchang and Chungking, February 16, 1938 - January 15, 1945. (2991.2/7414)

   This is a semi-monthly publication with articles on literature, current affairs, Manchuria, youth problems, etc. An article by Teng Ying-ch'ao (Mme. Chou En-lai) addressed to her fellow countrymen from Manchuria can be found in Vol. I, No. 2.

52. Hsin ch'ang-ch'eng she 新長城社 (ed.). Ti-hou k'ang-Jih min-chu ken-chü ti chieh-shao 敵後抗日民主根據地介紹 (Introduction to the Anti-Japanese Democratic Bases Behind the Japanese Lines). Fuyu, Chieh-fang, n.d. 112 pp. (4292.24/0743)

   Most of this book is identical with the Chung-kuo ti-hou k'ang-Jih min-chu ken-chü ti kai-k'uang (see item no. 50) but with more descriptive detail, especially of the military campaigns. The New China News Agency is given as the source for the book.

53. Hsin-hua jih-pao 新華日報 (New China Daily). Hankow, March - May 1938 (incomplete); and Chungking, June - December 1938; September, November - December 1939; February, March - June, and August 1940; and March 1941 - February 1947 (almost complete). (newspaper)

This was the most important CCP newspaper published in the KMT area.

54. Jen-min ch'u-pan she 人民出版社. K'ang Jih chan-chen shih-ch'i chieh-fang ch'ü kai-k'uang 抗日戰爭時期解放區概況 (Liberation Areas During the Sino-Japanese War). Peking, same, 1953. 132 pp. (4292.24/0450.1)

According to the publisher's note, this is a reprint of the Chung-kuo ti-hou k'ang-Jih min-chu ken-chü ti kai-k'uang originally published by the Hsin-hua shu-tien, Yenan, October 1944 (see item no. 50), with an additional chapter on the Shensi-Kansu-Ningsia Border Region (to 1945) and a revision of the introduction. The present volume contains a number of maps of the areas described in the book.

55. Li I-shan 李一刪. Chung-kung ko-chü hsia chih cheng-chih 中共割據下之政治 (Politics Under Communist Control). Chungking, Kuang-ming, 1943. 96 pp. (4292.24/4417)

A critical account of the origin of the border regions and their government, finance, land reforms, and social conditions.

56. Min-chu cheng-ch'üan 民主政權 (Democratic Regime). n.p., n. pub., 1948. 150 pp. microfilm. (4292.24/2014)

A useful reference book on the political systems of various Communist regions, divided into three sections: a general survey, an assessment of political experience, and the legal system.

57. Ning-sheng 寧生. Lun so-wei chieh-fang ch'ü cheng-ch'üan wen-t'i 論所謂解放區政權問題 (The So-Called Political

Regime of the Liberated Areas). n.p., Cheng-lun, 1946. 104 pp. (4292.24/3221)

A survey of the history of the Communist regions, with lengthy quotations from the Ho-p'ing jih-pao, Shih-chieh jih-pao, the Central News Agency, the New China Daily, and from other journals.

58. Shih-shih wen-t'i yen-chiu hui 時事問題研究會 (ed.). K'ang-chan chung ti Chung-kuo cheng-chih 抗戰中的中國政治 (Chinese Politics During the War of Resistance). Yenan, Chieh-fang, 1940. 553 pp. (2991/1365)

Edited by the Association for the Study of Current Affairs, Yenan, this is a compilation of materials selected from current newspapers and periodicals, and from the writings of Mao Tse-tung and less well-known figures. Included are Communist materials critical of the KMT and the National Government. The book consists of six parts: the first three deal with the organization of the National Government, the People's Political Council, and the "democratic movement" during the Sino-Japanese War; the last three are devoted to mass movements, the Shensi-Kansu-Ningsia Border Region and other Communist bases in North China, and to declarations, resolutions, or programs of various parties and political organizations. Each part is divided into several chapters arranged according to topics. In each selection, complete sources are given.

59. _____ (ed.). K'ang-chan chung ti Chung-kuo chiao-yü yü wen-hua 抗戰中的中國教育與文化 (Chinese Education and Culture During the War of Resistance). n.p., K'ang-chan shu-tien, 1940. 413 pp. (4911/6756)

Edited by the Association for the Study of Current Affairs, Yenan, this is a compilation of writings from current newspapers and periodicals, almost two-thirds of which are on the subject of education. Of the ten chapters on education, there is one on education in Manchuria, one on the Shensi-Kansu-Ningsia Border Region and the other Communist regions in North China; the rest of the ten deal with education in the National Government's areas. One chapter in the second part of the book contains articles on educational and cultural organizations and publications in the Communist regions.

60. _____. K'ang-chan chung ti Chung-kuo ching-chi 抗戰中的中國經濟 (Chinese Economics During the War of Resistance). n.p., K'ang-chan shu-tien, 1940. 656 pp. (4355/6576)

   A compilation of writings selected from current newspapers, periodicals, and books on the wartime economic situation in China as well as on the peasantry, industry, communication, foreign trade, finance, the cost of living, and the general standard of living. The last of the eight sections in the book is devoted to economic conditions in Shensi-Kansu-Ningsia, Shansi-Chahar-Hopeh, Shansi, Shantung, and other Communist-controlled regions.

61. Sun Wei-min 孫蔚民 and Cheng Wei 鄭煒. Min-chu chien-she chiang-hua 民主建設講話 (Talks on Democratic Reconstruction). n.p., n. pub., 1946. 166 pp. microfilm. (4292.24/1947)

   Approved by the Government of the Kiangsu-Anhwei Border Region, this textbook for middle schools and general young readers is arranged under six headings: general conditions in the border regions, the political system, economics, culture and education, the armed forces, and the judiciary. The appendix consists of five resolutions of the Political Consultative Conference.

62. Ta Kung Pao 大公報. Chungking, June 1940 - December 1945 (almost complete); January - May 1946 (incomplete); several issues in 1947; January 1948 (incomplete); and January 1949 (almost complete). (newspaper)

   Internationally known, this was the most influential independent newspaper in China during the Sino-Japanese War and shortly after. It went over to the side of the Communists in the late 1940's. For the Communist view of this newspaper during the war, see item no. 146, pp. 95-97.

63. Tung Pi-wu 董必武. Chung-kuo chieh-fang ch'ü shih-lu 中國解放區實錄 (A True Account of the Chinese Liberation Areas). San Francisco, Ho-tso, 1946. 48 pp. (4292.24/4131)

Written in 1945 by a Communist member of the Chinese Delegation to the United Nations Conference on International Organization, this pamphlet briefly describes government, economics, education, the army, and the workers' movement in the Chinese Communist-controlled areas. It is also available in an English version, entitled Memorandum on China's Liberated Areas (San Francisco, May 18, 1945; 31 pp.).

64. Wen-hua chiao-yü yen-chiu hui 文化教育研究會 (ed.). Ti-wo tsai hsüan-ch'uan chan-hsien shang 敵我在宣傳戰綫上 (Propaganda Warfare). [Yenan], same, 1941. 297 pp. microfilm. (2991/0240)

A comprehensive survey and analysis of the propaganda activities of the Japanese and puppet governments, and of Communist countermeasures. The book lists a number of newspapers, news agencies, magazines, and pamphlets published by the Japanese and their puppet governments in China.

V. THE PARTY

Two of the most important Party affairs during the war were the campaign for the rectification of "styles of work," launched throughout the CCP in 1942, and the Seventh Congress of the Party, held between April 23 and June 11, 1945, in Yenan. The basic materials concerning both events are abundantly available in the Hoover Library, although the text of Wang Shih-wei's interesting and sensational Yeh pai-ho-hua is unfortunately incomplete. The Congress adopted a new Party Constitution and elected a new Central Committee headed by Mao Tse-tung.

This section also includes a number of articles and speeches by Liu Shou-ch'i, collections of Party documents, and Kuomintang analyses of the CCP.

65. Chan-k'ai fan-sheng yü tzu-wo p'i-p'ing 展開反省與自我批評 (To Launch a Self-reflection and Self-criticism Campaign). Chantung, Hsin-hua, n.d. 86 pp. microfilm. (4292.79/7779)

Editorials from the Ta-chung jih-pao and articles by Hsiao Hua, Liu Shao-ch'i, and Kao Kang in connection with the Party rectification movement.

66. Ch'en Yün 陳雲　Tsen-yang tso i-ko kung-ch'an tang-yüan 怎樣做一個共產黨員　(How To Be a Communist Party Member). Canton, Hsin-hua, 1950. 22 pp. (4292.52/7913)

This article, written on May 30, 1939, is one of the documents included in the Cheng-feng wen-hsien (see item no. 67).

67. Cheng-feng wen-hsien 整風文獻　(Party Rectification Documents). 3rd ed. n.p., Chieh-fang, 1944. 352 pp. (4292.52/5701a)

The official handbook for study and discussion of the Party's rectification movement, which began with Mao Tse-tung's speech delivered at the opening of the Party School in Yenan on February 1, 1942. Mao launched an attack on three general errors in the Party's style of work: subjectivism in thought, sectarianism in Party relations, and formalism in literature and art. Twenty-one of the twenty-seven documents collected in this volume are available in English translation in Mao's China: Party Reform Documents, 1942-44 by Boyd Compton (Seattle: University of Washington Press, 1952).

68. Chieh-fang she 解放社 (comp.). K'ang-Jih min-tsu t'ung-i chan-hsien chih-nan 抗日民族統一戰綫指南　(A Guide to the Anti-Japanese National United Front). Vols. II-X. n.p., same, 1938-1940. (4292.11/2503)

This collection contains declarations, resolutions, and circular telegrams of the CC of the CCP and of the Communist military leaders. The bulk of the collection consists of speeches, writings, and statements by Communist leaders. The writings of Mao Tse-tung and Lo Fu appear in every volume; those of Wang Ming (Ch'en Shao-yü) appear in every volume except Vols. V and VIII. The writings of other leaders are available in the following volumes:

    Chou En-lai: Vols. III, and V-VIII

    Chu Teh: Vols. II, III, and V-VII

    Hsiang Ying: Vols. III, VII, and IX

Jen Pi-shih: Vol. III

K'ai Feng: Vols. II, and IV-VII

K'ang Sheng: Vol. X

Li Fu-ch'un: Vol. II

Lin Piao: Vols. II and V

Lin Tsu-han: Vol. VI

Liu Shao-ch'i: Vols. V, VII, and VIII

P'eng Te-huai: Vols. II, IX, and X

Po Ku: Vols. III-VI

Wang Chia-hsiang: Vols. VI, VII, IX, and X

69. Chung-kung chung-yang k'ang-ch'an hsüan-yen chi 中共中央抗戰宣言集 (Collected Statements of the Central Committee of the Chinese Communist Party). Sunan, Hsin-hua, 1949. 69 pp. (4292.24/5455)

Seventeen declarations and statements by the CC of the CCP made between August 1, 1935, and July 7, 1947, many of them on the anniversary of the outbreak of the Sino-Japanese War.

70. Chung-kung mi-mi 中共秘密 (Secrets of the Chinese Communist Party). 2nd ed. [Chuchiang], Chung-hsin, 1941. 20 pp. (2987/5423)

This pamphlet consists of three Communist documents selected to show the CCP's conspiracy against the National Government: (1) the resolution of the CC of the CCP on the current political situation and the tasks of the party, dated February 1, 1940; (2) an emergency announcement of the South China Bureau of the CC of the CCP regarding changes of the organizational form and working methods of the party; and (3) documents revealing secret techniques of party activities.

71. Chung-kuo kung-ch'an tang. Chung-yang shu-chi ch'u 中國共產黨中央書記處 (ed.). K'ang-chan i-lai chung-yao wen-chien hui-chi 抗戰以來重要文件彙集 (Collected Important Documents Since the Outbreak of the Sino-Japanese War). n.p., n. pub., 1942. 223 pp. (4292.24/5640.56)

    Edited by the Secretariat of the CC of the CCP, this book contains 67 important Communist documents dated from July 8, 1937, to July 7, 1942, and arranged in chronological order. Of these, 23 documents were issued by the CC of the CCP; 12 by Mao Tse-tung; and 2 by Liu Shao-ch'i, including the one on the fundamental problems of the guerrilla war against Japan (dated July 16, 1937, and originally written under the pseudonym of T'ao Shang-hsing). The rest are resolutions, declarations, or circular telegrams of the army leaders, regional border governments, and Yenan mass organizations.

72. Chung-kuo kung-ch'an tang. Chung-yang wei-yüan hui 中國共產黨中央委員會. Wei k'ang-chan ssu-chou nien chi-nien hsüan-yen 為抗戰四週年紀念宣言 (Declaration on the Occasion of the Fourth Anniversary of the Outbreak of the Sino-Japanese War). n.p., 1941. 1 p. (4292.24/5640.564f)

    In this manifesto, the CC of the CCP reaffirms its United Front policy and its willingness to co-operate with the KMT.

73. _____. Wei k'ang-chan liu chou-nien chi-nien hsüan-yen 為抗戰六週年紀念宣言 (Declaration on the Occasion of the Sixth Anniversary of the Outbreak of the Sino-Japanese War). n.p., Hsin-hua, 1943. various pagination. (4292.24/5640)

    In addition to the manifesto of the CC of the CCP, this volume contains several speeches or articles by Mao Tse-tung, Chu Teh, P'eng Te-huai, Ch'en Yi, Liu Po-ch'eng, and Teng Hsiao-p'ing in commemoration of the occasion.

74. [Chung-kuo kung-ch'an tang]. Liao-pei sheng wei-yüan hui. Hsüan ch'uan pu. 中國共產黨遼北省委員會宣傳部 (ed.). Shih-mo shih kung ch'an tang 什麼是共產黨 (What Is the Communist Party?). Revised ed. [Liaopei], Tung-pei, 1948. 115 pp. (4292.51/5640)

Edited by the Propaganda Department of the Liaopei Provincial Committee of the CCP and written in simple language for the purpose of helping new party members and the masses to understand Communism, this book consists of thirty topical lectures on the subject.

75. Chung-kuo kung-ch'an tang tang-chang 中國共產黨黨章 (The Constitution of the Chinese Communist Party). Huatung, Hsin-hua, 1950. 24 pp. (4292.13/5640b)

One of the several editions of the CCP Constitution adopted by the Seventh Congress of the Party on June 11, 1945. This Constitution was revised in 1956 and a new Constitution was adopted by the Eighth Congress on September 26 of the same year.

76. Chung-kuo kung-ch'an tang ti-ch'i tz'u tai-piao ta-hui yüan-shih ts'ai-liao hui-pien 中國共產黨第七次代表大會原始材料彙編 (Collected Primary Sources of the Seventh Congress of the Communist Party of China). n.p., [CCP], 1945. 192 pp. microfilm. (4292.417/5640)

Speeches and reports delivered by Communist leaders at the Seventh Congress of the CCP, a list of the members of the CC, and two editorials from the Liberation Daily commenting on the event.

77. Chung-kuo kung-ch'an tang ti liu-chung ch'üan-hui wen-chien 中國共產黨的六中全會文件 (Documents on the Sixth Plenum of the Central Committee of the Chinese Communist Party). Chungking, Hsin-hua jih-pao, 1939. 142 pp. (4292.11/2135.07)

This volume contains eight documents, including Mao Tse-tung's report to the Sixth Plenum of the CC of the CCP, October 12-14, 1938. Of the five editions of the report (entitled Lun hsin chieh-tuan, "On the New Stage") available in the Hoover Library, this is probably the best one.

78. Chung-kuo kung-ch'an tang yü chung-hua min-tsu 中國共產黨與中華民族 (The Chinese Communist Party and China). Shantung, Hsin-hua, 1943. 36 pp. microfilm. (2991/5640.56)

　　Three editorials from the Liberation Daily and one article by Wang Chia-hsiang, all written for the occasion of the 22nd anniversary of the establishment of the CCP.

79. Chung-kuo kuo-ming tang. Chung-yang kai-tsao wei-yüan hui 中國國民黨中央改造委員會. Chung-kung tang-ti tsu-chih yü k'ung-chih 中共黨的組織與控制 (Organization and Control of the Chinese Communist Party). Taipei, same, 1951. 110 pp. (4292.4/5667.54)

　　A résumé of discussions by the Sixth Section of the Central Reorganization Committee of the KMT, covering the following subjects concerning the CCP: (1) the CCP's philosophical basis; (2) the fundamental principles of the Party's organization; (3) the organizational system; (4) how Party members are controlled; (5) how civic organizations can be controlled; and (6) how the people can be controlled.

80. _____. Fei-tang ti tsu-chih yü ts'e-lüeh lu-hsien 匪黨的組織與策略路線 (Organization and Strategy of the Bandit Party). Taipei, Chung-yang wen-wu, 1952. 176 pp. (4292.4/5667)

　　A collection of fourteen essays relating to the CCP's organization, rectification movements, the mass lines, the New Democratic Youth League, etc., including a history of the Communist movement in Taiwan. These essays, written between 1950 and 1956, are considered analyses by KMT researchers.

81. Chung-kuo kuo-min tang. Chung-yang wei-yüan hui. Ti-liu tsu 中國國民黨中央委員會第六組 Fei-tang tsu-chih hsi-t'ung t'u-piao hui-pien 匪黨組織系統圖表彙編 (Tables of the Bandit Party's Organization). Taipei, same, 1953. 8 pp. (4292.4/5667.79)

　　Five excellent tables compiled by the Sixth Section of the CC of the KMT on the CCP's organization, membership, party-government relations, party-government relations after 1953 election, important meetings and declarations. The data includes material from the 1920's to the 1950's.

82. Fan Wen-lan 范文瀾 and others. Lun Wang Shih-wei ti ssu-hsiang i-shih 論王實味的思想意識 (On Wang Shih-wei's Ideology). Shantung, Hsin-hua, 1942. 66 pp. microfilm. (4292.79/0136)

A very important collection of articles criticizing Wang Shih-wei by Fan Wen-lan, Ai Ch'ing, Chang Ju-hsin, and Lo Mai. The appendix consists of (1) a chronology of the Academia Sinicia's meeting in Yenan, discussing Wang Shih-wei's case, and (2) a text of Wang's sensational Yeh pai-ho-hua. (Unfortunately, the text is incomplete).

83. Fei-tang tsu-chih chih yen-chiu 匪黨組織之研究 (A Study of the Bandit Party's Organization). Taipei, n. pub., 1953. 50 pp. (4292.4/7922)

A publication of the Research School of Revolutionary Practice, Taiwan, this paper analyzes the theory, strategy, tactics, and developments of the CCP organization.

84. Hsiu-yang chih-nan 修養指南 (Cultivation Guidance). Liaopei, Tung-pei shu-tien, 1948. 120 pp. (4292.52/2854)

A collection of articles and speeches by Mao Tse-tung, Liu Shao-ch'i, and others on how Communist Party members should "cultivate" themselves in two categories: (1) correct ideology and (2) opposition to "bureaucratic and warlord tendencies." Among the articles is Chang Ju-hsin's criticism of Wang Shih-wei, author of the sensational Yeh Pai-ho-hua.

85. Hung-mien ch'u-pan she 紅棉出版社 (comp.). Chung-kuo kung-ch'an tang k'ang-chan wen-hsien 中國共產黨抗戰文獻 (War Documents of the Chinese Communist Party). Vol. I. Hong Kong, same, 1946. 68 pp. (4292.24/2422)

A collection of eight CCP policy documents issued in 1937-38.

86. K'ang-Jih chiu-kuo chih-nan 抗日救國指南 (A Guide to Anti-Japanese and National Salvation). Vol. I. n.p., K'ang-Jih, 1937. 118 pp. (2991.1/2135.564)

    Edited by "K.N.," this "guide book" consists of twelve chapters. With the exception of the last chapter, which is the Ten-Point National Salvation Program endorsed by the enlarged meeting of the CC of the CCP at Lochuan in northern Shensi on August 25, 1937, each chapter is an article by a noted Communist leader: one by Ch'en Shao-yü on the "New Stage of the Japanese Aggression and the New Period of the Chinese People's Struggle"; four by Mao Tse-tung (two of which are dated July 23 and September 29, 1937, respectively); four by Lo Fu (one undated, the others dated April 11, August 2, and September 18, 1937, respectively); and one each by Li Fu-ch'un and K'ai Feng. All deal with either the current Sino-Japanese war or United Front problems, and most of them were included in the collection, K'ang-Jih min-tsu t'ung-i chan-hsien chih-nan (see item no. 68).

87. Kao Kang 高崗. Shih-shih k'o-k'o wei lao-pai-sheng hsing-li ch'u-pi 時時刻刻為老百姓興利除弊 (Always Promote That Which Is Profitable and Abolish That Which Is Evil for the People). n.p., Chi-Lu-Yü, n.d. 40 pp. microfilm. (4292.24/0222.1)

    Six speeches and articles by Kao Kang, dated 1943-45, on the "methods of leadership and the style of work."

88. Kuan-yü hsin ti chih-shih fen-tzu kan-pu ti i-hsieh wen-t'i 關於新的知識份子幹部的一些問題 (A Number of Problems Relating to the New Cadres Recruited from the Intelligentsia). [Yenan], n. pub., 1944. 24 pp. (4292.79/7002)

    Excerpts from the writings of Lenin, Stalin, and Mao Tse-tung on the subject. In addition, this pamphlet includes a resolution of the CCP, dated February 1, 1939, concerning the recruitment of party members from the intelligentsia.

89. Liu Shao-ch'i 劉少奇 Ch'ing-suan tang-nei ti Meng-sai-wei-chu-i ssu-hsiang 清算黨內的孟塞維主義思想 (Eliminate Menshevist Ideas Existing in the Party). n.p., n. pub., 1943. 12 pp. (4292.11/7294,38)

    Written for the 22nd anniversary of the founding of the CCP.

90. _____. Jen ti chieh-chi hsing 人的階級性 (On Man's Class Nature). Hsipei, Jen-min, 1941. 8 pp. (4292.1/7294)

    A brief discussion of man's nature from the viewpoint of the class struggle.

91. _____. Lun kung-ch'an tang yüan ti hsiu-yang 論共產黨員的修養 (On the Training and Cultivation of a Communist Party Member). Kalgan, Hsin-hua, 1946. (4292.52/7294)

    A lecture delivered at the Marx-Lenin Institute, Yenan, on August 7, 1939. It was originally published in the Chieh-fang, Nos. 82-84. Part of the article is included in the Cheng-feng wen-hsien (see item no. 67). Various editions have subsequently been published by various publishers. The text as revised by Liu in 1949 is also available in the Hoover Library. (4292.52/7294.1)

92. _____. Lun kuo-chi chu-i yü min-tsu chu-i 論國際主義與民族主義 (Internationalism and Nationalism). Chekiang, Hsin-hua, 1949. 35 pp. (4292.11/7294.06)

    An English translation of this text has been published by the Foreign Languages Press, Peking.

93. _____. Lun tang 論黨 (On the Party). Huapei, Hsin-hua, 1946. 105 pp. (4292.21/7294)

    A collection of six articles and speeches: (1) "On Man's Class Nature"; (2) "How To Be a Good Communist," written for the K'ang-ti pao, Ch'ien-feng pao, and Mai-chin pao on the occasion of the 19th anniversary of the founding of the CCP, July 1, 1940.

An English translation was subsequently published by the Foreign Languages Press, Peking, [1951]; (3) "On Inner-Party Struggle," a lecture delivered on July 2, 1941. (see item no. 95); (4) "In Opposition to Various Deviations Within the Party," an excerpt of a meeting record; (5) "Democratic Spirit and Bureaucracy," a lecture delivered at the Party School in Central China; and (6) "Eliminate Menshevist Ideas Existing in the Party," written for the occasion of the 22nd anniversary of the establishment of the CCP.

In addition, there is an exchange of letters between Liu Shao-ch'i and a comrade.

94. _____. Lun tang 論黨 (On the Party). Peking, Chieh-fang, 1950. 176 pp. (4292.13/7294)

This book contains (1) Liu's report on the revision of the Party constitution, delivered on May 14, 1945 at the Seventh Congress of the CCP; and (2) the Constitution of the CCP adopted by the Seventh Congress on June 11, 1945.

According to Liu's report, the CCP had 1,210,000 members in 1945. An English translation of the report has been published by the Foreign Languages Press, Peking.

95. _____. Lun Tang-nei tou-cheng 論黨內鬥爭 (On the Inner-Party Struggle). [Hong Kong], Cheng-pao, 1947. 49 pp. (4292.11/7294.09)

A lecture delivered on July 2, 1941, at the Party School in Central China. A number of English translations are available, including one published by the Foreign Languages Press, Peking [1950?], and one by the People's Publishing House, Bombay, 1951. It is included in the Cheng-feng wen-hsien (see item no. 67).

96. _____ and others. Lun ch'ün-chung lu-hsien 論羣眾路綫 (On the Mass Line). Hong Kong, Hsin min-chu, 1949. 71 pp. (4292.11/7294.01)

The first of the five articles in this book is by Liu Shao-ch'i, and the remaining four are by Ch'en Po-ta and others; all the writings deal with the masses.

97. Liu Tzu-chiu 劉子久. Kuan-yü hsüeh-hsi wen-t'i chi Huai-pei ch'ü tang-wei ti hsin 關於學習問題給淮北區黨委的信 (Letter to the Huaipei District Committee Concerning Study Problems). n.p., Chieh-fang, 1944. 28 pp. (4292.521/7212)

The writer of this letter was the secretary of the Huaipei District of the CCP. In the spring of 1944 he was sent to the Party School at Yenan for study. In this letter, dated July 5, 1944, the writer points out the weakness of the CCP in the Huaipei district (north of the Huai River) and discusses the cadre work in that area. The letter was also broadcast and circulated to other areas for reference.

98. Lun Kung-ch'an tang. 論共產黨 (On the Communist Party). Huapei, Hsin-hua, 1940. 265-428 pp. microfilm. (4292.2/0409)

This is apparently the second volume of a two-volume book. This part consists of the last two chapters (XI and XII), which deal with the "two-line struggle" in the party and the relations of the Party and the masses, and an appendix of Communist Party constitutions in various countries, including China.

99. Shan-tung sheng. Chiao-tung ch'ü. Tang-wei hsüan-ch'uan pu 山東省膠東區黨委宣傳部 (ed.). Kuan-yü kung-ch'an tang-yüan ch'i-chieh wen-t'i 關於共產黨員氣節問題 (Concerning the Integrity of Party Members). n.p., same, 1946. 35 pp. microfilm. (4292.52/7579)

Two articles, written in wartime, discuss defection of Communists under various excuses when they were captured. Reprinted by the Propaganda Department of the Party Committee of the Chiaotung Military Region for Party guidance.

100. Ssu-hsiang fan-sheng hsüan-chi 思想反省選集 (Selected Works on Thought Reform). n.p., [CCP], 1943. 109 pp. microfilm. (2259.9/1217)

A collection of four articles written by CCP members in North China during the party rectification campaign of 1942, and reprinted by the Hopeh-Shantung-Honan Committee of the Party.

101. Ta-chih 大智 (ed.). T'uan-chieh ti ta-hui sheng-li ti ta-hui 團結的大會勝利的大會 (A Congress of Unity and Victory). Kalgan, Hsin-hua, 1945. 50 pp. (4292.24/4386)

This volume contains five items: the first three are accounts of the 7th Congress of the CCP (April 23 - June 11, 1945) at Yenan, including the texts of speeches; the other two are editorials on the Congress reprinted from the Liberation Daily.

102. Tang ti chien-she 黨的建設 (The Party's Reconstruction). Taipei, Yang-ming, 1951. 183 pp. (4292.02/9210)

This is the third reprint of a CCP document made by the KMT for its own reference. (It was first reprinted in July 1938 and again in December of the same year.) The book is divided into ten chapters, with the following titles: Members of the Party; The Organization of the Party; The Principle of the System of Democratic Centralization; Discipline; Internal Contradictions of the Party; Cadre Policy; Party Leadership; Educational and Propaganda Work; Relations Between the Party and the Masses; and the Party's Work in the Army. These chapters were thought to reveal the methods and strategy of the CCP within the newly established United Front.

103. Tang-yüan chiao-ts'ai 黨員教材 (A Textbook for Party Members). n.p., n.pub., [1946]. 102 pp. microfilm. (4292.13/5640.5)

Twenty-seven lessons based on a report given by Liu Shao-ch'i at the Seventh Congress of the CCP.

104. Tung-pei shu-tien 東北書店 (ed.). Lun ling-tao fang-fa 論領導方法 (On the Method of Leadership). 2nd ed. Harbin, same, 1948. 63 pp. (4292.52/5150)

    Most of this book consists of articles and newspaper editorials discussing CCP "methods" and the Party's leadership of the masses. Also included are a decision made by the Central Political Bureau on June 1, 1943, on the method of leadership, and part of a speech by Kao Kang in January 1945 concerning party work techniques.

105. Wang Hou-sheng 王厚生 P'ing kung-ch'an tang ti tsu-chih 評共產黨的組織 (On the Communist Party's Organization). Kowloon, Tzu-yu, 1956. 152 pp. (4292.4/1172)

    Critical comments on the organization of the CCP as described in the Party Constitution of 1945.

106. Wen-hsien 文獻 (Documents). Nos. 1-8. Shanghai, October 10, 1938 - May 10, 1939. (2991.03/0423)

    This monthly aims at presenting historical documents of the Sino-Japanese War. It carries both domestic and international news, with reprints of writings and speeches of the Kuomintang and Communist leaders. Anti-Japanese guerrilla news is reported in almost every issue.

    Chu Teh's comments on the anti-Japanese military campaigns in North China and his speech on military strategy appear in issue Nos. 1 and 4, respectively.

    P'eng Te-huai's comments on the War of Resistance in North China appear in Nos. 5 and 7.

    Ch'en Shao-yü's speech at a mass meeting in Yenan denouncing Wang Ching-wei was published in No. 6.

    Lin Po-ch'ü's report at the First People's Council is available in No. 8.

    Issue No. 2 contains (1) Chou En-lai's analysis of the war; (2) Lin Piao on guerrilla war in North China; (3) Yeh Chien-ying on the anti-Japanese war situation in the Communist controlled area; and (4) an open letter of the Kiangsu Provincial Committee of the CCP (October 30, 1938). Issue No. 3 contains a special section for the Enlarged Sixth Plenum of the CC of the CCP, including the complete text of Mao Tse-tung's report, which is continued in No. 4. It includes an article on the Shensi-Kangsu-Ningsia Border Region and one on the reorganization of the New Fourth Army.

107. Wen-hua chiao-yü yen-chiu hui 文化教育研究會 (ed.). Hsüeh-hsi sheng-huo 學習生活 (Study Life). n.p., same, 1941. 218 pp. (4292.52/0240)

An important source book on the educational program for CCP cadres. The need for an educational and training program for cadre functionaries was decided upon in the Enlarged Sixth Plenum of the CC of the CCP in 1938. Consequently, the Central Cadre Educational Department was established in the following year for the purpose of carrying out the plan. The program was first put into practice in Yenan, then adopted in other Communist regions. This is a summary of the establishment and progress of the program during 1939-40.

VI. THE UNITED FRONT

A. GENERAL

With regard to the CCP's United Front policy during the first years of the Sino-Japanese War, the "deviation" of Ch'en Shao-yü (Wang Ming) was one of the significant events in the party history. The Hoover Library has a comprehensive collection of works written by Ch'en during this period.

Whether or not Ch'en was more faithful in carrying out the Comintern's policy, which was allegedly divergent from the Yenan position, it was Mao Tse-tung's strategy ("unity side by side with struggle and unity through struggle") that permitted Communist expansion and the eventual overthrow of the National Government on the mainland. This section includes theoretical discussions of the United Front by Communist leaders and Kuomintang writers. Also included are a number of leftist magazines and writings published in the first years of the War, some of them by writers who later became active in the Democratic League.

108. Chan-hsien 戰綫 (War Front). Nos. 1-5 and 9. Shanghai, September 13 - October 26, 1937. (2991.2/6535)

This magazine was published every five days, and was devoted to wartime political and military affairs. Among the members of the editorial committee were Chang Nai-ch'i, Chang Han-fu, and Ai Ssu-ch'i. Issue No. 2 (September 18, 1937) contains an article on the Koreans in the United Northeast Anti-Japanese Army.

109. Chang Chih-i 張執一 (ed.). K'ang-chan chung ti cheng-tang ho p'ai-pieh 抗戰中的政黨和派別 (The Wartime Political Parties and Groups). Chungking, Tu-shu sheng-huo, 1939. 135 pp. (4737/1341)

A useful and fair presentation of the history, programs, and leadership of the following parties and organizations: the KMT, the CCP, the Chinese Liberation Action Committee (The Third Party), the National Social Party, the Youth Party, the National Salvation Association, and the Chinese Revolutionary League. Programs are quoted from original documents of the respective organizations. The appendix is on Trotskyites and their publications.

110. Ch'en Shao-yü 陳紹禹. Ch'en Shao-yü (Wang Ming) chiu-kuo yen-lun hsüan-chi 陳紹禹(王明)救國言論選集 (Selected Works of Ch'en Shao-yü). Hankow, Chung-kuo ch'u-pan, 1938. 364 pp. (2991.2/7922)

This includes Ch'en Shao-yü's speeches and writings from 1935 to June 1938, including his speech on the United Front delivered at the Seventh Congress of the Communist International in the summer of 1935. These writings fully reflect his views on KMT - CCP cooperation during the early stage of the Sino-Japanese War. He was subsequently attacked for advocating the "class surrender doctrine" or "rightist deviation." In an open letter to a comrade, dated April 28, [1938], also signed by Chou En-lai and Ch'in Pang-hsien (Po Ku), Ch'en Shao-yü reveals, among other things, an interesting account of Chang Kuo-t'ao's defection from the party.

111. _____. Mu-ch'ien kuo-nei-wai hsing-shih yü ts'an-cheng hui ti-ssu tz'u ta-hui ti ch'eng-chi 目前國內外形勢與參政會第四次大會的成績 (The Current Domestic and Foreign Situation and the Achievements of the Fourth Plenary Session of the People's Political Council). n.p., Chieh-fang, 1939. 53 pp. (4890.191/7922)

A speech given at the staff meeting of the <u>New China Daily</u> on September 20, 1939, reporting on the Fourth Plenary Session of the People's Political Council of September 9-18, 1939. Ch'en advocated full support of the National Government in waging war against Japan. The book's appendix is Ch'en Shao-yü's speech at a meeting in commemoration of the third anniversary of Lu Hsün's death.

112. Chiu-wang 救亡 (National Salvation). No. 3. Changhai, September 7, 1937. (2991.03/4401)

There is no useful article in this issue.

113. Chiu-wang chou-k'an 救亡週刊 (National Salvation Weekly). No. 1. Shanghai, October 10, 1937. (2991.03/4071)

An organ of the Shanghai Vocational Association for National Salvation, containing discussions of national politics in general and of local professional interests in particular.

114. Ch'üan-min chou-k'an 全民週刊 (People's Weekly). Vol. I Nos. 7, 9-11, 14-25 - Vol. II, No. 1. Hankow, January 22 - June 4, 1938. (2991.01/8731)

Published by Shen Chün-ju, Li Kung-p'u, and other "liberal and democratic persons" who were not sympathetic to the KMT, this magazine presents writings relating to the Sino-Japanese War, with emphasis on education and public opinion. It stresses "exchange of national salvation ideas," "youth in wartime," and "exchange of experiences among writers."

115. Ch'üan-min k'ang-chan 全民抗戰 (People's War of Resistance). Nos. 8, 9, 33, 34, 36-40, 44, 46, 57-59, 95, 103, 153. Hankow and Chungking, July 29, 1937 - November 1, 1941. (2991.01/8756)

   Edited by Tsou T'ao-fen and Liu Shih, this periodical is primarily devoted to national politics, with special emphasis on national unity in the face of Japanese aggression. It was originally published every three days, then became a five-day magazine and finally a weekly. It was quite popular among students and the intelligentsia.

116. Chung Kung 鍾拱. T'uan-chieh k'ang-chan yü chung-kung 團結抗戰與中共 (Unity, the War of Resistance, and the Chinese Communist Party). Shanghai, Pai-hsing, 1941. 50 pp. (2991.2/8158)

   A concise, readable, anti-Communist pamphlet analyzing the Communist strategy and the United Front.

117. Chung-kuo k'ang-chan liang-nien pi-sheng 中國抗戰兩年必勝 (China Will Win the War in Two Years). n.p., Shih-shih, 1942. 46 pp. (2991.2/5656)

   This pamphlet contains four articles asserting the inevitability of the Chinese final victory against Japan and of the bright prospects for China. The writings appear to be editorials from Chinese Communist newspapers.

118. [Fan] Ch'ang-chiang 范長江. Sai-shang hsing 塞上行 (Journey Beyond the Passes). Tientsin, Ta Kung Pao, 1937. 338 pp. (3078/4173)

Written by a noted correspondent of the Ta Kung Pao, the last chapter of this book is an account of his trip to Sian and then Yenan in February 1937. His interviews with Chou En-lai on the Sian Incident and with Mao Tse-tung on the founding of the Communist base in Shensi are of historical value.

119. Hou Wai-lu 侯外廬. K'ang-Jih min-tsu t'ung-i chan-hsien lun 抗日民族統一戰綫論 (On the Anti-Japanese United Front). Hankow, Sheng-huo, 1938. 87 pp. (2991.2/2320)

Six selected articles that ably and quite systematically deal with the theory of the United Front.

120. Hsia Yen 夏衍 (ed.). Chung-Jih chan-cheng yü kuo-chi 中日戰爭與國際 (The Sino-Japanese War and the World). Shanghai, K'ang-chan ch'u-pan, 1937. 61 pp. (2991.03/3102)

In addition to three letters addressed to American Communist leaders by Chu Teh, Mao Tse-tung, and Chou En-lai respectively, this book contains sixteen articles by foreign Communists and labor leaders commenting on the Sino-Japanese War.

121. Hsiao Chien-ying 蕭隽英. K'ang-chan ch'ien-hou 抗戰前後 (Before and After the War of Resistance). [Hong Kong], Ta-chung sheng-lu, 1939. 83 pp. (2991.2/4224)

Written by a professor at Sun Yat-sen University and one-time president of a newspaper (Ch'ün-sheng pao), four of the six articles collected in this book deal with the United Front.

122. Hsin chan-hsien 新戰綫 (The New War Front). Vol. I, Nos. 3, 8, and 10 - Vol. II, No. 1. Canton, January 1 - September 5, 1938. (2991.2/0262)

A comprehensive general weekly with articles on the United Front and current domestic and foreign affairs. Most of the contributors were local Cantonese academicians and writers.

123. Hsiung Ch'i 熊琦 (ed.). Kuo Mo-jo hsien-sheng tsui-chin yen-lun chi 郭沫若先生最近言論集 (Collection of Kuo Mo-jo's Recent Speeches). Canton, Li-sao, 1938. 92 pp. (2991.03/0234)

　　　Nine speeches by Kuo Mo-jo on Japan and the Sino-Japanese War.

124. Hsü Yu-lai 徐友來. Chung-kuo kung-ch'an tang nei-mu 中國共產黨內幕 (Inside the Chinese Communist Party). Chuchiang, Chung-hsin, 1941. 62 pp. (4292.2/2944)

　　　An attack on the military and political activities of the CCP. The theme of the book is that the ultimate aim of the Party is to seize power from the KMT rather than to collaborate with it. No "inside" information is offered.

125. Hsüeh-shih sheng-huo 學識生活 (Learning and Life). Vol. I, No. 1; Vol. II, No. 3/4; and Vol. IV, Nos. 1 and 5. Chungking, April 25, 1940 - May 1, 1943. (9200/7123)

　　　A magazine designed to assist general readers in the study of social and natural sciences. Among the contributors are Liu Ya-tzu, Kuo Mo-jo, Shen Chün-ju, and Li Kung-p'u.

126. K'ang-chan 抗戰 (War of Resistance). Nos. 1-6 and 26-50. Shanghai, August 19, 1937 - March 3, 1938. (2991.2/5165)

　　　Edited by Tsou T'ao-fen and published every three days, this periodical purported to "present systematic analyses and reports of the national and international situation that are directly or indirectly related to the Sino-Japanese War on the one hand . . . and reflect the urgent demands of the masses during the war on the other hand." Among the frequent contributors were Kuo Mo-jo, Chin Chung-hua, and Mao Tun.

127. K'ang-chan pu-pan she 抗戰出版社 (ed.). Ti pa-lu chün 第八路軍 (The Eighth Route Army). Hankow, same, 1938. 136 pp. (4292.9/5622)

　　The title of this badly organized book is misleading. Although it provides a glimpse of life in the Eighth Route Army and biographical sketches of its leaders, the book contains more useful information on the Long March, the Sian Incident, and the United Front. Its appendix consists of seven documents: (1) Agnes Smedley's interview with Mao Tse-tung in Yenan on March 1, 1937; (2) Chu Teh's writing on the war against Japanese aggression; (3) P'eng Te-huai's writing on the prerequisites for victory in the war against Japan; (4) Lo Fu's article, dated June 20, 1937, reviewing the Communist movement of the previous ten years; (5) a CCP declaration on KMT-CCP cooperation; (6) Chiang Kai-shek's statement on the CCP's declaration mentioned above; and (7) Madame Sun Yat-sen's article on the last two statements.

128. K'ang-chan ming-lun chi 抗戰名論集 (Famous War Writings). n.p., Chan-shih, n.d. 92 pp. (2991.1/2135.53)

　　Selected writings of Communist leaders including those of Mao Tse-tung, Chu Teh, Lo Fu, P'eng Te-huai, Lin Po-ch'ü, and K'ai Feng. All appear to have been written shortly after the outbreak of the Sino-Japanese War in 1937, except Lin's article "From the Soviet to the Democratic Republican System," and the letters to Earl Browder by Mao Tse-tung, Chu Teh, and Chou En-lai, respectively (all dated June 24, [1937?]).

129. K'ang-ta i fen-hsiao. Cheng-chih ch'u 抗大一分校政治部 (ed.). Lun Ma Lieh chu-i chüeh-ting ts'e-lüeh ti chi-ko chi-pen yüan-tse 論馬列主義決定策略的幾個基本原則 (On the Fundamental Principles of Marxist-Leninist Strategy). Shantung, Political Department of Shantung Military Region, n.d. 119 pp. microfilm. (4292.2/5687)

　　Edited by the Political Department of the First Branch of the Anti-Japanese Military and Political Academy, this book contains Wang Ming's lengthy criticism of party cadres that did not fully understand the United Front policy. The appendix consists of decisions on basic policies in various Communist bases.

130. Kuan-yü kung-tang wen-t'i chih chien-t'ao yü wu-jen ying-ch'ü chih fang-chin 關於共黨問題之檢討與吾人應取之方針 (An Examination of the Communist Problem and Our Policy). n.p., n. pub., 1940. 24 pp. (4292.1/3049)

　　This is apparently a KMT publication devoted to examining the CCP's fundamental policies and current activities and suggesting attitudes and policies that should be adopted by the KMT. Among the Communist sources cited is the speech by Chang Hao (Lin Yü-ying) delivered in 1937 on the Communist Party line and strategy.

131. Kuo-chi shih-shih yen-chiu hui 國際時事研究會 (ed.). T'ung-i chan-hsien hsia ti Chung-kuo kung-ch'an tang 統一戰線下的中國共產黨 (The Chinese Communist Party Under the United Front). Hong Kong, same, 1938. 94 pp. (2991.2/6765)

　　Edited and published by the Association for the Study of International Affairs, this volume is a collection of articles written by CCP leaders, including the following: (1) Mao Tse-tung, Ch'en Shao-yü, and Chang Wen-t'ien, then the Secretary-General of the CCP (all on the United Front); (2) Lin Tsu-han (on the Soviet area) and Ts'ai Ho-sen (written in 1936 on the seven years' history of the Chinese Soviet movement); and (3) Wang Chia-hsiang and Wang Shou-tao (on the development of the Communist forces from the Red Army to the Eighth Route Army).

132. [Kuo-min cheng-fu]. Ssu-fa hsing-cheng pu. Tiao-ch'a chü 國民政府司法行政部調查局 (ed.). Kung-fei t'ung-chan kung-tso ti ts'e-lüeh yü yün-yung 共匪統戰工作的策略與運用 (The Communist Strategy and Application of the United Front). Taipei, same, 1960. 174 pp. (4292.71/1321)

　　Edited and published by the Bureau of Investigation of the Department of Justice of the National Government, this book is in four sections: (1) an analysis of the principle and nature of the Communist United Front policy; (2) the Communist strategy and application of the United Front policy from the 1920's to 1949; (3) the post-1949 period; and (4) conclusion. This is a detailed examination of the subject.

133. K'uo-ch'ing ssu-hsiang chieh ti mi-wu 廓清思想界的迷霧 (Clear Up Some Hazy Ideas). n.p., n. pub., [1938]. 107 pp. (4738/0364)

    Written from the KMT viewpoint, three of the four chapters of this book are criticisms of the current writings, speeches, and political views of Mao Tse-tung, Ch'en Shao-yü, and Chang Wen-t'ien.

134. Min-i 民意 (Public Opinion). Nos. 1-18, and 20-48. Hankow and Chungking, December 15, 1937 - November 9, 1938. (9200/7031.20)

    A leading KMT weekly of high quality. Local KMT publications often echoed discussion and comment on the important political problems treated in this organ. A subject index is available for every twelve issues, arranged in these categories: political commentaries, finance, foreign affairs, military affairs, education, the mass movement, literature, feature reports, and miscellaneous. Among the contributors are many leading KMT theorists. Issue No. 22 (May 11, 1938) contains a report of an interview with Chang Kuo-t'ao.

135. Min-tsu kung-lun 民族公論 (Public Opinion of the Nation). Vol. I, No. 6. Shanghai, February 20, 1939.

    This 186-page issue carries articles on current domestic and foreign affairs, including two articles by well-known Commumist writers: one by Hua Kang on French politics, and the other by Ch'en Po-ta on Sun Yat-sen's theory of "knowledge and action."

136. Mu-ch'ien hsing-shih ti fen-hsi 目前形勢的分析 (An Analysis of the Current Situation). n.p., Li-lun, 1936. 64 pp. (2991.2/1073)

    In addition to a number of Chinese translations of resolutions passed by the Seventh World Congress of the CI, this book contains the following documents concerning the anti-Japanese national united front: (1) a resolution of the Central Politburo of the CCP, December 25, 1935, on the "current political situation and the party's tasks"; (2) a circular telegram of the Central Government of the Soviet People's Republic of China, February 21, 1936, calling for a national anti-Japanese convention for the purpose of declaring war on Japan; (3) an anti-Japanese declaration of the North China Bureau of the CC of the CCP, March 10, 1936; and (4) a declaration of the Central Committee of the Communist Youth Corps of China on the students' patriotic movement. The remaining materials included are: (1) an article by Liang-p'ing on the change of policy toward rich peasants; (2) a declaration to the Mongolian people by the Central Government of the Soviet People's Republic of China, dated December 20, 1935 and signed by Mao Tse-tung; and (3) a student recruitment bulletin, dated February 1936, issued by the Red Army Academy (Hsi-pei k'ang-Jih hung-chün ta-hsüeh).

137. Pai Shui 白水. Chou En-lai yü Teng Ying-ch'ao 周恩來與鄧穎超 (Chou En-lai and Teng Ying-ch'ao). Hankow, I-hsing, 1938. 118 pp. (4292.3/2613)

   Of the collected articles in this volume, four are Chou En-lai's speeches and writings dealing with the early political and military situation in the Sino-Japanese War, five are his wife's speeches and writings relating to women's problems, and the remaining four are reporters' interviews.

138. Pao-wei Chung-kuo t'ung-meng 保衛中國同盟 (China Defense League). New No. 27. Hong Kong, March 15, 1941. (2991.01/2256)

   This bi-weekly was the Chinese edition of the mouthpiece of the organization with the same title, which was headed by T. V. Soong and Madame Sun Yat-sen. One of the two articles published in this issue is a Chinese translation of a report on conditions in southeast Shansi by Miss Kathleen Hall, a Red Cross worker who went there in December 1939.

139. P'ing-hsin 平心. Lun hsin Chung-kuo 論新中國 (New China). 2nd ed. Shanghai, Ch'ün-chung, 1950. 232 pp. (2991.2/1433)

Originally published in Shanghai in 1941 under the pseudonym Ch'ing-chih, this book is a collection of the author's essays and articles on current Chinese politics (especially the United Front) following the CCP line.

140. Shih-tai wen-hsien she 時代文獻社 (ed.). Chiu-kuo wu-tsui 救國無罪 (Saving One's Own Country Is Not a Crime). [Shanghai?], same, 1937. 171 pp. (4737.7/6202)

A record of the so-called "Incident of the Seven Gentlemen," covering the period between November 22, 1936, when the leaders of the National Salvation Association were arrested in Shanghai, and June 30, 1937, when they were released from prison. The seven leaders were Shen Chün-ju, Chang Nai-ch'i, Wang Tsao-shih, Tsou T'ao-fen, Li Kung-p'u, Sa Ch'ien-li, and Shih Liang. The book was compiled from current newspaper reports and court proceedings.

141. Ta-chung sheng-huo 大眾生活 (Public Life). New Nos. 1-22, 25, and 27. Hong Kong, May 17 - November 15, 1941. (2991.01/4626)

This left-wing weekly was originally published by Tsou T'ao-fen in Shanghai, but was banned by the KMT in 1936. Upon resumption of its publication, Tsou followed the original line and gave comprehensive coverage of national and international affairs. Among the well-known contributors are Ch'iao Mu (Ch'iao Kuan-hua) and Chin Chung-hua.

142. T'ao-fen wen-chi 韜奮文集 (Works of Tsou T'ao-fen). 3 vols. Hong Kong, San-lien, 1957. 550, 738, and 515 pp. (9159/2263.1)

The most comprehensive collected works of Tsou T'ao-fen, who died on June 2, 1944, and was posthumously admitted to CCP membership in September of the same year. Volume I contains his articles written between 1927 and 1940, arranged in chronological order. Volume II consists of his books of travels, and Volume III, four books including the one entitled "Since the War" (K'ang-chan i-lai).

143. Ti-k'ang 抵抗 (Resistance). Nos. 7-25. Shanghai, September 9 - November 9, 1937. (2991.2/5451)

　　　Edited by Tsou T'ao-fen and published every three days, this magazine carries articles on current national and international affairs. Among the well-known contributors are Hu Yü-chih, Chin Chung-hua, Fan Ch'ang-chiang, Liu Shih, and Liu Ssu-mu. Madame Sun Yat-sen's article on KMT - CCP relations appears in the No. 12 issue (September 26, 1937).

144. Wai-chiao pu ch'ing-pao 外交部情報 (Intelligence Reports of the Ministry of Foreign Affairs). Nos. 16-183. n.p., September 19, 1938 - March 20, 1939. mimeo. (2991.52/2009)

　　　These daily intelligence reports of the "Intelligence Division of the Ministry of Foreign Affairs" are probably from the puppet Renovated Government set up by the Japanese at Nanking after the fall of the capital. They are concerned with the National Government, Chinese Communists, and KMT-CCP relations. Some of the reports are in Japanese.

145. Wang Tu-chung 王大中. Chung-kuo kung-ch'an tang hsüan-ch'uan kung-tso tsung chien-t'ao 中國共產黨宣傳工作總檢討 (A Critical Examination of the Propaganda Work of the Chinese Communist Party). Chuchiang, Sheng-li, 1941. 66 pp. (4292.61/1145)

　　　An examination of the post-1937 propaganda tactics of the CCP from these angles: organization, contents, and development. It includes a useful list of Communist newspapers and magazines then published in China and abroad, and a brief analysis of Communist views of international relations.

146. Wen-hua chiao-yü yen-chiu hui 文化教育研究會 (ed.). Ko k'ang-Jih tang-p'ai ti hsuan-ch'uan huo-tung 各抗日黨派的宣傳活動 (The Propaganda Activities of Various Anti-Japanese Political Parties and Groups). [Chungking or Yenan], same, 1941. 229 pp. (4737/0240)

Compiled and published by the Association for Cultural and Educational Studies, this book consists of six chapters, which discuss the propaganda themes and activities of the KMT, the CCP, the National Salvation Association, the Chinese Liberation Action Committee (The Third Party), the Youth Party, the National Social Party, and the Vocational Education Group. Sources of their political programs are quoted at some length from original documents. A list of their newspapers and periodicals with annotations is extremely useful for reference.

147. Wu Han-chen 吳涵真. Chiu-kuo shih-jen t'uan tsu-chih kang-yao 救國十人團組織綱要 (An Organizational Outline for the Ten-Man National Salvation Group). n.p., n. pub., n.d. 1 p. (2991.2/2334)

This appears to be a left-wing educator's proposal for the establishment of a national salvation organization in the 1930's.

148. Yeh Ch'ing 葉青 (pseud. of Jen Cho-hsüan 任卓宣). Tang-p'ai wen-t'i 黨派問題 (Party Problems). n.p., Chung-chung, 1940. 124 pp. (4737/2123)

This pamphlet consists of eight articles written by a noted ex-Communist KMT theorist, who attempts to solve by theoretical discussions the problems posed by CCP collaboration with the KMT. The writings originally appeared in various newspapers and magazines.

B. CH'EN TU-HSIU

The following are writings and speeches made by Ch'en Tu-hsiu in 1937 and 1938, after his release from Nanking prison in September 1937. These pamphlets were all issued by the same publisher (whose office moved to several cities because of the war). Each pamphlet title is taken from the title of one of the speeches or articles in the collection, which deal mainly with Ch'en's views on the Sino-Japanese War, KMT-CCP relations, and related subjects. In this connection, attention is called to the posthumous publication of a collection of six letters and four articles written by Ch'en between March 1940 and

May 13, 1942, under the title Ch'en Tu-hsiu tsui-hou tui-yü min-chu cheng-chih ti chien-chieh (Ch'en Tu-hsiu's Final Views on Democracy) in item no. 194 of my earlier volume, <u>The Chinese Communist Movement 1921-1937</u>.

Also included in this section are works attacking the activities of the Trotskyites. It should be noted, however, that Ch'en Tu-hsiu declared later that he no longer belonged to the Trotskyite group or any other political organization. It is merely a matter of convenience that these works are grouped together.

149.   Ch'en Shao-yü 陳紹禹 and others. T'o-p'ai tsai Chung-kuo 托派在中國 (The Trotskyites in China). Chinhua, Hsin Chung-kuo, 1939. 184 pp. (4292.29/7922)

A collection of ten articles and speeches by Ch'en Shao-yü, K'ang Sheng, Hsü T'e-li, and others. Of special interest are those on the execution of Wang Kung-tu in Kwangsi, the arrests of Chang Mu-t'ao in Shansi, and Ch'en Po-ta's attack on Ch'en Tu-hsiu's views of the Sino-Japanese War.

150.   Ch'en Tu-hsiu 陳獨秀. K'ang-Jih chan-cheng chih i-i 抗日戰爭之意義 (The Significance of the War of Resistance Against Japan). Shanghai, Ya-tung, 1937. 18 pp. (2991.03/7942.56)

The title is taken from a speech delivered at the Central China University (Hua-chung ta-hsüeh), Wuchang, on October 6, 1937. The other article in this pamphlet was written for the anniversary of the Republican Revolution of October 10, 1911.

151.   _____. Kao Jih-pen she-hui chu-i che 告日本社會主義者 (To the Japanese Socialists). Kunming, Ya-tung, 1938. 25 pp. (2991.03/7942.261)

The title is taken from one of the six articles in this pamphlet, three of them dated July and August, 1938. Among the subjects dealt with are capitalism and socialism.

152. _____. Min-tsu yeh-hsin 民族野心 (National Ambition). Canton, Ya-tung, 1938. 18 pp. (2991.03/7942.70)

Five selected articles and speeches, which appear to have been written or delivered in July 1938 (the author was then in Chungking). Among the subjects discussed are capitalism in China and guerrilla war.

153. _____. Tsen-yang shih yu-ch'ien che ch'u-ch'ien yu-li che ch'u-li 怎樣使有錢者出錢有力者出力 (How to Persuade the Rich to Contribute Money and the Poor to Contribute Labor). Shanghai, Ya-tung, 1937. 18 pp. (2991.03/7942.84)

Five selected articles (one of them dated November 9, 1937), including one on Lu Hsün and his alleged views on the United Front.

154. _____. Ts'ung kuo-chi hsing-shih kuan-ch'a Chung-kuo k'ang-chan ch'ien-t'u 從國際形勢觀察中國抗戰前途 (The Future of the War of Resistance in Relation to the International Situation). Canton, Ya-tung, 1938. 18 pp. (2991.03/7942.26)

Two of the three articles in this pamphlet deal with KMT-CCP problems during the war.

155. _____. Wo-men tuan-jan yu-chiu 我們斷然有救 (We Will Definitely Survive). Canton, Ya-tung, 1938. 18 pp. (2991.03/7942.22)

In the four articles here the author discusses war and reconstruction and makes recommendations for political and economic systems to be adopted by the KMT.

156. _____. Wo tui-yü k'ang-chan ti i-chien 我對於抗戰的意見 (My Own View on the War of Resistance). Canton, Ya-tung, 1938. 39 pp. (2991.03/7942.23)

Three of the five articles are speeches delivered in Wuchang and Hankow, October - November 1938. An important article describes a ten-point wartime political program advocated by the author.

157. Ta-lu 大路. (The Great Road). Nos. 1, 3, and 8. Canton, n.d. - December 20, 1937. (4292.01/4366)

This weekly of current political affairs was not published regularly. Issue No. 8 includes an article on the activities and arrests of Wang Kung-tu and other alleged Trotskyites in Kwangsi province.

158. Wei-mo 微沫 (pseud.). Liang-nien i-lai t'o-p'ai tsui-hsing ti tsung-chieh 兩年以來托派罪行的總結 (The Criminal Activities of the Trotskyites in the Last Two Years). Kweilin, Hsin-chih, 1939. 123 pp. (4292.29/2439)

Basing his argument partly on Chinese Trotskyite publications that appeared after the outbreak of the Sino-Japanese War, the author denounces the strategy and program of the Trotskyites and their attitude toward the war. An article by P'eng Chen on Trotskyite activities in the Shansi-Chahar-Hopeh Border Region is included as an appendix.

C. KMT-CCP RELATIONS

The KMT-CCP United Front reached its high point in Hankow in 1938. Shortly after the fall of the city there were signs of deterioration of their relations. After the clashes in Hopeh in 1938, larger operations took place between the KMT-CCP guerrilla forces in Hopeh in 1939, and these continued into the spring of 1940. The New Fourth Army Incident of 1941 brought about a sharp deterioration in the internal situation and heightened the danger of civil war; wartime cooperation between the KMT and the CCP virtually ended then.

All the titles listed in this section were published between 1940 and 1945; they deal generally with relations between the two parties. Materials pertaining to the New Fourth Army Incident are arranged under separate heading.

159. Chang Cheng-ming 張政明 (ed.). Min-chu yü t'uan-chieh 民主與團結 (Democracy and Unity). Chungking, Tu-li, 1945. 199 pp. (2992/1137)

This book consists of four parts: (1) a collection of 24 editorials from Chinese newspapers published in Chungking between September 16, 1944, and April 3, 1945, commenting on the problems of democracy and unity in the nation; (2) English and American newspaper comments on the subject; (3) Chiang Kai-shek's speech delivered on March 1, 1945; and (4) Chang Chih-chung's important report made at the People's Political Council on KMT-CCP negotiations between May and August 1944, with all related records and documents.

In November 1945, seven months after the publication of this book, a "second edition" was published by the Min-tsu ch'u-pan she under the editorship of Wang Han-min. This "second edition" is identical in every way with the original, but no reference has been made to it.

160. Chang T'ieh-chün 張鐵君. Chung-kung wen-t'i p'ing-i 中共問題平議 (An Objective Discussion of the Chinese Communist Problems). Chungking, Cheng-lun, 1943. 74 pp. (2991.2/1381)

Comments and discussions of the CCP's theoretical basis and practice.

161. Cheng-chih yüeh-k'an 政治月刊 (Political Monthly). Vol. I, Nos. 4-5. Shanghai, April 20 - May 20, 1941. (2991.5/1371)

A magazine published in the Wang Ching-wei puppet regime. An article by Chin Chün-chih on the antagonism between the KMT and CCP appears in these two issues.

162. Chieh-fang she 解放社 (ed.). Tsai min-chu yü t'uan-chieh ti chi-ch'u shang chia-ch'iang k'ang-chan cheng-ch'ü tsui-hou sheng-li 在民主與團結的基礎上加強抗戰爭取最後勝利 (On the Basis of Democracy and Unity Strengthening the War of Resistance and Winning the Final Victory). n.p., same,

1944. various pagination. (2991.03/2503)

    Eight editorials from the Liberation Daily of June - July 1944 and a circular telegram issued by several Yenan organizations celebrating United Nations Day. The title is taken from an editorial of the newspaper, July 7, 1944.

163. Chin-jih chih mo-ts'a wen-t'i 今日之磨擦問題 (Today's Rift Problems). n.p., Chin-pu, 1940. 55 pp. (2991.2/8630)

    Following the publication of the Mo-ts'a ts'ung-ho erh lai in the spring of 1940 (see item no. 169), the same publisher compiled these official documents of the KMT and CCP in December of the same year in order to place the blame on the National Government for the rifts of the two parties. Among the documents included are: (1) the CCP demands of the KMT regarding the party, the 18th Group Army, the New Fourth Army, and the Shensi-Kansu-Ningsia Border Region, June 1940; (2) the KMT's answer to the above demands, July 2, 1940; (3) the KMT's decisions of July 16, 1940, regarding the area of the Border Region and of the Communist Army; (4) the CCP's counter-proposal of August 1940; and (5) Chou En-lai's proposal for the adjustment of war zones that were to be under the jurisdiction of Communist forces. This pamphlet provides useful background information in regard to the New Fourth Army Incident, which occurred shortly after its publication.

164. Chou En-lai 周恩來 and others. Kuan-yü hsien-cheng yü t'uan-chieh wen-t'i 關於憲政與團結問題 (On Constitutional Government and Unity). [Chekiang], Po-chung, 1944. 43 pp. (4890.18/7264)

    Reprints of (1) Chou En-lai's speech at the meeting held in Yenan commemorating the 19th anniversary of Sun Yat-sen's death; (2) a report by the New China News Agency on the constitutional movement in China; (3) statements and talks by Lin Po-ch'ü and Wu Yü-chang; and (4) a declaration of the Association for Promoting Constitutional Government, which was founded in Yenan on February 20, 1940.

165. Fan Feng-lin 樊鳳林. Chung-kung yü erh-chieh ts'an-cheng hui 中共與二屆參政會 (The Chinese Communists and the Second Congress of the People's Political Council). Chengtu, Chung-chih, 1941. 72 pp. (4890.192/4374)

The Chinese Communists refused to attend the Second Congress of the People's Political Council, which convened shortly after the New Fourth Army Incident. This book includes the following documents: (1) Chiang Kai-shek's speech, March 8, 1941; (2) a resolution of the People's Political Council; and (3) editorials by pro-KMT newspapers.

166. Hsin Chung-kuo pao-she 新中國報社 (ed.). Hsin Chung-kuo p'ing-lun chi 新中國評論集 (Selected Writings from the New China Journal). Shanghai, same, 1943. 248 pp. (2991.53/0564)

Section VII of this book contains eleven editorials and articles published in an organ of the Wang Ching-wei puppet regime. They were written between November 24, 1940, and November 25, 1942, and relate to KMT-CCP relations.

167. Hua-pei cheng-wu wei-yüan hui. Cheng-wu t'ing. Ch'ing-pao chü 華北政務委員會政務廳情報局 (comp.). Kuo-kung hsiang-k'o 國共相尅 (The Kuomintang and the Communists Destroy Each Other). [Peking], same, 1943. 37 pp. (2991.2/4111)

Compiled and published by the Information Office of the Political Affairs Bureau of the North China Administrative Council (Japanese-sponsored puppet regime), this book presents a concise chronological account of the KMT-CCP conflict from 1927.

168. Kung-ch'an tang chih tsui-o 共產黨之罪惡 (The Communist Party's Evil). n.p., 1940. 45 pp. (2991.2/5667)

Edited and published by Wang Ching-wei's "Propaganda Department of the Central Executive Committee of the Kuomintang," this pamphlet contains three articles and four editorials of the Chung-hua jih-pao, denouncing the CCP conspiracy.

169. Kuo-min ko-ming chün. Ti shih-pa chi-t'uan chün. Cheng-chih pu 國民革命軍第十八集團軍政治部. Mo-ts'a ts'ung-ho erh lai 磨擦從何而來 (Whence the Conflict?). n.p., same, 1940. 51 pp. (2991.2/8482)

    Compiled and published by the Political Department of the 18th Group Army, this book places the blame for the rift between the KMT and the CCP on the National Government. The book contains a number of secret government documents and directives aimed at containing Communist activities and expansion in North China, north Shensi, and in the Japanese-occupied territory.

170. Lin Chung-kuo 林忠國 Kung-ch'an tang p'o-huai k'ang-chien chih ching-kuo 共產黨破壞抗建之經過 (The Communist Obstruction of the War of Resistance and National Reconstruction). n.p., n. pub., 1941. 44 pp. (2991.2/4956)

    Primarily a KMT presentation of the fighting between KMT and CCP troops after their first clash in Hopeh in 1938.

171. Ta-chung jih-pao she 大眾日報社 (ed.). Ch'i-lai chih-chih nei-chan wan-chiu wei-wang 起來制止內戰挽救危亡 (Arise to Stop the Civil War and Save the Nation). Vol. II. n.p., same, 1943. 54 pp. (2991.2/4664)

    This volume contains letters and telegrams sent to Chiang Kai-shek and other leaders of the National Government by Chu Teh and other Communist military leaders and mass organizations with regard to the deteriorating relations between KMT and CCP. All the documents appear to have been issued in July 1943. According to the preface of the book, Volumes I and III (not available) are devoted, respectively, to related articles and public reaction.

172. Ts'an-cheng hui yü yen-lun tzu-yu 參政會與言論自由 (The People's Political Council and the Freedom of Speech). Shanghai, Shang-hai tsa-chih, 1941. 52 pp. (4890.19/2187)

    This pamphlet consists of (1) texts of letters exchanged between the People's Political Council and the seven Communist leaders, who refused to attend the Council meetings; (2) the Yenan Hsin chung-hua pao's editorials commenting on their position; and (3) reports of KMT persecution of the Chungking New China Daily, the K'ai-ming jih-pao (began publication in Hengyang, Hunan on August 13, 1939), and of the bookstore Sheng-huo shu-tien.

173. Tsou Yang 鄒陽. Kuo-kung chih-chien 國共之間 (Between the Kuomintang and the Communist Party of China). n.p., Li-shih, 1945. 78 pp. (2991.2/2272)

    Selected documents concerning KMT and CCP relations from 1937 to 1945. The editor maintains an impartial position.

174. Tu Yüan 杜遠. Kuo-kung ho-tso ti wei-lai 國共合作之未來 (The Prospect for Kuomintang and Communist Cooperation). Shanghai, Kuo-nan, 1937. 41 pp. (2991.2/4133)

    A concise non-partisan discussion of the KMT-CCP relations.

175. Wu Man-chün 吳曼君. I-ko cheng-fu i-ko tang 一個政府一個黨 (One Government, One Party). 2nd ed. Chungking, Sheng-li, 1941. 60 pp. (2991.2/2361)

    On the premise that China should have only one government (the Nationalist Government) and one party (the KMT), the author proposes that the only solution for CCP problems in China was the dissolution of all political parties except the KMT.

176. Yü Chung-hua 余仲華 (ed.). Chung-kung wen-t'i t'i-yao 中共問題提要 (A Compendium of Chinese Communist Problems). 2nd ed. n.p., Min-chih, 1945. 164 pp. (2987/8924)

Edited from the KMT viewpoint, this book deals primarily with the Communist military, economic, and political activities. Its supplement contains seventeen documents, which are useful for the study of KMT-CCP relations from 1938 to March 1945.

VII. THE NEW FOURTH ARMY INCIDENT

The New Fourth Army was built from remnants of the Red Army that had been left behind in Kiangsi and Fukien after the Communists started the Long March in October 1934. In October 1937, three months after the outbreak of the Sino-Japanese War, the New Fourth Army was formally created by order of the National Government. It was organized in February of the following year and went into action shortly afterwards. Numbering about 12,000 officers and men, it was operating by the end of 1940 in various districts of Anhwei, Kiangsu, Chekiang, and Hupeh. On January 7, 1941, Government forces attacked the Headquarters of the New Fourth Army in southern Anhwei on the grounds that the Army did not move to the north bank of the Yangtze as ordered. As a result Commander Yeh T'ing was wounded and taken prisoner and the Deputy Commander Hsiang Ying was killed. The Communists called this the "Southern Anhwei Incident." The following works furnish documentary material as well as newspaper comments of the event.

177. Chan-tsai k'ang-chan ti li-ch'ang shang tui-yü hsin-ssu-chün shih-chien chiang chi-chu kung-tao hua 站在抗戰的立場上對於新四軍事件講幾句公道話 (An Objective Observation on the New Fourth Army Incident from the Viewpoint of the War of Resistance). n.p., n. pub., 1941. 18 pp. (2991.2/0456)

Considering the New Fourth Army Incident as a matter of military discipline, this observation appears to be by someone who was sympathetic to the National Government.

178. Ch'en Chün 陳俊 (ed.). Hsin-ssu-chün man-chi 新四軍漫記 (On the New Fourth Army). Shanghai, T'ung-i, 1939. 186 pp. (4292.9/7924.06)

Mainly based on the writings of foreign correspondents, this book deals with the New Fourth Army and has two chapters on its commanders, Yeh T'ing and Hsiang Ying. Sources are not given.

179. Ch'en Ts'ung-i 陳從一. Huan-nan shih-pien ch'ien-hou 皖南事變前後. (Before and After the Southern Anhwei Incident). Shanghai, Hsin-hua, 1950. 79 pp. (4292.9/7921)

 A somewhat literary account of the author's life as a prisoner after the New Fourth Army Incident. He was with the 2nd Detachment of the Army when it was captured by KMT troops.

180. Ch'en Yi (Ch'en I) 陳毅. Huan-nan shih-pien ti chen-hsiang Su-pei shih-pien ti chen-hsiang 皖南事變的真相蘇北事變的真相 (The True Stories of the Clashes in Southern Anhwei and Northern Kiangsu). [Yenan], 1944. manuscript. various pagination. (4292.24/7904)

 A photostatic copy of Ch'en Yi's letter, dated August 28, 1944, to Colonel David D. Barrett, recounting clashes between KMT troops and the New Fourth Army in southern Anhwei and northern Kiangsu in the years 1939-41. Barrett was then in command of a detachment sent to Yenan by the Commanding General of the China-Burma-India Theatre for the purpose of maintaining liaison with the Chinese Communists. The manuscript also includes carbon copies of Barrett's letter (written after the war) to the U.S. Department of the Army, with background information and an English translation of Ch'en Yi's letter and report. (Five maps.)

181. Chiang Chih-chien 江志堅. Su-pei kuei-hung 蘇北歸鴻 (Letters from Northern Kiangsu). Chungking, Sheng-li, 1941. 96 pp. (4292.24/3147)

 Twenty-one letters written between September 15 and November 25, 1940, by a man who traveled through 17 Communist districts in northern Kiangsu in order to "rescue" his younger brother, who had joined the Communist forces. Local conditions were unfavorably reported in great detail in these letters.

182. Chien-kuo ch'u-pan she 建國出版社 (ed.). Kuan-yü hsin-ssu-chün shih-chien hua-ch'iao yü-lun i-pan 關於新四軍事件華僑輿論一班 (Public Opinion of the Overseas Chinese on the New Fourth Army Incident). Manila, same, 1941. 209 pp. (2991.2/1622)

This book is divided into three parts: (1) comments and editorials of overseas Chinese newspapers on the New Fourth Army Incident; (2) statements and circular telegrams of overseas Chinese organizations; and (3) a supplement, which includes an interview with Tan Kah Kee (Ch'en Chia-keng) on KMT-CCP relations. Little pro-KMT material is included.

183. Chung-hsin ch'u-pan she 中心出版社. Hsin-ssu-chün shih-chien chen-hsiang 新四軍事件真相 (The Factual Picture of the New Fourth Army Incident). Chuchiang, same, 1941. 74 pp. (2991/5322)

These selected documents and newspaper editorials on the New Fourth Army Incident are: (1) two telegrams from Ho Ying-ch'in and Pai Ch'ung-hsi to Chu Teh and P'eng Te-huai, dated October 19, 1940, and December 8, 1940; (2) an official announcement of the Military Council of the National Government, January 18, 1941; (3) Chiang Kai-shek's speech delivered on January 27, 1941; and (4) newspaper editorial comments. No Communist document is included in the book except an excerpt of a telegram from Chu Teh to Ho and Pai.

184. Chung-kung pu-fa hsing-wei chi p'o-huai k'ang-chan shih-shih chi-yao 中共不法行為及破壞抗戰事實紀要 (The Unlawful Acts of the Chinese Communist Party and a Record of Its Obstruction of the War of Resistance). Chuchiang, Chung-hsin, n.d. 23 pp. (2987/5413)

This pamphlet purports to show the unlawful acts of the CCP between 1937 and 1940 in order to refute the contention of Chu Teh and P'eng Te-huai (made in their telegrams dated December 25, 1939, and January 15, 1940) that the KMT was responsible for the rift between the two parties. It lists a number of events purporting to prove that the CCP had been obstructing the government's administration and financial system, attacking the government troops, and expanding its own army. According to a Communist source, this pamphlet was originally published by the Political Department of the Tienshui Field Headquarters of Generalissimo Chiang Kai-shek in February 1940.

185. Hsia Yang 夏陽. Huang-ch'iao chan-tou 黃橋戰鬥 (Fighting at Huangchiao). Nanking, Jen-min, 1956. 36 pp. (4292.9/1472.44)

   A brief account of an important battle in northern Kiangsu that paved the way for the establishment of a Communist base by the New Fourth Army.

186. Hsiang Ying 項英. Hsiang Ying chiang-chün yen-lun chi 項英將軍言論集 (Collected Speeches of Hsiang Ying). Chinhua, Chi-na, 1939. 92 pp. (2991.03/2222)

   Important source material on the founding of the New Fourth Army, its battle experience, and its development in its first year (1938), as narrated by its deputy commander.

187. Hsin-hua jih-pao Hua-pei fen-kuan 新華日報華北分館 (ed.). Ch'üan-kuo ch'i-lai chih-chih tang-ch'ien yen-chung wei-chi 全國起來制止當前嚴重危機 (The Whole Country Should Arise to Stop the Present Serious Crisis). n.p., same, 1941. 72 pp. (2991.2/8644)

   Edited and published by the North China Office of the New China Daily, this pamphlet includes: (1) editorials of the Yenan Hsin chung-hua pao and Chieh-fang on the deterioration of KMT-CCP relations; (2) P'eng Te-huai's report at a cadre meeting, November 22, 1940; and (3) texts of telegrams sent by Chu Teh, P'eng Te-huai, Yeh T'ing, and Hsiang Ying to Ho Ying-ch'in. Although the pamphlet was published on October 10, 1941, the manuscript had apparently been sent to the printer shortly before the outbreak of the "New Fourth Army Incident."

188. K'ang-ti 抗敵 (Resist the Enemy). No. 11. Chinghsien. April 16, 1940. (2991.01/5104)

This issue of the semi-monthly contains combat statistics of the New Fourth Army for March 1940.

189. Kung-tang p'o-huai k'ang-chan yin-mou ti tsung pao-lu 共黨破壞抗戰陰謀的總暴露 (Exposé of the Communist Conspiracy in Its Obstruction of the War Effort). n.p., n. pub., 1941. 228 pp. (4292.24/4914)

Compiled from the viewpoint of the National Government, this is a comprehensive survey of the unlawful acts of the CCP that led to the New Fourth Army Incident. A number of secret Communist documents are included.

190. Ou Chiang-tung 區江東 (ed.). K'ang chien kuo-ts'e hsia chih Chung-kuo kung-ch'an tang 抗建國策下之中國共產黨 (The Chinese Communist Party Under the National Policy of the War of Resistance and Reconstruction). Kweilin, T'ung-i, 1941. 172 pp. (2991.2/7135)

Published shortly after the New Fourth Army Incident in order to show the conspiracy of the CCP, this book includes several allegedly secret Communist documents, statements of defectors, and editorial comments on the incident from Chinese newspapers in China and abroad.

191. Shang-jao chi-chung ying 上饒集中營 (The Concentration Camp at Shangjao). Revised and enlarged ed. Shanghai, Jen-min, 1952. 278 pp. (2991.2/4173.1)

A collection of personal accounts by prisoners in a KMT concentration camp in Shangjao, Kiangsi. Most of the inmates were cadre and soldiers of the New Fourth Army. With a preface by Jao Sou-shih, dated January 13, 1945.

192. Tzu-ch'in 孜槳. Ch'u-tung chung ti hsin-ssu-chün 出動中的新四軍 (The New Fourth Army on the March). Hankow, Ch'ün-li, 1938. 84 pp. (4292.24/1419)

A personal account of the First Group of the First Detachment of the New Fourth Army, which set out for combat from their Hunan-Hupeh-Kiangsi border base on February 9, 1938.

193.　　Yin Yang 殷楊．Huan-nan t'u-wei chi 皖南突圍記 (Breakthrough in Southern Anhwei). Harbin, Tung-pei shu-tien, 1947. 46 pp. (4292.24/2452)

A somewhat literary work of 1942, this is a personal account of the New Fourth Army Incident, with several Communist documents.

VIII. THE ARMY

A. GENERAL

According to a wartime press interview with Yeh Chien-ying, Chief of the Staff of the 18th Group Army, the Chinese Communist army, including the regular and guerrilla forces, expanded from 92,000 in 1937 to 474,476 in 1944, in addition to 2,130,000 militia. The two largest units of the Chinese Communist army during the war were the Eighth Route Army and the New Fourth Army. The former was officially renamed the 18th Group Army of the National Army, although both names were used interchangeably in Communist publications. After World War II these forces were called the People's Liberation Army.

The territory controlled by the Communist forces consisted of a large area in North China under the jurisdiction of the 18th Group Army, a much smaller area in Central China under the New Fourth Army, and two very small areas (the East River and Hainan Island) in Kwangtung Province of South China.

This section lists sources that relate mainly to the Communist army in North and Central China. For the material concerning the East River Region and Hainan Island, see the "Kwangtung Base Area" section. Communist troops in many areas had to produce part or all of their own food and clothing in order to exist; for information about such production and the various activities of the Army in the regions other than North

China, consult the works listed under the headings of the various regions concerned.

194. Ch'eng Shih 程栻. Kung-chün nei-mo chieh-p'ou 共軍內幕解剖 (Inside the Communist Army). Hong Kong, Tzu-yu, 1951. 122 pp. (4292.9/2154)

    An analysis by an anti-Communist writer of the organization, training, and recruitment methods of the Communist army. It is a useful aid to understanding the local background of the New Fourth Army Incident and the rise of Ch'en Yi. The facts, however, should be carefully checked.

195. Ch'ien-hsien yüeh-k'an 前綫月刊 (The Front Monthly). Nos. 5 and 6. n.p., November - December 1940. microfilm. (2991.01/8225.71)

    An army publication of high quality. These issues include important reports of P'eng Te-huai, Yang Shang-k'un, and Lo Jui-ch'ing at the high-level cadre meeting of the North Bureau of the CC of the CCP.

196. Chin-ch'a-Chi chün-ch'ü cheng-chih pu 晉察冀軍區政治部 Hsin chan-shih k'o-pen 新戰士課本 (A Textbook for Training Troops). n.p., same, [1946]. 39 pp. (4292.9/8863.06)

    Edited and published by the Political Department of the Shansi-Chahar-Hopeh Military Region, this pamphlet consists of nine lessons used by the Eighth Route Army in training soldiers.

197. _____. Jen-min chan-cheng 人民戰爭 (The People's War). n.p., same, 1946. no pagination. (4292.9/8863.87)

    A pictorial pamphlet concerning the Shansi-Chahar-Hopeh Border Region from its establishment in 1938 to the Communist capture of Kalgan in December 1948.

198. _____. Pa-lu chün ho lao-pai-hsing 八路軍和老百姓 (The Eighth Route Army and the People). n.p., same, 1946. no pagination. (4292.9/8862.86)

　　A pictorial representation of the following campaigns: "Support the Government," "Love the People," "Support the Army," and "Cherish Soldiers' Dependents."

199. Chu Teh 朱德. Lun chieh-fang ch'ü chan-ch'ang 論解放區戰場 (On the Battle Front of the Liberated Areas). n.p., Chieh-fang, May 1945. 65 pp. (4292.9/2923)

　　A military report made by Chu Teh at the Seventh Congress of the CCP on April 25, 1945. He discussed the problems and achievements of the Communist forces in the War of Resistance against Japan and pointed out the future direction and tasks of the army. The text of this report has subsequently appeared in various editions. An English translation is available.

200. [Chung-kuo kuo-min tang.] Chung-yang kai-tsao wei-yüan hui. Ti-liu tsu 中國國民黨中央改組委員會第六組 (ed.). Chung-kung chün-shih 中共軍事 (The Chinese Communist Army). Taipei, same, 1951. 89 pp. (4292.9/5667.54)

　　Edited and published by the Sixth Section of the Central Reorganization Committee of the Kuomintang, this book is divided into six chapters dealing systematically with the organization, characteristics, strategy, and tactics of the Chinese Communist Army from its early development to 1950.

201. _____. (ed.). Huo-kuo ts'an-min ti kung-fei chün-shih 禍國殘民的共匪軍事 (Betrayal of the Nation and Suppression of the People by the Communist Bandits' Army). Taipei, Chung-yang wen-wu, 1952. 70 pp. (4292.9/5661)

　　This pamphlet is primarily devoted to a discussion of Party politics and party-army relations as well as political activities in the army and militia of the CCP.

202. Huang T'ao 黄濤. Chung-kuo jen-min chieh-fang chün ti san-shih nien 中國人民解放軍的三十年 (Thirty Years of the Chinese People's Liberation Army). Peking, Jen-min, 1958. 60 pp. (4292.9/4834)

　　A useful, concise, chronological account of the development of the Chinese Communist forces from 1927 to 1950.

203. Jen-min ch'u-pan she 人民出版社 (ed.). K'ang-Jih chan-cheng shih-ch'i Chung-kuo jen-min chieh-fang chün 抗日戰爭時期中國人民解放軍 (The People's Liberation Army During the War of Resistance). Peking, same, 1953. 231 pp. (4292.9/8722)

　　With slight revisions, this is a reprint of a book entitled K'ang-chan pa-nien lai ti pa-lu chün yü hsin-ssu-chün (item no. 209), a comprehensive report on the operations of Chinese Communist military forces from 1937 to March 1945.

204. Kung-fei chan-lueh chan-shu chih yen-chiu 共匪戰略戰術之研究 (A Study of the Strategy and Tactics of Communist Bandits). Taiwan, Ko-ming shih-chien, 1953. 35 pp. (4292.9/4766)

　　An informative KMT analysis of CCP military strategy from 1930 to 1949.

205. Kung-lun ch'u-pan she 公論出版社 (ed.). Chung-kung chih mi-mi chün-shih kung-tso 中共之秘密軍事工作 (The Secret Military Work of the Chinese Communists). n.p., same, 1941. 18 pp. (4292.9/8022)

　　This pamphlet describes how the Chinese Communists worked in their own army and in the war zones. It attacks their methods of subversion in the KMT forces.

206. Kuo Chi-chiao 郭寄嶠. Kung-fei chün-shih chih p'ou-hsi 共匪軍事之剖析 (An Analysis of the Military Machine of

the Chinese Communist Bandits). Taiwan, Yang-ming, 1951. 96 pp. (4292.9/0232)

An informative KMT analysis of the CCP military strategy, organization, intelligence system, political work, and education in the army, with statistics and maps. The book is organized in topical and chronological order (1927-50).

207. Pa-lu chün chün-cheng tsa-chih 八路軍軍政雜誌 (The Military and Political Affairs Magazine of the Eighth Route Army). Nos. 2, and 8-9. n.p., February 15 - September 25, 1939. (4292.9/8633)

An organ of the Political Department of the Eighth Route Army, this periodical carries current Communist news and writings. Among the important articles published in issue No. 2 are: (1) Mao Tse-tung's preface, entitled "War of Resistance and Foreign Assistance," which was written on January 20, 1939, for the English translation of his "Lun ch'ih-chiu chan" (On the Protracted War); (2) Wang Chia-hsiang's writings on the united front; and (3) Lo Jui-ch'ing on the cadre-education problem in the army. Issue No. 8 (August 25, 1939) includes articles by Liu Po-ch'eng on guerrilla warfare experience in North China (continued in issue No. 9), Wang Chen on the defeat of the Japanese attack on Shansi-Chahar-Hopeh area, and Lü Cheng-ts'ao on guerrilla warfare in open territory. Mao Tse-tung's interview with a correspondent of the New China Daily, September 1, 1939, on the new international situation, and his speech at a cadre meeting in Yenan on September 14, 1939, on the "second imperialist war" appear in issue No. 9.

208. Shih-shih wen-t'i yen-chiu hui 時事問題研究會 (ed.). K'ang-chan chung ti Chung-kuo chün-shih 抗戰中的中國軍事 (Chinese Military Affairs During the War of Resistance). n.p., K'ang-chan shu-tien, 1940. 237 pp. (2991/6576.56)

Edited by the Association for the Study of Current Affairs, Yenan, this is a compilation of writings selected from current newspapers and periodicals on the Sino-Japanese War, with special emphasis on the Communist Army, guerrilla forces, and mass organizations. Sources are given in each selection.

209. Ti shih-pa chi-t'uan chün. Tsung cheng-chih pu. Hsüan-ch'uan pu 第十八集團軍總政治部宣傳部 (ed.). K'ang-chan pa-nien lai ti pa-lu chün yü hsin-ssu-chün 抗戰八年來的八路軍與新四軍 (The Eighth Route Army and the New Fourth Army During Eight Years of War). n.p., n. pub., [1945]. 226 pp. (4292.9/8482)

    Edited by the Propaganda Department of the General Political Department of the 18th Group Army, this is a comprehensive operational report of the Chinese Communist army from 1937 to March 1945. See Jen-min ch'u-pan she, ed., K'ang-Jih chan-cheng shih-ch'i Chung-kuo jen-min chieh-fang chün (item no. 203).

210. _____. Chung-chi kuo-wen tu-pen 中級國文讀本 (Intermediate Chinese Readings). Vol. I. n.p., same, 1942. 110 pp. (5205/8482)

    This textbook contains readings considered suitable for the Communist Army; some of the selected writings are of historical value.

211. Yeh Chien-ying 葉劍英. Chung-kung k'ang-chan i-pan ch'ing-k'uang ti chieh-shao 中共抗戰一般情況的介紹 (The General Situation of the Chinese Communist War Effort Against the Japanese). n.p., Chieh-fang, July 1944. 38 pp. (4292.9/4984)

    A talk by Yeh Chien-ying, Chief of Staff of the 18th Group Army, to a group of Chinese and foreign reporters on June 22, 1944. On the basis of intelligence received in March 1944, Yeh analyzed the Japanese situation in China. According to his information, the total Japanese forces in China (probably excluding Manchuria) at that time were 34.5 divisions, totalling 560,000 men. He also reviewed the achievements of the Chinese Communist army through the War of Resistance against Japan. According to him, the Chinese Communist army, including the regular and guerrilla forces, expanded from 92,000 in 1937 to 474,476 in 1944, in addition to 2,130,000 militia.

B. WAR EFFORT

Most of the works selected under this heading are periodicals and books on the Eighth Route Army. Some compare the war efforts of the KMT and the CCP forces.

212. Chan-ti t'ung-hsün 戰地通信 (War Correspondence). Nos. 7-10, 12-18, 20, 22-26, and 29-30. Hong Kong, December 19, 1937 - March 1, 1938. (2991.01/6430)

This weekly of war reports occasionally carried news concerning the Communist leaders. For example, issue No. 10 (January 9, 1938) contains an interview in Yenan with Mao Tse-tung (December 5, 1937), who discussed the prospects of the Sino-Japanese War. An interview with P'eng Te-huai in Hankow, January 19, 1938, on the war in North China was published in issue No. 15 (February 13, 1938). Chu Teh on "Experience and Lessons of the Eighth Route Army Against Japan in the Last Half-Year" is available in issue No. 17 (February 27, 1938).

213. Ch'ien-hsien 前綫 (The War Front). Nos. 2 and 3/4. n.p., February 6 - February 12, 1938. (4292.9/8223)

This weekly was edited and published by the General Political Department of the 18th Group Army. Among the useful articles in issue No. 2 are Hsiao K'o on guerrilla warfare, Lu Ting-i on KMT-CCP relations, and Ho Lung on anti-Japanese warfare in northwest Shansi. Issue No. 3/4 contains an article by Chu Teh on the war experience and lessons of the Eighth Route Army and other articles by Jen Pi-shih, Teng Hsiao-p'ing and Tso Ch'üan (the last two on education for new recruits). It also contains a text of the CCP Politburo's resolution, dated December 13, 1937, calling for the convention of the Seventh Congress of the CCP.

214. Chin-jih hsin-wen 今日新聞 (Today's News). n.p., 1939. mimeo. (2991.01/8607)

Chinese Communist army as well as national and international news dispatches, issued by the New China News Agency on September 22, 1939.

215. Hao-jan 浩然 (ed.). Hung-ch'ü shih-lun t'e-chi 紅區時論特輯 (Selected Writings on Current Affairs in the Red Area). n.p., Sheng-lu, 1938. 156 pp. (2991.2/3623)

No source is given for this collection of 25 articles and news dispatches. They appear to have been selected from current newspapers or periodicals. Among the writings of interest are: (1) P'eng Te-huai's talk on the war against Japan (November 15, 1937); and (2) an excerpt from the Ta Kung Pao correspondent's interview with Jen Pi-shih, head of the Political Department of the Eighth Route Army, originally published on November 2, 1937. The book is poorly edited, and its title is misleading; the writings were not published in the Red area.

216. Ho Ch'ang-kung 何長工. Hung-chün ti-pa chün tang ti sheng-huo 紅軍第八軍黨的生活 (Party Life in the Eighth Route Army). n.p., n.d. (4292.9/2271)

This appears to be a magazine article written in the 1930's by the political commissar of the 5th Column, which later became part of the Eighth Route Army. It deals with the CCP organization and leadership in the army.

217. Hsin Chung-kuo ch'u-pan she 新中國出版社 (ed.). Hsin Chung-kuo tsai chin-chan chung 新中國在進展中 (New China Is Marching Forward). Shanghai, same, 1937. 52 pp. (2991.2/0562)

Poorly edited. The only document not readily available in other books is an interview with Chu Teh and P'eng Te-huai by Wang Shao-t'ung.

218. Hsin hsüeh-shih 新學識 (New Knowledge). Vol. II, Nos. 3, 5, 11, and 12. Hankow, November 10, 1937 - April 25, 1938. (2991.01/0270)

A semi-monthly which sometimes contains articles relating to the Chinese Communist movement. For example, No. 5 (December 10, 1937) contains [Chou] Li-po's article on P'eng Te-huai, who had discussed the war situation. An article on the Trotskyites and the Sino-Japanese War appears in No. 11 (April 10, 1938). An interview with Liao Ch'en-yün (Ch'en Yün?) in Yenan was published in No. 12. (It may be noted that Ch'en Yün was also known as Liao Ch'eng-yün.)

219. Huang Feng 黄峯 (ed.). Ti pa-lu chün hsing-chün chi: K'ang-chan shih-tai 第八路軍行軍記：抗戰時代 (The Eighth Route Army: the Period of War of Resistance). Vol. II. Hankow, n. pub., 1938. 208 pp. (4292.9/4825)

Selected articles and correspondence on the Eighth Route Army in the first year of the Sino-Japanese War. Authors are identified but no original publication sources are given.

220. K'ang-chan chung ti pa-lu chün 抗戰中的八路軍 (The Eighth Route Army During the War of Resistance). n.p., Pa-lu chün, 1942. 36 pp. (4292.9/8482.56)

A pictorial pamphlet published by the General Political Department of the 18th Group Army and the Military and Political Affairs Magazine Society of the Eighth Route Army (Pa-lu chün chün-cheng tsa-chih she), containing photographs of the Eighth Route Army at work and at war. The Hoover Library has a copy autographed by Chu Teh for Edgar Snow.

221. K'ang-chan ta-hsueh 抗戰大學 (War of Resistance). Vol. I, No. 3/4 and Vol. II, No. 4. Canton and Kweilin, December 25, 1937 and February 10, 1939. (2991.2/5647)

This semi-monthly contains articles by Lo Fu and Liao Ch'eng-chih as well as news of the New Fourth Army and of the Shansi-Chahar-Hopeh Border Region.

222. K'ang-Jih yu-chi chan-cheng ti i-pan wen-t'i 抗日游擊戰爭的一般問題 (General Problems in the Anti-Japanese Guerrilla War). Yenan, Chieh-fang, 1938. 98 pp. (2991.1/2135.56)

Edited by the Association for Anti-Japanese War Studies, this book sums up the Communist guerrilla experience in the civil war as well as in the ten-month-old anti-Japanese war. With the exception of Mao Tse-tung's article on "Strategic Problems in Anti-Japanese Guerrilla War," dated May 1938, the remaining six chapters of the book were written by Ch'en Ch'ang-hao, Liu Ya-lou, Hsiao Ching-kuang, and Kuo Hua-jo. It is not clear, however, whether these were collective writings, or whether each chapter should be attributed to an individual writer.

223. Kao k'o-fu 高克甫 (ed.). Ti pa-lu chun tsai Shan-hsi 第八路軍在山西 (The Eighth Route Army in Shangsi). Shanghai, Nan-hua, 1938. 281 pp. (4292.9/0245)

Compiled from Edgar Snow's writings and Chinese newspaper reports on the commanders, strategy, and mass mobilization of the Eighth Route Army, this book provides fragmentary information on the Army in the first year of the Sino-Japanese War. Among the interesting articles are interviews by a Ta Kung Pao correspondent with Mao Tse-tung, Chu Teh, P'eng Te-huai, and Jen Pi-shih.

224. Kuan-yü shih-pa chi-t'uan chün hsing-tung cheng-hsiang 關於十八集團軍行動真象 (On the Activities of the 18th Group Army). n.p., n. pub., n.d. 1 p. (2991.2/7048)

A statement issued by the spokesman of the 18th Group Army in Chungking, refuting the reports of the Central News Agency on their activities.

225. Kuo-min ko-ming chün. Ti shih-pa chi-t'uan chün. Cheng-chih pu 國民革命軍第十八集團軍政治部 (ed.). Pa-lu chün pai-t'uan ta-chan t'e-chi 八路軍百團大戰特輯 (Special Volume on the Hundred-Regiment Offensive). n.p., Pa-lu chün, 1941. 190 pp. (4292.9/8482.86)

Edited by the Political Department of the 18th Group Army, this volume includes statements by Chu Teh, P'eng Te-huai, Ho Lung and other Communist military leaders on the significance of the successful large-scale counteroffensive staged by the Communist forces against the Japanese in North China, beginning August 20, 1940. Included are also numerous military communiques and daily reports of the "hundred-regiment battles."

226. Lu Chieh 魯杰 (ed.). Ch'ü-chu Jih-pen ch'iang-tao ch'u Chung-kuo 驅逐日本強盜出中國 (To Drive the Japanese Bandits from China). Hankow, Ta shih-tai, 1938. various pagination. (2991.03/2643)

    Thirty selected articles on the Sino-Japanese War dealing with mobilization and military affairs, by Mao Tse-tung, Chou En-lai, P'eng Te-huai, Lin Piao, Liao Ch'eng-chih, among others.

227. Ma Han-ping 馬寒冰. Wang Chen nan-cheng chi 王震南征記 (Southern Expedition of Wang Chen). Hankow, Chung-kuo ch'u-pan, 1947. 55 pp. (4292.24/7233)

    In November 1944 the 359th Brigade of the 120th Division of the 18th Group Army under the command of Wang Chen set out from Yenan to engage in guerrilla warfare. This book is an account of the journey which took them through seven provinces ending at the Hunan-Kwangtung-Kiangsi border.

228. Mei-yu Kung-ch'an tang chiu mei-yu Chung-kuo 沒有共產黨就沒有中國 (There Will Be No China Without the Communist Party). n.p., n. pub., n.d. 66 pp. (2991.2/3440)

    The title is taken from an editorial of August 25, 1943, of the Liberation Daily, one of the five articles included in this pamphlet. The other articles compare the war efforts of the KMT and CCP, and describe Communist actions against the puppet army.

229. Niu Shan 牛山 (ed.). Pa-lu chün ti ch'ing-nien chan-shih 八路軍的青年戰士 (The Young Fighters in the Eighth

Route Army). Yenan, Chung-kuo ch'ing-nien, 1939. 53 pp. (4292.9/92527)

This pamphlet describes the active role of young soldiers in the Eighth Route Army, 45 per cent of them being under the age of 23. A supplement contains an article by Chang Ting-ch'eng on the role of youth in the New Fourth Army.

230. Pa-lu chün. Liu-shou ping-t'uan. Cheng-chih pu 八路軍留守兵團政治部 (comp.). Kuo-kung liang-tang k'ang-chan ch'eng-chi pi-chiao 國共兩黨抗戰成績比較 (A Comparison of the Achievements of the Kuomintang and the Chinese Communist Party in the War of Resistance). n.p., same, 1943. 90 pp. (2991/8863.64)

Compiled and published by the Political Department of the Garrison Troops of the Rear Headquarters of the Eighth Route Army, these are editorials, articles, and news items from the <u>Liberation Daily</u> of August and September 1943, selected to show the KMT's emphasis on combating the Communists rather then fighting the Japanese. Several chapters of the book deal with Japanese collaborators among KMT members.

231. Ti-jen k'ou-chung ti pa-lu chün hsin-ssu-chün yü Chung-kuo kung-ch'an tang 敵人口中的八路軍新四軍與中國共產黨 (The Eighth Route Army, the New Fourth Army, and the Chinese Communist Party--in the Eyes of the Enemy). n.p., Hsin-hua, n.d. 45 pp. (4292.9/0865)

This volume was compiled from a Japanese news agency (Domei), Japanese newspapers, and puppet newspapers in order to show that the Communist forces were considered formidable by the Japanese. Sources are given.

232. Wang Chia-hsiang 王稼祥 and others. Cheng-chih kung-tso lun-ts'ung 政治工作論叢 (Political Work in the Army). Vol. I., n.p., Pa-lu chün, 1941. 221 pp. (4292.9/1123)

A collection of 21 articles by Wang Chia-hsiang, (Director of the Political Department of the 18th Group Army), Lu Ting-i,

Wang Shou-tao, Lo Jui-ch'ing, Hsiao Hsiang-jung, T'an Cheng, and others. Most of the articles deal with political work in the army; some discuss guerrilla warfare experiences in North China and policies toward Japanese and puppet troops. The last article sums up political work in the Shansi-Chahar-Hopeh Military Region. All the articles were selected from the army periodical, <u>Pa-lu chün chün-cheng tsa-chih</u> (see item no. 207).

233. Wang Hsiang-li 王向立. Jen-min ti chün-tui 人民的軍隊 (People's Army). Huatung, Kuang-hua, 1948. 112 pp. (4292.9/1120)

A collection of the author's rather literary writings and reports on the Chinese Communist forces in various border regions with regard to combat, production drives, study, army-people relations, officer-soldier relations, etc.

234. Wu Jui 吳銳 and others. Nan-cheng pei-chan erh-shih-wu nien 南征北戰二十五年 (Through Twenty-five Years of War). Peking, Chung-kuo ch'ing-nien, 1956. 158 pp. (4292.9/2381)

The story of a company from its establishment in August 1928 in the Hopeh-Anhwei-Honan border area, through the Long March, the anti-Japanese war in North China, and participation in the fight against KMT troops in Central China after World War II.

C. THE MILITIA

The People's militia were not regular forces, but were still an important adjunct to the Chinese Communist army. Its function was to maintain peace and order in rear areas and to engage in spontaneous guerrilla warfare in active defensive operations. Available works included in this section are mainly secondary sources.

235. Chung-kuo jen-min chieh-fang chün. Hua-pei chün-ch'ü. Cheng-chih pu 中國人民解放軍華北軍區政治部 (ed.).

Min-ping ying-hsiung 民兵英雄 (Militia Heroes). Peking, T'ung-su tu-wu, 1954. 84 pp. (4292.9/5687.77)

Edited by the Political Department of the North China Military Region of the Chinese People's Liberation Army, this book consists of seven militia stories set during and after the Sino-Japanese War. Of doubtful historical value.

236. Li-chan 力斬. Chan-tou chung ti chieh-fang ch'ü min-ping 戰鬥中的解放區民兵 (The People's Militia of Liberation Areas in Combat). [Hong Kong], Chung-kuo ch'u-pan, 1947. 44 pp. (4292.9/4252)

The author attempts to present a systematic analysis of the nature, duties, organization, operation, and development of the militia in the Communist-controlled areas. The text refers to operations in the Sino-Japanese War and to tentative exploits in the postwar struggle against the Nationalist army. While the book is not well organized and leaves much room for improvement, it is one of the few useful works on the subject. Its appendix consists of Provisional Regulations of the Organization of the People's Militia in the Shansi-Chahar-Hopeh Border Region, passed by the Administrative Council of the Shansi-Chahar-Hopeh Border Region in 1945.

237. Ta-chung jih-pao she 大眾日報社 (ed.). Min-ping kung-tso shou-ts'e 民兵工作手冊 (Militia Handbook). n.p., same, [1942]. 76 pp. (4292.9/8632)

This handbook attempts to tell how to organize militia and also touches on training, strategy, and ordnance sources. It is not a systematic treatise on the subject, but rather a compilation of fragmentary accounts, stories, anecdotes, and news reports, most of them appearing to have taken place in the Shansi-Chahar-Hopeh Border Region. In addition to a number of obscure authors, the sources given in the book are Liberation Daily, Ch'ien-wei pao, and I-meng tao-pao.

238. Ti shih-pa chi-t'uan chün. Tsung cheng-chih pu. Hsüan-ch'uan pu 第十八集團軍總政治部宣傳部 (ed.). Ti-hou

chan-ch'ang shang ti min-ping 敵後戰場上的民兵 (The Militia Behind Enemy Lines). n.p., same, 1945. 86 pp. (4292.9/6248.02)

Edited and published by the Propaganda Department of the General Political Department of the 18th Group Army, this book describes the people's militia in the Communist areas and its activities through 1944, with special emphasis on the importance of combining the military with the civilian population.

239. Ting Li 丁勵. Chung-kung ti min-ping chih-tu 中共的民兵制度 (The Militia System of the Chinese Communists). Hong Kong, Yu-lien, 1954. 78 pp. (4292.9/1272)

A well-organized book, one-third of it dealing with the development of the militia system from the Kiangsi Soviet to 1949.

240. Yen-fou she 鹽阜社)ed.). Min-ping tai-piao ta-hui shou-ts'e 民兵代表大會手冊 (Handbook for the Conference of the Militia). n.p., same, 1945. 60 pp. (4292.9/7123)

This pamphlet tells militia stories, discusses militia strategy, and deals with the militia conference convened at Yenfou [Hunan?].

IX. THE BORDER REGIONS

Communist-controlled regions behind Japanese lines were generally referred to by the Communists as anti-Japanese bases. Administratively, they were called "Border Regions" under the Border Region Governments or Administrative Council. In most cases the military and border regions were identical in extent, although there were military regions that had no border region governments or administrative councils, and there were also border regions that were divided into more than two military regions. At the end of 1944 there were 16 anti-Japanese bases, of which only 5 had full-fledged Border Region Governments; 8 had administrative councils, and 3 were military regions that had no governments or councils. By the end of the war, there were 19 "liberated areas," as they were called after 1945.

A. THE SHENSI-KANSU-NINGSIA BORDER REGION

1. General

This was the original base of the Chinese Communist movement after the Long March. It was one of the poorest of all the Communist areas. This section contains an important source on the history of the Communist movement in Shensi prior to the arrival of the Communist forces from Kiangsi and a useful survey of the Border Region in the first two years of the Sino-Japanese War. Section X of my previous volume contains a number of primary sources on the early Yenan period of 1935-37.

241. Ch'en Kuo-hsin 陳國新 and others. So-wei pien-ch'ü 所謂邊區 (The So-called Border Region). Chungking, Tu-li, 1939. 56 pp. (3060/4022)

This book contains fourteen articles selected from periodicals or books. Most of the writings are by authors who had lived in North Shensi, but had become disillusioned with the CCP. References are made to the bombing of Yenan by the Japanese, the legal system, the North Shensi Public Academy, and the Anti-Japanese Military and Political Academy.

242. Ch'en Yen 陳言. Shen Kan tiao-ch'a chi 陝甘調查記 (Report on Shensi and Kansu). 2 vols. Peiping, pei-fang, 1936. 174 and 80 pp. (3060/7906)

Volume I, Chapter II, Section VIII of the book deals with the origin and development of the Chinese Communist movement in Shensi.

243. Ch'i Li 齊禮 . Shen-Kan-Ning pien-ch'ü shih-lu 陝甘寧邊區實記 (A True Account of the Shensi-Kansu-Ningsia Border Region). n.p., Chieh-fang, 1939. 176 pp. (4292.24/0231)

    A useful account of the Shensi-Kansu-Ningsia Border Region in 1937 and 1938. The first three chapters of the book cover the following topics: area, population, political administration, governmental organization, economics, finance, judicial system, elective system, and improvement of living conditions. Chapters IV to VI deal with the united front, mass movements, and mass organizations. Chapter VII is a survey of six academies and schools, and the last chapter is devoted to the political indoctrination of Garrison Troops of the Rear Headquarters of the Eighth Route Army. The book is based on the writer's own study as well as data supplied by his Communist comrades who had been long-time residents in the area.

244. Pien-ch'ü tang ti li-shih wen-t'i chien-t'ao 邊區黨的歷史問題檢討 (An Examination of Questions Concerning Party History in the Border Region). n.p., [CCP], 1943. microfilm. (4292.24/022.37)

    Published by the Northwest Bureau of the CC of the CCP, this is an important source on the Party history in Shensi prior to the arrival of the Party center in 1935. It is a speech delivered by Kao Kang at an high-level cadre meeting in the Shensi-Kansu-Ningsia Border Region on November 17-18, 1942.

245. Shen-Kan-Ning pien-ch'ü fu-yüan ti shuo-ming 陝甘寧邊區幅員的說明 (Area and Population of the Shensi-Kansu-Ningsia Border Region). [Yenan], n. pub., [1944?]. 2 pp. mimeo. (4292.24/7433.74)

    According to this source, which appears to be the Communist government, the total area of the Shensi-Kansu-Ningsia Border Region was 129,608 square miles and the population under its control was 2,000,000. However, because of changes resulting from the Kuomintang occupation, the Border Region area was 98,960 square miles and the population 1,500,000 at the end of 1943.

2. Yenan

Until it was banned by the KMT authorities, one of the songs that appealed most to Chinese youth in the first years of the Sino-Japanese War was about Yenan. It was the headquarters of the CC of the CCP from January 1937 to March 1947. Most of the works in this section are journalists' reports; some were written by disillusioned youths.

246. Chao Ch'ao-kou 趙超構. Yen-an i-yüeh 延安一月 (A Month in Yenan). 2nd ed. Nanking, Hsin-min, 1946. 252 pp. (3060.13/4844)

   On May 17, 1944, a group of 21 men made up of 9 Chinese journalists, 6 foreign correspondents, and 6 officials of the National Government left Chungking for a 70-day visit to Northwest China. Most of them returned to Chungking on July 25. From May 31 to July 12 they were in the Shensi-Kansu-Ningsia Border Region, and they spent 34 of these 43 days in Yenan. This book is a collection of reports written by the chief editorial writer of the Hsin-min pao. It covers the following aspects of the regional government: life, currency, finance, politics, army, cooperatives, educational system, land policy, marriage law, Yenan University, the Lu Hsüan School of Arts, newspapers, cultural policy, cadre training, and the organization of the masses. The most interesting part of these reports is the author's record of his impressions of the Communist leaders, such as Mao Tse-tung, Chu Teh, Lin Piao, Ho Lung, Po Ku, and other important figures. The author attempts to be objective.

247. Ch'i Shih-chieh 齊世傑. Yen-an nei-mu 延安內幕 (Inside Yenan). Chungking, Hua-yen, 1943. 25 pp. (3060.13/0242)

   Written by a former Communist, this pamphlet describes with bitterness the social conditions and hardships of life in Yenan.

248. Chin Tung-p'ing 金東平. Yen-an chien-wen lu 延安見聞錄 (Report from Yenan). Chungking, Tu-li, 1944. 164 pp. (3060.13/8151)

    The author, who was a Shang-wu jih-pao reporter, was one of the journalists who visited northern Shensi in the summer of 1944 (see item no. 246). The first three chapters deal with the Chinese Communist movement from the Kiangsi Soviet period to Shensi. Chapter IV is a critical account of Communist rule in Yenan while the last chapter includes several anecdotes concerning the visit.

249. Hsin-min shu-tien 新民書店 (ed.). Yen-an feng-kuan 延安風光 (Yenan Scenes). Hong Kong, same, 1949. 71 pp. (3060.13/0750)

    A pamphlet of 34 poorly printed pictures of Yenan, with brief explanatory notes.

250. Huang Yen-p'ei 黃炎培. Yen-an kuei-lai 延安歸來 (Return from Yenan). Shanghai, Kuo-hsün, 1945. 74 pp. (3060.13/4894)

    The author was one of the five members of the People's Political Council who visited Yenan July 1-5, 1945. This book is his account of the trip. Of special significance are the record of his conversation with Mao Tse-tung and his impression of the Communist military leaders. (See also item no. 257).

251. Jen-min ch'u-pan she 人民出版社 (ed.). Chin-jih ti Yen-an 今日的延安 (Today's Yenan). Sian, same, 1956. no pagination. (3060.13/7187)

    A pictorial presentation of Yenan. Good photography.

252. Jen T'ien-ma 任天馬. Huo-yüeh ti Fu-shih 活躍的膚施 (The Active Yenan). Shanghai, Shang-hai tsa-chih, 1938. 104 pp. (3060.13/2117)

An account of the writer's journey to Yenan, then known as Fushih, in the spring of 1937. He appears to have toured the city with a number of students from Peiping. The highlights of the trip were his meetings with Mao Tse-tung, Ting Ling, Lin Piao, Lin Po-ch'ü, and other Communist leaders.

253. Li Li-ch'u 李藜初. Shen-pei yin-hsiang chi 陝北印象記 (Impressions of North Shensi). Yenan, Chieh-fang, 1937. 98 pp. (4292.24/4423)

Selected articles written by a number of journalists. Of uneven quality.

254. Liu Pai-yü 劉白羽. Yen-an sheng-huo 延安生活 (Life in Yenan). n.p., Hsien-shih, 1946. 47 pp. (3060.13/7221)

Literary writings portraying life in Yenan.

255. Lu P'ing 魯平 (ed.). Sheng-huo tsai Yen-an 生活在延安 (Life in Yenan). n.p., n. pub., 1938. 182 pp. (3060.13/2614)

A collection of 17 articles by authors ranging from unknown writers to noted journalists who had visited Yenan. An article by Ho Sung, dated December 1937, reporting the arrival of Ch'en Shao-yü at Yenan from Russia (pp. 57-66) is significant in view of the Japanese and Western sources which date the return of Ch'en in the spring of 1938.

256. Ma Chi-ling 馬季鈴 and others. Shen-pei niao-k'ao 陝北鳥瞰 (A Bird's-Eye View of North Shensi). Chengtu, Chung-chih, 1941. 144 pp. (3060.13/7228.1)

A collection of 16 articles written by ten youths after their defection from Yenan, containing useful information on the Anti-Japanese Military and Political Academy, the North Shensi Public Academy, the Lu Hsün School of Arts, and the Women's College (headed by Wang Ming).

257. Tso Shun-sheng 左舜生. Chin san-shih nien chien-wen tsa-chi 近三十年見聞雜記 (Random Notes and Reminiscences of the Last Thirty Years). Kowloon, Tzu-yu, 1952. 142 pp. (2259.9/4122.1)

    Written by a leader of the Youth Party (or Young China Party), the book (pp. 79-93) contains an interesting account of his visit to Yenan (July 1-5, 1945) and his meetings with Mao Tse-tung, Chu Teh, Ch'en Shao-yü, Chang Wen-t'ien, Madame Chou En-lai, and other Communist leaders. His observations on Mao Tse-tung may provide an insight into Mao's temperament and outlook. The book also contains his interpretation of the KMT-CCP negotiations in 1946-47. The author who was one of the five members of the People's Political Council visited Yenan in 1945. (See item no. 250).

258. Ts'ui Yün-ch'ang 崔允常. Shen-pei lun-kuo hua 陝北輪廓畫 (A General Picture of North Shensi). Kweilin, Hsin Chung-kuo, 1939. 58 pp. (4292.24/2129)

    A description of politics, economics, government, education, cultural, and social conditions of Yenan obtained from the author's friend, who had been disillusioned after training there.

259. Wang Chung-ming 王仲明 (ed.). Shen-pei chih hsing 陝北之行 (Journey to North Shensi). [Chungking?], Ch'iu-chih, 1945. 116 pp. (3060.13/1126)

    A collection of 16 articles, radio broadcasts, and interviews with Chinese newspapermen who went on the trip mentioned in item no. 246. With the exception of one article on Mao Tse-tung, the book contains little biographical data on the Communist leaders but is full of statistics and information on finance, land policy, education, army, population, and the political institutions of the Shensi-Kansu-Ningsia Border Region.

260. Wu Wen 伍文 (ed.). Yen-an nei-mu 延安內幕 (Inside Yenan). Shanghai, Ssu-hai, 1946. 65 pp. (4292.31/2104)

This book presents the elite of Yenan, compiled from the writings of visitors. Chinese and Westerners are apparently included, although no sources are given.

261. Wu-yüeh ti Yen-an pien-chi wei-yüan hui 五月的延安編輯委員會 (ed.). Wu-yüeh ti Yen-an 五月的延安 (Yenan in May). n.p., n. pub., n.d. 184 pp. (3060.13/1721)

   A collection of 55 student essays, most on the subject "Yenan in May."

262. Yüan Ching-hsin 原景信. Shen-pei chien-ying 陝北剪影 (An Image of North Shensi). [Hankow?], Hsin Chung-kuo, 1938. 53 pp. (3060.13/7962)

   A hostile report by a Sao-tang pao correspondent of his journey to northern Shensi in March - April, 1938, with information on the Anti-Japanese Military and Political Academy, Shensi Public Academy, life in Yenan, and the political situation in the border area. The book also includes (1) a summary of Mao Tse-tung's remarks in an interview on the KMT-CCP cooperation, and (2) an interview with Chang Kuo-t'ao, who spoke at some length about mass organization in the border regions.

3. Political Systems

The following are primary sources on the Assembly and the political functioning of the Shensi-Kansu-Ningsia Border Region. The most basic and important documents appear to be present here.

a. The Assembly

263. Chung-kuo k'o-hsüeh yüan. Li-shih yen-chiu so. Ti-san so 中國科學院歷史研究所第三所 (ed.). Shen-Kan-Ning pien-ch'ü ts'an-i hui wen-hsien hui-chi 陝甘寧邊區參議會文獻彙輯 (Collected Documents of the Assembly of the

Shensi-Kansu-Ningsia Border Region). Peking, K'o-hsüeh, 1958. 379 pp. (4292.24/7433.2)

Between January 1939 and 1946 the Assembly of the Shensi-Kansu-Ningsia Border Region held four plenary sessions. The present volume, edited by the Institute of History of the Academy of Sciences, is a reprint of four collections of documents concerning these sessions, namely: (1) Shen-Kan-Ning pien-ch'ü ti-i chieh ts'an-i hui shih-lu (see item no. 264); (2) Shen-Kan-Ning pien-ch'ü ti-erh chieh ts'an-i hui hui-k'an (see item no. 268); (3) Shen-Kan-Ning pien-ch'ü ti-erh chieh ts'an-i hui ti-erh tzu ta-hui ts'o-lu; and (4) Shen-Kan-Ning pien-ch'ü ti-san chieh ts'an-i hui ti-i tzu ta-hui hui-k'an. The last two titles were originally edited and published by the Standing Committee of the Second Assembly and the Standing Committee of the Third Assembly, respectively. It may be noted that Kao Kang's speeches, originally published in item no. 268, have been deleted from the second title in the reprint.

264. [Shen-Kan-Ning] pien-ch'ü cheng-fu 陝甘寧邊區政府 (comp.). Shen-Kan-Ning pien-ch'ü ti-i chieh ts'an-i hui shih-lu 陝甘寧邊區第一屆參議會實錄 (The Record of the First Assembly of the Shensi-Kansu-Ningsia Border Region). n.p., n. pub., 1939. 104 pp. (4292.24/7433)

A collection of documents and resolutions of the First Assembly of the Shensi-Kansu-Ningsia Border Region, including the elective law, land law, judicial proceedings, and Lin Po-ch'ü's report on the work of the Border Government in 1937-38.

265. _____. Pan-kung t'ing 辦公廳 (comp.). Chia-chin chun-pei chin tung chü-hsing ti san-ko ta-hui 加緊準備今冬舉行的三個大會 (Intensified Preparations for the Three Meetings to Be Convened This Winter). n.p., same, 1944. 53 pp. (4292.24/7433.47)

Documents relating to plans for three meetings, including the Second Plenary Session of the Second Assembly, scheduled to be held on December 1, 1944.

266. _____. Shen-Kan-Ning pien-ch'ü ti-erh chieh ts'an-i hui chung-yao wen-hsien 陝甘寧邊區第二屆參議會重要文獻 (Important Documents of the Second Assembly of the Shensi-Kansu-Ningsia Border Region). n.p., same, 1944. 99 pp. (4292.24/7433.1)

Fourteen documents relating to events of the First Plenary Session of the Second Assembly, November 6-21, 1941, including Mao Tse-tung's speech, a program for Border Region administration, regulations on human rights, election of delegates to the Assembly, etc. All these are available in the following larger compilation (see item no. 268).

267. _____. Shen-Kan-Ning pien-ch'ü ts'an-i hui ch'ang-chu hui ti-shih-i tz'u cheng-fu wei-yüan hui ti-wu tz'u lien-hsi hui-i chih chüeh-ting chi yu-kuan ching-chi wen-hua chien-she ti chung-yao t'i-an 陝甘寧邊區參議會常駐會第十一次政府委員會第五次聯席會議的決定及有關經濟文化建設的重要提案 (The Decisions and the Important Proposals of the Joint Session of the 11th Meeting of the Standing Committee of the Assembly and the 5th Meeting of the Government Council of the Shensi-Kansu-Ningsia Border Region Concerning Economics, Culture, Reconstruction, and Other Matters). [Yenan?], same, 1944. 97 pp. (4292.24/7433)

Among the decisions made at this joint session was the one to summon the Second Plenary Session of the Second Assembly on December 1, 1944. This book contains the texts of 35 proposals submitted to the joint session.

268. Shen-Kan-Ning pien-ch'ü ti-erh chieh ts'an-i hui ch'ang-chu wei-yüan hui 陝甘寧邊區第二屆參議會常駐委員會 (comp.). Shen-Kan-Ning pien-ch'ü ti-erh chieh ts'an-i hui hui-k'an 陝甘寧邊區第二屆參議會彙刊 (Collected Documents of the Second Assembly of the Shensi-Kansu-Ningsia Border Region). n.p., same, 1942. 252 pp. (4292.24/7433.1)

These documents are classified as follows: (1) procedures and elections of the Assembly; (2) key speeches and official policy statements; (3) a report on the Border Region Government; (4) resolutions; (5) administrative regulations; and (6) bills proposed in the Assembly.

b. Others

269. K'ang-Jih ken-chü-ti cheng-ts'e t'iao-li hui-chi: Shen-Kan-Ning chih-pu 抗日根據地政策條例彙集：陝甘寧之部 (Policies and Statutes of the Anti-Japanese Bases: Shensi-Kansu-Ningsia). 3 vols. n.p., n. pub., 1942. 782 pp. (4661.95/5645)

This comprehensive collection of policies and statutes of the Shensi-Kansu-Ningsia Border Region contains 243 items issued from 1937 to 1942. It is arranged in eight categories: programs, government organization, mass organizations and movements, peasants and the land, culture and education, the protection of human rights.

270. Kao Kang 高崗. I-chiu-ssu-wu nien pien-ch'ü ti chu-yao jen-wu ho tso-feng wen-t'i 一九四五年邊區的主要任務和作風問題 (The Main Tasks and Working Spirit of the Border Region in 1945). n.p., n. pub., 1945. 20 pp. (4292.24/0222)

In this speech delivered at a cadre meeting of the Northwest Bureau of the CC of the CCP in Yenan on January 9, 1945, Kao Kang discussed two main tasks for the year (increased production and improvement of the elective system) and examined the shortcomings of the party cadres in the Border Region.

271. Shen-Kan-Ning pien-ch'ü cheng-fu. Min-cheng ting 陝甘寧邊區政府民政廳 (ed.). Shen-Kan-Ning pien-ch'ü hsiang-hsüan tsung-chieh 陝甘寧邊區鄉選總結 (The Village Election of the Shensi-Kansu-Ningsia Border Region). [Yenan?], n. pub., 1941. 118 pp. (4292.24/7433.71)

A detailed account of the preparations, regulations, and proceedings of the village election held in the Border Region in 1941.

272. Shen-Kan-Ning pien-ch'ü cheng-fu. Pan-kung t'ing 陝甘寧邊區政府辦公廳 (ed.). Shen-Kan-Ning pien-ch'ü cheng-ts'e t'iao-li hui-chi hsü-pien 陝甘寧邊區政策條例彙集續編 (Policies and Statutes of the Shensi-Kansu-Ningsia Border

Region: A Supplement). n.p., same, 1944. 273 pp. (4661.95/5645.1)

This appears to be a supplement to <u>K'ang-Jih ken-chü-ti cheng-ts'e t'iao-li hui chi: Shen-Kan-Ning chih-pu</u> (item no. 269), containing documents for 1943 and 1944.

273. Shen-Kan-Ning pien-ch'ü chien-cheng shih-shih kang-yao 陝甘寧邊區簡政實施綱要 (A Concise Administrative Program for the Shensi-Kansu-Ningsia Border Region). n.p., Ta-chung, 1943. 33 pp. (4292.24/7433.81)

This program was approved by the Border Government at the third meeting of the Government Council.

274. Shen-Kan-Ning pien-ch'ü hsüan-chü wei-yüan hui 陝甘寧邊區選舉委員會 (ed.). Hsüan-chü wen-chien 選舉文件 (Documents of the Election). Vol. I. [Yenan?], same, 1945. 29 pp. (4292.24/7433.37)

Selected documents relating to the three-level elections (village, district, and the Border Region) scheduled to be held between October 15 and December 31, 1945, as decided by the Second Plenary Session of the Second Assembly.

275. Shen-Kan-Ning pien-ch'ü shih-cheng kang-ling 陝甘寧邊區施政綱領 (The Political Platform of the Shensi-Kansu-Ningsia Border Region). [Yenan?], CCP, 1941. 1 p. (4292.24/5640.74f)

This is a 21-article platform of the CCP for the election of the Second Assembly of the Shensi-Kansu-Ningsia Border Region. This program, which was submitted by the Central Bureau of the Border Region of the CCP, was approved by the Central Political Bureau of the CCP on May 1, 1941.

4. Land and Social Reforms

The available sources concerning social reforms bear only on the problem of handling vagrants and witch doctors. Some of the documents on land policy are related also to the Shansi-Chahar-Hopeh Border Region.

276. Chung-kung chung-yang kuan-yü k'ang-Jih ken-chü-ti t'u-ti cheng-ts'e ti chüeh-ting 中共中央關於抗日根據地土地政策的決定 (The Chinese Communist Party's Decision Concerning Land Policy in the Anti-Japanese Bases). n.p., n. pub., [1942]. 18 pp. (4396/5455)

　　A resolution passed by the Central Political Bureau of the CCP on January 28, 1942.

277. Chung-kuo kung-ch'an tang. Chin-ch'a-Chi chung-yang chü. Hsüan-ch'uan pu 中國共產黨晉察冀中央局宣傳部. T'u-ti cheng-ts'e chung-yao wen-chien hui-chi 土地政策重要文件彙集 (Collected Important Documents on Land Policy). n.p., same, 1946. 101 pp. microfilm. (4395/5640.2)

　　Published by the Propaganda Department of the Shansi-Chahar-Hopeh Bureau of the CC of the CCP, this is a collection of the Party decisions on land policy with excerpts from the writings of Mao Tse-tung, Liu Shao-ch'i, and others on the same subject between 1927 and 1946. Most of the documents are related to the Shensi-Kansu-Ningsia and Shansi-Chahar-Hopeh Border Regions.

278. Chung-kuo kung-ch'an tang. Hsi-pei chung-yang chü. Tiao-ch'a yen-chiu shih 中國共產黨西北中央局調查研究室. Shen-Kan-Ning pien-ch'ü erh-liu-tzu ti kai-tsao 陝甘寧邊區二流子的改造 (Reform of Vagrants in the Shensi-Kansu-Ningsia Border Region). Shantung, Hsin-hua, n.d. 40 pp. (4292.8/5640)

　　According to a Communist investigation, in 1937 about 5 per cent of the 30,000 population of the Yenan district and 16 per cent of the population of Yenan City (under 3,000) were vagrants.

This pamphlet by the Inspection and Research Office of the Northwest Bureau of the CC of the CCP tells how the reform of vagrants was undertaken in the Border Region.

279. Chung-kuo kung-ch'an tang yü t'u-ti ko-ming 中國共產黨與土地革命 (The Chinese Communist Party and the Agrarian Revolution). Hong Kong, Cheng-pao, [1948?]. 78 pp. (4395/2135)

Selected writings of Mao Tse-tung, Fang Fang, and CCP documents on land reform from 1927 to 1947, arranged in chronological order. A lengthy article by Hsi-tung on land reforms in the Kiangsi Soviet was translated from the Japanese version because the Chinese original was not available.

280. Shen-Kan-Ning pien-ch'ü cheng-fu. Pan-kung t'ing 陝甘寧邊區政府辦公廳 (ed.). Chan-k'ai fan-tui wu-shen ti tou-cheng 展開反對巫神的鬥爭 (Anti-Witchcraft Campaign). n.p., same, 1944. 86 pp. (4298.8/7433)

Collected stories and writings on the campaign against witch doctors, launched in 1944 by the Government of the Shensi-Kansu-Ningsia Border Region.

5. Production Drives

Because of the poverty of the Border Region, the difficulty of obtaining supplies from the outside, and the economic blockade imposed by the National Government after 1939, two production campaigns were undertaken by the troops and government bodies in the Shensi-Kansu-Ningsia Border Region. The first, begun in 1938, aimed chiefly at the improvement of living conditions; the second, begun in 1941, aimed at self-support. The extensive production campaign in the Communist base areas behind the enemy lines was started in 1942. By 1943 it had become a widespread movement. Every person was to be a producer. "Labor heroes" were named as a means of encouraging people to increase their productive efforts. The organization of cooperatives was actively promoted. The following pamphlets, books, and documents are exclusively from Communist sources. Some are related to trade regulations and factory management.

281. Ch'i Sheng 齊生. Chieh-fang ch'ü ti kung-ch'ang ching-ying yü kuan-li 解放區的工廠經營與管理 (Factory Management in the Liberated Areas). n.p., Pei-chi hsing, 1946. 26 pp. (4426/0221)

This appears to be a reprint of a treatise on factory management in the Communist area during the Sino-Japanese War. The subject is briefly but ably presented.

282. Chung-kuo kung-ch'an tang. Hsi-pei chung-yang chü. Tiao-ch'a yen-chiu shih 中國共產黨西北中央局調查研究室 (ed.). Chieh-shao nan-ch'ü ho-tso she 介紹南區合作社 (Introducing the Nan-ch'ü Cooperative). n.p., same, 1944. 71 pp. (4478.18/5640)

Edited and published by the Inspection and Research Office of the Northwest Bureau of the CC of the CCP, this is an account of the development of a well-known cooperative located south of Yenan.

283. _____. I-chiu-ssu-san nien sheng-ch'an yün-tung chung ti ching-yen 一九四三年生產運動中的經驗 (The Production Drive of 1943). n.p., same, 1944. various pagination. (4292.75/5640)

An important collection of writings relating to the production drive in the Shensi-Kansu-Ningsia Border Region in 1943. At least three of the six titles collected here are available in pamphlet form, namely: "Pien-ch'ü ti lao-tung hu-chu," "Chieh-shao nan-ch'ü ho-tso she," and "Erh-liu-tzu ti kai-tsao." (See item nos. 284, 282, and 278, respectively.) The remaining three are concerned with irrigation projects, the improvement of agricultural products, and the settlement of refugees in the Border Region.

284. _____. Pien-ch'ü ti lao-tung hu-chu 邊區的勞動互助 (Cooperative Farm Labor in the Border Region). n.p., same, 1944. (4398.181/5640.37)

    This book deals with the following aspects of cooperative labor in the Shensi-Kansu-Ningsia Border Region: (1) its various forms and practices existent in the villages; (2) its development from 1937 to 1943; (3) its function and effect on agricultural production; (4) its new form and nature; and (5) results.

285. Li-keng 力耕. Chieh-fang ch'ü ti sheng-ch'an yün-tung 解放區的生產運動 (Production Drives in Liberated Areas). Hong Kong, Chung-kuo ch'u-pan, 1947. 34 pp. (4292.75/4255)

    Included in this book are writings relating to the production drives in the Shensi-Kansu-Ningsia Border Region after 1942.

286. Lo Ch'iung 羅瓊. Shen-Kan-Ning pien-ch'ü min-chien fang-chih yeh 陝甘寧邊區民間紡織業 (The Popular Weaving Industry in the Shensi-Kansu-Ningsia Border Region). n.p., Chung-kuo, 1946. 48 pp. (4448/6114)

    Based on reports and materials presented to a joing meeting of cooperatives in the Shensi-Kansu-Ningsia Border Region in June 1944, this book is a useful aid to understanding the growth of small-scale weaving industries in the Border Region. It also describes at some length how the Border Government solved the clothing problem after the KMT economic blockade in 1939.

287. Mao Tse-tung 毛澤東. Ching-chi wen-t'i yü ts'ai-cheng wen-t'i 經濟問題與財政問題 (Economic and Financial Problems). Shantung, Hsin-hua, 1946. 171 pp. microfilm. (4355/2135c)

    The bulk of the book contains selections from the writings of Mao Tse-tung and others dealing with wartime production, chiefly agricultural and industrial, in the Shensi-Kansu-Ningsia Border Region. Detailed figures and statistics are given.

288.   Pa-lu chün. Lien-fang chün. Cheng-chih pu. Hsüan-ch'uan pu 八路軍聯防軍政治宣傳部 (comp.). Pu-tui lao-tung ying-hsiung ti tai-piao 部隊勞動的英雄代表 (Representative Labor Heroes Among the Troops). n.p., same, 1944. 141 pp. (4292.31/8863.071)

   Compiled and published by the Propaganda Department of the Political Department of the Joint Defense Forces of the Eighth Route Army, this book contains stories of 15 army "labor heroes" in the Border Region, who were outstanding in their contributions to the production drive.

289.   Pa-lu chün. Liu-shou ping-t'uan. Cheng-chih pu 八路軍留守兵團政治部 (comp.). I-chiu-ssu-san nien liu-shou ping-t'uan sheng-ch'an chien-she 一九四三年留守兵團生產建設 (Production Record of Garrison Troops in 1943). n.p., same, 1944. 99 pp. (4398.181/8867)

   Edited and published by the Political Department of the Garrison Troops of the Rear Headquarters of the Eighth Route Army, this is an account of the production of the Garrison Troops in industry, agriculture, grazing, trade and cooperatives.

290.   _____. Liu-shou ping-t'uan ti ying-hsiung men ho mu-fan che 留守兵團的英雄們和模範者 (Heroes and Models in the Garrison Troops). Vol. I. n.p., same, 1944. 65 pp. (4292.31/8863)

   Stories of seventeen labor heroes and exemplary members of the Garrison Troops of the Rear Headquarters of the Eighth Route Army.

291.   _____. Pu-tui lao-tung ying-hsiung 部隊勞動英雄 (Labor Heroes in the Army). n.p., same, 1943. 84 pp. (4292.31/8863.0

   In November 1943 the Labor Heroes' Conference was held in Yenan. The personnel who were in charge of propaganda in the Political Department of the Garrison Troops of the Rear Headquarters of the Eighth Route Army interviewed delegates from the Garrison Troops. Some of them were the same persons described in the Pu-tui lao-tung ying-hsiung ti tai-piao (see item no. 288), but the stories in this pamphlet are much shorter and less informative.

292. _____. Wei feng-i tsu-shih erh tou-cheng 為豐衣足食而鬥爭 (Struggle for Food and Clothing). n.p., same, 1943. 49 pp. (4395.8863)

   Relating to the 1943 production drive campaign.

293. Shen-Kan-Ning pien-ch'u cheng-fu. Pan-kung t'ing 陝甘寧邊區政府辦公廳 Wei kung-yeh p'in ti ch'üan-mien tzu-chi erh fen-tou 為工業品的全面自給而奮鬥 (Struggle for Complete Self-Sufficiency in Industrial Production). [Yenan?], same, 1944. 106 pp. (4432.181/7433)

   Published by the Government Office of the Shensi-Kansu-Ningsia Border Region, this book is important to the understanding of industrial development in the Border Region. It contains speeches delivered by Liu Shao-ch'i, Kao Kang, Teng Fa, and Kao Tzu-li at the joint conference of 203 factory workers and employee-delegates representing 39 factories and 6 textile cooperatives, held in May 1944. The book also contains other materials and documents relating to the meeting.

294. Shen-Kan-Ning pien-ch'ü ho-tso she ko-pu yeh-wu kuei-tse 陝甘寧邊區合作社各部業務規則 (Regulations of Various Departments of the Cooperatives in the Shensi-Kansu-Ningsia Border Region). [Yenan?], n.d. 5 pp. manuscript (carbon copy). (4478.181/7433)

   A list of regulations governing the operation of various departments of the cooperatives in the Border Region.

295. Shen-Kan-Ning pien-ch'ü ho-tso shih-yeh shih-cheng yüan-tse 陝甘寧邊區合作事業施政原則 (Administrative Principles of Cooperatives in the Shensi-Kansu-Ningsia Border Region). [Yenan?], n.d. 1 p. manuscript (carbon copy). (4478.181/7433.1)

This manuscript contains 15 articles on the administrative principles of cooperatives in the Border Region.

296. Shen-Kan-Ning pien-ch'ü mao-i kung-ssu yeh-wu hsü-chih 陝甘寧邊區貿易公司業務須知 (Regulations of Trade Companies in the Shensi-Kansu-Ningsia Border Region). n.p., n. pub., 1944. 59 pp. (4540/7433)

This concerns efforts of trade companies in the Border Region to correct mistakes that had resulted in business losses.

297. Shen-Kan-Ning pien-ch'ü tsu-chih lao-tung hu-chu ti ching-yen 陝甘寧邊區組織勞動互助的經驗 (Experiences in Organizing Mutual Labor Assistance in the Shensi-Kansu-Ningsia Border Region). n.p., Hua-pei, 1944. 50 pp. (4398.181/7433)

This pamphlet consists of three articles: (1) an article identical with one in the Pien-ch'ü ti lao-tung hu-chu (see item no. 284) on the experience of organizing mutual labor assistance in the Shensi-Kansu-Ningsia Border Region; (2) a brief introduction to the mutual labor movement in the Shansi-Chahar-Hopeh Border Region; and (3) on collective labor.

298. Tsu-chih ch'i-lai 組織起來 (Let Us Organize). n.p., Tung-pei shu-tien, 1947. 32 pp. (4398.181/2244)

This pamphlet deals with the peasant household quota production plan in the Shensi-Kansu-Ningsia Border Region.

299. Tsu-chih ch'i-lai 組織起來 (Let Us Organize). n.p., Chin-Sui, 1944. 337 pp. (4292.75/2244)

Published by the Shansi-Suiyuan Bureau of the CC of the CCP, this is an important source on production campaigns in the Shensi-Kansu-Ningsia and Shansi-Suiyuan Border Regions. All the materials and documents were selected from the Liberation Daily and K'ang-chan jih-pao of 1942-44, including: (1) a speech delivered by Mao Tse-tung on November 29, 1943, at a reception given for labor heroes of the Shensi-Kansu-Ningsia Border Region; (2) Kao Kang's speeches at the Conference of Labor Hero Representatives of the Border Region (originally appeared in the Liberation Daily of November 27, 1943) and at the reception given for the labor hero representatives by the Northwest Bureau of the CC of the CCP (originally published in the Liberation Daily of December 11, 1943); and (3) declarations of several labor hero meetings (1943-44) in the two Border Regions.

300. Tung-pei hsing-cheng wei-yüan yui. Pan-kung t'ing 東北行政委員會辦公廳 (ed.). Tsen-yang tsu-chih ch'i-lai 怎樣組織起來 (How to Organize for Production). Dairen, same, 1947. 146 pp. (4396/5121)

Reprints of seven articles relating to wartime production campaigns in the Shensi-Kansu-Ningsia and Shansi-Suiyuan Border Regions for the reference of those who were undertaking a similar task in Northeast China (Manchuria). Edited and published by the Office of the Northeast Administrative Council.

301. Wang Ping 王冰 (ed.). Sheng-ch'an wen-hsien 生產文獻 (Documents on Production). Shantung, Hsin-hua, 1946. 98 pp. (4398.181/1133)

In addition to selected wartime speeches of Mao Tse-tung, Kao Kang, and Li Fu-ch'un on production campaigns, this book includes (1) Communist Shantung Governor Li Yü's directive on production work in 1946, and (2) a directive on economic work in 1945 by the Shantung Bureau of the CC of the CCP. On the back of the cover there is listed a Production Campaign Series issued by the Inspection and Research Office of the Northwest Bureau of the CC of the CCP.

6. Garrison Troops

The activities of the Garrison Troops in the Border Regions were mainly "cultural studies" and campaigns to improve relations between the army and the people. Works on their production efforts are listed in the preceding section.

302. Chang Yu-ch'ih ho san-lien ti wen-hua hsüeh-hsi 張友池和三連的文化學習 (Chang Yu-ch'ih and Cultural Studies in the 3rd Company). n.p., Pa-lu chün lien-fang, 1945. (4292.9/6748)

Published by the Political Department of the Joint Defense Forces of the Eighth Route Army, this is a story of a soldier who succeeded in educating himself as well as in helping his comrades to study.

303. "Fa-chan sheng-ch'an", "yung-cheng ai-min" wen-hsien chi "發展生產""擁政愛民"文獻集 (Documents on "Increase Production," "Support the Government" and "Love the People" Campaigns). n.p., Pa-lu chün lien-fang, 1944. 65 pp. (4398.181/8863)

Published by the Political Department of the Joint Defense Forces of the Eighth Route Army, this book contains eight documents on the production drive in 1943 and 1944, written by Chu Teh, Mao Tse-tung, and Ho Lung; and four documents of the Northwest Bureau of the CC of the CCP on a drive to improve cooperation between the army and the people, including a speech by Chu Teh and a directive by the Northwest Bureau in 1944.

304. Kao Wei-sung 高維嵩. Ching san-lü pa-t'uan erh-lien ti wen-hua huo-tung 警三旅八團二連的文化活動 (The Cultural Activities of the 2nd Company of the 8th Regiment of the 3rd Garrison Brigade). n.p., Pa-lu chün lien-fang, 1944. 29 pp. (4292.9/0222)

Published by the Political Department of Joint Defense Forces of the Eighth Route Army, this pamphlet was written by a commissar of a company whose cultural activities were considered outstanding. The author tells how the soldiers were encouraged to take part in reading, writing, dramatic entertainments, and other activities under his leadership.

305. [Pa-lu chün.] Lien-fang chün. Cheng-chih-pu. Hsüan-ch'uan pu 八路軍聯防軍政治部宣傳部 (ed.). Chün-min chih-chien 軍民之間 (Army-People Relations). n.p., same, 1946. 83 pp. (4292.9/8863.373)

Thirty-four anecdotes concerning army-civilian relations, edited and published by the Propaganda Department of the Political Department of Joint Defense Forces of the Eighth Route Army.

306. Pa-lu chün. Liu-shou ping-t'uan. Cheng-chih pu 八路軍留守兵團政治部. I-nien lai ti yung-cheng ai-min kung-tso 一年來的擁政愛民工作 (Works on "Support the Government and Love the People" Campaign in the Last Year). n.p., same, 1944. 35 pp. (4292.9/8863.18)

Edited and published by the Political Department of the Garrison Troops of the Eighth Route Army, this report summarizes the improvement of the army-civilian relations during 1943. It tells how the soldiers helped the people in production and other works.

307. _____. Yung-cheng ai-min 擁政愛民 (Support the Government and Love the People). n.p., same, 1944. 17 pp. (4292.9/8863.51)

A summary of the achievement in army-civilian relations during 1943.

308. Pu-tui sheng-huo 部隊生活 (Army Life). No. 110. [Yenan], October 31, 1944. (4292.9/0723f)

Published every three days by the Political Department of the Garrison Troops of the Rear Headquarters, this issue of the newspaper is primarily concerned with cultural and educational problems of the soldiers.

309. [Ti shih-pa chi-t'uan chün.] Tsung cheng-chih pu 第十八集團軍總政治部 (ed.). Ch'i-ch'i-ling t'uan ti-erh lien 七七0團第二連 (The 2nd Company of the 770th Regiment). n.p., Pa-lu chün lien-fang, 1944. 22 pp. (4292.9/8631)

Edited by the General Political Department of the 18th Group Army, this is a report on the improvement of production, training, and army-civilian relations achieved by the 2nd Company of the 770th Regiment of the 385th Brigade.

310. _____. Ching-ch'i t'uan ti ti-ch'i lien 警七團的第七連 (The 7th Company of the 7th Garrison Regiment). Shantung, Hsin-hua, 1944. 38 pp. (4292.9/8863.44)

An account of the model soldier Chang Chih-kuo and his company's achievements in improving production, army-civilian relations, and other related activities.

311. _____. Hsüan-ch'uan pu 宣傳部 . Chün-min kuan-hsi 軍民關係 (Army-People Relations). Shanghai, Shang-hai tsa-chih, 1949. 49 pp. (4292.9/8482.37)

Edited by the Propaganda Department of the General Political Department of the 18th Group Army, this pamphlet deals with relations between the army and the people.

312. _____. Kuan-ping kuan-hsi 官兵關係 (Officer and Soldier Relations). n.p., same, 1945. 102 pp. (4292.9/8863.377)

This book sums up the experience of the Garrison Troops of the Rear Headquarters of the Joint Defense Forces with respect to their efforts to improve relations between officers and soldiers.

313. _____. Ling-tao tso-feng 領導作風 (Spirit of Leadership). Shanghai, Shang-hai tsa-chih, 1949. 86 pp. (4292.9/5640.83)

This appears to be a reprint of a book originally published by the Propaganda Department of the General Political Department of the 18th Group Army in 1945. After the high-level cadre conference held in the winter of 1942, the Garrison Troops of the Shensi-Kansu-Ningsia Border Region launched two successive rectification movements: the first was a campaign against the "warlord tendency" in the army, and the second was a study of the report of T'an Cheng on political indoctrination. This book sums up the experience gained in these campaigns. It develops two themes: (1) how to indoctrinate cadres, and (2) how to follow the "mass line." The supplement describes the political indoctrination of two model companies: the 2nd Company of the 8th Regiment of the 3rd Garrison Brigade and the 1st Company of the 1st Regiment.

7. Education

There were two kinds of schools in the Border Region: those under direct supervision by the Communist Party for the training of Party cadre and army personnel, such as the Party School at Yenan and the Anti-Japanese Military and Political Academy; and those under the Educational Department of the Border Region Government, such as Yenan University.

With two exceptions, all materials in this section are Communist sources; they include statements of educational policy and regulations, catalogs and descriptions of the institutions, and speeches by Communist leaders at educational conferences.

314. Ch'en Chien-hua 陳建華. K'ang-ta yü ch'ing-nien 抗大與青年 (Youth and the Anti-Japanese Military and Political Academy). Chungking, n. pub., 1940. 38 pp. (4292.24/2263.1)

   An unfavorable report and reminiscences by a student who spent eleven months at the Anti-Japanese Military and Political Academy at Yenan.

315. Ch'eng Chin-wu 程今吾. Yen-an i hsüeh-hsiao 延安一學校 (A School in Yenan). Shanghai, Hsin-hua, 1949. 148 pp. (4956/2181)

   An account of life in a school from September 1944 to March 1946; the school was one established for the dependents of the Eighth Route Army officers and soldiers.

316. Chiao-yü chen-ti she 教育陣地社 (ed.). Chiao-yü chieh ti ying-hsiung mu-fan 教育界的英雄模範 (Exemplary Teachers). Kalgan, Hsin-hua, 1946. 100 pp. (4912.181/4074)

This book includes articles on the activities of four model teachers in the Shansi-Chahar-Hopeh Border Region, and reports on four elementary schools by the Government of the Shensi-Kansu-Ningsia Border Region.

317. _____. Hsin min-chu chu-i wen-hua chiao-yü 新民主主義文化教育 (Culture and Education in New Democracy). Kalgan, Hsin-hua, 1946. 96 pp. (4932/4374)

This book contains Mao Tse-tung's writings on culture and education under New Democracy, his speeches on literature delivered at the Yenan meetings of May 2 and 23, 1942, and on October 30, 1945, at the Cultural and Education Meeting of the Shensi-Kansu-Ningsia Border Region. It also includes a talk by Lo Mai at the latter meeting on November 15, 1945.

318. _____. Ken-chü ti p'u-t'ung chiao-yü ti kai-ko wen-t'i 根據地普通教育的改革問題 (The Problems of Educational Reform in the Border Region). Kalgan, Hsin-hua, 1946. 50 pp. (4911/4074.45)

A collection of government directives, four editorials from the Liberation Daily, and part of a speech on education delivered by Lin Po-ch'ü on January 6, 1944.

319. Chung-kuo nü-tzu ta-hsüeh chao-sheng chien-chang 中國女子大學招生簡章 (The Admission Regulations of the Women's College). [Yenan], n. pub., 1939. 3 pp. (4997.181/5641)

Regulations, comprised of 10 articles, issued in the name of the college president, Wang Ming.

320. Hsin chiao-yü hui 新教育會 (ed.). Chieh-fang ch'ü ch'ün-chung chiao-yü chien-she ti tao-lu 解放區群眾教育建設的道路

(Mass Educational Reconstruction in the Liberated Areas). 2nd ed. Harbin, Tung-pei shu-tien, 1948. 155 pp. (4991.8/0407)

Edited by the New Educational Society, this is a collection of 18 articles on the new educational philosophy and system, with the citation of model examples from the Shensi-Kansu-Ningsia and the Shansi-Chahar-Hopeh Border Regions, including the educational campaign in the winter of 1944.

321. Hsü Shu-huai 徐舒懷. K'ang-ta kuei-lai 抗大歸來 (Return from the Anti-Japanese Military and Political Academy). 2nd ed. Hankow, Chiu-shih, 1939. 53 pp. (4292.24/2989)

A critical description of school life in the Communist academy, by a disillusioned student.

322. Mao Tse-tung 毛澤東 and others. K'ai-chan ta kuei-mu ti ch'ün-chung wen-chiao yün-tung 開展大規模的群眾文教運動 (Let's Launch a Large-Scale Cultural and Educational Campaign for the Masses). Hong Kong, Chung-kuo ch'u-pan, 1947. 89 pp. (4991.8/2135)

The materials contained in this book are related to the Cultural and Educational Conference of the Shensi-Kansu-Ningsia Border Region, October 11 - November 18, 1944. Included are speeches by Mao Tse-tung, Kao Kang, and Lo Mai, editorials of the Liberation Daily, an article by Chou Erh-fu, and the texts of seven resolutions of the conference.

323. Pien-ch'ü chiao-yü t'ung-hsün 邊區教育通訊 (Educational Correspondence from the Border Region). Vol. I, No. 1 - Vol. II, No. 3. Yenan, November 1, 1945 - September 1, 1946. (4912.181/3740)

An official publication of the administration of Shensi-Kansu-Ningsia, with writings on policy, teaching methods, progress, and problems of educational work in the Border Region. Articles by Hsü T'e-li appear in Vol. I, No. 1, and Vol. II, No. 3 (September 1, 1946). The report of Lin Po-ch'ü on cultural and educational policy is published in issue Vol. I, No. 6 (May 20, 1946).

324. Shen-Kan-Ning pien-ch'ü cheng-fu. Chiao-yü t'ing 陝甘寧邊區政府教育廳. Chung-teng kuo-wen 中等國文 (Intermediate Chinese). 2 vols. n. p., Hsin-hua, 1946. 245 and 267 pp. (5205/7433)

Edited by the Department of Education of the Shensi-Kansu-Ningsia Border Region Government, this selection of Chinese readings for textbooks contains no classics; the readings are generally related to contemporary social and political topics, and include Mao Tse-tung's speech delivered in Yenan on February 20, 1940, at the establishment of the Association for Promoting Constitutional Government.

325. Shen-Kan-Ning pien-ch'ü cheng-fu. Pan-kung t'ing 陝甘寧邊區政府辦公廳 (comp.). Shen-Kan-Ning pien-ch'ü chiao-yü fang-chen 陝甘寧邊區教育方針 (The Educational Policy of the Shensi-Kansu-Ningsia Border Region). n.p., same, 1944. 60 pp. (4912.181/7433)

Edited and published by the Government office of the Shensi-Kansu-Ningsia Border Region, this volume is a collection of official documents and directives, dated January 6 to May 21, 1944, relating to educational policy and reforms concerning high schools, Yenan University, and other related matters in the Shensi-Kansu-Ningsia Border Region. The appendix includes reprints of four editorials from the Liberation Daily of 1941-44.

326. _____. Ssu-ko min-pan hsiao-hsüeh 四個民辦小學 (Four Elementary Schools). n. p., same, 1944. 69 pp. (4912.181/6270)

An account of four elementary schools in Yenan and vicinity.

327. Shen-Kan-Ning pien-ch'ü wen-chiao ta-hui hsüan-chi 陝甘寧邊區文教大會選輯 (Selected Documents on the Cultural and Educational Meeting of the Shensi-Kansu-Ningsia Border Region). n.p., Chahar Chiao-yü t'ing, 1945. 48 pp. (4912.181/3619)

Published by the Education Department of the Chahar Provincial Government, these selected documents concern the Cultural and Educational Meeting, October - November 1945, and

include an editorial from the Liberation Daily and a speech by
Kao Kang. The speeches by Mao Tse-tung and Lo Mai are
identical with those appearing in Hsin-min-chu chu-i wen-hua
chiao-yü (see item no. 317).

328.   Tung-yüan she 動員社 (ed.). K'ang-ta tung-t'ai 抗大動態
(Activities in the Anti-Japanese Military and Political Academy).
[Wuhan?], n. pub., 1939. 230 pp. (4292.24/2263).

More than ten staff members of the Mobilization Society of
Wuhan visited Yenan and stayed for more than a month with the
students at the Anti-Japanese Military and Political Academy.
This book, a product of that trip, presents the Communist viewpoint on the history, development, educational policy, and other
aspects of the Academy.

329.   Wen-chiao kung-tso hsin fang-hsiang 文教工作新方向 (New
Direction of Cultural and Educational Works). n.p., Chi-Lu-Yü,
n.d. 50 pp. microfilm. (4912.181/3619.1)

Containing an editorial from the Liberation Daily and speeches
by Mao Tse-tung, Li Fu-ch'un, T'an Cheng, and others at the
Cultural and Educational Meeting of the Shensi-Kansu-Ningsia
Border Region, 1945.

330.   Wu Han-chang 吳漢章 and Chang Chih-p'ing 張治平. Yen-an
shih-li ti-i wan-ch'üan hsiao-hsüeh-hsiao 延安市立第一完全小
學校 (The First Public Elementary School of Yenan). [Yenan],
n. pub., 1946. mimeo. 6 pp. (4912.18/2330)

Written by the two principals of the school, this pamphlet
gives a brief account of its development from its founding in
1939 to 1946, with tables and statistics on the faculty, administration, student body, and finance.

331.   Yen-an ta-hsüeh kai-k'uang 延安大學概況 (General Information on Yenan University). [Yenan?], n. pub., 1944. mimeo.
8 pp. (4997.18/1434)

This catalog furnishes information on the history, organization, faculty, courses, administration, student life, and educational policy at Yenan University.

B. THE SHANSI-CHAHAR-HOPEH BORDER REGION

Founded in January 1938, this was the first border region established by the Chinese Communists outside of the Shensi-Kansu-Ningsia base. The central core of this area was the mountainous region forming the border between Shansi, Chahar, and Hopeh, but the base area also extended into the fertile North China plain. The economy of the mountainous regions is similar to that of the Yenan area, although the plains include very fertile agriculture lands. The following materials are related to these affairs of the Border Region: war, education, law, and mutual labor assistance. A comprehensive collection of laws, ordinances, and statutes of the Border Region is available.

332. Chan-ch'ang 戰場 (The Battlefield). No. 12. n.p., August 1944. (4292.9/6454)

   A pictorial magazine published by the 129th Division of the 18th Group Army.

333. Chiao-yü chen-ti 教育陣地 (Educational Battlefield). Vol. V, No. 6 - Vol. VI, No. 3; and Vol. VII, Nos. 1-2. Kalgan, December 16, 1945 - August 16, 1946. (4912.171/4074)

   An important educational monthly in the Shansi-Chahar-Hopeh Border Region, carrying educational news, reports, and discussions of educational problems.

334. Chiao-yü chen-ti she 教育陣地社 (comp.). Hsin chiao-yü lun-wen hsüan-chi 新教育論文選集 (Selected Essays on New Education). Kalgan, Hsin-hua, 1946. 116 pp. (4903/4074)

   A collection of nineteen essays collected from the editorials of the Chin-Ch'a-chi jih-pao of 1944-46 and the Chiao-yü chen-ti monthly, 1943-46.

335. _____. K'ang-chan shih-ch'i pien-ch'ü chiao-yü chien-she 抗戰時期邊區教育建設 (Education in the Border Region During the Sino-Japanese War). 2 vols. Kalgan, Hsin-hua, 1946. 107 and 102 pp. (4911/4074)

Indispensable sources on the development of education in the Shansi-Chahar-Hopeh Border Region during the Sino-Japanese War of 1937-45.

336. Chin-Ch'a-Chi hua-pao 晉察冀畫報 (The Chin-Ch'a-Chi Pictorial). Nos. 1-9/10. n.p., July 7, 1942 - December 1945. (4292.24/1315)

Published by the Political Department of the Shansi-Chahar-Hopeh Military Region, the first few issues of this magazine contain pictures and articles stressing guerrilla warfare and achievements of the Communist forces commanded by Nieh Jung-chen in the Shansi-Chahar-Hopeh Border Region during the Sino-Japanese War. The first issue has English captions.

337. Chin-Ch'a-Chi pien-ch'ü hsing-cheng wei-yüan hui 晉察冀邊區行政委員會 (comp.). Hsien-hsing fa-ling hui-chi 現行法令彙集 (A Collection of Current Laws and Ordinances). 2 vols. n.p., same, 1945. 704 pp. (4661.95/1313)

Compiled by the Administrative Council of the Shansi-Chahar-Hopeh Border Region, the laws and ordinances of the Border Region collected in these volumes are classified under the following categories:

(1) Basic Programs

(2) Civil Administration: (a) political powers, such as government organization, the elective system, and cadres; (b) social policy, including the land law, the marriage law, the law of inheritance, mass organizations, people's militia, and veterans; (c) social control; (d) public safety; (e) public health.

(3) Education

(4) Finance

(5) Trade and industry

(6) Judicial system

These volumes include only those laws and ordinances issued before November 1945. A number of existing regulations and statutes of minor importance are not included.

338. _____. Shih-yeh ch'u 實業處 (comp.). Lao-tung hu-chu ti tien-hsing li-tzu ho ching-yen 勞動互助的典型例子和經驗 (Typical Cases and Experiences of Mutual Labor Assistance). n.p., same, n.d. 50 pp. (4398.181/1313.92)

Edited and published by the Industrial Bureau of the Administrative Council of the Shansi-Chahar-Hopeh Border Region, this book contains seven case studies and three accounts of experiences in the mutual labor assistance program in the Border Region. They appear to have been written in 1945. Some were examples from the Shensi-Kansu-Ningsia Border Region.

339. _____. Nung-hui 農會 (ed.). Chin-Ch'a-Chi pien-ch'ü ti lao-tung hu-chu 晉察冀邊區的勞動互助 (Mutual Labor Assistance in the Shansi-Chahar-Hopeh Border Region). n.p., same, 1946. 72 pp. (4398.181/1313.13)

Edited and published by the Industrial Bureau and the Peasant Association of the Administrative Council of the Shansi-Chahar-Hopeh Border Region, this book furnishes information on mutual labor assistance in the Border Region for use in the "newly liberated areas." It is based on data collected in the region in 1944.

340. Chou Erh-fu 周而復. Chieh-fang ch'ü Chin-Ch'a-Chi hsing 解放區晉察冀行 (Journey to the Shansi-Chahar-Hopeh Liberation Area). 2nd ed. Shanghai, Shang-hai shu-pao, 1949. 130 pp. (2991/7212)

Twenty short articles reporting events to 1945, such as Japanese atrocities in North China, and life and production in the Shansi-Chahar-Hopeh Border Region. The portrait of Nieh Jung-chen is useful.

The author appears to have been a member of one of the cadres sent to the area by the Yenan headquarters of the 18th Group Army. He witnessed the convention of the First People's Assembly in the Border Region, January 15, 1943.

341. [Chou] Li-po 周立波. Chin-Ch'a-Chi pien-ch'ü yin-hsiang chi 晉察冀邊區印象記 (Impressions of the Shansi-Chahar-Hopeh Border Region). Hankow, [Tu-chu sheng-huo], 1938. 205 pp. (4292.24/7203.13)

A fragmentary account of the author's trip in the Shansi-Chahar-Hopeh Border Region between December 1937 and February 1938, with special emphasis on guerrilla warfare against the Japanese. Some of the propaganda bulletins of the Eighth Route Army, in both Mongolian and Japanese, are reproduced in facsimile.

342. Jen-min ti ta-hsüeh 人民的大學 (The People's University). Sunan, Hsin-hua, 1949. 90 pp. (4997.14/4118)

An introduction to the United North China University founded in the Shansi-Chahar-Hopeh Region in 1939, with biographical data on its president Ch'eng Fang-wu and other faculty members.

343. K'ang-Jih ken-chü-ti cheng-tse t'iao-li hui-chi: Chin-Ch'a-Chi chih-pu 抗日根據地政策條例彙集:晉察冀之部 (Policies and Statutes of the Anti-Japanese Bases: Shansi-Chahar-Hopeh). n.p., n. pub., 1941. 475 pp. (4661.95/5645)

A collection of policies and statutes of the Shansi-Chahar-Hopeh Border Region, containing 140 documents issued between 1938 and 1941. The classification is similar to the other collection in the same series (see item no. 269).

344.　Ti shih-pa chi-t'uan chün.　Tsung cheng-chih pu.　Hsüan-ch'uan pu 第十八集團軍總政治部宣傳部 (comp.).　Pa-lu chün ti ying-hsiung yü mu-fan 八路軍的英雄與模範 (Heroes and Models of the Eighth Route Army).　Vol. I.　n.p., Tung-pei, 1946.　114 pp.　(4292.31/8482.86)

　　Compiled by the Propaganda Department of the General Political Department of the 18th Group Army, this book consists of stories of nineteen labor heroes from the Shansi and Hopeh Communist areas.　The compiler's preface is dated 1944.

C.　THE SHANSI-HOPEH-SHANTUNG-HONAN BORDER REGION

　　This border region was administratively under one Border Region Government.　Militarily, it was divided into two regions: the Shansi-Hopeh-Honan Military Region (including the Taihang Area and the Taiyueh Area) and the Hopeh-Shantung-Honan Military Region (including the original Hopeh-Shantung-Honan Area and the Chinan Area).

　　Much of the Shansi-Hopeh-Honan Region was mountainous and unproductive, with a relatively small population.　In general, its economy resembled in most respects that of the Shensi-Kansu-Ningsia Border Region.　The Hopeh-Shantung-Honan Region lay entirely in the alluvial plains of North China and it resembled in every respect the plains area of the Shansi-Chahar-Hopeh Border Region.

　　The much-publicized "Hundred-Regiment Battles" were fought in this Border Region.　Most of the materials included in this section are primary sources, including laws and ordinances, documents on land reform, and economic and financial reports.

345.　[Chi-nan hsing-shu 冀南行署].　Chi-nan hsing-shu ti-i tz'u ts'ai lien hui pao-kao yü tsung-chieh 冀南行署第一次財聯會報告與總結 (Report and Summary of the First Joint Financial Meeting of the Chinan Administrative Office).　n.p., same, 1946.　30 pp.　microfilm.　(4581.95/1426)

　　Marked confidential material consisting of two documents: a summary and a report of the first joint financial meeting of the Chinan (south Hopeh) Administrative Office.

346. Chi-nan yin-hang T'ai-hang ch'ü hang. Kung-shang kuan-li tsung-chü yen-chiu shih 冀南銀行太行區行工商管理總局研究室 (ed.). T'ai-hang ch'ü shui-wu kung-shang kung-tso li-nien lai chung-yao chüeh-ting chih-shih ming-ling 太行區稅務工商工作歷年來重要決定指示命令 (Important Directives and Ordinances of Tax and Business in the Taihang Area). n.p., same, 1945. 198 pp. microfilm. (4596.9/1482)

    Documents, regulations, statistics, and experience reports concerning taxes and business in the Taihang Area for the years 1940-45, published by the Bank of Chinan.

347. Ch'i Wu 齊武. I-ko ko-ming ken-chü ti ti ch'eng-ch'ang 一個革命根據地的成長 (The Development of a Revolutionary Base). Peking, Jen-min, 1958. 323 pp. (4292.24/0214)

    A comprehensive and informative account of the founding and growth of the Shansi-Hopeh-Shantung-Honan Border Region from the outbreak of the Sino-Japanese War through 1949. It includes reprints of two documents: (1) Reconstruction Policy of the North China Bureau of the CC of the CCP in the Shansi-Hopeh-Honan Border Region, dated April 5, 1941; and (2) the Revised Provisional Regulations on Land Use in the Shansi-Hopeh-Shantung-Honan Border Region.

348. Chin-Chi-Lu-Yü chün-ch'ü cheng-chih pu 晉冀魯豫軍區政治部 (ed.). Sung Jen-ch'iung kuan-yü cheng-chih kung-tso ti pao-kao 宋任窮關於政治工作的報告 (A Report on Political Work by Sung Jen-ch'iung). n.p., same, 1947. 16 pp. microfilm. (4292.9/3932.70)

    This is Sung's report on political work in the army at the Party School of the Shansi-Hopeh-Shantung-Honan Military Region on June 15, 1947, published by the Political Department of the Shansi-Hopeh-Shantung-Honan Military Region.

349. Chin-Chi-Lu-Yü pien-ch'ü cheng-fu 晉冀魯豫邊區政府 (comp.). Fa-ling hui-pien 法令彙編 (Collected Laws and Ordinances). n.p., same, 1942. 118 pp. (4661.95/1121)

Compiled and published by the Government of the Shansi-Hopeh-Shantung-Honan Border Region, this is a collection of laws and ordinances of the Border Region, classified under five categories: general, civil, finance, reconstruction, education and justice.

350. _____. Fa-ling hui-pien 法令彙編 (Collected Laws and Ordinances). 2nd ed. n.p., same, 1946. 64 pp. microfilm. (4661.95/1121.1)

Compiled and published by the Government of the Shansi-Hopeh-Shantung-Honan Border Region, this is a collection of land laws, labor laws, marriage laws, tax laws, and other provisional regulations issued between 1942 and 1945 in the Border Region.

351. Chin-Chi-Lu-Yü pien-ch'ü Chi-Lu-Yü ti-shih hsing-cheng tu-ch'a chuan-yüan kung-shu 晉冀魯豫邊區冀魯豫第十行政督察專員公署 . Chien-ming ho-li fu-tan chan-hsing pan-fa 簡明合理負担暫行辦法(Provisional Regulations for Simple and Fair Taxes). n.p., same, 1945. 15 pp. microfilm. (4591/1121.86)

A detailed tax scale for land taxes, reprinted from the Hopeh-Shantung-Honan Administrative Office of the Government of the Shansi-Hopeh-Shantung-Honan Border Region.

352. Chin-Chi-Lu-Yü pien-ch'ü tiao-ch'a yen-chiu shih 晉冀魯豫邊區調查研究室 . Kuo-min ching-chi tiao-ch'a ch'u-pu yen-chiu 國民經濟調查初步研究 (Preliminary Investigation of the People's Livelihood and Economy). n.p., T'ao-fen, 1944. 58 pp. microfilm. (4358/1121)

A primary source giving detailed figures and statistics on personal wealth, the cost of living, taxes, and savings in the Taihang Area of 1944.

353. Chin-Chi-Lu-Yü Yüan-ch'ü tzu-chüeh t'uan-chieh yün-tung ti ching-yen 晉冀魯豫原曲自覺團結運動的經驗 (Experience of the Voluntary Cooperation Campaign at Yuanchu in the Shansi-Hopeh-Shantung-Honan Border Region). n. p., n. pub., n. d. 20 pp. microfilm. (4292.24/1121)

Communist sources on land reforms and mass campaigns at Yuanchu (in Shehsien district).

354. [Chung-kuo kung-ch'an tang.] Chi-Lu-Yü ch'ü tang wei-yüan hui 中國共產黨冀魯豫區黨委員會. Ch'ün-yün chih-shih hui-pien 群運指示彙編 (Collected Directives on the Mass Movement). n. p., same, 1945. 44 pp. microfilm. (4661.95/1121.3)

Directives issued by the Hopeh-Shantung-Honan Committee of the CCP with respect to various mass campaigns.

355. _____. I-chiu-ssu-ch'i nien shang-pan nien lai ch'ü tang-wei kuan-yü t'u-kai yün-tung ti chung-yao wen-chien 一九四七年上半年來區黨委關於土改運動的重要文件 (Important Documents Concerning Land Reforms Issued in the First Half of 1947 by the Hopeh-Shantung-Honan Committee of the Communist Party of China). n. p., same, 1947. 77 pp. microfilm. (4395/1464)

Twelve documents selected and published by the Hopeh-Shantung-Honan Committee of the CCP.

356. _____. Hsüan-ch'uan pu 宣傳部. Tang-yüan chi-pen chih-shih 黨員基本知識 (Basic Knowledge for Party Members). 2nd ed. n. p., same, 1947. 156 pp. microfilm. (4292.5/5412)

A treatise on the CCP, workers and peasants, revolutionary aims and tactics, etc.

357. Kung-tso t'ung-hsün 工作通訊 (Work Correspondence). No. 32. n. p., June 15, 1947. microfilm. (2992/1217)

Published by the Hopeh-Shantung-Honan Committee of the CCP, this is a special issue on guerrilla warfare.

358. [Pa-lu chün]. Lien-fang chün. Cheng-chih pu. Hsüan-ch'uan pu 八路軍聯防軍政治部宣傳部 (ed.). Chan-tou tsai T'ai-hang-shan shang 戰鬥在太行山上 (Fighting in the Taihangshan Mountains). n.p., same, 1944. 94 pp. (4292.9/6748.67)

    Selected military reports of combat, 1942-44, in the Shansi-Hopeh-Honan Military Region, edited and published by the Propaganda Department of the Political Department of the Joint Forces of the Eighth Route Army.

359. Pei-fang tsa-chih 北方雜誌 (The Magazine of the North). Vol. I, Nos. 2-6. Hantan, July 15 - December 19, 1946. (9200/1000.34)

    An organ of the Cultural Association (Wen-lien) of the Shansi-Hopeh-Shantung-Honan Border Region, this monthly is a general magazine of literature and culture, with occasional political commentaries.

360. Pei-fang t'ung-hsün 北方通訊 (Correspondence from the North). Vol. I, Nos. 6-10; Vol. II, Nos. 1, and 3; and 2 special issues. n.p., March 30 - October 19, 1947. mimeo. (4997.171/1102)

    An official magazine of Northern University, serving as a bulletin and reporting various kinds of activities of the University faculty and students. The two special issues are not mimeographed: one is a special number published for the first graduation class of the College of Arts and Education; the other is concerned with creative writing.

361. Pei-fang t'ung-hsün 北方通訊 (Correspondence from the North). Nos. 1-2. n.p., January 13 and 18, 1948. mimeo. (4997.171/1102.1f)

Published by Northern University in connection with the land reform work undertaken by the faculty and students of the university under the presidency of Fan Wen-lan.

362. T'ai-hang ch'ü hsing-cheng kung-shu 太行區行政公署. T'ai-hang ch'ü ssu-fa kung-tso kai-k'uang 太行區司法工作概況 (Judiciary Work in the Taihang Area). n.p., same, 1946. 53 pp. microfilm. (4724/4271)

An official report on the judiciary work in the Taihang Area (1937-45).

363. _____. T'ai-hang ch'ü i-chiu-ssu-liu nien chung-yao wen-chien hui-chi 太行區一九四六年重要文件彙集 (Collected Important Documents of the Taihang Administrative Office for the Year 1946). n.p., same, 1946. 154 pp. microfilm. (4661.95/1121.2)

Documents are arranged under sections on civil government, finance, education, reconstruction, the judiciary, etc.

364. Ting Ling 丁玲. I-erh-chiu shih yu Chin-Chin-Chi-Lu-Yü ch'ü 一二九師與晉冀魯豫邊區 (The 129th Division and the Shansi-Hopeh-Shantung-Honan Border Region). Peking, Hsinhua, 1950. 58 pp. (2991/4433)

Writing in July 1944 at Yenan, the noted authoress described the establishment and development of the Border Region, founded by the 129th Division and commanded by Liu Po-ch'eng. Her account was based on interviews with Liu and other Communist leaders of the Border Region.

D. THE SHANTUNG BASE AREA

The Chinese Communist base in Shantung was broken into a number of separate political and military areas: Chiaotung, Pinghai, Pohai, Luchung, and Lunan. Materials pertaining to this base are arranged in geographical rather than topical divisions. Under the first heading are sources pertaining to the whole base, including newspapers of post-1945 issues. Materials relating to the Chiaotung Area are abundant, and they are grouped under the second heading. Under the third heading are materials relating to all areas other than Chiaotung and Lunan--those concerning the latter being conspicuously absent. Almost all the materials contained in these sections are primary sources on microfilm.

1. <u>General</u>

365. Chi-tung hsing 冀東行 (Journey to Eastern Hopeh). Hong Kong, Hsin-sheng, 1948. 60 pp. microfilm. (3056/0263)

    Eight letters written by a young man reporting on various aspects of life in eastern Hopeh under Communist rule.

366. Chiao-tung hsin-hua shu-tien 膠東新華書店 (ed.). Wen-hua chiao-yü cheng-ts'e 文化教育政策 (Cultural and Educational Policy). Chiaotung, same, 1946. 56 pp. microfilm. (4917/7504)

    In addition to the five policy regulations concerning the primary and high schools in Shantung, this volume includes two summary reports on the same subjects.

367. Chung-kuo kung-ch'an tang. Shan-tung fen-chü. Hsüan-ch'uan pu 中國共產黨山東分局宣傳部 . Ta-tien ch'a-chien tou-cheng tsung-chieh 大店查減鬥爭總結 (At the Conclusion of the Rent Reduction Campaign in Tatien). n.p., same, 1944. 72 pp. microfilm. (4395/4047)

    Published by the Propaganda Department of the Shantung Regional Bureau of the CCP, the writings contained in this extra issue of the <u>Tou-cheng sheng-huo</u> are related to land reforms in Tatien, Lunan district, Pinhai Military Region.

368. Hsin-ssu-chün Shan-tung chün-ch'ü ssu-ling pu 新四軍山東軍區司令部 (ed.). Hsin-ping chün-shih chiao-ts'ai 新兵軍事教材 (Military Manual for New Recruits). Shantung, Hsin-hua, 1944. 120 pp. microfilm. (8905/0631)

    Thirty-five lessons for new recruits and for the training of militias, edited by the Headquarters of the Shantung Military Region.

369. Shan-tung chün-ch'ü. Cheng-chih pu. Hsüan-ch'uan pu 山東軍區政治部宣傳部 (ed.). Yung-ai mu-fan 擁愛模範 (Models for the "Support the Government and Love the People" Campaign). [Chiamussu], Tung-pei, 1947. 48 pp. (4292.9/5687)

    Edited by the Propaganda Department of the Political Department of the Shantung Military Region, this book contains articles on seven minor army officers and soldiers who were named models for the "Support the Government and Love the People" campaign.

370. Shan-tung hua-pao 山東畫報 (Shantung Pictorial). No. 25. Shantung, July 1, 1945. (4292.9/2554)

    A pictorial published by the Political Department of the Shantung Military Region, with an article by Commander Lo Jung-huan on the Shantung Liberated Area.

371. Su Shih-p'ing 宿士平 (ed.). Shan-tung jen-min ti hsin-sheng 山東人民的新生 (Rebirth of the People from Shantung). Shantung, Hsin-hua, 1946. 100 pp. microfilm. (3057/3641a)

    Twenty-five articles and reports by obscure writers on the Communist regime in Shantung.

372. Tang-ch'ien ti chin-chi jen-wu 當前的緊急任務 (The Present Urgent Tasks). n.p., n. pub., [1945]. 34 pp. microfilm. (2992/2546)

The title is taken from an editorial in the Liberation Daily. The other seven articles contained in this volume are Ta-chung jih-pao editorials, four of them related to the Shantung Military Region. Those that are dated are of August 1945.

373. Ti shih-pa chi-t'uan chün. Shan-tung chün-ch'ü ssu-ling pu. Chün-shih chiao-ts'ai pien-shen wei-yüan hui 第十八集團軍山東軍區司令部軍事教材編審委員會 (ed.). Nei-wu t'iao-ling chi-lü t'iao-ling ts'ao-an 內務條令紀律條令草案 (Draft of Internal and Disciplinary Regulations). n.p., same, 1944. 49 pp. microfilm. (8924/8482)

Drafted by the Military Manual Compilation Committee of the Headquarters of the Shantung Military Region of the 18th Group Army and issued under the names Lo Jung-huan and Li Yü, Commander (concurrently Political Commissar) and Deputy Political Commissar of the Region respectively, these draft regulations deal with internal army relations and duties.

374. Tou-cheng 鬥爭 (Struggle). No. 56. n.p., 1946. microfilm. (4292.01/7225.2)

Although this microfilm material is identified in handwriting as the 56th issue of Tou-cheng, it is actually a 90-page printed document, entitled "On the Mass Line and the Mass Movement in Shantung," published by the Chiaotung Committee of the CCP. It is a report given by Li Yü at a local Communist conference in September 1945 on land reforms in Shantung.

It may be mentioned that the Tou-cheng monthly is an organ of the Huatung Bureau of the CC of the CCP. It emerged from the combining of the Tou-cheng sheng-huo and Chen-li.

375. T'u-ti tsung-chieh pao-kao 土地總結報告 (A Summary Report on Land Reforms). n.p., n. pub., [1944?]. 65 pp. microfilm. (4395/4422)

A preliminary report on land reforms in Shantung, where the campaign for the reduction of rent and interest began in 1942. The appendix is a land lease regulation for Shantung.

2. Chiaotung

376. Chan-shih p'eng-yu 戰士朋友 (Fighters' Friends). No. 12. [Chiaotung], April 1945. mimeo. (4292.9/6474)

   A sort of comic book published for the soldiers by the Political Department of the Chiaotung Military Region, Shantung.

377. Chiao-tung chün-ch'ü. Cheng-chih pu 膠東軍區政治部 (ed.). Liang-chung tso-feng 兩種作風 (Two Styles of Work). n.p., same, 1945. 39 pp. microfilm. (4292.9/7537)

   A collection of articles on the "Support the Cadre and Love the Soldiers" campaign.

378. _____. Ch'ien-hsien pao she 前線報社. Wen Tien-hsiang pan ho Chang Hsü-yu p'ai 溫典祥班和張緒友排 (Squad Leader Wen Tien-hsiang and Platoon Leader Chang Hsü-yu). n.p., same, 1946. 37 pp. microfilm. (4292.9/7537.35)

   Stories of two model soldiers with respect to improvement of officer-soldier relations.

379. Chiao-tung chün-ch'ü. Cheng-chih pu. Tsu-chih pu 膠東軍區政治部組織部 (ed.). Kuan-yü ch'üeh-ting chieh-chi ch'u-shen wen-t'i 關於確定階級出身問題 (Concerning Class Origin). n.p., same, 1946. 42 pp. microfilm. (4130/7537)

   Excerpts from <u>Kung-ch'an tang jen</u>, <u>Tou-cheng sheng-huo</u>, <u>Kung-ch'an tang-yüan</u>, <u>Nung-min shih i-chia</u>, and other publications dealing with the proper classification of people by class origin.

380. Chiao-tung hua-pao 膠東畫報 (The Chiaotung Pictorial). Nos. 1-7. Chiaotung, June 20, 1944 - April 1945. (4292.24/7554)

This magazine, with some illustrations and comics, deals mainly with life, production, and anti-Japanese activities among Communist soldiers in Chiaotung. It appears to aim at a rural and non-intellectual reading public.

381. Chiao-tung ta-chung 膠東大眾 (The Chiaotung Masses). Nos. 27-31. [Chiaotung], January 1 - March 15, 1946. (2992/7546)

An organ of the Chiaotung Cultural Association. These issues of this semi-monthly carry articles of high quality on current social, political, and literary matters. It first appeared in 1941, but ceased publication after issue No. 26 during the war. Issue No. 27 appears to be the first issue when the magazine resumed publication after the war; it contains a useful article on the cultural development in Chiaotung during the eight years' War of Resistance.

382. Ch'ün-li pao 群力報 (Mass Strength Journal). Nos. 163-178, and 230. Chiaotung, January 1 - August 25, 1947. (4292.25/1544)

Published once or twice a week, this Communist newspaper carries mainly local army news.

383. Lai-tung hsien cheng-fu i-chiu-ssu-liu nien shang pan-nien min-cheng kung-tso tsung-chieh 萊東縣政府1946年上半年民政工作總結 (A Summary of Civil Affairs of the District Government of Laitung in the First Half of 1946). n.p., 1946. [29 pp.]. manuscript on microfilm. (3057.45/4561)

Detailed reports by the local government on land policy, the war effort, the mass movement, etc.

384. Lai-tung hsien cheng-fu min-chu yün-tung tsung-chieh pao-kao 萊東縣政府民主運動總結報告 (A Summary Report of the District Government of Laitung on the Democratic Movement in the District). n.p., 1946. [16 pp.]. manuscript on microfilm. (3057.45/4561.1)

A detailed report of the government organization, propaganda, education, and election system under the Communist rule in Laitung District.

385. Lai-yang hsien cheng-fu kuan-yü pa chiu shih yüeh-fen chi-ko wen-t'i ti pao-kao 萊陽縣政府關於八,九,十月份幾個問題的報告 (Report of Several Problems in the District Government of Laiyang During August, September, and October). Laiyang, 1946. 17 pp. manuscript on microfilm. (3057.47/4761)

The problems mentioned in this Communist document are concerned with the civil war, production, organization, militia, etc.

386. Pa-lu chün. Shan-tung Chiao-tung chün-ch'ü. Cheng-chih pu 八路軍山東膠東軍區政治部 (ed.). Hsüeh-chan pa-nien ti Chiao-tung tzu-ti ping 血戰八年的膠東子弟兵 (Chiaotung Soldiers in the Eight Years of a Bloody War). n.p., Hsin-hua, 1945. 226 pp. (4292.9/8863.26)

Edited by the Political Department of the Chiaotung Military Region of the Eighth Route Army, this book consists of excerpts from local newspapers and periodicals about Communist troops engaged in guerrilla warfare in the Chiaotung Military Region, one of the six Communist regions in Shantung. The Chiaotung Military Region was established on July 1, 1942, in order to unify all the local guerrilla forces in the eastern part of the province.

387. Shan-tung sheng. Chiao-tung ch'ü. Hsing-cheng kung-shu 山東省膠東區行政公署(ed.). Shan-tung sheng cheng-fu Shan-tung chün-ch'ü kung-pu chih ko-chung t'iao-li kang-yao pan-fa hui-pien 山東省政府山東軍區公佈之各種條例綱要辦法彙編 (Collected Statutes, Regulations, and Outlines Issued by the Shantung Provincial Government and the Shantung Military Region). n.p., same, 1945. 58 pp. microfilm. (4661.95/2597)

Eighteen documents issued in August 1945 concerning various postwar problems, such as measures to be taken after the capture of cities. Edited by the Chiaotung Administrative Office of Shantung Province.

388. _____. Shan-tung sheng Chiao-tung ch'ü cheng-li t'u-ti teng-chi ch'en-pao teng-chi chan-hsing pan-fa 山東省膠東區整理土地等級陳報登記暫行辦法 (Provisional Regulations on Reports, Registrations, and Classifications of Land in Chiaotung Area, Shantung Province). n.p., same, 1946. 8 pp. microfilm. (4395/2597)

Three regulations consisting of ten, ten, and seven articles respectively.

389. _____. Shan-tung sheng Chiao-tung ch'ü min-kuo sa-wu nien-tu cheng-liang pan-fa 山東省膠東區民國卅五年度徵糧辦法 (Grain Levy Regulations of Chiaotung, 1946-47). n.p., same, [1947?]. 8 pp. microfilm. (4591/2597)

Two regulations consisting of thirteen and twelve articles respectively.

390. Shan-tung Chiao-tung chün-ch'ü chi Chiao-tung ch'ü hsing-cheng kung-shu lien-ho kung-pu ling 山東膠東軍區及膠東區行政公署聯合公佈令 (Joint Order of the Chiaotung Military Region and the Administrative Office of the Chiaotung Area). n.p., n. pub., 1947. 2 pp. microfilm. (4292.9/6748.38)

Concerning army schools.

391. Tung-hai ch'ü i-nien lai cheng-ch'üan kung-tso tsung-chieh pao-kao 東海區一年來政權工作總結報告 (A Summary Report of Political Work in the Tunghai Area During the Last Year). Wenteng, [Commissioner's Office of Chiaotung-Tunghai, Wenteng, Shantung], 1941. various pagination. microfilm. (3057/5371)

A lengthy, comprehensive report.

3. Other Areas

392. Kung-tso t'ung-hsün 工作通訊 (Work Correspondence). No. 24. n.p., July 30, 1947. microfilm. (4395/5433)

    Published by the Pohai Committee of the CCP, this issue includes directives on land reforms, mass campaigns, and speeches by local Communist leaders.

393. Lu-chung hsing-cheng kung-shu 魯中行政公署. Lu-chung ch'ü k'ang-Jih min-chu cheng-ch'üan chien-she ch'i-nien lai ti chi-pen tsung-chieh chi chin-hou chi-pen jen-wu 魯中區抗日民主政權建設七年來的基本總結及今後基本任務 (A Summary of the Reconstruction of the Anti-Japanese Democratic Regime in Luchung in the Last Seven Years and Its Future Tasks). n.p., same, 1945. 56 pp. microfilm. (3057/2521)

    A comprehensive and detailed political report by the authorities of the Luchung (central Shantung) Administrative Office at the First Congress of the Assembly in July 1947.

394. Lu-chung wen-hsieh 魯中文協 (ed.). Tung-hsüeh tsung-ho chiao-ts'ai 冬學綜合教材 (A Comprehensive Teacher's Manual for the Winter Session). n.p., same, 1945. 40 pp. microfilm. (4292.5/2509)

    Eighteen lessons combining studies with practical life, edited by the Cultural Association of Luchung.

395. Min-ping 民兵. (The Militia). No. 45. Shantung, August 21, 1947. (4292.9/7478f)

    Published by the Political Department of the Pinhai Military Region, this four-page issue is mainly devoted to the land reform undertaken by the Communist army. It appears to be an army paper published every five days, and its circulation was "strictly prohibited for outsiders."

396. Pin-hai nung-ts'un 濱海農村 (Pinhai Peasantry). No. 264. Shantung, August 23, 1947. (4292.25/3354)

    A one-page Communist newspaper published every two days, carrying local news. It began publication on June 1, 1945.

397. [Shan-tung chün-ch'ü.] P'o-hai ch'ü. Cheng-chih pu 山東軍區渤海區政治部. Chien-k'u fen-tou ying-chieh kuang-ming 艱苦奮鬥迎接光明 (Struggle for a Bright Future). n.p., same, 1947. 32 pp. microfilm. (2992/4447)

    Published by the Political Department of the Pohai Area of the Shantung Military Region, this volume includes seven articles: the New Year (1947) messages by Mao Tse-tung and Chu Teh and editorials from the <u>Liberation Daily</u>.

E. THE KWANGTUNG BASE AREA

    The two Communist bases in Kwangtung Province, one located in the East River area and the other on Hainan Island, were the only Communist areas in South China. Most of the works in this section are concerned with Communist activities on Hainan Island, including post-1945 materials.

398. Chung-kuo hsin min-chu chu-i ch'ing-nien t'uan. Hua-nan kung-tso wei-yüan hui. Hsüan-ch'uan pu 中國新民主主義青年團華南工作委員會宣傳部 (ed.). I-ko huo-cho liu-shih ko 一個活捉六十個 (Each One Captured Sixty Men Alive). Canton, Ch'ing-nien, 1950. 46 pp. (2992/5607)

    Ten selected articles on the capture of Hainan Island by the Communist forces, including one account of the development of Communist guerrilla forces there.

399. Feng Pai-chü 馮白駒. Chung-kuo kung-ch'an tang ti kuang-hui chao-yao tsai Hai-nan tao-shang 中國共產黨的光輝照耀在海南島上 (The Communist Party of China Is Shining

Bright on Hainan Island). Canton, Jen-min, 1951. 14 pp. (3073.34/3227)

Written by the most prominent Communist leader in Hainan since 1929, this long article gives little history of the Communist movement there.

400. ———— and others. Kuang-tung jen-min k'ang-Jih yu-chi chan-cheng hui-i 廣東人民抗日游擊戰爭回憶 (Reminiscences of the Guerrilla Warfare in Kwangtung During the Sino-Japanese War). Canton, Jen-min, 1951. 30 pp. (2991.2/0587)

Six articles written by Feng Pai-chü, Tseng Sheng, and other Communist guerrilla leaders in various parts of Kwangtung. The writings were selected from the Canton Nan-fang jih-pao.

401. Li I-sheng 李毅生. Fen-chan erh-shih-san nien ti Hai-nan tao 奮戰二十三年的海南島 (The Twenty-three Years of Struggle on Hainan Island). Hankow, Jen-min, 1951. 66 pp. (3073.34/4402)

Based on the writer's own recollections and study, this is a short history of the Chinese Communist movement on Hainan Island from the founding of the Hainan Local Committee in June 1926, to 1949, with a biographical sketch of Feng Pai-chü.

402. Lin Ying 林盈. Ch'iung-yai ku-tao shang ti tou-cheng 瓊崖孤島上的鬥爭 (Struggle on Lonely Hainan Island). 2nd ed. [Hong Kong], Hsin min-chu, 1947. 52 pp. (3073.34/4911)

Although this book is primarily devoted to the activities of the Chinese Communist Anti-Japanese forces in Hainan during the Sino-Japanese War, it also furnishes a brief description of the Communist political organizations, programs, marriage laws, land laws, elective system, etc.

F. OTHER REGIONS

This section includes material pertaining to Communist bases other than the five regions listed above. Within this category, there is more material concerned with the Shansi-Suiyuan Border Region than the rest.

403. Chin-Sui pien-ch'ü hsing-cheng kung-shu. Min-chiao ch'u. 晉綏邊區行政公署民教處. I-chiu-ssu-ssu nien tung-hsüeh yün-tung tsung-chieh 一九四四年冬學運動總結 (A Summary Report of the 1944 Winter Session). n.p., same, n.d. mimeo. 20 pp. (4912.171/1237)

   This report by the Educational Department of the Administrative Office of the Shansi-Suiyuan Border Region discusses the accomplishments and weaknesses of the study campaign in the winter session of 1944.

404. Chin-Sui pien-ch'ü kang-chan yü chien-she kai-k'uang 晉綏邊區抗戰與建設概況 (General Situation of the Shansi-Suiyuan Border Region). n.p., n. pub., n.d. 34 pp. mimeo. (4292.24/1237)

   This is a general survey of the area, touching on population, the elective system, administration, culture, education, the judicial system, trade, and living standards in the Shansi-Suiyuan Border Region. It appears to be a Communist publication intended for internal reference.

405. Chou Li-po 周立波. Nan-hsia chi 南下記 (Journey to the South). n.p., Kuang-hua, 1948. 76 pp. (4292.24/7203)

   This book contains fourteen short articles describing the author's experiences and the Communist leaders he met when he accompanied the Communist troops on a march from Yenan to join the Fifth Division of the New Fourth Army in Hupeh in November 1944. Among the Communist figures mentioned in this book are Wang Chen, Wang Shou-tao, and Li Hsien-nien.

406. Hsin ch'ün-chung 新群眾 (The New Masses). Vol. I, Nos. 4, 5, and Vol. II, No. 3. n.p., March 20 - August 31, 1946. (4292.01/0216)

   A Communist periodical published in the Hopeh-Shansi Border Region, containing miscellaneous writings on agriculture, the legal system, and local and current affairs. A translation of Israel Epstein's report on Mao Tse-tung appears in Vol. I, No. 4. This magazine was designed for mass consumption, and it contains no valuable writings.

407. Hsin-ssu-chün Su-chung chün-ch'ü ti-ssu ti-fang wei-yüan hui 新四軍蘇中軍區第四地方委員會. Lao-tung cheng-ts'e yü t'u-ti cheng-ts'e ch'u-pu chien-ch'a 勞動政策與土地政策初步檢查 (Preliminary Review of the Labor and Land Policies). n.p., same, 1945. 106 pp. microfilm. (4395/4586)

   Detailed land reform data for the years 1940-45 in an area under the control of the New Fourth Army, published by the Fourth Local Committee of the Suchung Military Region of the New Fourth Army.

408. K'ang-chan yü wen-hua 抗戰與文化 (Culture and War of Resistance). Vol. VI, No. 6. Sian, April 30, 1942. (4130/1942)

   This monthly issue contains an article on the Communist activities in Shantung as well as a survey of the foreign policy of the CCP as reflected in its publications.

409. K'ang-han li-kung 抗旱立功 (Combat the Drought). Nos. 2, 3, and 5. Licheng, June 21 - July 25, 1947. mimeo. (4292.5/5601f)

   A one-page mimeographed newspaper of local agricultural production news.

410. Kuan-chung pao 關中報 (The Kuanchung Journal). Nos. 265 and 268. [Shensi?], December 21, 1944 - January 16, 1945. (4292.24/7754f)

This appears to be a Communist army newspaper published every five days.

411. [Kuo-min ko-ming chün. Ti pa-lu chün.] Lien-fang chün. Cheng-chih pu. Hsüan-ch'uan pu 國民革命軍第八路軍聯防軍政治部宣傳部 (ed.). Fan-shen 翻身 (Turnover). n.p., same, 1946. 84 pp. (4395/8863.22)

Edited by the Propaganda Department of the Political Department of the Joint Defense Forces of the Eighth Route Army, this pamphlet consists of 15 reports of landlord liquidation cases in Shantung, Shansi, Kiangsu-Anhwei border, and other areas.

412. Li-ch'eng hsiao-pao 黎城小報 (The Licheng Journal). Nos. 97, 102, 103, 105, and 106. Licheng, November 4 - December 12, 1947. mimeo. (4292.25/2454f)

A one-page mimeographed newspaper edited by the Joint Office of Licheng district, Shansi, carrying mainly local agricultural production news.

413. Min-chu chien-she 民主建設 (Democratic Reconstruction). Nos. 2 and 3. Huatung, April and June 1946. (4292.25/7010)

The official organ of the Government of the Kiangsu-Anhwei Border Region, containing laws, regulations, official documents, and articles. Most of the articles deal with economic, agricultural, and financial problems in the Border Regions.

414. Sui-te fen-ch'ü wen-chiao ta-hui mi-shu ch'u 綏德分區文教大會秘書處 (ed.). Ta-chung hei-pan pao 大眾黑版報 (The Blackboard Newspaper for the Masses). n.p., same, 1944. 26 pp. (4991.8/2287)

Edited and published by the Secretariat of the Cultural and Educational Conference, Suiteh, this book tells how to publish rural newspapers for the village masses. It is based on the reports and experience of its participants.

415. Wen-tsung 文綜 (Literary Collections). No. 1. Jukao, January 10, 1946. (9200/0429)

   A magazine published in the Communist region of Jukao, Kiangsu Province, with articles on current political events, literature, and the peasantry.

416. Yü O pien-ch'ü shih-cheng kang-ling 豫鄂邊區施政綱領 (Administrative Programs of the Honan-Hupeh Border Region). n.p., n. pub., 1942. 22 pp. (4396/5455.1)

   This pamphlet contains three documents and one statement from a "Yenan observer." These documents are: (1) the program approved by the First Plenary Session of the First Congress of the Border Region, March 22, 1942; (2) the CCP's decision concerning land policy in the anti-Japanese bases, approved by the Politburo of the Party on January 28, 1942; and (3) a supplement to the above-mentioned land policy. The Yenan observer's comments deal with wartime land reforms.

PART THREE

THE POSTWAR PERIOD, 1945-49

X. GENERAL WORKS

A. GENERAL

This section contains handbooks, chronologies of events, periodicals, documents, bibliographies of Communist publications, and general discussions of postwar Chinese politics.

417. Cheng-pao 正報 (The Upright Journal). Nos. 1-115. Hong Kong, July 21, 1946 - November 13, 1948. (9200/1144)

   This periodical was generated from a two-day journal (not available) published (in Hong Kong?) after World War II as an organ of the Chinese Communist column in East River, Kwangtung Province. A ten-day magazine for the first ten issues, it became a weekly with contents in these categories: (1) comments and editorials of current domestic politics; (2) reprints of the Liberation Daily's editorials; (3) feature articles (many by well-known Communists); (4) official documents and statements of the CCP; (5) reports on Communist areas; and (6) war news, etc. It ceased publication after issue No. 115.

418. Hsiang-ch'ün 向羣 (ed.). Chung-kuo wen-t'i wen-hsien 中國問題文獻 (Documents on Chinese Problems). Vol. I. n.p., Ta-chung wen-hua, 1946. 210 pp. (4890.22/2215)

   A collection of 31 documents, which include declarations of the CCP, the Democratic League, and of the Third Party immediately after the war; KMT-CCP negotiations; the Political Consultative Conference; the cease-fire orders; and the nationalization of armies. The appendix consists of a chronology of important national and international events and a statement on the policy and organization of the Democratic National Reconstruction Association.

419. Hsin-hua she 新華社 (ed.). Shih-mo jen ying-fu chan-cheng tse-jen 什麼人應負戰爭責任 (Who Should Be Responsible for the War). Hong Kong, Hsin min-chu, 1949. 82 pp. (2992/0243)

   Edited by the New China News Agency, this is a chronology of important political events in China from August 3, 1945, to April 1, 1949, compiled from the Communist viewpoint with special emphasis on the civil war.

420. Hua-shang pao 華商報 (ed.). I-chiu-ssu-ch'i nien shou-ts'e 一九四七年手冊 (The 1947 Handbook). Hong Kong, same, 1947. various pagination. (9317/4043)

   Edited and published by a leftist newspaper in Hong Kong, this handbook includes the following sections that are related to the subject of this bibliography: current political parties, cultural and educational organizations in the Communist areas, conditions of various Communist regions, men in the news, resolutions of the Political Consultative Conference, and a list of newspapers and magazines suspended by the KMT authorities.

421. _____. I-chiu-ssu-chiu nien shou-ts'e 一九四九年手冊 (The 1949 Handbook). 3rd ed. Hong Kong, same, 1949. various pagination. (9317/4043.3)

   Contrary to the case in the 1947 Handbook, the Communist regions receive more attention in this volume than the area controlled by the National Government. The subjects related to this bibliography are similar to those in the 1947 Handbook, covering events up to the end of March 1949 and including a number of important Communist documents.

422. Keng-yün 耕耘 (ed.). Hsin min-chu shou-ts'e 新民主手冊 (New Democracy Handbook). Shanghai, Cheng-i, 1947. 147 pp. (4292.06/5553)

   A compilation of source materials and writings comparing internal conditions in Kuomintang-controlled regions after World War II with conditions in the "liberated areas." The editor declares himself no Communist but makes it clear that the CCP rule was better for his fellow-countrymen during the turbulent period.

423. [Kuo-min cheng-fu. Kuo-fang pu. Shih-cheng chü 國民政府國防部史政局]. Kuo-fang pu shih-cheng chü tzu-liao mu-lu: Kung-fei shih tzu-liao chih-pu 國防部史政局資料目錄：共匪史資料之部 (A Check List of Collections in the Historical and Political Bureau of the Ministry of National Defense: Communist Bandit Source Materials). Nanking, same, 1947. 54 pp. (4292.62/6710)

Compiled and published by the Historical and Political Bureau of the Ministry of National Defense of the National Government, this is a bibliography of Chinese Communist publications published after 1945, collected by the Bureau between February and May 1947. It totals 1,617 titles arranged in fifteen categories. The supplement contains fourteen titles relating to the Korean Communist movement.

424. Li Pu 李普. Kuang-jung kuei-yü min-chu 光榮歸於民主 (Honor Belongs to Democracy). Chiamussu, Tung-pei shu-tien, 1946. 136 pp. (4292.24/4486)

A discussion of politics and military affairs in various Communist regions, with stories and anecdotes favorable to the regime.

425. Sa Ying 沙英. Chung-kuo ssu ta chia-tsu ti wei-chi 中國四大家族的危機 (The Crisis of the Big Four Families in China). Harbin, Kuang-hua, 1948. 109 pp. (4355/3243).

A collection of 17 articles on economic, financial, and military crises in the National Government, as well as foreign trade, student riots, and the activities of "democratic and liberal groups." With the exception of one article, all the writings had been published in the Tung-pei jih-pao; the title of the book is taken from one of the articles.

426. Ts'ao Chü-jen 曹聚仁. Ts'ai-fang erh-chi 採訪二記 (The Second Report). 2nd ed. Hong Kong, Ch'uan-k'en, 1955. 303 pp. (2992/5612)

A noted journalist's memoirs of the events between the end of World War II and the Communist capture of Shanghai in the spring of 1949, with excellent analyses of KMT-CCP relations, the Democratic League, and the general political situation in China.

427. _____. Ts'ai-fang san-chi 採訪三記 (The Third Report). n.p., n. pub., n.d. 215 pp. (2992/5612.1)

Personal account of and political comments on events from the Communist capture of Shanghai to the end of the Korean War, with an excellent analysis of the Communist leaders.

428. Yang Chi 楊紀 (ed.). I-chiu-ssu-ch'i Chung-kuo yao-lan 一九四七中國要覽 (1947 China at a Glance). Shanghai, Chung-kuo yao-lan, 1947. various pagination. (9316/5617)

Compiled from current newspapers and magazines (to May 1947) by an editor of the Ta Kung Pao, the materials contained in this handbook that relate to the subjects of this bibliography are: political parties, major war battles in the Sino-Japanese War, and a chronology of important national and international events, 1937-47.

B. NEWSPAPERS

More than 80 newspapers are listed under this section, because almost all the available issues in the Chinese Collection of the Hoover Library were published after 1945; the holdings vary from several issues to complete sets. With a few exceptions, they are not cataloged but are filed in alphabetical order in the stacks. When the issues are available beyond 1950, indications of their holdings apply only to the end of 1949.

Most of the newspapers are dailies. Translations of their titles would be of little value, and no attempt has been made to annotate all of them; their political affiliations are noted whenever possible. See also item no. 53.

429. Ch'ang-ch'un jih-pao 長春日報. Changchun, January - May 1947. (incomplete).

430. Cheng-i pao 正義報. Kunming, July 1946 - December 1947. (almost complete).

431. Chi-Jo-Liao jih-pao 冀熱遼日報. Chengteh, March - August 1946. (almost complete).

432. Ch'i-ch'i jih-pao 七七日報. Hsuanhuatien, February - June 1946. (almost complete).

   A Communist publication in the Lishan district of the Hupeh-Honan-Anhwei Border Region.

433. Chieh-fang jih pao 解放日報. Shanghai, May 28, 1949 --. (complete).

   A leading organ of the CCP. See item no. 44.

434. Chieh-fang pao 解放報. Peiping, February 22 - May 1946. (complete).

   A Communist organ published every three (later, two) days. It began publication on February 22, 1946, and was banned by KMT police on May 29 of the same year.

435. Chien-kuo jih-pao 建國日報. Canton, March 1946 - November 1947. (incomplete).

   A leading newspaper in Kwangtung Province since 1940's. Close to the wartime army high command of the province.

436. Chin-Ch'a-Chi jih-pao 晉察冀日報. Kalgan, March - September 1946 and February 1948. (incomplete).

   A leading Communist newspaper in the Shansi-Chahar-Hopeh Border Region. In September 1945 it moved to Kalgan.

437. Chin-pu jih-pao 進步日報. Tientsin, February 27, 1949 --. (almost complete).

   Reorganized from the Ta Kung Pao after Communist capture of Tientsin.

438. Ch'ing-nien Chung-kuo 青年中國. Shanghai, December 1946 - December 1947. (incomplete).

   A weekly published by the Youth Party.

439. Chung-cheng jih-pao 中正日報. Changchun, February - June 1947. (incomplete).

440. Chung-hua shih-pao 中華時報. Shanghai, May 1, 1946 - April 30, 1947. (almost complete).

441. Chung-shan jih-pao 中山日報. Canton, March 1946 - August 1947. (incomplete).

   A KMT newspaper in Canton.

442. Chung-Su jih-pao 中蘇日報. Mukden, November 1946 - May 1947. (incomplete).

443. Chung-yang jih-pao 中央日報. Chengtu, October 1943 - June 1946. (almost complete).

    An official organ of the KMT. The two most important ones were published in Chungking and Nanking.

444. _____. Chungking, March - June 1945, and March - May 1946. (incomplete).

445. _____. Shanghai, April - October 1946. (incomplete).

446. _____. Nanking, September 1945 - December 1947 (almost complete), and January 1948 - April 1949. (incomplete).

447. _____. Canton, March - October 1949. (almost complete).

448. Ho-p'ing jih-pao 和平日報. Chungking, March - June 1945 and March - May 1946. (incomplete).

    Renamed from the KMT army organ, Sao-tang pao.

449. _____. Shanghai, October - December 1946 (incomplete), and March 1947 - March 1948. (almost complete).

450. _____. Hankow, March - June 1946, and January - March 1947. (incomplete).

451. _____. Mukden, November 1946 - December 1947. (almost complete).

452. Hsin Chung-hua pao 新中華報. Yenan, March 12, 1939, January - December 1940 (incomplete), February 27, March 12 and May 1, 1941.

   A Communist organ edited by Liao Ch'eng-chih.

453. Hsin-hsin hsin-wen 新新新聞. Chengtu, January - December 1947. (incomplete).

454. Hsin kuo-min jih-pao 新國民日報. Sian, March - June 1947. (incomplete).

455. Hsin-min pao 新民報. Chungking, March - April 1946. (incomplete).

456. _____. Nanking, January - July 1948. (incomplete).

457. _____. Peiping, January 1948 - June 1950. (incomplete).

458. Hsin-pao 新報. Mukden, December 1946 - July 1947. (incomplete).

459. Hsin sheng-ming pao 新生命報. Liaoning, December 1946 - January 1948. (incomplete).

460. Hsin-sheng pao 新生報. Changchun, September - October 1946. (incomplete).

461. Hsin-Su pao 新蜀報. Chungking, March 1946 - April 1947. (incomplete).

    A local newspaper.

462. Hsin-wen pao 新聞報. Shanghai, December 1947 - May 1949. (incomplete).

    A leading newspaper.

463. Hua-chung jih-pao 華中日報. Hankow, March - May 1946. (incomplete).

464. Hua-pei jih-pao 華北日報. Peiping, October 1945 - November 1948. (almost complete).

465. I-shih pao 益世報. Peiping, June 1947 - November 1948. (almost complete).

    A Catholic newspaper.

466. Jen-min jih-pao 人民日報. Hantan, May 1 - June 27, 1946. (almost complete).

    The leading Communist organ of the Shansi-Hopeh-Shantung-Honan Border Region.

467. _____. Wuan, July 1946 - April 1948. (almost complete).

468. _____. Shihchiachuang, June 1948 - February 1949. (almost complete).

    Emerged (in June 1948) from the amalgamation of the Hantan Jen-min jih-pao and the Kalgan Chin-Ch'a-Chi jih-pao.

469. _____. Dairen, April - September 1949. (incomplete).

470. _____. Peiping, February - March 1949. (almost complete)

471. _____. Peiping, March 1949 --. (complete).

    Became the mouthpiece of the CC of the CCP.

472. K'ang-chan jih-pao 抗戰日報. Hsinghsien, December 1941 - April 1946. (incomplete). (4292.24/5664f)

    A Communist newspaper carrying more national than local news.

473. K'ang-chan pao 抗戰報. Suiteh, September - December 1944 (incomplete), and 2 issues of August - September 1945. (4292.24/5164f)

    First published on August 13, 1939, this newspaper (published every five days) carried primarily local news of agricultural production and other activities of Communist forces. Issue No. 419 has the full text of the resolution of the Cultural and Educational Conference of Suiteh, Suiyuan.

474. Kuan-tung jih-pao 關東日報. Dairen, July 1948 - March 1949. (almost complete).

475. Kuang-ming jih-pao 光明日報. Peiping, June 1949 --. (complete).

  An official organ of the Democratic League, which began publication in June 1949.

476. Kuang-ming pao 光明報. Tsingtao, January 15 and 25, 1948. microfilm.

477. Kung-jen jih-pao 工人日報. Peiping, July 1949 --. (complete).

  Organ of the Federation of Labor Unions in China.

478. Kuo-min hsin-pao 國民新報. Peiping, November 1946 - May 1947. (incomplete).

479. Kuo-min jih-pao 國民日報. Changsha, November 1946 - December 1947. (almost complete).

480. Liao-ning jih-pao 遼寧日報. Wafangtien, October 1948 - January 1949. (almost complete).

481. Lien-ho jih-pao 聯合日報. Shanghai, September - November 1945, and April 1946 - May 1947. (almost complete).

482. Min-chu pao 民主報. Chungking, March - May 1946. (incomplete).

483. Min-yen pao 民言報. Tsingtao, November 1946 - January 1948. (almost complete).

484. Nan-ching wan-pao 南京晚報. Chungking, March - April 1946. (incomplete).

485. Pien-ch'ü ch'ün-chung pao 邊區群眾報. Yenan, March 1944 - January 1947. (almost complete).

    A Communist organ.

486. P'o-hai jih-pao 渤海日報. [Pohai], September - November 1946, December 1947, and January - April 1948. (incomplete).

487. Shang-wu jih-pao 商務日報. Chungking, April 1945 - December 1947. (incomplete; only several issues in 1945-46).

488. Shen-pao 申報. Shanghai, December 1945 - May 1949. (incomplete; several issues only in 1945 and 1947).

    A leading newspaper.

489. Shih-chia-chuang jih-pao 石家莊日報. Shihchiachuang, March - April 1948. (incomplete).

490. Shih-chieh jih-pao 世界日報. Chungking, May 1945 - December 1947. (almost complete).

    A leading newspaper.

491. _____. Peiping, January 1946 - February 1949. (almost complete).

492. Shih-chieh wan-pao 世界晚報. Peiping, November - December 1945. (almost complete).

493. Shih-hua pao 實話報. Dairen, July 1948 - July 1949. (almost complete).

494. Shih-tai jih-pao 時代日報. Shanghai, March - June 1946. (almost complete).

495. Ta-chung jih-pao 大眾日報. Chiaotung, July 1946 - October 1947. (almost complete).

496. _____. Lin-i, October - November 1946. (almost complete).

497. _____. Shantung Liberated Area, February - August 1947 (almost complete) and several issues in 1948 (microfilm).

    First published on January 1, 1939, this was an important newspaper in the "Shantung Liberated Area."

498. Ta-chung pao 大眾報. Chiaotung, September 1947 - August 1948. (9 issues only). microfilm.

    A Communist newspaper published in the Chiaotung Military Region, carrying local and national news. It began publication on August 13, 1938.

499. Ta-kang pao 大剛報. Hankow, March - June 1946, and March 1947 - January 1948. (almost complete).

    A well-known newspaper.

500. Ta-kuang pao 大光報. Canton, January - December 1947. (almost complete).

    A mouthpiece of the Kwangtung Provincial Government.

501. Ta Kung Pao 大公報. Shanghai, November 1945 - April 1949. (almost complete).

    See item no. 62.

502. _____. Tientsin, December 1945 - May 1948. (almost complete).

503. Ta-lien jih-pao 大連日報. Dairen, May 1948 - March 1949. (almost complete).

504. Tung-pei jih-pao 東北日報. Mukden, March - December 1946 and March - September 1949. (incomplete).

505. Tung-pei shih-pao 東北時報. Changchun, August - November 1946. (almost complete).

506. Yen-an jih-pao 延安日報. Yenan, September - December 1947. (incomplete).

507. Yen-t'ai jih-pao 煙台日報. Chefoo, November 1946 - March 1947. (incomplete). partially microfilm.

    First published on September 18, 1945, this newspaper carries news on the civil war and the Communist regions.

508. Wen-hui pao 文滙報. Shanghai, September 1945 - May 1947, and June - December 1949. (almost complete).

    A leading newspaper.

509. Wu-han jih-pao 武漢日報. Hankow, March 1946 - December 1948. (incomplete).

XI. MANCHURIA

    Included in this section are Communist policy statements and documents; journalists' reports; and periodicals with articles on Manchurian problems, documents on educational reforms, and above all, documents on the United Northeast Anti-Japanese Army. There are only a few items related to land reforms; such items are listed in Section XVIII.

510. Chang Chan 張瞻. Tung-pei san-yüeh chi 東北三月記 (Three Months in the Northeast). n.p., P'ing-tsin, 1946. 41 pp. (2992/1366)

    A Ta-kang pao correspondent's report of Manchuria during his stay there from January to April 1946, with a report of an interview with Chang Chia-ao (Chang Kia-ngau) and a report of Madame Chiang Kai-shek's visit. In a number of places, the author's name appears as Chang Tan, and it is difficult to determine which is correct.

511. Chi Yün-lung 紀雲龍. Yang Ching-yü ho k'ang-lien ti-i lu-chün 楊靖宇和抗聯第一路軍 (Yang Ching-yü and the First Route Army of the United Northeast Anti-Japanese Army). n.p., Tung-pei, 1946. 122 pp. (4292.3/4203)

    An informative and detailed account of the career of a Communist guerrilla leader, who was killed in 1940, and his army in Manchuria. This book is based on official Japanese and "Manchukuo" documents as well as Chinese Communist sources, with passing comment on the Korean Communists.

512. Chien-ping 尖兵 (Point). Vol. IX, No. 7/8. Nanchang, May 16, 1946. (2992/9828)

This semi-monthly carries anti-Communist articles. Issue Vol. IX, No. 5/6 is a special number on the Manchuria problem, but it is not available.

513. Chih-shih 知識 (Knowledge). Vol. I, No. 3 - Vol. II, No. 3; Vol. X, No. 2; Vol. XI, No. 1; and Vol. XII, No. 2, Chiamussu, Harbin, and Mukden, September 1, 1946 - August 1, 1949. (4292.01/8605)

This semi-monthly was a general periodical for young readers, with special emphasis on student life, education, current affairs, and the development of Manchuria. Vol. I, No. 3 contains a useful article on middle school education in "liberated areas." A biographical sketch of Yang Ching-yü by Chi Yün-lung and an article on the United North China University appear in Vol. I, No. 4 (September 15, 1946). Issue Vol. I, No. 6 (November 1, 1946) has an article on Li Chao-lin, former commander of the Third Route Army of the United Northeast Anti-Japanese Army.

All issues contain some useful news and occasional reports on the activities of known literary figures in Communist areas. The magazine ceased publication after issue Vol. XXII, No. 2, when it was combined with two other periodicals (Tung-pei ch'ing-nien and Sheng-huo pao) and published under the name Sheng-huo chih-shih.

514. Chou Erh-fu 周而復. Tung-pei heng-tuan mien 東北橫斷面 (The Northeast Journey). n.p., Chin-jih, 1946. 159 pp. (2992/7212)

A journalist's fragmentary report of his travels in Manchuria from April to June 1946. He interviewed Lin Piao, Chang Hsüeh-shih, and Chou Pao-chung.

515. _____. Sung-hua-chiang shang ti feng-yün 松花江上的風雲 (Events Across the Sungari River). Hong Kong, Chung-kuo ch'u-pan, 1947. 132 pp. (2992/7212.1)

This is a sequel to the previous volume. It was originally published as a series in the Shanghai Shih-tai chou-pao under the title "Tung-pei feng-yün." It tells of postwar Manchuria, especially the history of the United Northeast Anti-Japanese Army, the organization of the United Democratic Army, and their military leaders.

516. Chung-kuo jen-min chieh-fang chün. Hua-pei chün-ch'ü. Cheng-chih pu 中國人民解放軍華北軍區政治部 (ed.). Tung-pei wan-ch'üan chieh-fang 東北完全解放 (Complete Liberation of the Northeast). n.p., same, 1948. 37 pp. (3052/5687)

A collection of the New China News Agency's broadcasts with regard to the civil war in Manchuria.

517. [Chung-kuo kung-ch'an tang. Tung-pei chü] 中國共產黨東北局 Kuan-yü ch'ien tung-pei ti-hsia tang tsu-chih chih tang-yüan yü k'ang lien kan-pu ti chüeh-ting 關於前東北地下黨組織之黨員與抗聯幹部的決定 (Decision Concerning Underground Party Members and Cadres of the United Northeast Anti-Japanese Army). n.p., same, 1948. 2 pp. microfilm. (4292.5/7085)

Dated January 1, 1948, this decision of the Northeast Bureau of the CCP calls for careful examinations as the basis for accepting or rejecting former underground Party members wishing to return to the Party organization and to re-establish relations with the Party.

518. Feng Chung-yün 馮仲雲. Tung-pei k'ang-Jih lien-chün shih-ssu nien k'u-tou chien-shih 東北抗日聯軍十四年苦鬥簡史 (A Brief History of the Bitter Struggles of the United Northeast Anti-Japanese Army). [Harbin], Ch'ing-nien, 1946. 91 pp. (2988/3221)

Written by the former political commissar of the Third Route Army of the United Northeast Anti-Japanese Army, this volume gives a detailed account of the leaders, organization and development of the anti-Japanese guerrilla forces which sprang up after the "Manchurian Incident" of 1931. According to the author, the United Army consisted of eleven "armies," the first seven of which were directly organized by the Manchuria Bureau of the CCP. After the outbreak of the Sino-Japanese War in 1937, these armies were grouped into three "route armies."

519. Feng-huo tung-pei 烽火東北 (Conflagration in the Northeast). Hong Kong, Wen-ts'ung, 1947. 52 pp. (2992/0322)

This is issue No. 7 of the publisher's series, carrying an article on the civil war in Manchuria and a "public opinion poll" on the KMT-CCP peace negotiations.

520. Hsin cheng-lun 新政論 (New Political Commentaries). Nos. 1-2. Chungking, January 31 - April 15, 1946. (2992/0210)

This non-Communist magazine contains no important material on the Chinese Communist movement, but its issue No. 2 is a special number on Sino-Soviet relations.

521. Hsin-hua jih-pao 新華日報 (ed.). Tung-pei wen-t'i 東北問題 (Manchuria Problems). n.p., same, 1946. 162 pp. (2992/0464)

Edited and published by the New China Daily, this is a collection of important statements made between November 28, 1945, and June 15, 1946, by Chu Teh, Chou En-lai, Lin Piao, and the CCP on the Manchuria situation; it includes several editorials by the New China Daily and the Yenan Liberation Daily on the same subject, as well as a number of articles on the United Northeast Anti-Japanese Army.

522. Hung Huang 洪荒. Tsui-hou ti cha-tzu 最後的渣滓 (The Dregs). Mukden, Tung-pei shu-tien, 1949. 31 pp. (2992/3841)

    Alleged misbehavior and corruption of the National Government's armies and personnel in Manchuria as reported by a Communist journalist who stayed with the People's Liberation Army in Manchuria in the spring of 1949.

523. Jo-ho sheng jen-min tai-piao hui-i ching-kuo chi chüeh-i an 熱河省人民代表會議經過及決議案 (The People's Congress of Jehol Province and Its Resolutions). n.p., n. pub., [1947?]. 28 pp. (4766.1/4398)

    The People's Congress of Jehol Province convened in Chengteh in November 1946. This pamphlet contains an account of the event, its resolutions, and the approved political programs submitted by the Provincial Committee of the CCP.

524. Kao Hsi-ping 高惜冰. Yüan-tung hung-huo ti chien-yin hou-ko 遠東紅禍的前因後果 (The Cause and Effect of the Red Catastrophe in the Far East). Taipei, Fan-kung, 1950. 74 pp. (2992.7/0293)

    The introduction of this pamphlet indicates vaguely that the author took part in government work in Manchuria from the end of World War II to the government's withdrawal from there. To readers who do not know about the author, Chapter III of this volume is useful in that it contains his personal observations of Communist actions there. The other chapters of the book deal with the Yalta agreement, the negotiations between the National Government and the Communists, and the natural resources of Manchuria. As former Governor of Antung, one of the Northeast provinces (Manchuria), the author could have added many more interesting and valuable experiences to his account.

525. Li Tu 李杜 and others. Tung-pei ti hei-an yü kuang-ming 東北的黑暗與光明 (Darkness and Brightness in Manchuria). n.p., Li-shih, 1946. 102 pp. microfilm. (3052/5166)

A collection of 14 articles and documents: 6 each on the United Northeast Anti-Japanese Army and on the deaths of Chang Hsin-fu and Li Chao-lin, and 1 each by the New China News Agency and the CCP spokesman on the Manchurian situation.

526. Liu Pai-yü 劉白羽. Shih-tai ti yin-hsiang 時代的印象 (Impressions of the Time). Harbin, Kuang-hua, 1948. 267 pp. (2992/7221.62)

A collection of writings divided into three sections. Section I of the book contains articles reporting life in Yenan; they were written after the author's arrival in Chungking in 1944 to work as a co-editor with Hu Sheng of the literary section of the <u>New China Daily</u>. Section II's articles are concerned with his visit in Manchuria, April - June 1946, as a reporter of the New China News Agency. The articles contained in Section III deal with another visit to Manchuria in the winter of 1946. The writings in Section I are somewhat literary, but those in Sections II and III are useful and informative, particularly on the United Northeast Anti-Japanese Army and the United Democratic Army.

527. Sheng-huo pao 生活報 (The Life Journal). Nos. 18, 38, 41-43, and 45. Harbin and Mukden, July 26, 1948 - January 16, 1949. (4292.25/2134f)

Published every five days, this newspaper carried both domestic and national news. Articles of particular interest are those on Liu Po-ch'eng and Liao Yao-hsiang, the latter being the KMT commander of the New Sixth Army. Published in Mukden from issue No. 45.

528. Tung-pei chiao-yü she 東北教育社 (ed.). Lun tung-pei chiao-yü ti kai-ko 論東北教育的改革 (On Educational Reform in the Northeast). 3rd ed. Tung-pei, Hsin-hua, 1950. 116 pp. (4912.11/5140.05)

In addition to nine educational regulations and ordinances, this book includes speeches by Lin Feng, Feng Wen-pin, and Tung Shun-ts'ai. The speech by Tung sums up the educational changes in Manchuria from 1946 to 1949.

529. _____. Tung-pei ssu-nien lai chiao-yü wen-chien hui-pien 東北四年來教育文件彙編 (Collected Documents on Education in the Northeast for the Last Four Years). Tung-pei, Hsin-hua, 1949. 125 pp. (4912.11/5140.51)

Of the 19 documents contained in this volume, 5 are editorials of the Tung-pei jih-pao; the rest are regulations and directives issued by the Communist educational authorities in Manchuria between September 24, 1946 and August 10, 1949.

530. Tung-pei ch'ien-feng 東北前鋒 (The Advance Guard of the Northeast). Nos. 8-9. Chungking, February 1-16, 1946. (3052/5188.231f)

This newspaper carries pro-KMT articles and discussions of Manchuria problems.

531. Tung-pei hua-pao 東北畫報 (The Northeastern Pictorial). Vol. I, Nos. 2, 3, and 42-83 (incomplete). n.p., May 1, 1946 - March 31, 1951. (3052/5154)

This monthly pictorial published pictures, cartoons, woodcuts, and occasionally reports and songs primarily concerned with the postwar Manchuria and anti-KMT propaganda. Issue No. 46 is devoted exclusively to the civil war.

532. Tung-pei wen-hua 東北文化 (The Northeast Culture). No. 2/3/4. Chungking, January 7, 1946. (3052/5102f)

With articles on various aspects of the political situation in Manchuria. Among the contributors are Chow Ching-wen (Chou Ch'ing-wen) and Liu Ya-tzu.

533. Wang Chien-ch'u 王健礎. Mu-fang chih-tao yüan Sung Yung-chang 模範指導員孫永章 (Sung Yung-chang, a Model Commissar). 2nd ed. n.p., Chung-kuo jen-min, 1948. 42 pp. (4292.9/1121)

Published by the Propaganda Bureau of the Political Department of the Northeast Military Zone of the Chinese People's Liberation Army for the reference of other party political workers in the army, this is an account of the successful political work of a CCP member after he became a company commissar in November 1945.

534. Wei Tung-pei ti ho-p'ing min-chu erh tou-cheng 為東北的和平民主而鬥爭 (Struggle for Peace and Democracy in the Northeast). Vol. I. n. p., Ta-chung wen-hua, [1946]. 124 pp. (2992/3512)

Included in this book are five editorials of the Liberation Daily (selected from February 25, 1946, through April 12 of the same year) and nine statements (by Chu Teh and other Communist writers) and articles; all are concerned with the Manchuria problem. One of the articles deals with the history of the United Northeast Anti-Japanese Army.

XII. THE PARTY

This section includes newspaper editorials, CCP documents, manuals for Party members, KMT analyses of the postwar CCP, and a number of works on the recruitment and training of intellectuals. Some of the basic decisions can be found in Mao Tse-tung's Selected Works, Vol. IV, which is listed in Section III of this bibliography.

Since this bibliography does not repeat any title that has been listed in the previous bibliography covering the years 1921-37, attention should be given to item no. 233 of the previous volume. That item is a collection of 15 important statements and documents issued by the CCP from May 30, 1937, to January 1, 1949, and entitled I-chiu-ssu-ch'i nien i-lai Chung-kuo kung-ch'an tang chung-yao wen-chien chi (Important Documents of the Chinese Communist Party Since 1947) (148 pp. 4292.7/1464). The Second Plenum of the CC, elected by the Seventh Congress of the CCP, decided in March 1949 to shift the main emphasis of the Party work from the countryside to the cities. In this connection, the works in Section XXI, "Industrial and Trade Policies," are closely related.

535. Cheng-pao ch'u-pan she 正報出版社 (ed.). Kuan-yü chih-shih fen-tzu ti kai-tsao 關於知識份子的改造 (On Reform of the Intelligentsia). Hong Kong, same, 1948. 37 pp. (4292.79/1422)

   This pamphlet contains (1) three policy decisions on the intelligentsia by the Northeast and the Chungyuan Bureaus of the CC of the CCP, (2) excerpts of Mao Tse-tung's commentaries on the intelligentsia, and (3) one article each by Jen Pi-shih and Hsia Yen.

536. Ch'i-chi hsüan-yen chi ch'i yen-chiu 七七宣言及其研究 (The July 7 Manifesto and Its Meaning). [Hong Kong?], Cheng-pao, [1946]. 38 pp. (2922/1143.44)

   The Manifesto of the CC of the CCP on the 9th anniversary of the outbreak of the Sino-Japanese War, July 7, 1946, and five short articles written by obscure authors expounding the meaning of the manifesto.

537. Chieh-fang she 解放社 (ed.). Chih-shih fen-tzu yü chiao-yü wen-t'i 知識份子與教育問題 (The Intelligentsia and Their Educational Problems). Shanghai, Hsin-hua, 1949. 53 pp. (4292.79/2503)

   A collection of 11 articles and directives of the Communist regions on the subject, arranged in chronological order (1939 to 1949).

538. Ch'ün-chung jih-pao she 群眾日報社 (ed.). Ch'e-ti kai-pien wo-men ti ling-tao tso-feng 澈底改變我們的領導作風 (Thoroughly Change the Style of Our Leadership). n.p., same, 1948. 32 pp. microfilm. (4292.5/1664)

   Contains four articles: two editorials by the Tung-pei jih-pao, one editorial by the Ch'un-chüng jih-pao (from which the title of this pamphlet is taken), and one article on the classification of classes.

539. Chung-kuo jen-min chieh-fang chün. Hua-tung yeh-chan chün. Cheng-chih pu 中國人民解放軍華東野戰軍政治部 (ed.). Tang-yüan chaio-ts'ai 黨員教材 (A Textbook for Party Members). n.p., same, 1947. 82 pp. microfilm. (4292.5/9644.1)

    A textbook about the CCP for its new and old members in the East China Field Army, published by the Field Army's Political Department.

540. Chung-kuo kung-ch'an tang. Chung-yang Hua-pei chü. Tang-hsiao chiao-wu ch'u 中國共產黨中央華北局黨校教務處 (ed.). Chung-kuo kung-ch'an tang tang-chang chiao-ts'ai 中國共產黨黨章教材 (A Textbook for the Constitution of the Chinese Communist Party). Chitung, Hsin-hua, 1948. 151 pp. (4292.13/5640.2)

    Edited by the Party School of the North China Bureau of the CC of the CCP, this textbook was provided for students in cadre schools of the district (county) or lower level for use in their study of the Party constitution. A revised edition of the book published by the Peking People's Publishing House in 1949 is for cadre schools above the district level. (Hoover 4292.13/5640.21)

541. Chung-kuo kung-ch'an tang. Hua-tung chung-yang chü 中國共產黨華東中央局 (ed.). Kuan-yü hsin chieh-fang ch'ü ta-liang fa-chan tang ti wen-t'i 關於新解放區大量發展黨的問題 (Concerning Party Expansion in the Newly Liberated Areas). Huatung, same, 1946. 21 pp. microfilm. (4292.25/5640)

    A report by Li Lin, this is an extra issue of the <u>Tou-cheng sheng-huo</u>.

542. Hsin min-chu chu-i ch'eng-shih cheng-ts'e 新民主主義城市政策 (The New Democratic City Policy). Hong Kong, Hsin min-chu, 1949. 198 pp. (4689/7294)

    Most of this book consists of documents and regulations relating to the city policy of the CCP, arranged in ten sections: (1) excerpts from speeches by Mao Tse-tung, Jen Pi-shih, Liu

Shao-ch'i, and Li Li-san, and directives issued by the Northeast Bureau of the CCP; (2) political principles and programs issued by the Headquarters of the Chinese People's Army; (3) city political organizations; (4) public safety; (5) transportation; (6) finance; (7) trade and taxes; (8) control of news and other communication media; (9) city housing; and (10) miscellaneous civic problems, such as settlements of disputes and the handling of city beggars.

543. Hsin-hua jih-pao tzu-liao shih 新華日報資料室 (ed.). Lun chih-shih fen-tzu 論知識份子 (On the Intelligentsia). 3rd ed. Sunan, Hsin-hua, 1949. 102 pp. (4292.79/0464)

  Edited by the New China Daily, this is a collection of 11 articles by Mao Tse-tung, Jen Pi-shih, Ch'eng Fang-wu, Ch'en Yi, and others selected from magazines on the role and weakness of the intelligentsia in the proletarian revolution.

544. Hsin-ssu-chün chien Shan-tung chün-ch'ü tang-wu wei-yüan hui 新四軍兼山東軍區黨務委員會. Kuan-yü pu-tui chih-hsing hsin tang-chang nei chi-ko wen-t'i ti chieh-shih yü ch'u-pu kuei-ting ts'ao-an 關於部隊執行新黨章內幾個問題的解釋與初步規定草案 (Preliminary Draft and Explanations of Several Problems Concerning the Enforcement of the New Party Constitution in the Army). n.p., same, n.d. 10 pp. microfilm. (4292.5/0633)

  A bulletin dated February 1, [1946?], issued by the Party Committee of the Shantung Military Region.

545. Hsin-ti jen-wu yü hsin-ti li-liang 新的任務與新的力量 (The New Tasks and the New Strength). [Harbin], Tung-pei shu-tien, 1948. 12 pp. (4292.52/0221)

  This pamphlet consists of only two articles: (1) the editorial of the Tung-pei jih-pao, November 9, 1948, on the recruitment and cultivation of new cadres; and (2) an excerpt from Lenin's article, "The New Tasks and the New Strength," written in 1905.

546. Hung Yen-lin 洪彥林. Tsen-yang tso kung-tso tsung-chieh 怎樣作工作總結 (How to Work at the Conclusion of Campaigns). 2nd ed. Hong Kong, Hsin min-chu, 1949. 124 pp. microfilm. (4196/3804)

   A study of methods on investigation, work, and mass lines.

547. I-chiu-ssu-ch'i nien tou-cheng jen-wu yü ch'ien-t'u 一九四七年鬥爭任務與前途 (The Tasks and Future for the Year 1947). [Hong Kong?], Cheng-pao, [1947]. 19 pp. (2992/1464)

   The texts of the Liberation Daily editorial and the radio broadcasts on New Year's Day 1947 by Mao Tse-tung and Chu Teh.

548. Kan-pu hsüeh-hsi 幹部學習 (Study Materials for the Cadres). Nos. 1-2, 5-6, 9-10, 12, 14/5. [Mukden?], November 1948 - August 1949. (4292.01/4071.37)

   Compiled and published by the Propaganda Department of the Northeast Bureau of the CC of the CCP once or twice a month, selected exclusively from the Tung-pei jih pao, the materials collected in these volumes are CCP resolutions, directives, editorials, and articles that reflect the party line on current national and international affairs. Issue No. 6 (April 1949) is primarily devoted to foreign affairs, and issue No. 9 (June 1949) contains a special documentary section for the First All-China Youth Congress. Most of the documents in issue No. 12 (August 1949) are related to the preparations for the People's Political Consultative Conference.

549. Kuan-yü ch'eng-shih cheng-ts'e ti chi-ko wen-hsien 關於城市政策的幾個文獻 (Several Documents Concerning City Policy). 2nd ed. Huapei, Hsin-hua, 1949. 46 pp. (2992/7040)

   A collection of 11 documents, including: (1) a directive concerning the newly captured cities issued by the Northeast Bureau of the CC of the CCP; (2) regulations issued by the Tsinan Military Control Committee regarding entering the cities; (3) a resolution passed by the Sixth Congress of the All-China Federation of Labor, which was held in Harbin in August 1948; and (4) a directive issued by the Chungyuan Bureau of the CC of the CCP to win over the intelligentsia.

550. Kung-tso t'ung-hsün 工作通訊 (Work Correspondence). No. 8. n.p., June 25, 1948. microfilm. (4292.25/1166)

Published by the Political Department of the Northwest Field Army of the Chinese People's Liberation Army, this issue contains articles dealing with army men and the party.

551. Shih-lun hsüan-chi 時論選集 (Selected Writings on Current Affairs). Vol. II. n.p., Chen-li, 1947. 29 pp. (2992/6032)

The contents of this volume are identical with the <u>I-chiu ssu-ch'i nien tou-cheng jen-wu yü ch'ien-t'u</u> (see item no. 547) with the addition of an article by Lu Ting-i on the postwar international situation.

552. Tang-nei huo-yeh wen-chien 黨內活頁文件 (A Loose-Leaf Collection of Party Documents). n.p., [CCP], 1946. 100 pp. microfilm. (4292.79/5412)

Published by the Propaganda Department of the Hopeh-Shantung-Honan Committee of the CCP, this is a collection of 18 documents relating to the experience of current party work, particularly in the direction of anti-bureaucracy, anti-warlordism, mass lines, and land reforms.

553. Ti-ch'i ping-t'uan cheng-chih pu 第七兵團政治部 (ed.). Tang-yüan chiao-ts'ai 黨員教材 (Manual for Party Members). n.p., same, 1949. 54 pp. microfilm. (4292.5/9644)

Based on the texts previously used in various troops, this manual was purported to be used in the army. It consists of 16 lessons dealing with the party organization, meetings, the training of party members, etc.

554.   T'ung-i ch'u-pan she 統一出版社 (ed.). Jih-pen t'ou-hsiang hou ti Chung-kuo kung-ch'an tang 日本投降後的中國共產黨 (The Postwar Chinese Communist Party). n.p., same, [1948]. 128 pp. (4292.25/2122)

   This appears to be a confidential publication circulated for reference within the KMT. It is a collective work recording CCP activities from the Japanese surrender in 1945 to the end of 1947. It is divided into the following chapters: (1) strategy, (2) organization, (3) peace negotiation, (4) armed revolts, (5) political system, (6) economy and finance, (7) land reform, (8) masses, (9) the CCP's relations with international communism, and (10) future development. Very useful.

555.   Yang K'uei-chang 楊奎章. Ch'eng-hsiang kuan-hsi wen-t'i 城鄉關係問題 (Problems of Urban-Rural Relations). Kowloon, Chung-yüan, 1949. 54 pp. (4292.7/4240)

   A discussion of the decision "to shift the center of gravity of Party work . . . from rural areas to the cities," as adopted by the Second Session of the Seventh Plenum of the CC of the CCP, March 1949.

XIII.   KUOMINTANG-COMMUNIST RELATIONS

A.   GENERAL

   On August 28, 1945, Mao Tse-tung flew to Chungking from Yenan, accompanied by U. S. Ambassador Patrick Hurley, to discuss with Chiang Kai-shek the postwar problems of peace, democracy, and unity. This began the negotiation period which finally ended in February 1947, when Chou En-lai and the other Communist representatives were ordered by the National Government to leave Nanking. This period was characterized in China by the newly coined phrases, "talk-talk-fight-fight," "fight-fight-talk-talk," "talk while fighting," and "fight while talking."

   The available materials in this section are abundant; most of them are newspapers and periodicals carrying articles on the political situation in general and the KMT-CCP relations of 1945-46 in particular.

Works pertaining to the Political Consultative Conference and the Marshall mission, two important events of the 1945-46 period, are listed under the following two headings respectively.

556. Cheng-ch'ü ch'üan-mien ti-k'ang ti sheng-li 爭取全面抵抗的勝利 (Struggle for Victory in All-Out Resistance). [Peiping?], Hsin-hua, [1946]. 40 pp. (2992/2181)

　　This pamphlet contains four cease-fire documents from the KMT-CCP negotiations in Nanking (September - October 1946), ten editorials from the Liberation Daily of the same period on the civil war and the withdrawal of American troops from China, and Mao Tse-tung's statement to a correspondent of the New York Herald Tribune on September 29, 1946.

557. Chi-Chin jih-pao she 冀晉日報社 (ed.). Mu-ch'ien shih-chü chih-nan 目前時局指南 (Guide to Current Situation). n.p., same, 1946. 57 pp. microfilm. (2992/1164)

　　Containing one article by Ch'en Po-ta and five editorials from the Liberation Daily criticizing Chiang Kai-shek and his policy.

558. Chiao-tung hsin-hua shu-tien 膠東新華書店 (ed.). Ho-p'ing chien-she hsin Chung-kuo 和平建設新中國 (To Rebuild China by Peaceful Means). Chiaotung, same, 1946. 37 pp. (2992/7504)

　　Fifteen selected articles and documents, including: (1) a political program submitted by the CCP representatives to the Political Consultative Conference; (2) comments on the conference and opinions on the constitution and reorganization of the National Government by Communist newspapers; and (3) criticisms of the Second Plenum of the CEC of the KMT (March 1946) by the Liberation Daily and the Communist leaders.

559. Chieh-fang jih-pao 解放日報. Mu-ch'ien hsing-shih 目前形勢 (The Current Situation). Vol. II. n.p., Tung-pei jih-pao, 1948. 11 pp. (2992/2064)

A reprint of two editorials from the Liberation Daily as broadcast from Yenan by the New China News Agency on August 29 and September 12 [1946] respectively. One editorial commented on KMT-CCP relations of the previous year and the other predicted the inevitable defeat of the KMT army.

560. _____. Po Chiang Chieh-shih. 駁蔣介石 (Refute Chiang Kai-shek). Kalgan, Chin-Ch'a-Chi, 1946. 56 pp. (2992/2064.14)

Five selected editorials from the Liberation Daily of March - April 1946, one of which refuted Chiang Kai-shek's report at the People's Political Council on April 1, 1946. In addition, the pamphlet includes one editorial of the New China Daily commenting on the Second Plenum of the Central Executive Committee of the KMT (March 1946).

561. Chien-kuo chou-pao 建國週報 (China Reconstruction News). Nos. 1-30. London, August 21, 1945 - May 15, 1946. mimeo. (2991.01/5634.1)

When the K'ang-chan chou-pao, originally published by Chinese in London during the Sino-Japanese War, resumed publication after World War II, it adopted the present name and carried international and pro-KMT Chinese news. It ceased publication after issue No. 30, because another Chinese journal, Ch'iao-sheng pao, was expected to replace it. The last few issues were confusingly dated and numbered.

562. Chin-Ch'a-Chi jih-pao she 晉察冀日報社 (ed.). Shih-lun hsüan-chi 時論選集 (Selected Works on Current Events). Vol. I. Kalgan, Hsin-hua, 1946. 116 pp. (2992/1316.60)

Thirteen important documents and writings on postwar KMT-CCP relations, beginning with the "Declaration Concerning the Present Situation" issued by the CC of the CCP on August 25, 1945. Among the documents collected are statements on the peace negotiations and proposals, and editorials of the Liberation Daily of April 1946.

563.   Ch'ing-nien p'ing-lun 青年評論 (The Youth Review). Vol. I, No. 1. Wuchang, May 18, 1947. (2992/5800)

   This issue, which contains articles commenting on KMT-CCP relations, appears to adopt a right-of-the-center position.

564.   Ch'ün-chung tsa-chih she 羣眾雜誌社. Wo-men ti chu-chang 我們的主張 (Our Stand). n.p., same, 1946. 28 pp. (2992.7/1600)

   Six editorials selected from the Liberation Daily, the New China News Agency, and the Ch'ün-chung (The Masses) commenting on the KMT-CCP negotiations, attacking Chiang Kai-shek's policy, and advocating cessation of civil war on CCP terms.

565.   Chung-kuo nei-chan chung ti liang-t'iao lu-hsien 中國內戰中的兩條路綫 (The Two Roads in the Chinese Civil War). [Hong Kong?], Cheng-pao, [1946]. 42 pp. (2992/1143.56)

   The seven articles included in this pamphlet appear to be Communist newspaper editorials.

566.   Hsiao-hsi 消息 (News). Nos. 1-10. Shanghai, April 7 - May 9, 1946. (2992/3223)

   Published on Sundays and Thursdays, this periodical is informative on the current political situation and the activities of newspapermen and Communist leaders. Tsou T'ao-fen's posthumous memoirs were published here as a series.

567.   Hsiao Min-sung 蕭敏頌. Lun cheng-chih min-chu hua yü chün-tui kuo-chia hua 論政治民主化與軍隊國家化 (On Democratized Politics and Nationalized Army). Hong Kong, Chih-yüan, 1946. 38 pp. (2992/4288)

   Three articles on coalition government, nationalization of the army, and the Political Consultative Conference. The author's position tends to support the National Government, but he adopts an impartial attitude. The three articles were written between November 4, 1945, and January 2, 1946.

568. Hsiao Tsung 蕭聰 (ed.). Chung-kuo min-chu chih-lu 中國民主之路 (The Road to Democracy in China). Hong Kong, Hsien-tai, 1946. 219 pp. (2992/4213)

An important source book on KMT-CCP relations, divided into eight parts: (1) the period of the Sino-Japanese War, 1937-45; (2) postwar problems and the events leading to Mao Tse-tung's visit to Chungking; (3) KMT-CCP negotiations, August - October 1945; (4) the spread of civil war; (5) the Marshall mission and the cease-fire; (6) Political Consultative Conference; (7) the protests of the CCP and the Democratic League regarding the human rights and liberties allegedly violated by the National Government; and (8) the work of the Executive Headquarters at Peiping in connection with Marshall's peace mediation. Following a brief account in each part are all the important related documents. The editor's narration is critical of the National Government.

569. Hsin-hua jih-pao 新華日報 (ed.). Wei ho-p'ing erh fen-tou 為和平而奮鬥 (Struggle for Peace). Chungking, same, 1945. 84 pp. (2992.7/7211)

This volume contains the following documents: (1) the manifesto of the CC of the CCP on the current situation, August 25, 1945; (2) records of Mao Tse-tung's speeches, press interviews, and statements made during his visit in Chungking beginning August 28, 1945; (3) records of KMT-CCP negotiations signed on October 10, 1945; and (4) editorials by the Liberation Daily and the New China Daily News commenting on the peace negotiations during the period between August 29 and October 2, 1945.

570. Hsin-hua wen-chai 新華文摘 (The New China Digest). Vol. I, No. 6, Vol. II, Nos. 7-8, and Vol. III, No. 9. Shantung and Huatung, February 15, 1946 - October 20, 1948. (4292.01/0405)

Articles of particular interest in these issues are: "An Important Key to the Reorganization of the National Government" (by Hua Kang); "My Father General Yeh-T'ing" (Vol. I, No. 6); a biographical sketch of Lo Ping-hui and Mao Tse-tung's letter to him, dated May 20, 1946, reproduced in facsimile (Vol. I, No. 7, which also includes a chronology of war writings by Hsü T'e-li); an account of the Communist capture of Tsinan, Shantung, and Lin Po-ch'ü's speech delivered at Yenan on July 1, 1948, on "Mao Tse-tung's Thought" (Vol. III, No. 9).

571. Hsin-sheng tsa-chih 新生雜誌 (The New Life Magazine). No. 1. Tientsin, November 16, 1948. (2992/0200)

A KMT or pro-KMT magazine focussing on current national politics with no articles of high quality.

572. Hsin shih-ch'i ti lu-hsien 新時期的路綫 (The Line for the New Age). n.p., Chi-Lu-Yü, 1945. 21 pp. microfilm. (2992/0642)

Editorials of the Liberation Daily as well as articles and military orders by Mao Tse-tung and Chu Teh after the Japanese surrender.

573. Hsin wen-hua 新文化 (New Culture). Vol. II, Nos. 4-9 and Vol. III, No. 6. Shanghai, August 10, 1946 - February 5, 1947. (2992/0202)

A medium level theoretical and scholarly semi-monthly opposed to the KMT, with occasional articles on current events.

574. Hsin wen-hua fu-wu she 新文化服務社 (ed.). Chiu-kuo pi-hsü mieh Chiang 救國必須滅蔣 (Chiang Kai-shek Must Be Overthrown in Order to Save the Nation). n.p., same, 1947. 30 pp. microfilm. (2269/4451.78)

Four editorials from the Liberation Daily and one article each by Wu Yü-chang and Tung Pi-wu, all condemning Chiang Kai-shek and his government.

575. Jen-min shih-tai 人民時代 (The People's Era). Vol. II, Nos. 2, 3, 6, and 7. Hsinghsien, July 15 - October 1, 1946. (2992/8762)

   A general and literary periodical with occasional comments on current political affairs.

576. Ko-ming chen-li ch'u-pan she 革命真理出版社 (ed.). Cheng-chih pao-t'u p'ing-lun 政治暴徒評論 (Comments on Political Brigands). n.p., same, 1946. 32 pp. (2992/4841)

   Twelve selected articles, most of them editorials by Chungking newspapers commenting unfavorably on the Yenan Liberation Daily editorial (April 6, 1946) entitled "Po Chiang Chieh-shih" (Refute Chiang Kai-shek), which was reprinted by the Chungking New China Daily two days later.

577. Kuang-fu ch'u-pan she 光復出版社(ed.). I-nien-lai Chung-Jih cheng-chü ti yen-pien 一年來中日政句的演變 (The Development and Change of the Sino-Japanese Relations in the Last Year). Taipei, same, 1947. 28 pp. (2992/9222)

   The first of the two articles in this volume is a reprint of a concise account of KMT-CCP relations (October 1945 - October 1946) from the Wen-hui pao of October 10, 1946.

578. Kuo-min cheng-fu chu-hsi kuang-chou hsing-yüan. Cheng-chih pu 國民政府主席廣州行轅政治部 (ed.). Chung-kung wang ho-ch'u ch'ü 中共往何處去 (The Prospects for the Chinese Communists). Canton, same, 1946. 18 pp. (2992/6710)

   A brief account and analysis of the CCP published by the Political Department of the Canton Headquarters of the President of the National Government.

579. [Kuo-min ko-ming chün. Ti pa-lu chün.] Lien [-fang chün.] Cheng [-chih pu.] Hsüan-ch'uan pu 國民革命軍第八路軍聯防軍政治部宣傳部 . Shih-shih wen-hsien hsüan-chi

時事文獻選集 (Selected Documents on Current Affairs). n.p., n. pub., 1946. 176 pp. (2992/8863)

    Edited by the Propaganda Department of the Political Department of the Joint Defense Forces of the Eighth Route Army, this volume consists of 29 important documents concerning KMT-CCP relations in the first six months after the end of World War II. It is arranged in chronological order beginning with the communique of October 10, 1945, which summarizes KMT-CCP negotiations on a number of issues, including Manchuria, the Political Consultative Conference, reorganization and nationalization of the army, and broadening of the National Government's basis.

580. Kuo-ming 國命 (The National Destiny). Vol. I, No. 5. Chengtu, August 20, 1946. (2992/6582)

    A semi-monthly with articles discussing KMT-CCP relations. Issue No. 4, which is not available, is a special number devoted to the political parties in China.

581. Li-shih wen-hsien she 歷史文獻社 (ed.). Cheng-chün fu-yüan wen-hsien 整軍復員文獻 (Documents Concerning the Reorganization of the Army and Demilitarization). n.p., same, 1946. 55 pp. (2992.7/7502)

    A collection of documents concerning the proposed reorganization of the Communist forces and related KMT-CCP agreements during the period between September 1945 (Mao Tse-tung's interview with a Reuters' reporter) and June 6, 1946 (Manchurian 15-day cease-fire order issued by Chiang Kai-shek and Chou En-lai). The documents are arranged in chronological order, and include the demilitarization regulations and other related policies of the Shansi-Chahar-Hopeh Border Region.

582. _____. T'ing-chan wen-hsien 停戰文獻 (Documents Concerning the Cease-Fire). n.p., same, 1946. 89 pp. (2992.7/7502.26)

    This volume contains 43 documents and writings, dated between December 8, 1945, and May 1946, concerning peace negotiations and the KMT-CCP truce. It includes statements by leaders of the Democratic League and non-partisan groups and organizations.

583. Mao Tse-tung tsai Chung-ch'ing 毛澤東在重慶 (Mao Tse-tung in Chungking). 3rd ed. Shanghai, Ho-chung, 1946. 68 pp. (4292.3/2135.24b)

 Of the nine articles collected in this pamphlet, only the ones from the Ta Kung Pao and the New China Daily relate to Mao's sojourn in Chungking in 1945.

584. Lo Mai 羅邁 and others. Shui tsai t'o 誰在拖 (Who Is Lagging?). Hong Kong, Ts'ao-yüan, 1946. 69 pp. (2992/6133)

 Ten selected articles mainly concerned with the Political Consultative Conference and the reorganization of the armies, both Nationalist and Communist. With the exception of Lo Mai's writings and Ch'en Po-ta's "Chiang Kai-shek Should Be Patriotic," the articles are unsigned.

585. Pei-fang wen-hua 北方文化 (Culture of the North). Nos. 1-7, and 10-12. Kalgan, March 1 - August 16, 1946. (9200/1002)

 Published by the Culture Society of the North (headed by Ch'eng Fang-wu), this semi-monthly is a high-quality magazine of literature and culture. Occasionally, it publishes articles on current events and political commentaries.

586. P'o-ch'an ti cheng-chih li-lun 破產的政治理論 (A Bankrupt Political Theory). n.p., n. pub., n.d. 40 pp. (2992/1021)

 These eight articles are selected from the Liberation Daily of March-April 1946. Among the subjects criticized were the Second Plenum of the KMT Central Executive Committee and the arrests of the Peiping Chieh-fang pao workers by the police on April 3, 1946.

587. P'ing-lun pao 評論報 (The Critique). Nos. 1-3, 6, and 18. Shanghai, November 9, 1946 - May 6, 1947. (2992/0404)

   A weekly periodical on current domestic politics. It carries articles on KMT-CCP negotiations and the "Third Force."

588. [Shan-tung sheng. Chiao-tung] ch'ü tang-wei hsüan-ch'uan pu 山東省膠東區黨委宣傳部 (ed.). Fan-tui nei-chan pao-wei ho-p'ing pao-wei chieh-fang ch'ü 反對內戰保衛和平保衛解放區 (Oppose Civil War, Safeguard Peace, and Safeguard the Liberated Areas). n.p., n. pub., 1946. 16 pp. microfilm. (2992/7926)

   Containing two editorials by the Ta-chung jih-pao, and one each from the Chün-cheng chou-pao and the Liberation Daily.

589. Shih-chieh hsin-ch'ao 世界新潮 (The New World Tide). Vol. II, Nos. 1-2. Canton, February 26 - March 23, 1947. (2992/4607)

   Most of the writings contained in these semi-monthly issues are concerned with current economic problems facing the National Government.

590. Shih-hsien ho-p'ing min-chu ti wen-hsien 實現和平民主的文獻 (Documents Relating to the Realization of Peace and Democracy). [Hong Kong], n. pub., [1946]. 39 pp. (2992/3121)

   This pamphlet contains the following documents: (1) Chiang Kai-shek's broadcast on New Year's Day, 1946; (2) comments on the Political Consultative Conference by Chu Teh, Chou En-lai, and the Liberation Daily; (3) the CCP spokesman's comments on the Manchuria situation (February 13, 1946); and (4) a Chinese translation of President Truman's statement of December 14, 1945, on the China policy of the American government.

591. Shih-shih jih-pao tzu-liao shih 時事日報資料室 (ed.). Chung-kuo t'ung-i wen-t'i 中國統一問題 (The Problem of Unification in China). n.p., same, 1946. 194 pp. (2992/6564)

This book is focussed on the political situation in China after the Japanese surrender through the end of the Political Consultative Conference in January 1946, with original documents relating to various issues of the period.

592. Su-Huan erh fen-ch'ü Jen-min pao she 蘇皖二分區人民報社 (ed.). Hsin-nien hsien-tz'u 新年獻詞 (New Year's Messages). n.p., same, 1947. 24 pp. microfilm. (2992/4218)

A collection of New Year's messages by Mao Tse-tung, Chu Teh, the Liberation Daily, as well as Chou En-lai's statement and Chang Ting-ch'eng's talk.

593. Ta-tao 大道 (The Way). No. 3. Chungking, October 20, 1945. (2992/4333)

This issue of a semi-monthly publication contains several pro-National Government articles concerning national unity, democracy, and the KMT-CCP peace negotiations.

594. Tung-pei jih-pao she 東北日報社 (ed.). Chung-kuo chü-ta pien-hua ti i-nien 中國巨大變化的一年 (A Year of Great Changes in China). Chiamussu, Tung-pei shu-tien, 1947. 329 pp. (2992/5164.56)

This volume contains 41 editorials from the Liberation Daily, 4 Tung-pei jih-pao editorials, 10 editorials or comments from the New China News Agency, and other Communist documents, all published between July 1946 and June 1947 and arranged in chronological order. Also included are many important Communist documents relating to party policy, KMT-CCP negotiations, the Marshall mission, and political, economic, and foreign affairs.

595. [_____]. Shih-lun hsüan-chi 時論選輯 (Selected Works on Current Events). Chiamussu, Tung-pei shu-tien, 1948. 148 pp. (2992/5164.1)

Most of the 45 articles included in this volume, a sequel to the one listed above, are the New China News Agency editorials and comments of July-December 1947, as published in the <u>Tung-pei jih-pao</u>. With the exception of several documents relating to the land law passed on September 13, 1947, and the Communist financial and economic policies in Manchuria, the writings are arranged in chronological order.

596. W. R. B. (comp.). Chin-jih chung-kung 今日中共 (Today's Chinese Communist Party). n.p., Ho-p'ing, 1946. 44 pp. (4292.2/8654)

This pamphlet appears to have been written shortly after the Political Consultative Conference, when the KMT and the CCP were on relatively friendly terms. Included are translations, excerpts from Communist publications, favorable and unfavorable fragmentary material on the CCP including material on the Seventh Congress, the political structure and organization of the CCP and schools in Yenan, etc. The compiler is identified only as "W. R. B."

597. Wen Ku-yin 聞谷音. Chung-kung fan shou-hsiang hsing-tung chih p'i-p'an 中共反受降行動之批判 (Criticism of the Chinese Communist Actions Relating to the Japanese Surrender). n.p., Ta-kung, 1946. 82 pp. (2991.11/7480)

A presentation condemning the Chinese Communist military authorities for disobeying the orders of the National Government with respect to the Japanese surrender.

598. Yang Erh 楊耳 and others. Kuo-shih t'ung 國事痛 (Sorrow for National Affairs). 2nd ed. Chiamussu, Tung-pei shu-tien, 1947. 58 pp. (2992/4214)

This is the only piece of fiction included in this bibliography. It is a political novel based on the historical events from August 15, 1945, to August 15, 1946, from the Communist viewpoint. It is so well written that it won an award of 50,000 Chinese dollars from the Propaganda Department of the Northeast China Bureau of the CC of the CCP. It first appeared serially in newspapers.

599.　Yü-lun chou-pao 輿論周報 (The Public Opinion Weekly). No. 26. Ningsia, November 23, 1947. (3078.5/7074)

　　Contains writings on current activities of the Communists in the Northwest.

B. THE POLITICAL CONSULTATIVE CONFERENCE

　　The Political Consultative Conference met in Chungking, January 10-31, 1946. It was attended by 38 persons: 8 from the KMT; 7 from the CCP; 4 from the Youth Party; 2 from the Democratic League; 2 from the Democratic-Socialist Party; 2 from the National Salvation Association; one each from the Vocational Education Group, the Rural Reconstruction Group, and the Third Party; and 9 members with no party affiliations. It adopted five resolutions: on government reorganization, the National Assembly, the program for peaceful reconstruction of the country, the draft constitution, and the resolution on military questions. The following materials are reports and documents as well as newspaper comments of the Conference.

600.　Chieh-fang jih-pao 解放日報. Chiang Chieh-shih yüan-tan yen-shuo yü cheng-chih hsieh-shang hui-i 蔣介石元旦演說與政治協商會議 (Chiang Kai-shek's Speech on New Year's Day and the Political Consultative Conference). Shantung, Hsin-hua, 1946. 12 pp. (4890.22/2064)

　　An editorial from the Liberation Daily, dated [January] 7, [1946], commenting on Chiang's speech and the Political Consultative Conference scheduled to be held three days hence.

601.　Chin-Chi-Lu-Yü chün-ch'ü. Cheng-chih pu 晉冀魯豫軍區政治部 (ed.). Cheng-chih min-chu hua yü chün-tui kuo-chia hua 政治民主化與軍隊國家化 (Democratization of the Government and Nationalization of the Armies). n.p., same, 1946. 51 pp. (4890.22/8482)

　　Edited and published by the Political Department of the Shansi-Hopeh-Shantung-Honan Military Region, this book contains comments by CCP leaders on the conclusion of the Political

Consultative Conference, editorials from the <u>Liberation Daily</u>, and the texts of the five resolutions adopted by the conference.

602. Chin-Chi-Lu-Yü pien-ch'ü cheng-fu. Mi-shu ch'u 晉冀魯豫邊區政府秘書處 (ed.). Yu-kuan cheng-chih hsieh-shang hui-i wen-chien hui-chi 有關政治協商會議文件彙集 (Selected Documents on the Political Consultative Conference). n.p., same, [1946?]. 65 pp. (4890.22/4713)

    Reprinted from the Taihang edition of the <u>New China Daily</u> by the Secretariat of the Government of the Shansi-Hopeh-Shantung-Honan Border Region, this volume includes only 14 documents, dated January 17 through March 1, 1946, relating to the political and military affairs of the conference. The documents, however, have many typographic errors and omissions.

603. Ho-p'ing min-chu ti tao-lu 和平民主的道路 (The Road to Peace and Democracy). n.p., n. pub., n.d. 90 pp. (4890.22/2170)

    A collection of 16 documents relevant to America's China policy and, especially, to the KMT-CCP cease-fire agreements. The documents, dated December 10, 1945, to January 16, 1946, are arranged in chronological order.

604. Hsüeh-hsi chih-shih she 學習知識社 (ed.). Cheng-chih hsieh-shang hui-i wen-hui 政治協商會議文彙 (A Selection of Documents on the Political Consultative Conference). n.p., same, 1946. 180 pp. (4890.22/7180)

    Selected documents, speeches, reports, articles, and newspaper comments on the Political Consultative Conference. It is not carefully edited; the preface is signed "Liu."

605. Kuo-chi ch'u-pan she 國際出版社 (ed.). Cheng-chih hsieh-shang hui-i 政治協商會議 (The Political Consultative Conference). 2 vols. Shanghai, same, 1946. 102 and 168 pp. (4890.22/6722)

Edited and published by the International Publishers, Volume (Part) I contains measures for the convocation of the conference, the inaugural speech of Chiang Kai-shek, and the addresses made at the opening session by leaders of the various parties represented. Relevant documents as well as reference materials that provide a background on the political situation before the conference are also included. Volume (Part) II includes the proceedings and results as well as reports and other relevant documents, compiled after the conclusion of the conference. Both volumes are printed with English texts.

606. Li Hsü 李旭 . Cheng-chih hsieh-shang hui-i chih chien-t'ao 政治協商會議之檢討 (A Review of the Political Consultative Conference). Nanking, Shih-tai, 1946. 132 pp. (4890.22/4441)

    A pro-KMT examination of the achievements of the Political Consultative Conference. The first chapter is an account of the conference; the second presents the contents of the five resolutions; the third contains newspaper editorials and articles commenting on the conference (no Communist sources are included); the fourth gives public opinions as reflected by civil organizations; and the fifth collects comments from abroad. The agreement on military affairs is given in the appendix.

607. Li-hua 立華 (ed.). Cheng-chih hsieh-shang hui-i wen-hsien 政治協商會議文獻 (Documents on the Political Consultative Conference). Peiping, Chung-wai ch'u-pan, 1946. 138 pp. (4890.22/0145)

    An excellent collection of documents relating to the Political Consultative Conference, which includes the speeches made by the delegates at the conference.

608. Li-shih wen-hsien she 歷史文獻社 (ed.). Cheng-hsieh wen-hsien 政協文獻 (Documents Relating to the Political Consultative Conference). n.p., same, 1946. 236 pp. (4890.22/7502)

    A pro-CCP collection of documents concerning the Political Consultative Conference. In addition to documents and speeches, this volume includes a number of editorials and comments from the <u>Liberation Daily</u> and the <u>New China Daily</u> not available in other selections listed in this section. It includes material (January through April 23, 1946) concerning the immediate aftermath of the conference and severely criticizing Chiang Kai-shek.

609. Ying-ming 嚶鳴 and Tz'u-cheng 慈正. Cheng-chih hsieh-shang hui-i shih-mo chi 政治協商會議始末記 (An Account of the Political Consultative Conference). Canton, Chung-hsin, 1946. 222 pp. (4892.22/6462)

    A pro-KMT account of the Political Consultative Conference, divided into seven sections: (1) prelude; (2) proceedings; (3) resolutions; (4) profiles; (5) anecdotes; (6) biographical sketches of the 38 delegates to the conference; and (7) pro-KMT newspaper comments.

610. Wen-hui ch'u-pan she 文匯出版社 (ed.). Cheng-chih hsieh-shang hui-i ts'e-hsieh 政治協商會議側寫 (A Profile of the Political Consultative Conference). Vol. I. Canton, same, [1946]. 44 pp. (4890.22/0322)

    A collection of Chungking newspaper reports on the Political Consultative Conference, most of them by Kao Chi of the <u>Ta Kung Pao</u>. All the articles describe the events, meetings, personalities, and recount anecdotes.

C. THE MARSHALL MEDIATION

    General George C. Marshall came to China in December 1945 as President Truman's representative with a mission to arrange for a cessation of hostilities between the armies of the National Government and the Chinese Communists; to find a settlement of the internal strife in China through a conference of all major political parties; to halt civil strife, to broaden the base of Chinese Government and to bring about a "united, democratic China." Marshall returned to the United States in March 1946, and returned to China for the second time in April of the same year, only to leave again on January 7, 1947.

Truman's statement "On Recent Sino-American Relations and China's Present Situation" (issued on December 18, 1946) and Marshall's "Statement to the American People on China's Present Situation" (made before leaving China for the U. S. to succeed James Byrnes as U. S. Secretary of State and released by the U. S. State Department on January 7, 1947) summarize the efforts and the failure of the mediation. Included in this section are not only Chinese sources on the mission but also current articles on international relations.

611. Chang Li-hsing 張力行. Ma-hsieh-erh shih-hua chi-shih 馬歇爾使華紀實 (The Marshall Mission in China). Taipei, Chan-tou, 1955. 95 pp. (2992.7/1342)

　　　Written by a Chinese interpreter (with the rank of Lieutenant Colonel) in the Marshall mission, this is a clear and concise account of General Marshall's mediation efforts, from his arrival in China on December 16, 1945, through his departure in January 1947. The book includes a number of official documents and some interesting personal reports and observations by the author, who is critical of the Chinese Communists. It provides a brief survey of what Marshall accomplished and an appraisal of his failure.

612. Chiang-chün pi-pai 蔣軍必敗 (Chiang's Army Will Inevitably Be Defeated). n.p., n. pub., [1946]. 63 pp. (2992/4336)

　　　Reprints of news dispatches of the New China News Agency and editorials of the Liberation Daily and the New China Daily of 1946 relating to the current political and military situation. The two dominant themes of the selected materials are Chiang's defeat and the opposition to the China policy of the United States.

613. Ch'iao Mu 喬木 (pseud. of Ch'iao Kuan-hua 喬冠華) and others. Lun shih-chieh mao-tun 論世界矛盾 (On World Contradictions). Hong Kong, Hua-ts'ui, [1947]. 52 pp. (2992/0461)

　　　The title of this pamphlet is taken from Ch'iao Mu's article on the world situation. In addition to articles on current domestic politics, economics, and the war in Manchuria, there is an open letter from Feng Yü-hsiang to his fellow countrymen dated May 26 1947, appealing for a peaceful solution of the KMT-CCP conflict.

614. Chin-Ch'a-Chi jih-pao she 晉察冀日報社 (ed.). Wei tu-li ho-p'ing min-chu erh tou-cheng 為獨立和平民主而鬥爭 (Struggle for Independence, Peace, and Democracy). n.p., same, 1946. 46 pp. (2992/1316.34)

    Eleven articles, including Mao Tse-tung's statement (June 1946) opposing American military assistance to Chiang Kai-shek, Chu Teh's speech delivered in Yenan (July 26, 1946), and comments by the Liberation Daily and the "Yenan people" on the joint statement of J. Leighton Stuart and George C. Marshall (August 1946).

615. Ch'üan chieh-fang ch'ü jen-min tung-yüan ch'i-lai fen-sui Chiang Chieh-shih ti chin-kung 全解放區人民動員起來粉碎蔣介石的進攻 (Mobilize All the People in the Liberated Areas to Smash Chiang Kai-shek's Attack). n.p., Tung-pei shu-tien, 1946. 91 pp. (2992.7/8207)

    Nineteen articles selected from the Liberation Daily, the New China News Agency, the Tung-pei jih-pao, and the statements of Communist leaders between June and August 1946, denouncing the China policy of the United States. The appendix to the book is a chronology of the "dictatorial" actions of Chiang Kai-shek and the National Government in the year August 1945 to August 1946. Under the entry of May 29, 1946, there is a list of KMT-prohibited newspapers, periodicals, and news agencies in Peiping. The title of the volume is taken from the editorial in the Liberation Daily of August 18, 1946.

616. Ho-erh-li ta-shih ti "kung-hsien" 赫爾利大使的"貢獻" (The "Contributions" of Ambassador Patrick Hurley). n.p., Ch'ün-chung ch'u-pan, n.d. 39 pp. (2992.7/4124)

    Comments on Patrick Hurley, Joseph Stilwell, the arrests of the Amerasia editor and others in the United States, selected from the Liberation Daily, the New China News Agency, and the Amerasia magazine.

617. Hsin-hua jih-pao 新華日報 (ed.). Hsin Chung-kuo ti shu-kuang 新中國的曙光 (The Light of Dawn of New China). n.p., Chung-kuo ch'u-pan, 1946. 104 pp. (2992.7/0464)

This book is divided into the following three parts: (1) translations of various China policy statements made by President Truman, James Byrnes, and General Marshall and comments by Chinese Communists; (2) records of Chou En-lai's press conference, Communist documents and comments relating to the cease-fire and to the Political Consultative Conference; and (3) comments and speeches by Chou En-lai, Chu Teh, and Communist newspapers on the success of the Political Consultative Conference. All the materials are related to the period between December 1945 and February 1946. The title of the book is taken from the title of the editorial in the New China Daily of January 11, 1946.

618. Hua-pei hsin-hua shu-tien pien-chi pu 華北新華書店編輯部 (ed.). Chung-kuo ho-p'ing chih-lu 中國和平之路 (The Road to Peace in China). n.p., same, 1946. 41 pp. (2992.7/4104)

This pamphlet includes translations of China policy statements made by President Truman and James Byrnes, and comments by the spokesmen of the CCP, dated between December 1945 and February 1946.

619. Jen-min chou-pao 人民周報 (The People's Weekly). Vol. I, No. 5. [Kalgan?], July 12, 1946. (2992/8774)

Several articles in this issue attack the China policy of the United States. Some of the writings are reprints from the Tung-pei jih-pao and the Liberation Daily, and they include a reply to the Ta Kung Pao's criticism of the CCP.

620. Liu-yüeh i-lai kuo-kung t'an-p'an chung-yao wen-hsien 六月以來國共談判重要文獻 (The Important Documents Relating to the Kuomintang and Communist Negotiations Since June). n.p., n. pub., n.d. 42 pp. (2992.7/0724)

Fourteen documents dated from June 6 (the Manchurian cease-fire order) through October 9, 1946, including documents on the CCP protest against the sale of American surplus war goods to China. Many of the original documents are Chou En-lai's memoranda to General Marshall. The cover indicates that this is "confidential material for reference only."

621. Lun chan-chü 論戰局 (On the War Situation). n.p., Tung-pei min-chu, 1946. 26 pp. (2992.7/0267)

  Selected articles and documents concerning the Marshall mediation, including three editorials from the <u>Liberation Daily</u>, one editorial comment by the New China News Agency, the declaration of the CC of the CCP on current situation as of October 17, 1946, and an exchange of notes among Chiang Kai-shek, Chou En-lai, and George C. Marshall during September and October of 1946. This volume was published by the General Political Department of the United Northeast Democratic Army. The title is taken from the editorial in the <u>Liberation Daily</u> of November 4, 1946.

622. Meng-pang jen-shih ti cheng-yen 盟邦人士的諍言 (Words of Caution from our Allies). [Chungking?], Hsin-hua, 1944. various pagination. (2992/6584)

  Chinese translations of 16 articles critical of the National Government, published in English, American, and Russian newspapers and periodicals. The authors include T. A. Bisson, L. K. Rosinger, and Brooks Atkinson. The title of the volume is taken from the editorial of the <u>Liberation Daily</u> for July 6, 1944, which serves as the introduction of the book.

623. Shan-tung hsin-hua shu-tien 山東新華書店 (ed.). Kuo nei-wai hsing-shih 國內外形勢 (Foreign and Domestic Situation). [Shantung], same, 1947. 124 pp. (4292.25/2504)

  Of the articles selected in part from editorials of the New China News Agency and the <u>Chin-Ch'a-Chi jih-pao</u>, seven deal with the civil war and six with international relations. In addition, the appendix contains three articles on the Soviet Union, the alleged American economic crisis, and the increasing strength of world communism.

624. Shih-lun 時論 (Current Commentaries). n.p., 1946. 24 pp. (2992.7/5170)

    Published by the General Political Department of the United Northeast Democratic Army, this pamphlet contains seven articles and documents, dated between June 22, 1946, (Mao Tse-tung's statement on American military aid to China) and October 23, 1946 (the <u>Liberation Daily</u>'s editorial appealing to the United Nations to condemn American intervention in China).

625. Tang-ch'ien shih-chü chung-yao wen-t'i 當前時局重要問題 (The Important Problems of the Current Situation). n.p., Cheng-pao, [1946]. 47 pp. (2992/9867)

    Five articles and documents, including the <u>Liberation Daily</u>'s comments (August 13, 1946) on the joint statement of George C. Marshall and Leighton Stuart of August 10, 1946, and records of Chou En-lai's press conferences, dated August 26, 1946.

626. Tu-li min-chu ho-p'ing 獨立民主和平 (Independence, Peace, and Democracy). [Chungking], Hsin-hua jih-pao, 1946. 96 pp. (2992/4021)

    This volume contains the following documents: (1) the manifesto of the CC of the CCP, July 7, 1946; (2) Mao Tse-tung's statement on American military assistance to China, June 22, 1946; (3) the statement of July 15, 1946, on the current situation by the members of the Democratic League who were delegates to the Political Consultative Conference; (4) several editorials of the <u>Liberation Daily</u> commenting on American military aid to the National Government; and (5) peace appeals by various individuals and organizations. Published by the <u>New China Daily</u>.

XIV. THE CIVIL WAR

The agreement of October 10, 1945, signed by representatives of the KMT and the CCP, resolved to avoid a civil war; but almost immediately fighting resumed between Government and Communist forces and spread to several provinces by the end of the month. A cease-fire agreement, signed on January 10, 1946, was brought about through General Marshall's efforts. From April on, hostilities in Manchuria and elsewhere developed into large-scale conflicts, interrupted by temporary truces from time to time. At the end of June 1946, the National Government started an all-out offensive south of the Great Wall; but its troops were compelled to switch from the offensive to the defensive a year later. The war progressed successfully for the Communists in 1948 and 1949, and the National Government leaders began to see the truth in the old Chinese saying, "a defeated army is like a collapsed mountain." Most of the sources included in this section are Communist newspaper commentaries on military affairs, and documents and directives concerning the war; some are periodicals and materials from KMT sources.

627. Chang Han-sai 張寒塞 (ed.). Jen-min ti yung-shih men 人民的勇士們 (The People's Warriors). n.p., Pei-fang ch'u-pan, 1949. 69 pp. (4292.9/1333.87)

   A collection of 17 short battle reports; only useful for local details.

628. Cheng-lun 政論 (Political Commentaries). New No. 11. Peiping, November 1, 1948. (2992/1102)

   Containing articles on the military situation in North China and current national economics.

629. Cheng-pao she t'u-shu pu 正報社圖書部 (ed.). Jen-min chieh-fang chan-cheng liang-chou-nien tsung-chieh ho ti-san nien ti jen-wu 人民解放戰爭兩週年總結和第三年的任務 (Summary of the Second Year and the Tasks for the Third Year of the People's War of Liberation). Hong Kong, same, 1948. 52 pp. (4292.9/1436)

An editorial by the New China News Agency with seven supplementary documents including war statistics and the development of the "liberated area" in the second year of the "People's War of Liberation" (July 1, 1947, to June 30, 1948).

630. Chieh-fang she 解放社 (ed.). Chiang ko-ming chin-hsing tao-ti 將革命進行到底 (Carry on the Revolution to the Bitter End). Shanghai, Hsin-hua, 1949. 214 pp. (2992/2483)

　　A selection of important statements and documents issued by the CCP, Mao Tse-tung, Chu Teh, and other Communist leaders from January to April 1949, that is, from the Communist capture of Peiping to the "liberation" of Nanking. Among the current topics discussed were "war criminals," opposition of foreign intervention, Taiwan, the peace overtures of Li Tsung-jen, etc. These are official versions, since the news dispatches first published in newspapers often contain telegraphic errors.

631. Chien-fei hua-chung ti-wei yü min san-san-shih-ch'i shih-erh yüeh san-shih jih chih-shih tang cheng chün wu ta jen-wu 奸匪華中地委於民三十七年十二月三十日指示黨政軍五大任務 (Directive of the Huachung Committee of the Chinese Communist Party, December 30, 1948, to Local Party, Political, and Military Authorities Concerning Five Tasks). n.p., [KMT], 1948. manuscript on microfilm. (2992/4574)

　　Excerpts from CCP documents captured by the KMT army. The directive deals with the war effort, support for the front, production, winter education, and captured cities.

632. Chin-Ch'a-Chi jih-pao she 晉察冀日報社 (ed.). Wei chih-chih nei-chan erh tou-cheng 為制止內戰而鬥爭 (Struggle to End the Civil War). n.p., same, [1945]. 134 pp. (2992/1316)

　　Reports by the New China News Agency on the KMT armies and their postwar military conflicts with the Communist forces. This book also contains the <u>Liberation Daily</u> comments on KMT-CCP relations in November 1945.

633. Ch'ing-chiao tao-pao 清剿導報 (Suppressing Communist Reports). No. 1. Chaoan, April 15, 1948. (2992/3234)

 Official documents relating to the suppression of the Communists in eastern Kwangtung early in 1948, edited and published by local military headquarters.

634. Ch'üan-li chun-pei ta fan-kung 全力準備大反攻 (To Prepare an All-Out Counter-Offensive). n.p., Hsin min-chu pao, [1947?]. 68 pp. microfilm. (2992/0704)

 The title is taken from an editorial of the New China News Agency, May 4 [1947]. The book consists of six of the New China News Agency's editorials and two statements by CCP spokesmen on the current situation. The main theme of the selection is that the Communists had now turned from defensive to offensive in the civil war.

635. Chüeh-wu ch'i-lai hsiang kuo-min tang fan-tung p'ai k'ung-su fu-ch'ou 覺悟起來向國民黨反動派控訴復仇 (Let's Awaken, Accuse, and Take Revenge on the Reactionary Kuomintang). n.p., n. pub., 1947. 32 pp. microfilm. (8922/7944)

 Reprinted by the Political Department of Chitung Military Region, this is a textbook for new recruits. The contents of the lessons are about the Eighth Route Army, treatment of prisoners of war, etc.

636. Chung-kuo jen-min chieh-fang chan-cheng san-nien chan-chi tsung-chieh 中國人民解放戰爭三年戰績總結 (Total Combat Statistics on the Three Years of the Chinese People's War of Liberation). Sunan, Hsin-hua, 1949. 48 pp. (4292.9/5687.56)

 Annual combat statistics for the years July 1, 1946, to June 30, 1949, issued by the Headquarters of the Chinese People's Liberation Army.

637. Chung-kuo kung-ch'an tang. Chi-Lu-Yü ch'ü tang-wei. She-hui pu 中國共產黨冀魯豫區黨委社會部. Kuo-min tang ti sui-ching cheng-ts'e 國民黨的綏靖政策 (The Kuomintang Pacification Policy). n.p., same, 1947. 22 pp. microfilm. (2992/5412)

   Published by the Hopeh-Shantung-Honan Committee of the CCP, these captured documents, allegedly issued by the KMT and the Kiangsu military authorities of the National Government, outline the ways of "pacifying" the Communists.

638. Fu-hsiao ch'u-pan she 拂曉出版社 (ed.). Chiu-ching shui tsai fa-tung nei-chan 究竟誰在發動內戰 (Who Is Actually Initiating the Civil War?). n.p., same, 1945. 48 pp. (2992/5622)

   Reports on the KMT military situation and excerpts of alleged KMT anti-Communist documents, selected from news broadcasts of the New China News Agency.

639. Hsin-min shu-tien 新民書店 (ed.). Chieh-fang chün sheng-huo 解放軍生活 (Life in the Liberation Army). Hong Kong, same, 1949. 68 pp. (4292.9/0750)

   In simple language and with poorly printed pictures, this pamphlet outlines the political education, entertainment, training, production drives, and other activities in the Communist forces. Of doubtful value.

640. Hua-pei hsin-hua shu-tien pien-chi pu 華北新華書店編輯部 (ed.). Kao Shu-hsün chiang-chün Han-tan ch'i-i t'e-chi 高樹勳將軍邯鄲起義特輯 (Selected Documents Concerning the Hantan Coup d'État of General Kao Shu-hsün). Licheng, same, 1945. 57 pp. (2992/4104)

   On October 20, 1945, Kao Shu-hsün, the former Deputy Commander-in-Chief of the 11th War Zone, led his New Eighth Army and deserted the National Government for the Communists in southern Hopeh. Subsequently, he became the Commander-in-Chief of the Democratic Reconstruction Army. This pamphlet contains Kao's declarations and other related documents of the event.

641. Hung-ch'i p'iao-p'iao pien-chi pu 紅旗飄飄編輯部 (ed.). Chieh-fang chan-cheng hui-i lu 解放戰爭回憶錄 (Reminiscences of the Liberation War). Peking, Chung-kuo ch'ing-nien, 1961. 377 pp. (2992/2011)

    A collection of 22 articles, most of them were written by Communist generals. Reprinted from various newspapers and magazines. Of uneven quality.

642. Jen-min ch'u-pan she 人民出版社 (ed.). Ti-san tz'u kuo-nei ko-ming chan-cheng kai-k'uan 第三次國內革命戰爭概況 (The Third Revolutionary Civil War). Peking, same, 1954. 243 pp. (2992/8722)

    An excellent reference work classified in four parts: (1) a survey of the civil war between July 1946 and June 1949 and war statistics covering the period from July 1946 to June 1950, issued by the Headquarters of the Chinese People's Liberation Army; (2) a chronology of important events between August 1945 and October 1949; (3) war maps; and (4) a table of important battles between July 1946 and June 1950.

643. Jen-min ti chün-tui 人民的軍隊 (The People's Army). Nos. 1-19. n.p., February 24 - September 25, 1946. (4292.9/8723f)

    A newspaper published irregularly (every ten days to over a month) by the Political Department of the Shansi-Hopeh-Shantung-Honan Military Region of the Eighteenth Army Group, carrying almost exclusively noncombat news of the troops (such as education and production drive campaigns), articles by Liu Po-ch'eng, and instructions from the Political Department.

644. Kuan Lin-cheng 關麟徵. Wei shih-mo yao chiao-fei yü chiao-fei tsung-t'i chan yao-i 為什麼要剿匪與剿匪總體戰要義 (Why Must We Suppress the Bandits, and the Essence of

191

Total War Against the Bandits). 2nd ed. Chengtu, Pa-t'i, 1948. 16 pp. (2992/7702)

Two speeches delivered by the Commandant of the Central Military Academy at Chengtu on April 13 and June 1, 1948 respectively, analyzing the Communist military machine.

645. Kuo-fang pu 國防部 (ed.). Chung-yang chih-hsing wei-yüan hui ti-ssu tz'u ch'üan-t'i hui-i tso-chan pao-kao 中央執行委員會第四次全體會議作戰報告 (War Report to the Fourth Plenum of the Sixth Central Executive Committee). [Nanking], same, 1947. 14 pp. (2992/6570)

A confidential report of the Ministry of National Defense of the National Government to the Fourth Plenum of the CEC of the KMT about the Communist forces, containing valuable military information, statistics, and tables.

646. Mu Hsin 穆欣. Nan-hsien hsün-hui 南線巡迴 (Journey to the Southern Front). 2nd ed. revised. Peking, San-lien, 1953. 211 pp. (2992/2278)

A journalist's report of the military conquests of the 4th Group Regiment of the 2nd Field Army of the People's Liberation Army from the time of its crossing of the Yangtze River in March 1949 through February 1950, when it marched to Kunming. The book was first published in 1950.

647. Shang-hai hsin-hsüeh yen-chiu yüan 上海心學研究院 (ed.). Ch'ü-chi pi-hsiung chi 趨吉避兇集 (To Pursue Good Fortune and Avoid That Which Brings Calamity). [Shanghai?], n. pub., 1946. 15 pp. microfilm. (2992/2337)

A collection of the New China News Agency's dispatches relating to the Eighth Route Army as well as to the defection of KMT officers and soldiers. The bogus editor and title were used to disguise the book's contents.

648. Shih-shih hsüeh-hsi ts'ai-liao 時事學習材料 (Study Material for Current Events). Sunan, Hsin-hua, 1949. 219 pp. (2992/0464.65)

    This book contains primarily editorials on the civil war from the Liberation Daily (August 18, 1946 - March 9, 1947) and the New China News Agency (April 12, 1947 - July 29, 1948), and a lengthy comment on the Marshall mission. One section is devoted to a summing up of the second year of the "People's War of Liberation" issued by the Headquarters of the Chinese People's Liberation Army on July 30, 1948. Also included are four official military bulletins giving statistical information regarding the war against the Nationalist armies.

649. Tsung-tung-yüan yü tsung-p'eng-k'uei 總動員與總崩潰 (Total Mobilization and Total Collapse). Tsingtao, Chien-kuo shu-tien, 1947. 25 pp. microfilm. (2992/2267)

    A camouflaged publication containing six editorials of the Ta-chung pao and one editorial from the Chin-Chi-Lu-Yü Jen-min jih-pao (June - July, 1947) on the civil war.

650. Tung-pei jih-pao she 東北日報社 (ed.). Chan-chü tsai k'ai-shih pien-tung 戰局在開始變動 (The War Situation Has Begun to Change). Chiamussu, Tung-pei shu-tien, 1947. 18 pp. (2992/5164.67)

    Four editorials selected from the Liberation Daily and the Tzu-wei pao, December 1946 - April 1947. The title is taken from an editorial in the Liberation Daily; other editorials comment on the military situation in Manchuria and the Third Plenum of the CEC of the KMT.

651. _____. Ta-tao Chiang Chieh-shih chien-li hsin Chung-kuo 打倒蔣介石建立新中國 (Overthrow Chiang Kai-shek and Establish a New China). [Chiamussu], Tung-pei shu-tien, 1949. 137 pp. (2992/5248)

    Forty-five editorials and news items of the New China News Agency between July 1948 and January 1949 published in the

Tung-pei jih-pao concerning the civil war in North China and Manchuria, the peace talks, "war criminals," and the declared policy of the Democratic League. The title of the book is taken from the editorial of the Tung-pei jih-pao of July 7, 1948.

652. Tung-yüan ch'i-lai nu-li fen-tou feng-sui Chiang Chieh-shih ti chin-kung 動員起來努力奮鬥粉碎蔣介石的進攻 (Let's Mobilize and Strive to Smash Chiang Kai-shek's Attack). n.p., [CCP], [1946]. 56 pp. microfilm. (2992/2645)

   A collection of nine editorials and comments from the Liberation Daily and the New China News Agency bitterly attacking Chiang Kai-shek, published jointly by the Propaganda Department of the Hopeh-Shantung-Honan Committee of the CCP and the Political Department of the Hopeh-Shantung-Honan Military Region.

653. Wang ssu-ling-yüan ts'ai hou-ch'in hui-i shang ti tsung-chieh pao-kao 王司令員在後勤會議上的總結報告 (Commander Wang's Report at the Meeting of Administrative Services). n.p., 1948. manuscript on microfilm. (2992/1186)

   A document, dated January 14, 1948, captured from the Communists in Shensi and edited by an officer of the KMT army.

654. Yang Ping-an 楊冰安. Chung-kuo jen-min chieh-fang chan-cheng 中國人民解放戰爭 (The Chinese People's War of Liberation). Shanghai, Hsin chih-shih, 1955. 116 pp. (4292.25/4233)

   A Communist account of the Chinese civil war, 1945-49.

XV. THE DEMOCRATIC AND LIBERAL GROUPS

A. GENERAL SURVEY

Before leaving China for the U. S. on January 7, 1947, General George C. Marshall, reporting the breakdown of his mediation mission in China, stated: "The salvation of the situation, as I see it, would be the assumption of leadership by the liberals in the Government and in the minority parties, a splendid group of men, but who as yet lack the political power to exercise a controlling influence." The following sections are concerned with these minority parties and liberals. They had clung to a "neutral," "independent," and "third-party" stand, seeking a reformist middle road. At first they were courted by both sides, but as events developed they were driven to align themselves with either the Communists or the National Government.

655. Chung-kuo ko hsiao tang-p'ai hsien-k'uang 中國各小黨派現況 (The Present Condition of the Minority Parties of China). n.p., n. pub., 1946. 144 pp. (4737/5629)

This appears to be a KMT confidential publication. It provides useful information on the history, program, organization, publications, and leadership of seven political parties and groups: the Democratic League, the Youth Party, the National Social Party, the Chinese Liberation Action Committee, the Vocational Education Group, the Democratic National Reconstruction Association, the National Salvation Association, and the Rural Reconstruction Group. The accounts of the last two groups are very brief. In the story of the Democratic League, emphasis is given to its relationship with the CCP.

656. Hsiao Wen-che 蕭文哲. Hsien-tai Chung-kuo cheng-tang yü cheng-chih 現代中國政黨與政治 (The Present Political Parties and Politics in China). Nanking, Chung-wai, 1946. 182 pp. (4737/4205)

The first part of the book is a survey of the history, programs, and organization of the current political parties and groups in China. The second part is devoted to comments on the attitudes of the major parties toward the reorganization of the National Government, the army, political programs, the National Assembly, and the constitution. Among the author's other publications are two books on Chinese government and political thought.

657. Hsiao Yeh-na 蕭也納 and Wang Erh-te 王尔得. Chung-kung ti min-chu tang-p'ai 中共的民主黨派 (The Communist-Controlled Democratic Parties and Groups). Kowloon, Tzu-yu, 1951. 80 pp. (4737/4242)

    A brief critical account of the history, organization, and leaders of the Revolutionary Committee of the Kuomintang, the Democratic League, the Democratic National Reconstruction Association, the Association for Promoting Democracy, the Peasants' and Workers' Democratic Party, the Chih Kung Tang, the September 3 Society, and of the Taiwan Democratic Self-Government League. All these groups participated in the People's Political Consultative Conference (held in Peiping in September 1949) sponsored by the CCP. The author stresses the Communist infiltration and control of these organizations.

658. Hsin Chung-kuo wen-hsien ch'u-pan she 新中國文獻出版社 (ed.). Chung-kuo hsin min-chu yün-tung chung ti tang-p'ai 中國新民主運動中的黨派 (The Chinese Political Parties and Groups in the New Democratic Movement). Shanghai, same, 1946. 122 pp. (4737/0560)

    This book is divided into three chapters. The first chapter consists of two articles by Teng Ch'u-min and Liu I, on political parties and development of Chinese political parties, respectively. The second chapter is a collection of articles on various current political parties and groups in China (the one on the CCP is by P'an Tzu-nien). Although the editor has not indicated the sources except for the authors' names, these articles are apparently reprints from the special issue No. 104 of Tsai-sheng (The National Renaissance). The last chapter includes documents relating to KMT-CCP relations, declarations and programs of the Democratic National Reconstruction Association (founded in Chungking December 20, 1945), and a chronology of important events in 1945.

659. Hu-ch'ün kou-tang hsien-hsing chi 狐群狗黨現形記 (A Set of Rogues). Chiamussu, Tung-pei shu-tien, 1948. 53 pp. (4737/4149)

    A collection of critical articles about the Political Study Clique, the Democratic-Socialist Party, the Youth Party, the Chung Ho Tang, and the leaders of these political groups. With the exception of four articles by the New China News Agency, the authors appear to be obscure writers.

660. Hua-pei hsin-hua shu-tien pien-chi pu 華北新華書店編輯部 (ed.). Ta hou-fang ti min-chu yün-tung 大後方的民主運動 (The Democratic Movement in the Interior). Licheng, 1946. 142 pp. (2992/4104)

    Collected news dispatches of the New China News Agency, dated from autumn of 1945 through the end of February 1946 and classified into the following categories: (1) the National Government's treatment of the press; (2) opposition to the civil war; (3) the Kunming Student Incident, December 1, 1946; (4) a coalition government advocated by the "democratic and liberal persons"; (5) the Chiaochangkou Incident, February 10, 1946, wherein Kuo Mo-jo and others were assaulted in a meeting celebrating the success of the Political Consultative Conference; and (6) peaceful solution of the Manchuria problem advocated by the Democratic League. The appendix has two documents. One is a brief history of the Democratic League and the other a declaration on the current situation issued by the Central Cadre Committee of the Third Party of China, November 12, 1945.

661. Min-chu wen-ts'ung ch'u-pan she 民主文叢出版社 (ed.). Cheng min-chu ti Chung-kuo cheng-tang 爭民主的中國政黨 (The Chinese Political Parties in Their Struggle for Democracy). Shanghai, same, 1946. 56 pp. (4737/7003)

    Selected material including Chiang Kai-shek's speech at the opening session of the Political Consultative Conference, excerpts from Mao Tse-tung's writings, the "Ten Great Policies" of the Democratic League by Chang Lan, declarations of the Democratic National Reconstruction Association, and the programs of the Third Party and of the National Social Party.

662. Tsung-heng t'ien-hsia 縱橫天下 (The World). Vol. II, No. 2/3. Canton, September 20, 1947. (4737/2411)

This issue is devoted exclusively to the current political parties and groups, with a brief history of each organization. With the exception of Huang Yen-p'ei's article on the Vocational Education Group, none of the contributors were well-known to the public.

663. Wei ta-fa-shih 衛大法師 (pseud. of Wei Chü-hsien 衛聚賢?). Chung-kuo ko-tang ko-p'ai hsien-chuang 中國各黨各派現狀 (The Present Condition of Various Parties and Groups in China). Shanghai, Shuo-wen, 1946. various pagination. (4737/2217)

Among the political parties and groups described in this book are the KMT, the CCP, the Democratic League, the Youth Party, the National Social Party, the Chinese Liberation Action Committee, the Vocational Education Group, the Democratic National Reconstruction Association, the Rural Reconstruction Group, the Min-pen she, and other minor organizations.

664. Yü Jun-t'ang 余潤棠 and Yao Ch'uan-k'eng 姚傳鏗 (eds.). Chung-kuo tang-tai cheng-tang lun 中國當代政黨論 (On the Present-Day Political Parties of China). Canton, Tsung-heng, 1948. 116 pp. (4737/8939)

The first chapter discusses the nature of political parties in general, and the second deals with the development of Chinese political parties. Two-thirds of the book is devoted to the last chapter, which introduces more than twenty current Chinese political parties and groups. Except for the leading parties, the accounts are very brief. There are informative accounts of the split of the Democratic-Socialist Party in 1947 and the activities of the Democratic League in Hong Kong after being declared illegal by the National Government.

B. THE DEMOCRATIC LEAGUE

At the beginning the Democratic League consisted of the minor parties and other groups outside of the KMT and the CCP. It sought for a reconciliation of the two rivals. From 1940 to the summer of 1944 it was known as the "Federation of Democratic Political Groups." Beginning in 1943, more and more individuals who had no party affiliations were recruited to its membership. It was reorganized under the name of the Democratic League of China in September 1944. In October 1945, 70 per cent of its membership were individuals without other party affiliations. Its leadership came from the upper strata of the intellectuals.

In the second half of 1946 some of the League leaders, who were more sympathetic to the Communists, began to feel persecution from the KMT authorities. On October 27, 1947, the Government authorities declared the League an "illegal organization." Subsequently, a new headquarters was established in Hong Kong. Under this heading are League documents and its official publication organs.

665. Chung-kuo min-chu t'ung-meng tsung-pu 中國民主同盟總部 (ed.). [Chung-kuo] min-chu t'ung-meng erh-chung ch'üan-hui cheng-chih pao-kao 中國民主同盟二中全會政治報告 (The Political Report to the Second Plenum of the Central Committee of the Democratic League). [Shanghai], same, 1947. 27 pp. (4737.1/5670.70)

Edited and published by the Headquarters of the Democratic League, this political report to the Second Plenum of the CC of the League was approved on January 10, 1947.

666. _____. Chung-kuo min-chu t'ung-meng san-chung ch'üan-hui 中國民主同盟三中全會 (The Third Plenum of the Central Committee of the Democratic League). [Hong Kong], same, 1948. 29 pp. (4737.1/5670.3)

This volume contains three documents approved by the Third Plenum of the CC of the Democratic League in January 1948: (1) a political report; (2) a manifesto; and (3) an emergency declaration denying its being an "illegal organization" as declared by the spokesman of the Ministry of the Interior of the National Government on October 27, 1947, and refusing to accept the dissolution measures adopted by the League Headquarters in Nanking on November 5, 1947.

667. _____. Min-chu t'ung-meng wen-hsien 民主同盟文獻 (Documents on the Democratic League). Shanghai, same, 1946. 167 pp. (4737.1/5670)

   A collection of forty-two documents dated from October 10, 1941, to December 23, 1946, arranged in chronological order. This is an important record of the Democratic League for that period. The bulk of the documents, however, date from October 1944; only two relate to the earlier period.

668. Hsien-tai hsin-wen 現代新聞 (Contemporary News). Vol. I, Nos. 1-7. Shanghai, May 10 - June 15, 1947. (2992/1207)

   A weekly of the Democratic League with articles by Chang Po-chün, Lo Lung-chi, Chang Nai-ch'i, Ma Yin-ch'u, and other leaders and members of the League.

669. Huang Kan-yin 黃干因 (ed.). Min-meng p'i-p'an 民盟批判 (A Critique of the Democratic League). [Hong Kong], Chung-pao, 1946. 37 pp. (4737.1/4816)

   A collection of articles critical of the program, leaders, and foreign policy of the League, selected from the Ho-p'ing jih-pao, and the Hong Kong Kung-p'ing pao, including several articles published in the Hong Kong Kuo-min jih-pao by Huang Kan-yin himself.

670. Kuang-ming ch'u-pan she 光明出版社 (ed.). Chung-kuo min-chu t'ung-meng ti hsing-chih yü jen-wu 中國民主同盟的性質與任務 (The Nature and Tasks of the Chinese Democratic League). Canton, same, 1950. 39 pp. (4731.1/5670.1)

   This volume consists of four documents approved by the Enlarged Meeting of the Fourth Plenum of the CC of the Democratic League in December 1949: (1) the Constitution of the

League; (2) an acceptance of the Common Program of the People's Political Consultative Conference as the program for the League; (3) a declaration; and (4) a political report.

671. Kuang-ming pao 光明報 (Light). New Nos. 1-22. Hong Kong, September 18, 1946 - July 19, 1947. (4737.1/9164)

   In October 1941 the leaders of what was later known as the Democratic League began publication of the Kuang-ming pao in Hong Kong. The newspaper ceased publication after three months as a result of the Japanese capture of Hong Kong. In 1946 it resumed publication every ten days as a magazine and an organ of the League, with Sa K'ung-liao as the "acting supervisor" for Liang Sou-ming. It carries articles on KMT-CCP relations, democracy, the "third force," and documents relating to the League. The joint investigation report of Liang Sou-ming and Chou Hsin-min on the assassinations of Li Kung-p'u and Wen I-to appears in issue No. 5. It contains no contributions from the pro-KMT faction of the League.

672. Kuang-ming pao 光明報 (Light). New Vol. I, No. 1 - Vol. IV, No. 2. Hong Kong, March 1, 1948 - September 16, 1949. (4737.1/9164.1)

   This semimonthly is apparently a resumed publication of the above item. Lu I served as the "supervisor and editor-in-chief" of this journal. Because the official newspaper Kuang-ming jih-pao of the Democratic League began publication in Peiping in July 1949, this magazine ceased publication after Volume IV, issue No. 2.

673. Min-chu 民主 (Democracy). Nos. 1-53/54. Shanghai, October 13, 1945 - October 31, 1946. (9200/7401)

   Edited by Cheng Chen-to, this is an organ of the Democratic League, with articles of high quality by Ma Hsü-lun and other leading members of the League. It was banned by the Shanghai police on October 14, 1946.

674. Min-chu 民主 (Democracy). Nos. 13-36. Kweilin, June 23, 1946 - January 11, 1947. (9200/7401.44)

    First published on January 10, 1946, this journal began publication as a weekly from issue No. 13, and was suppressed by police after issue No. 36. This set is a cumulative edition with a cumulative subject index classified into: (1) editorials; (2) commentaries on current affairs; (3) feature articles; (4) literature; (5) book reviews; (6) miscellaneous articles; (7) feature reports; and (8) documents (exclusively on the Democratic League).

675. Min-chu chou-k'an 民主週刊 (The Democratic Weekly). Vol. I, No. 1 - Vol. III, No. 19. Kunming, December 9, 1944 - August 2, 1946. (4737.1/7032.61)

    An organ of the Democratic League with articles on current national politics by Lo Lung-chi, Fei Hsiao-t'ung, Wen I-to, Tseng Chao-lun, and other liberals. Each volume consists of 26 issues. The cumulative edition of Vol. II, Nos. 14-26 has a subject index with these categories: general, current comments, politics, military affairs, economics, international affairs, society, education, book reviews, correspondence, literature, poetry, and prose. No articles by the pro-KMT faction of the League appear in the magazine.

676. Min-chu chou-k'an 民主週刊 (The Democratic Weekly). Nos. 1-15. Peiping, January 21 - December 18, 1946. (4737.1/7032.11)

    The Peiping edition is an official organ of the Democratic League, with different contents from its Kunming edition (item no. 675). The articles here are increasingly critical of the KMT and the China policy of the United States.

677. Min-chu hsing-chi k'an 民主星期刊 (The Democratic Weekly). Nos. 1, 5, 9, 12, 17-24, 54, and 59. Chungking and Peiping, October 1, 1945 - November 9, 1946. (9200/7064f)

Published by T'ao Hsing-chih and edited by Teng Ch'u-min, this periodical (in newspaper size) presents the opinions of the "Third Force," with articles by Tso Shun-sheng, Kuo Mo-jo, Ma Yin-ch'u, Chang Shen-fu, Mao Tun, and others. The first editorial, written by Chang Lan, defines the plans and editorial policy of the magazine.

678. Min-chu pan-yüeh k'an 民主半月刊 (The Democratic Semi-Monthly). Nos. 1-4. Peiping, January 10 - March 1, 1947. (9200/7097)

This periodical appears to be an organ of the Democratic League, with many articles by Chang Hsi-jo. National affairs, Manchurian problems, student demonstrations, and opposition to America are common subjects of the articles. Issue No. 3 contains the political report to the Second Congress of the CC of the Democratic League, dated January 10, 1947.

679. Min-hsien yüeh-k'an she 民憲月刊社 (ed.). Ho-p'ing min-chu t'ung-i chien-kuo chih-lu 和平民主統一建國之路 (The Road to Peace, Democracy, Unification, and Reconstruction). Vol. I. Hong Kong, same, 1946. 59 pp. (4737.1/5670.2)

This is the first volume of a collection of the documents relating to the Democratic League, including a brief history of the organization. Most of the documents are available in the Min-chu t'ung-meng wen-hsien (see item no. 667). Poorly edited.

680. Yüan-wang 願望 (Wish). Nos. 1, 4, 5, and 15-19. Hong Kong, January 16 - May 29, 1946. (9200/7801)

Edited by Hu Shou-yü and Liang Jo-ch'en, this weekly appears to have been an organ of the Democratic League in Canton and Hong Kong. It carried articles of current national politics, but few were contributed by the national figures in the League.

C. THE DEMOCRATIC-SOCIALIST PARTY

This party was formed in August 1946 by the amalgamation of the National Social Party (founded by Carsun Chang in 1931) and the Democratic Constitutionalist Party (so named in November 1945), with Chang as the chairman and Wu Hsien-tzu vice-chairman. But shortly afterward, there developed serious dissension in the party, which led to a complicated fight for leadership.

681. Chung-kuo min-chu she-hui tang chuan-chi 中國民主社會黨專輯 (A Special Publication on the Democratic-Socialist Party of China). [Shanghai], Tsai-sheng, [1946]. 78 pp. (4737.3/1423)

This volume contains Carsun Chang's lectures on democratic and constitutional government as well as programs, declarations, and other documents of the Democratic-Socialist Party.

682. Jen-tao 人道 ("Humanities"). Nos. 1, 2, and 4-6. Hong Kong, January 9 - February 20, 1948. (9200/8033)

Edited by Wu Hsien-tzu, this weekly carries articles on politics, economics, culture, foreign affairs, democracy, and KMT-CCP relations.

683. [Li Ta-ming] 李大明. Chung-kuo min-chu hsien-cheng tang ti li-ch'ang 中國民主憲政黨的立場 (The Position of the Democratic Constitutionalist Party of China). [San Francisco], n. pub., 1948. 37 pp. (4737.5/1700)

A speech delivered by the leader of the Democratic Constitutionalist Party at a Party Congress in San Francisco.

684. Tsai-sheng 再生 (The National Renaissance). Nos. 104 (Chungking, December 5, 1945), 105-140 and 171-204 (Shanghai, March 25, 1946 - February 29, 1948), Vol. I, Nos. 9, 12, and

Vol. II, No. 1 (Canton, November 1, 1948 - April 15, 1949). (4737.3/1421)

An official organ of the National Social Party, this periodical was first published as a monthly in Peiping in 1932, advocating "democracy and freedom of thought." (The Hoover Library has a complete set of the first volume, consisting of twelve issues, dated May 20, 1932 to April 20, 1933). Later, it was published in Hankow, and then in Chungking. No. 104 (semi-monthly) is a special issue on current Chinese political parties. Beginning with issue No. 105 (March 25, 1946), the magazine (now a weekly) was published in Shanghai. The cumulative edition of Nos. 105-130 contains an index, with authors' names, arranged into six topical sections: (1) constitutional politics; (2) philosophy, culture, science, politics, education, and others; (3) domestic politics; (4) foreign affairs; (5) miscellaneous articles; and (6) the Democratic-Socialist Party (issue No. 129 is a special issue on that Party). Among frequent contributors to these issues were Carsun Chang, Sun Pao-i, Fei Hsiao-t'ung, and P'an Kuang-tan. Wu Tsao-ch'ih was in charge of the Canton edition. For several years after 1949, the magazine was published in Hong Kong; issues from this period are also available at the Hoover Library.

685. Wu Hsien-tzu 伍憲子. Chung-kuo min-chu hsien cheng-tang tang shih 中國民主憲政黨黨史 (A History of the Democratic Constitutionalist Party of China). n.p., n. pub., n.d. 206 pp. (4737.5/2131)

Written by the chairman of the Democratic Constitutionalist Party, this is an account of the party's history beginning with K'ang Yu-wei's activities in 1890's. The present name was adopted in a party congress held in Montreal, Canada, in November 1945, with the author as the chairman and Li Ta-ming the vice-chairman. In the summer of 1946 agreement was reached to amalgamate with the National Social Party to form the Democratic-Socialist Party. However, shortly before the organizational meeting, scheduled for June 1947, the leaders of the Democratic Constitutionalist Party decided to withdraw from the amalgamation on account of certain policies of, and internal dissension within, the National Social Party.

The book has a preface by Li Ta-ming, dated April 16, 1952, San Francisco. It may be mentioned that the Hoover Library has an incomplete set of the Lei-feng magazine (edited by Wu Hsientzu), which began publication in May 1928.

D. THE YOUTH PARTY

This party was formed in Paris in 1923, but the name was not officially adopted until the Fourth Congress of the party held in Mukden in 1929. Under this heading are items dealing with Party history, documents, and periodicals edited by party members.

686. Cheng-chih lu-hsien 政治路線 (Political Line). Vol. I, Nos. 1-2. Chengtu, November 1 - December 1, 1946. (2992/1362)

   A general and comprehensive monthly with articles on current political problems and documents. Issue No. 2 contains Tso Shun-sheng's statement and the texts of the letters exchanged between Chiang Kai-shek and Carsun Chang (Chang Chün-mai). The magazine attempts to adopt a "neutral" political position between the KMT and the CCP. Most of the contributors are leaders or members of the Youth Party.

687. Chung-kuo ch'ing-nien tang cheng-kang 中國青年黨政綱 (The Political Programs of the Youth Party of China). n.p., n. pub., n.d. 18 pp. (4737.2/5658.91)

   This document, dated December 12, 1945, appears to have been published by the Youth Party itself.

688. Chung-kuo ch'ing-nien tang tang-shih tzu-liao 中國青年黨黨史資料 (Source Material on the History of the Youth Party of China). Vol. I. Taipei, Min-chu ch'ao, 1955. 153 pp. (4737.2/5658)

   Of the documents and articles contained in this volume, only a few declarations and resolutions are related to the period 1937-49. The articles are by leading members of the Youth Party and reveal some inside information on Party history.

689.   Feng-yün 風雲 (Wind and Clouds). Vol. I, Nos. 1-11. Shanghai, August 1, 1948 - January 1, 1949. (9200/7113)

   Edited by Shen Yün-lun, this semi-monthly carries articles on liberals, democracy, and the Sino-American relations. The editor, a member of the Youth Party, declares that although most of the contributors are also members of the Youth Party, this magazine cannot be considered an official organ of that party.

690.   Tso Hung-yü 左宏禹 (ed.). K'ang-chan chien-kuo chung chih Chung-kuo ch'ing-nien tang 抗戰建國中之中國青年黨 (The Youth Party in the War of Resistance and Reconstruction). n.p., Kuo-hun, 1939. 68 pp. (4737.2/4132)

   The editor, who appears to be a member of the Youth Party, here presents a brief history of the Party, statements by the party and its leader Tseng Ch'i, an exchange of letters between Chiang Kai-shek and Tso Shun-sheng, and newspaper editorials commenting on cooperation among the political parties in China.

E. OTHER GROUPS AND INDIVIDUALISTS

   The following sources cannot be classified into a number of subdivisions because either some of their political affiliations cannot be readily identified or they have insufficient numbers to merit separate headings. Included are works on the Democratic National Reconstruction Association, the Third Party, the National Salvation Association, and other groups and individualists who had not identified themselves with any political machine and who would therefore be difficult to categorize.

691.   [Ch'en Chün-yen] 陳俊彥. Chung-kuo ti-san shih-li ch'u-hsien 中國第三勢力出現 (The Appearance of a Third Force in China). [Hong Kong], same, [1950?]. 30 pp. (4737.91/5681)

   A collection of three documents: the manifesto, the constitution, and the statement of an obscure anti-Communist organization, the Chinese League for Freedom (Chung-hua min-tsu tzu-yu lien-meng).

692.   Chi-nai 集納 (Symposium). Nos. 1-4, and 6. Peiping, February 15 - June 20, 1946. (2992/2922)

   Contains articles by Hua Kang (on the broadening of the National Government), Ma Hsü-lun, Teng Ch'u-min, Ch'iao-mu (or Ch'iao Mu) and others. It is not clear whether the name of the last-mentioned writer is Hu Ch'iao-mu or Ch'iao Kuan-hua. Among other useful articles are those on land problems, on Ho Lung, on the disappearance of Yü Ta-fu, and a letter from Mr. and Mrs. Hu Yü-chih describing their life of exile in Sumatra during World War II.

693.   Ch'i-p'ien pi-hsü chieh-ch'uan 欺騙必須揭穿 (Deceit Must Be Uncovered). Hong Kong, Tzu-yu shih-chieh, 1948. 59 pp. microfilm. (2992/4732)

   This volume includes articles on the civil war and a symposium on the "third force" problem participated in by noted leftists and "democratic individualists." The main argument is that there was no neutral road to take in the KMT-CCP struggle.

694.   Chou-lun 周論 ("Universitas"). Vol. I, Nos. 1-24; Vol. II, Nos. 1-3, and 14-17. Peiping, January 16 - November 5, 1948. (9200/7202)

   The contributors to this magazine are noted university professors of history and philosophy. The publication aims to be "scientific, objective, and calm" in discussing scholarly and current issues. Articles on student demonstrations are available. Available are also author and subject indexes for Volume I (24 issues). The subject index is arranged under the following categories: international relations and diplomacy, politics, economics, society, law, education and youth, miscellaneous articles, and correspondence.

695.   Chou-pao 周報 (The Weekly). Nos. 8, 21/22, 23, 26, and 46. Shanghai, October 27, 1945 - July 20, 1946. (2992/7244)

   This magazine occasionally carries articles concerning the KMT-CCP negotiations and related proposals advanced by organizations such as the Association for Promoting Democracy in China. Among the contributors are Ma Hsü-lun and Shih Fu-liang. Kuo Mo-jo's critique of Wang Yün-sheng's view on Chinese history appears in issue No. 46.

696. Chung-chien 中建 (China Reconstructs). Peiping Edition. Vol. I, Nos. 1-10. Peiping, July 20 - December 5, 1948. (2992/5014b)

This is the Peiping edition of a Shanghai semi-monthly, with contributions by Chang Tung-sun, Fei Hsiao-t'ung, Ma Yin-ch'u, Chang Chih-jang, Hsü Te-yen and many other well-known scholars, professors, and liberals. Issue No. 1 is the same as Vol. II, No. 4 (or Whole No. 52) of the Shanghai edition, which is not available. The magazine later published a Comprehensive Edition in Shanghai (see the following item). The present Peiping editions contain articles on current problems of the intelligentsia. Issue No. 8 contains an article on the Association for the Study of Anarchism and a useful report of the current left-wing writers and publications in Hong Kong.

697. _____. Comprehensive Edition. Vol. I, Nos. 1-3. Shanghai, February 10 - March 10, 1949. (2992/5014.1)

Issue No. 1 is devoted to the KMT-CCP negotiations.

698. Chung-hua lun-t'an 中華論壇 (The China Tribune). Vol. I, Nos. 10/11, and 12; Vol. II, Nos. 1, 2, and 4-6. Chungking and Shanghai, December 1, 1945 - November 1, 1946. (4737.9/5404)

An official organ of the Third Party. It was edited by Chang Po-chün and carried articles of high quality on domestic politics and social problems. Issue Vol. I, No. 10/11 contains a special section of documents relating to the Third Party. Beginning with Vol. I, No. 12 (August 16, 1946), publication of this semi-monthly was moved from Chungking to Shanghai.

699. Chung-kuo chih-kung tang tang-chang 中國致公黨黨章 (The Constitution of the Chih Kung Tang). n.p., n. pub., n.d. 26 pp. (4737.4/5618)

   The revised constitution of the Chih Kung Tang, approved by the Third Congress of that party on May 4, 1946. It consists of seven chapters totaling 72 articles.

700. Chung-mei p'ing-lun 中美評論 (The Sino-American Review). Nos. 1-3, Mukden, June 20 - July 20, 1946. (2992/5800.3)

   Published every ten days, this organ of the Sino-American Association in Mukden carries articles on current economic, political, and foreign affairs. Among the contributors are Chang Chün-mai (Carsun Chang), Ma Yin-ch'u, Kuo Mo-jo, Fei Hsiao-t'ung, Ma Hsü-lun, Mao Tun and T'ien Han.

701. Ho-p'ing she 和平社 (ed.). Hsia-kuan hsüeh-an 下關血案 (The Massacre at Hsiakuan). n.p., same, 1946. 84 pp. (2992/2614)

   A collection of reports and documents concerning the Hsiakuan Incident of June 23, 1946. On that day Ma Hsü-lun and other "representatives" of Shanghai people and organizations arrived at the Nanking railway station from Shanghai to appeal to the National Government to declare a cessation of the civil war. They were assaulted by a "mob" upon their arrival. Among the documents included are messages of sympathy from Chou En-lai and other Communist leaders.

702. Hsin-wen p'ing-lun 新聞評論 (News Commentaries). Nos. 7-13. Peiping, February 9 - June 15, 1946. (2992/0700f)

   The contents of this weekly (published every ten days in magazine form from issue No. 13) are increasingly critical of the KMT, with articles on student activities, on the Political Consultative Conference, on the current political situation, in refutation of Ho Yung-chi's writings, and statements of the Democratic League's spokesman on Manchuria. Among the contributors are Chang Shen-fu and Tseng Chao-lun.

703. Jen-min pao 人民報 (The People's Journal). New Series No. 1. Canton and Hong Kong, July 20, 1946. (2992/8074)

This magazine was first published in Hong Kong and then in Canton. It was banned by the Canton local authorities after the No. 30 issue. This is a "temporary edition," with articles discussing the "middle road." The contributors' political leaning appears to be left of center.

704. Jen-min shih-chi 人民世紀 (The People's Century). Nos. 1, 2, and 4. Peiping, December 30, 1945 - March 11, 1946. (9200/8742f)

The first two issues were published weekly as newspapers. Issue No. 4 appears in the form of a magazine. The contents are: discussions of student activities, democracy, the current national political situation, foreign policy, and, above all, Manchurian problems.

705. Jen-yen chou-k'an 人言週刊 (People's Opinions Weekly). Nos. 2, 9, 13, and 14. Peiping, February 21 - May 4, 1946. (9200/8031f)

This journal carries news and articles on current national politics. Issue No. 13 contains an open letter from Yang Kang to newspapermen in China, protesting the imprisonment and death of her brother, Yang Tsao, a noted journalist who died in a KMT prison.

706. K'o-kuan 客觀 (Objectivity). Vol. I, No. 6 - Vol. II, No. 5. Canton, October 2, 1948 - April 16, 1949. (9200/3641)

A semimonthly carrying articles on current political events. None of the contributors are well-known writers, except Huang Yen-p'ei, whose article, dated March 1949 (probably a reprint) is entitled "Why Did I Go to the Liberated Area?" (Vol. II, No. 5).

707. Kuan-ch'a 觀察 (The Observer). Vol. I, No. 1 - Vol. V, No. 18. Shanghai, September 1, 1946 - December 24, 1948. (9200/4139)

Edited by Ch'u An-p'ing, this was a very popular weekly serving as a political forum for the Chinese liberals and the intelligentsia. Two volumes, each consisting of 24 issues, were published every year, carrying articles by professors, liberals, and leading members of the Democratic League. Issue Volume II, No. 24 (February 8, 1947) contains an article by Ch'u on the origin and purported nature of the magazine. The periodical was banned by the KMT authorities after issue Volume V, No. 18 (December 24, 1948), only to resume publication in Peking on November 1, 1949. The Hoover Library holdings of the post-1949 issues are Volume VI, Nos. 1-14 (November 1, 1949 - May 16, 1950).

708. Kuang-hua chou-pao 光華週報 (The Kuanghua Weekly). Vol. I, Nos. 1-6. Peiping, September 18 - October 21, 1945. (9200/9434)

A weekly with occasional articles on democracy and current domestic affairs. Not a leftist publication.

709. Kuo-hsün 國訊 (The National News). Nos. 194-441 (incomplete). Chungking and Shanghai, February 1939 - January 17, 1948. (9200/6501)

Edited by Huang Yen-p'ei, Tao Hsing-chih, Yang Wei-yü and other vocational educationalists, the contents of this ten-day magazine may be grouped into the following categories: the Sino-Japanese War, military affairs, politics, finance, education, diplomacy, and feature reports. It was first published in Shanghai (December 1931 to October 4, 1937); then in Chungking (August 13, 1938, to 1945) with Hong Kong and Kweilin editions (the Hong Kong edition was suspended after Pearl Harbor); and again in Shanghai (1945 to September 18, 1946). After a suspension of six months, it resumed publication as a weekly, beginning with issue No. 411 (May 4, 1947), until January 1948.

710. _____. New Series, Vol. I, Nos. 1-05. Hong Kong, October 10, 1947 - January 3, 1948. (9200/6501.1)

Among the noted contributors to this postwar Hong Kong semimonthly edition of the above magazine are Huang Yen-p'ei, Chang Tung-sun, Wang Yün-sheng, Liu Ya-tzu, Ma Hsü-lun, and Sa K'ung-liao. An article on the dissolution of the Democratic League by the KMT is in issue No. 4. Most of the articles are on national affairs.

711. Lin Chen 林真. Chung-kuo nei-mu 中國內幕 (Inside China). Shanghai, Hsin-wen tsa-chih, 1948. 46 pp. (2992/4948)

A collection of articles (1947-48) on the current political situation, including a report on Lo Lung-chi's life after the Democratic League had been outlawed by the National Government.

712. Liu Wang Li-ming 劉王立明 and others. Hsüeh-ch'ang 血賬 (Bloody Account). Hong Kong, Hsin min-chu, 1948. 30 pp. (2992/2163)

This pamphlet contains Liu Wang Li-ming's brief history of the Chinese Association for Civil Rights established on November 8, 1946, as a direct result of the assassination of Li Kung-p'u and Wen I-to. Another useful article concerns the alleged persecution of the leading members of the Democratic League by the KMT authorities.

713. Lu chih-yu i-t'iao 路祇有一條 (There Is Only One Way). Hong Kong, Tzu-yu shih-chieh, 1947. 51 pp. microfilm. (2992/6341)

Among the articles published in this volume are one by Ch'iao Mu (on the civil war) and one by Teng Ch'u-min (on the neutral attitude toward the KMT-CCP struggle).

714. Min-chu sheng-huo 民主生活 (The Democratic Life). Nos. 1, 2, 4, 5, 8, and 9. Chungking and Peiping, January 9 - March 13, 1946. (9200/7023)

    Edited by Sung Yün-pin and published by Shen Chün-ju, this is an organ of the National Salvation Association. Articles by well-known liberals and "democratic individualists." Some of the issues available in the Hoover Library are of the Peiping edition.

715. Min-chu shih-tai 民主時代 (The Democratic Age). No. 3. Canton, December 1, 1947. (9200/7062)

    A monthly magazine containing articles by Sa Meng-wu and other "orthodox" political scientists.

716. Min-chu shih-tai 民主時代 (The Democratic Age). Nos. 1 and 4. Hong Kong, June 1 - July 16, 1949. (9200/7062.23)

    Containing articles on the Chinese civil war and translations of the political system of the Soviet Union.

717. Min-hsin chi 明心集 (To Make Our Intentions Clear). n.p., n. pub., 1946. 42 pp. microfilm. (4292.79/6232)

    Collected accounts given by Ch'en Chin-k'un, Li Fu-jen, Yen Pao-han, and Chang Kuo-ch'üan for their going over to the Communist regime. Their actions took place under various circumstances and at different times. The bulk of the book consists of articles, speeches, and letters by Ch'en Chin-k'un, a noted professor of the famous law school in China, Chaoyang College of Law (also known as Chaoyang University). Li, who explained his action in the form of a letter to Lo Lung-chi, and Yen are "democratic individualists." Chang was a political worker in the KMT army with the rank of brigadier-general.

718. Min-yen 民言 (Public Opinion). Nos. 4/5-6. Tientsin, March 16 - April 10, 1946. (9200/7406)

A semimonthly of current national affairs; critical of the KMT Government.

719. Shih-chi p'ing-lun 世紀評論 (The Century Review). Vol. I, No. 1 - Vol. IV, Nos. 1-2, and 14-20. Nanking, January 4, 1947 - November 6, 1948. (9200/4200)

This is a high-quality weekly with articles contributed by university professors and liberals who were not active in politics or political organizations. Each volume consists of 24 issues, the contents of which may be classified according to the following categories: special political features, national affairs, the civil war, literature, book reviews, special reports, etc.

720. Shih-tai chou-k'an 時代週刊 (The Time Weekly). No. 26. Nanking and Chungking, December 15, 1946. (2992/6231)

An anti-Communist magazine with articles criticizing Lo Lung-chi and Wang Yün-sheng and analyzing the military conference held in Yenan shortly before the publication of this issue.

721. Shih-tai p'i-p'ing 時代批評 ("Modern Critique"). Hong Kong, Vol. I, No. 1 - Vol. IV, No. 79 (incomplete) (June 16, 1938 - September 16, 1941); and Vol. IV, No. 85 - Vol. VI, No. 113 (June 16, 1947 - May 15, 1949). (9200/6250)

Founded and edited by Chow Ching-wen (Chou Ch'ing-wen), the author of Ten Years of Storm (translated by Lai Ming and published by Holt, Rinehart, and Winston in 1960) and one-time Secretary-General of the Democratic League, this periodical of national and foreign affairs has consistently advocated a democratic and socialistic political system for China.

A native of Northeastern Provinces (Manchuria), Chow has been an ardent advocate for the release of Chang Hsüeh-liang. Most of the time during the years between 1938 and 1941, he was critical of both the KMT and the CCP; thus the semimonthly published in this period necessarily excluded articles by many noted writers of various political views.

The periodical ceased publication after Pearl Harbor, having produced 84 issues. It resumed publication on June 16, 1947 (Vol. IV, No. 85), and was published as a monthly from issue Volume V, No. 97 until June 1949 when Chow left Hong Kong for Peiping to take part in the People's Political Consultative Conference. In the 1940's, Chow became active in the Democratic League. As a result, the 29 postwar issues of the magazine were also enlivened by the contributions of noted writers and political figures. With Chow's departure from Hong Kong, the periodical was suspended, only to be resumed on August 25, 1958, after he had returned to Hong Kong from the mainland, disillusioned with the Peking Government. (At first he was very reticent about the Communist regime. Then he broke silence and bitterly attacked the Communist government, especially after publication of this periodical was resumed).

For Chow's own review of the magazine, see his article, entitled "On the 23rd Anniversary of Modern Critique," in issue Volume X, No. 12 (June 16, 1960). The article also reveals Chou En-lai's role in the convocation of the People's Political Consultative Conference.

722. Shih-tai wen-hua ch'u-pan she 時代文化出版社 (ed.). Chung-kuo wang ho-ch'u ch'ü 中國往何處去 (Whence Goes China?). Vol. I. Shanghai, same, 1949. 327 pp. (9200/6470.1)

After the suppression of the weekly Shih yü wen (see the next item), the publisher compiled a two-volume collection of articles selected from that magazine. Volume I is arranged under the following categories: 8 articles on the "third force"; 3 on foreign policy; 17 on the civil war; and 8 on democracy and international relations. Volume II, which is not available, is devoted to (1) liberalism; (2) the Japan policy of the United States; (3) the intelligentsia; and (4) land reform.

723. Shih yu wen 時與文 (Time and Literature). Vol. I, No. 1 - Vol. III, No. 23. Shanghai, March 14, 1947 - September 24, 1948. (9200/5470)

The contents of this weekly may be classified under the following heads: international relations, national affairs, finance, military affairs, literature, and feature reports, with articles discussing the "third force," the civil war, and the foreign policy of China. A number of articles on foreign affairs were contributed by Huan Hsiang. The magazine was suppressed by police after issue Volume III, No. 23. See also the above item.

724. Ta-ti chou-pao 大地週報 (The World Weekly). Nos. 1-11. Peiping, December 1, 1945 - March 10, 1946. (2992/4434)

  Among the contributors to this magazine are Liu Ya-tzu and Chang Tung-sun. Its political background, however, is far from clear. It contains articles on the Political Consultative Conference.

725. Teng Yen-ta hsien-sheng hsün-nan shih-wu chou-nien chi-nien hui 鄧演達先生殉難十五週年紀念會 (ed.). Teng Yen-ta ti tao-lu 鄧演達的道路 (Teng Yen-ta's Road). [Shanghai?], same, 1946. 86 pp. (4737.9/1332)

  Edited and published by the Committee for the Commemoration of the 15th Anniversary of Teng Yen-ta's Death, this book consists of four articles (one each by Chang Po-chün and P'eng Tse-min, one biographical sketch of Teng Yen-ta, and one on his life and activities) and five documents relating to the political views, programs, declarations, and history of the Third Party. Some of the documents are reprinted from the Chung-hua lun-t'an, Vol. I, No. 10/11 (December 1, 1945).

726. Ts'ang-hai hsing 滄海行 (Journey to the World). Hong Kong, Tzu-yu wen-ts'ung, 1947. 62 pp. (2992/3642)

  Articles of particular interest in this pamphlet are those published on the first anniversary of the assassination of Wen I-to (July 15, 1947) and a survey of the current military situation.

727. T'ung-i chan-hsien chu wen-t'i 統一戰線諸問題 (Problems of the United Front). Kowloon, Tzu-yu shih-chieh, 1948. 57 pp. (4292.25/2162)

This is the 11th issue of the <u>Freedom Series</u> (Tzu-yu ts'ung-k'an), with articles by Yü Huai, Shen Chih-yüan, and others. Yü attacked the "Third Force" and Shen discussed various problems of the United Front policy.

728. Tzu-yu p'i-p'an 自由批判 (Free Criticism). Vol. I, Nos. 1, 2, 4, and 9. Peiping, July 1 - November 11, 1948. (2992/2559)

A periodical published every ten days covering a wide scope of subjects including articles on the intelligentsia, liberalism, and the "middle road." A reprint of a useful survey of the current Chinese magazines and newspapers published in Hong Kong appears in issue No. 4.

729. Wan-hsiang 萬象 (The Kaleidoscope). Vol. I, Nos. 1-3, and 6. Shanghai, October 9 - November 13, 1948. (9200/4223.31)

First published in Chungking, June 1943, the articles of this weekly are primarily concerned with political figures in the National Government. Issue No. 2 contains an account of dissensions in the Democratic-Socialist Party.

730. Wen-ts'ui 文萃 (The Digest). Vol. I, Nos. 1-50; Vol. II, Nos. 1-11, 14-17, and 22. Shanghai, October 9, 1945 - March 6, 1947. (9200/044.1)

Most of the articles in the early issues of this weekly are reprints from the CCP and liberal newspapers and magazines published in Chungking and Kunming. Among the writers are Communists and leading members of the Democratic League. The contents may be classified into four categories: (1) social and economic conditions in Communist and KMT regions; (2) political views of various groups other than the KMT and the CCP; (3) analysis of international relations (with many articles by Ch'iao Mu); and (4) literature. After it was forced to shut down by the KMT in March 1947, it began secret publication in serial form (ts'ung-k'an) for a short period of time. The Hoover Library also has the following issues of the Peiping edition of the magazine: Nos. 16-20 (March 24 - May 19, 1946). (9200/0444.1)

731. Wo-men fan-tui nei-chan 我們反對內戰 (We Oppose the Civil War). n.p., Tzu-yu, 1945. 62 pp. (2992/2273)

A collection of eleven articles by Chou Chien-jen, Ma Hsü-lun, and others, opposing the civil war.

732. Yeh Feng 野風 (The Wild Wind Weekly). No. 3. Shanghai, March 11, 1949. (2992/6271)

The articles of this issue deal with the marriage of Chu Teh and K'ang K'o-ch'ing, make comments on several high officials of the National Government, and criticize Liang Sou-ming.

XVI. STUDENT DEMONSTRATIONS

The CCP considered the student demonstrations in the KMT-controlled areas as part of a second front against the National Government. The works available in this section are related only to demonstrations in Shanghai and Kunming.

733. Ch'en Lei 陳雷. Hsiang p'ao-k'ou yao fan ch'ih 向砲口要飯吃 (Demand for Food). Shanghai, Hu-pin, 1947. 134 pp. (2992/7916)

Current newspaper and magazine stories and reports of student hunger riots and anti-civil war demonstrations in various cities between May and July of 1947.

734. Ch'ing-nien sheng-huo 青年生活 (Youth Life). Vol. I, No. 1. Liaoning, December 1948. (4292.01/5823)

A periodical for young readers in Manchuria. This issue includes a special section for two events of the student movements in Peiping and Kunming on December 9, 1935, and December 1, 1946, respectively.

735. Hu En-tse 胡恩澤. Hui-i ti-san-tzu kuo-nei ko-ming chan-cheng shih-chi ti Shang-hai hsüeh-sheng yün-tung 回憶第三次國內革命戰爭時期的上海學生運動 (Reminiscences of the Student Movement in Shanghai During the Third Revolutionary War). Shanghai, Jen-min, 1958. 60 pp. (4180.1/4263)

A sympathetic frangmentary account of student political activities in Shanghai between 1945 and 1949. The slogans of these activities were anti-hunger, anti-persecution, anti-America, anti-Chiang Kai-shek, etc.

736. Hu Lin 胡麟. I-er-i ti hui-i 一二一的回憶 (Reminiscences of December 1). Hong Kong, Hai-hung, 1949. 70 pp. (4180.1/4205)

A clear, concise, personal, and sympathetic account of the events leading to the killing of four schoolteachers and students by police in Kunming on December 1, 1946. The incident was a result of anti-civil war meetings and student demonstrations. The appendix contains the regulations of the All-China Students' Association, approved by the 14th National Student Congress on March 5, 1949.

737. Pa tsu-kuo t'ui-hsiang tu-li tzu-yu chieh-fang 把祖國推向獨立自由解放 (Push the Motherland Toward Freedom, Liberty, and Liberation). Shanghai, St. John's University, 1948. 30 pp. microfilm. (4180.1/1244)

This student publication of St. John's University, Shanghai, carries almost exclusively student demonstration news and anti-America articles.

738. Teng-ta 燈塔 (Lighthouse). n.p., n.d. microfilm.
(4180.1/9146)

   Issued by the Political Propaganda Section of the Propaganda Department on the first anniversary of the founding of the All-China Students' Federation, which is probably not the same one set up in March 1949, because the present publication is dated June 19. The year of publication, however, cannot be verified. The contents (student demonstrations, etc.) appear to be related to the civil war period.

739. Yü Tsai hsien-sheng chi-nien wei-yüan hui 于再先生紀念委員會 (ed.). I-erh-i min-chu yün-tung chi-nien chi 一二一民主運動紀念集 (Commemorative Writings on the Democratic Movement of December 1). Shanghai, Chen-hua, 1946. 212 pp. (4180.1/1122)

   This volume contains articles written in commemoration of the death of Yü Tsai, a schoolteacher, and three students, who were killed by the police in Kunming on December 1, 1946, including accounts of commemorative meetings in various cities and many speeches by the "democratic and liberal persons."

XVII. THE NEW DEMOCRATIC YOUTH LEAGUE

   The First Congress of the New Democratic Youth League met in Peiping in April 1949. This section includes not only a number of documents on the League but also works related to the Communist youth movement in general; some pertain to the pre-1945 period.

740. Ch'ing-chiu wen-hsien 青救文獻 (Documents of the United Northwest Youth National Salvation Association). n.p., Chung-kuo ch'ing-nien, 1939. 219 pp. (4292.53/1158)

   Selected documents issued by the United Northwest Youth National Salvation Association from its establishment in April 1937 to July 1939, including its regulations and documents of its first and second congresses.

741. Chung-kuo ch'ing-nien 中國青年 (Chinese Youth). Nos. 7-9. Yenan, August 15 - September 16, 1939. (2991.2/5658)

    These are the few issues of the official organ of the CY, which made a brief reappearance in 1939-40 in Yenan, having ceased publication after 1927. It resumed publication again in 1948 (see item nos. 107-8 in my previous volume <u>The Chinese Communist Movement, 1921-1937</u>).

    Issue No. 8 is a special number commemorating the 25th International Youth Day. Yang Sung's article on the significance of the Russo-German Non-Aggression Pact and a report on the student congress in the Shensi-Kansu-Ningsia Border Region appear in issue No. 9.

742. Chung-kuo ch'ing-nien she 中國青年社 . Chung-kuo hsin min-chu chu-i ch'ing-nien t'uan t'uan-chang chiang-hua 中國新民主主義青年團團章講話 (On the Constitution of the New Democratic Youth League of China). Peking, Ch'ing-nien, 1950. 108 pp. (4292.53/5668.56)

    A "preliminary draft" of commentaries on the organization, discipline, nature, and members' rights and obligations of the New Democratic Youth League of China; originally published in the Shantung <u>Ch'ing-nien wen-hua</u>.

743. _____. Kuan-yü pu-tui chung chien-li hsin min-chu chu-i ch'ing-nien t'uan 關於部隊中建立新民主主義青年團 (Concerning the Establishment of the New Democratic Youth League in the Army). Peking, same, 1950. 20 pp. (4292.53/5658.70)

    This pamphlet contains (1) a resolution of the New Democratic Youth League of China and of the Political Department of the Chinese People's Revolutionary Military Committee concerning the establishment of the League in the army; (2) an article on "youth work" in the Communist forces; and (3) an article on the experience of the League's activities in a company of the Fourth Field Forces (Ti-ssu yeh-chan chün).

744. _____. Tsai fan feng-so tou-cheng chung chien-li yü chuang-ta ch'ing-nien t'uan 在反封鎖鬥爭中建立與壯大青年團 (Growth of the Youth League During the Blockade). Shanghai, same, 1949. 61 pp. (4292.53/4748)

Two of the eleven documents in this book are resolutions of the CC of the CCP relating to the New Democratic Youth League of China. The remaining ones are related to the League in the Huatung Region (Eastern China).

745. _____. Tsen-yang chien-li hsin min-chu chu-i ch'ing-nien t'uan 怎樣建立新民主主義青年團 (How to Establish the New Democratic Youth League). [Peking], same, 1949. 53 pp. (4293.53/5668.84)

This book contains the following material concerning the New Democratic Youth League of China: (1) 6 resolutions and bulletins of the CC of the CCP and the League's Central Committee; (2) 7 articles by Feng Wen-pin; and (3) 3 editorials of the Chung-kuo ch'ing-nien; and articles by other writers.

746. _____. Wei t'uan-chieh chiao-yü ch'ing-nien i-tai erh tou-cheng 為團結教育青年一代而鬥爭 (Struggle for the Unity and Education of the Younger Generation). Peiping, same, 1949. 104 pp. (4292.53/5607.811)

A collection of documents relating to the First Congress of the New Democratic Youth League of China. This is the best of several collections on the same subject.

747. Chung-kuo ch'ing-nien t'ung-hsin 中國青年通訊 (Chinese Youth Correspondence). Nos. 3 and 5. August 5 - September 11, 1939. mimeo. (4292.53/5658.58)

Edited by the Joint Office of the Chinese Youth National Salvation Organizations at Yenan, issue No. 3 of this magazine carries news and studies concerning the youth movement; issue No. 5 is a chronology of important events in the youth movement from 1937 to 1939.

748. Chung-kuo hsin min-chu chu-i ch'ing-nien t'uan 中國新民主主義青年團 (The New Democratic Youth League of China). Hong Kong, Hsin min-chu, 1949. 91 pp. (4292.53/5607.07)

  The materials contained in this book fall into the following categories: (1) New Democratic Youth League's constitution and programs; (2) reports and speeches delivered by Jen Pi-shih, Chu Teh, and Feng Wen-pin at the First Congress of the New Democratic Youth League in April 1945; (3) the New China News Agency's reports on the League and its First Congress; and (4) the membership list of the Central Committee of the League.

749. _____. Chung-yang tsu-chih pu 中央組織部 (ed.). Ch'ing-nien t'uan wen-ta 青年團問答 (Inquiries and Explanations Concerning the Youth League). Vol. I. Peking, Ch'ing-nien, 1951. 33 pp. (4292.53/5607.58)

  Edited by the Department of Organization of the New Democratic Youth League, this is a useful compilation of questions and answers relating to the organization of the League. The inquiries were raised during the year following the establishment of the League.

750. Chung-kuo hsin min-chu chu-i ch'ing-nien t'uan. Ho-pei sheng T'ang-shan shih kung-tso wei-yüan hui 中國新民主主義青年團河北省唐山市工作委員會 (ed.). Ch'ing-nien shou-ts'e 青年手册 (Youth Handbook). Tangshan, I-chih, 1950. 59 pp. (4292.53/5607.582)

  Edited by the Working Committee of the New Democratic Youth League in the City of Tangshan, Hopeh Province, this handbook includes brief accounts of several "youth memorial days" commemorating student incidents taking place after 1936 and of "revolutionary youth organizations" established since 1919.

751. _____. T'uan-yüan chiao-ts'ai 團員教材 (Manual for Members of the Youth League). 13th ed. Tangshan, same, 1951. 29 pp. (4292.53/5607.66a)

First published in 1949, this pamphlet consists of several articles (two of them by Feng Wen-pin) discussing the routine work of a League branch, such as calling meetings, organizational principles of the League, and so on.

752. Chung-kuo hsin min-chu chu-i ch'ing-nien t'uan ti-i tz'u ch'üan-kuo tai-piao ta-hui wen-hsien 中國新民主主義青年團第一次全國代表大會文獻 (Documents Relating to the First Congress of the New Democratic Youth League of China). n.p., Hsin-hua, 1949. 86 pp. (4292.53/5607.81)

The contents of this book are identical with that of item no. 748, with the exception that the present volume contains Chiang Nan-hsiang's report at the First Congress of the League and three documents issued by the League's Central Committee.

753. Min-chu ch'ing-nien 民主青年 (Democratic Youth). Vol. II, Nos. 1-3 and Supplement. Peiping, February 25, 1946 - June 16, 1946. (4180.1/7058)

This semimonthly was probably an organ of the Democratic League, and carries articles on education, youth problems, student movements, and other topics. Issue No. 1 contains an article by Ch'en Chia-k'ang, reporting on the World Youth Congress held in London in November 1945. The Supplement (February 1, 1946) is a special number presenting youth's views on the Political Consultative Conference.

754. Min-chu ch'ing-nien 民主青年 (Democratic Youth). Nos. 2, 3, and 4. Kalgan, February - April 1946. (4292.01/7058.13)

Edited by the Min-chu ch'ing-nien she and printed by the Chin-Ch'a-Chi jih-pao, this is a medium-level magazine for educated young readers presenting articles on a variety of subjects, such as current affairs, education, popular science, youth problems, student movements, and literature. Hsiao San's "Comrade Mao Tse-tung's Childhood" begins in issue No. 4, after which the magazine was published under the new title Shih-tai ch'ing-nien (see item no. 756).

755.   Min-chu ch'ing-nien 民主青年 (Democratic Youth). Nos. 13, 15, 17, 18, 41, 49, 50, 54, 63 and 66. Dairen, October 1, 1947 - June 1, 1949. (4292.01/7058)

Published by the United Kwantung Democratic Youth Association, this semimonthly contains writings on youth problems, current affairs, literary essays and fiction. Issue No. 41 (September 1, 1948) includes Ch'en Po-ta's writings and an article on Yang Ching-yü. The text of a speech of Lin Po-ch'ü at a cadre meeting on July 1 [1948] in Yenan is reprinted in issue No. 54 (February 1, 1949). Issue No. 66 includes a number of documents relating to the All-China Youth Congress. After the establishment of the New Democratic Youth League, this magazine became an organ of the Port Arthur and Dairen Branch of the organization. The Hoover Library holdings (post-1949) are Nos. 99, 101, 104, 106, 110, 113, 121, and 122 (May 1, 1950 - January 21, 1951).

756.   Shih-tai ch'ing-nien 時代青年 (Youth of Our Time). Nos. 5-7, and 11-13. Kalgan, May 20 - September 5, 1946. (4292.01/7058.13)

Formerly called the Min-chu ch'ing-nien (see item no. 754), this periodical for young readers began publication under the present title with issue No. 5 in order to distinguish itself from the Democratic League magazine of the same name in Peking. It had also become a better magazine, published semimonthly with higher quality articles. The last part of Hsiao San's "Comrade Mao Tse-tung's Childhood" appears in issue No. 7 (or Vol. II, No. 1) (June 5, 1946).

XVIII. LAND REFORM

One of the most important factors that contributed to the military victory of the CCP was the land reform which had been carried out in Communist regions. It won the active support of the peasants in the war against the KMT. The agrarian policies of the Party were clearly defined by the promulgation of the "Outline of Land Law" in 1947 and publications of "How to Analyze the Classes," "Resolutions Concerning Some Problems Arising from Agrarian Struggles," Mao Tse-tung's "Speech at a Conference of Cadres in the Shansi and Suiyuan Liberated

Area" (April 1, 1948), and Jen Pi-shih's "Some Problems of Land Reform."

The primary and secondary sources in this section on the Communist postwar land reforms range from editorial comments to case studies in various regions. Some of the important land laws are also included. The two systematic studies, however, are done by the KMT and anti-Communist writers.

757. Chieh-fang she 解放社 (ed.). Lun hsin chieh-fang ch'ü t'u-ti cheng-ts'e 論新解放區土地政策 (On the Land Policy of the New Liberated Areas). n.p., Hsin-hua, 1949. 25 pp. (4395/2503)

A collection of directives or programs issued in 1948 by the CC, the Chungyuan Bureau, and the Northeast Bureau of the CCP, as well as editorials of the Yü-hsi jih-pao on land policy and reforms.

758. Chin-Ch'a-Chi hsin-hua shu-tien 晉察冀新華書店 (ed.). T'u-ti kai-ko yü cheng-tang 土地改革與整黨 (Land Reforms and Rectifications of the Party). n.p., same, 1948. 23 pp. (4395/1310)

This pamphlet includes (1) a directive of the CC of the CCP, February 22, 1948, on land reforms and Party rectifications in "old liberated areas" and "semi-old liberated areas"; (2) a directive of the Shansi-Chahar-Hopeh Bureau of the CCP to Party committees of various levels on carrying out the above instructions; and (3) a report of land reform experiences at Suiteh and Pingshan.

759. Chin-Ch'a-Chi jih-pao she 晉察冀日報社 (ed.). Ch'üan-t'i nung-min ch'i-lai p'ing-fen t'u-ti 全體農民起來平分土地 (All Peasants Arise to Divide the Land). [Kalgan?], Hsin-hua, 1948. 31 pp. (4395/1316.87)

Ten articles on land reform, selected from the Chin-Ch'a-Chi jih-pao's editorials (November-December 1947).

760. Chin-Chi-Lu-Yü pien-ch'ü cheng-fu. Ti-i t'ing 晉冀魯豫邊區政府第一廳 (ed.). Chien-tsu chien-hsi i-wen chieh-ta 減租減息疑問解答 (Questions and Answers About Reduction of Rent and Interest). n.p., Hsin-hua, n.d. 40 pp. (4395/1121)

   Edited by the First Office of the Shansi-Hopeh-Shantung-Honan Border Government, this pamphlet consists of questions and answers regarding the regulations promulgated on October 25, 1940, concerning the reduction of rent and interest.

761. Chin I-hung 金一鴻. Chung-kung t'u-kai yü Chung-kuo t'u-ti wen-t'i 中共土改與中國土地問題 (Chinese Communist Land Reforms and the Land Problems of China). Kowloon, Tzu-lu, 1950. 162 pp. (4395/8113)

   The first chapter presents the CCP's land reforms from the Kiangsi Soviet to the establishment of the People's Republic of China. The remaining two chapters of the book deal with general land problems in China as well as the KMT's land policy. In preparing the manuscript, the author appears to have done extensive research work on the subject.

762. Chin-Sui pien-ch'ü sheng-ch'an wei-yüan hui 晉綏邊區生產委員會 (ed.). Hsin Chieh-fang ch'ü ti ch'ün-chung sheng-ch'an 新解放區的群眾生產 (Production of the Masses in the Newly Liberated Areas). n.p., same, 1946. 17 pp. (4292.75/1237)

   A discussion of production problems in the regions which came under Communist control after 1945, edited by the Production Committee of the Shansi-Suiyuan Border Region.

763. Chung-kuo kung-ch'an tang. Chung-yang wei-yüan hui 中國共產黨中央委員會. Chung-kuo t'u-ti fa ta-kang 中國土地法大綱 (The Outline of Land Law). Hantan, Hsin-hua, 1949. 6 pp. (4395/5640)

   Two documents: (1) the Outline of Land Law, approved by the All-China Land Conference on September 13, 1947; and

(2) resolutions of the CC of the CCP, October 10, 1947, on the promulgation of the Outline of Land Law.

764. Chung-kuo kung-ch'an tang. Hua-tung chü. Min-yün pu 中國共產黨華東局民運部 (ed.). Huai-an O-ch'ien hsiang t'u-ti kai-ko ching-yen chieh-shao 淮安鵝錢鄉土地改革經驗介紹 (Introducing Land Reform Experiences in Ochien Village, Huaian District). n.p., same, 1947. 28 pp. microfilm. (4395/5445)

This pamphlet includes (1) three articles on land reform in Ochien village published in the Huachung New China Daily, (2) six news reports on related subjects, and (3) one article discussing the writing of land contracts.

765. Chung-kuo kung-ch'an tang. Nen-chiang sheng wei-yüan hui 中國共產黨嫩江省委員會. T'u-ti kai-ko chung ti chi-ko wen-t'i ho san-ko tien-hsing ching-yen 土地改革中的幾個問題和三個典型經驗 (Several Land Reform Problems and Experiences of Three Typical Cases). Tsitsihar, Tung-pei shu-tien, 1948. 60 pp. (4395/4414)

Edited by the Nenchiang Provincial Committee of the CCP, this pamphlet includes Jen Pi-shih's report, and reports of experiences in Kuohsien (in Shensi Province) Pingshan, and Huang-chia-ts'un (in Suiteh).

766. Chung-kung ti t'u-ti kai-ko cheng-ts'e 中共的土地改革政策 (Land Reform Policy of the Chinese Communist Party). 3rd ed. [Taipei], Yang-ming, 1951. 104 pp. (4395/5424)

A KMT publication, containing reprints of six Communist land reform documents of 1948.

767. Fen-sui ti-chu fan-pa yin-mou 粉碎地主翻把陰謀 (To Smash the Landlords' Treachery). n.p., Ch'ün-chung jih-pao, 1948. 32 pp. microfilm. (4395/9140)

Newspaper reports of landlords' alleged attempts to obstruct land reforms in various villages. The locations of the incidents are not clear, but the obscure village names appear to be in Manchuria.

768. Kung-fei t'u-ti cheng-ts'e chih yen-chiu 共匪土地政策之研究 (A Study of the Communist Land Policy). Taipei, Yang-ming, 1957. 146 pp. (4395/4417)

A KMT publication of a detailed study of the subject. The first two of the five chapters in the book deal with the CCP's land policy and its developments; the next two chapters are concerned with the post-1949 period, and the last chapter is an examination of the KMT land policy in comparison with that of the CCP.

769. Lenin and others. Lun ch'ün-chung kuan-tien 論群眾觀點 (On the Mass Viewpoint). Weihsien, Chi-nan, 1946. 65 pp. microfilm. (4290.13/0164)

In addition to Lenin's article, this book consists of articles by Kao Kang, Li Yü, and the Huachung New China Daily.

770. Li-keng 力耕 (ed.). Chieh-fang ch'ü ti t'u-ti cheng-ts'e yü shih-shih 解放區的土地政策與實施 (Land Policy and Practice in the Liberated Areas). Hong Kong, Chung-kuo ch'u-pan, 1947. 64 pp. (4395/4255)

The first of the three chapters contained in this book discusses the basic Communist theory of land reform; the second consists of several articles dealing with current land policy; and the third presents CCP land policy and practice during and after the Sino-Japanese War. The last chapter consists mainly of CCP documents.

771. Liu Shao-ch'i 劉少奇 and others. T'u-kai cheng-tang tien-hsing ching-yen 土改整黨典型經驗 (Typical Experiences

in Land Reforms and Party Rectification). Hong Kong, Chung-kuo ch'u-pan, 1949. 60 pp. (4395/7294)

Among the documents included in this volume on land reforms in 1948 are: (1) a directive of the Shansi-Hopeh-Shantung-Honan Bureau of the CCP; (2) Jen Pi-shih's speech of January 12, 1948; (3) reports of land reform in Kuohsien (Shansi), in Huang-chia-ts'un (Suiteh district in the Shensi-Kansu-Ningsia Border Region), and in Pingshan (Shansi-Charhar-Hopeh Border Region); the last being written by Liu Shao-ch'i with an introductory note (March 1948) by Mao Tse-tung; and (4) a directive of the CC of the CCP, February 22, 1948, on land reforms in "old-liberated areas" and "newly liberated areas."

772. Lun hsin chieh-fang ch'ü t'u-ti cheng-ts'e 論新解放區土地政策 (On Land Reform Policy in the Newly Liberated Areas). Hong Kong, Hsin min-chu, 1949. 25 pp. (4395/0020)

Included in this pamphlet are (1) an excerpt from Mao Tse-tung's talk delivered at a cadre meeting on April 1, 1948; (2) the rent and interest reduction program of the Chungyuan Bureau of the CCP, October 8, 1948; and (3) a directive of the Northeast Bureau of the CC of the CCP dated December 23, 1948.

773. [Po I-po 薄一波]. Chih-hsing chung-yang wu-ssu chih-shih ti chi-pen tsung-chieh chi chin-hou jen-wu 執行中央五四指示的基本總結及今後任務 (Carry Out the May Fourth Directive of the Central Committee Regarding Future Tasks). n. p., [CCP], 1947. 15 pp. microfilm. (4395/4413)

Published by the Propaganda Department of the Hopeh-Shantung-Honan Committee of the CCP, this is a concluding report at a regional land conference on June 2 [1947].

774. Shen Chih-yüan 沈志遠 (ed.). Chung-kuo t'u-ti wen-t'i yü t'u-ti kai-ko 中國土地問題與土地改革 (Chinese Land Problems and Land Reforms). Hong Kong, Hsin-chung, 1948. 80 pp. (4395/3143)

Second of a special magazine series, Li-lun yü hsien-shih ts'ung-k'an, with articles by Ch'en Po-ta, Shen Chih-yüan, Ti Chao-pai, and others.

775. T'u-ti kai-ko hou ti cheng-ts'e 土地改革後的政策 (Policy After Land Reforms). n.p., n. pub., 1946. 33 pp. microfilm. (4396/4414)

A Communist textbook for political indoctrination.

776. Tung-pei jen-min cheng-fu. Nung-lin pu 東北人民政府農林部 (ed.). T'u-ti cheng-ts'e fa-ling hui-pien 土地政策法令彙編 (A Collection of Land Laws and Policies). Mukden, same, 1950. 241 pp. (4395/5187)

Edited and published by the Ministry of Agriculture of the Northeast People's Government, these 59 documents on land laws and policies were issued between 1947 and 1950 by the CC of the CCP, the Northeast Bureau of the Party, the Northeast People's Government, and other Communist regions.

777. Tung-pei jih-pao she 東北日報社 (ed.). Ch'ün-chung kung-tso shou-ts'e 群眾工作手册 (Handbook for Work with the Masses). Chiamussu, Tung-pei shu-tien, 1947. 131 pp. microfilm. (4395/5164)

Reference material for land reform in Manchuria.

778. Wei shun-chieh tang ti tsu-chih erh tou-cheng 為純潔黨的組織而鬥爭 (Struggle to Purify the Party's Organization). Hong Kong, Cheng-pao, 1948. 85 pp. (4395/3239)

Selected documents and writings on land reform, including (1) speeches made by P'eng Chen and Nieh Jung-chen at the Land Conference of the Shansi-Chahar-Hopeh Border Region, (2) an article by Teng Ying-ch'ao, and (3) land reform directives from various Communist regions. The title of the book is taken from Chin-Sui jih-pao's editorial of November 27 [1947].

779. Wu-lung hsien cheng-fu t'u-ti kai-kao tsung-chieh 五龍縣政府土地改革總結 (Land Reforms in Wulung District). n.p., 1946. [10 pp.] manuscript on microfilm. (4395/1061)

    A summary report of the District Government of Wulung on land reforms.

XIX. THE LABOR MOVEMENT

    The Communist labor movement was understandably inactive during the Sino-Japanese War, as the Communists had been operating in rural areas. In addition to miscellaneous primary sources on the labor movement in Kalgan, Shanghai, and other border regions, this section contains several collections of documents relating to the Sixth Congress of the All-China Federation of Labor. The Congress met in Harbin in August 1948, and it elected Ch'en Yün as Chairman and Liu Ning-i, Li Li-san and Chu Hsüeh-fan as Vice-Chairmen. It decided to restore the Federation of Labor Unions in China. It had almost been two decades since the Fifth Congress had met secretly in Shanghai in 1929.

780. Chang-shih kung-jen shou-chieh tai-piao ta-hui hui-k'an 張市工人首屆代表大會彙刊 (Publication of the First Congress of Workers' Representatives in Kalgan). [Kalgan], [same conference], 1945. 25 pp.. (4460.363/1018)

    This publication consists of a brief account of the First Congress of Workers' Representatives in Kalgan (December 21-25, 1945), programs and resolutions of the Congress, and regulations and documents concerning the Kalgan General Labor Union.

781. Chao I-po 趙一波 (ed.). Chung-kuo chih-kung yün-tung wen-hsien 中國職工運動文獻 (Documents on the Chinese Labor Movement). Vol. I. Shanghai, Shih-nien, 1946. 134 pp. (4474/4813)

    Of the documents contained in the volume, only those concerning the organization of the labor unions in the early Yenan period are related to this bibliography; the rest are concerned with the earlier period, the 1920's and 1930's. Arranged in chronological order, most of the material is taken from the labor yearbook, Chung-kuo lao-tung nien-chien. The records of the first four congresses of the All-China Labor Federation are useful for reference. The documents relating to the Kiangsi Soviet are collected from the editor's own private sources.

782. Chieh-fang she 解放社 (ed.). Chung-kuo chih-kung yün-tung ti tang-ch'ien jen-wu 中國職工運動的當前任務 (The Present Tasks of the Labor Movement in China). Shanghai, Hsin-hua, 1949. 94 pp. (4474/2032)

    This book consists of seven documents relating to the Sixth Congress of the All-China Federation of Labor, two commentaries from the New China News Agency, and a text of labor insurance regulations issued by the Northeast Administrative Council on December 27, 1948.

783. Chin-Ch'a-Chi pien-ch'ü tsung kung-hui 晉察冀邊區總工會 (ed.). Tang-ch'ien chih-kung yün-tung ti chi-ko wen-hsien 當前職工運動的幾個文獻 (Several Documents Relating to the Present Labor Movement). n.p., same, 1946. 63 pp. (4460.17/1313)

    Edited and published by the General Labor Union of the Shansi-Chahar-Hopeh Border Region, these documents fall into three categories: (1) resolutions of the Executive Committee of the Union; (2) programs, regulations, and work reports of the General Labor Union of the Peiping-Suiyuan Railway; (3) programs, regulations, and activities of the General Labor Union of Kalgan.

784. Kung-jen pao she 工人報社 (ed.). Chin-Ch'a-Chi pien-ch'ü kung-jen wu-i chi-nien hua-ts'e 晉察冀邊區工人五一紀念畫冊 (A Pictorial Commemoration of the May First Anniversary by the Workers of the Shansi-Chahar-Hopeh Border Region). [Kalgan], same, 1946. no pagination. (4460.171/1313.13)

Photos with captions about the life of the workers in the Shansi-Chahar-Hopeh Border Region.

785. Ch'üan-kuo min-chu fu-nü lien-ho hui ch'ou-pei wei-yüan hui 全國民主婦女聯合籌備委員會 (ed.). Hsin she-hui ti hsin nü-kung 新社會的新女工 (New Women's Labor in a New Society). Shanghai, Hsin-hua, 1949. 51 pp. (4467/8670)

In addition to three editorials and comments from the New China News Agency and its East China and Northeast branches, this book contains eight articles describing the successful work of several women workers in North Chian, Manchuria, and other places. Edited by the Preparatory Committee of the All-China Democratic Federation of Women.

786. Chung-hua ch'üan-kuo tsung kung-hui 中華全國總工會 (ed.). Chung-kuo chih-kung yün-tung wen-hsien 中國職工運動運文獻 (Documents Relating to the Chinese Labor Movement). Peking, Kung-jen, 1949. 146 pp. (4460.10/5486.11)

Of these documents, seven are related to the Sixth Congress of the All-China Federation of Labor; four are editorials and comments from the New China News Agency (1948-49); two were issued by the Shanghai Military Control Committee (1949); two by the Northeast Administrative Council (1948-49); and one by the North China People's Government (1949).

787. Hua-pei tsung kung-hui ch'ou-pei wei-yüan hui 華北總工會籌備委員會 (ed.). Ti-liu tz'u ch'üan-kuo lao-ta chüeh-i 第六次全國勞大決議 (Resolutions of the Sixth Congress of the All-China Federation of Labor). Chungyuan, Hsin-hua, 1949. 60 pp. (4452/4121)

Edited by the Preparatory Committee of the General Labor Union of North China, this volume includes resolutions of the Sixth Congress of the All-China Federation of Labor and other related documents. Also included are the organizational regulations and the list of officers of the Federation, as well as speeches by Li Li-san and Chu Hsüeh-fan. The appendix contains three documents concerning labor regulations in Manchuria.

788. Kung-jen ti hsin t'ien-ti 工人的新天地 (The Worker's New World). Kowloon, Kung-jen wen-hua, 1948. 35 pp. (4451/1820)

This pamphlet contains miscellaneous news of workers, particularly those in Hong Kong and Shanghai. It also includes an article by Chu Hsüeh-fan about his trip to Manchuria.

789. Li Kuang 黎光 (ed.). Ti-liu tz'u ch'üan-kuo tao-tung ta-hui 第六次全國勞動大會 (The Sixth Congress of the All-China Federation of Labor). Kowloon, Kung-jen wen-hua, 1948. 74 pp. (4460.40/8692.6)

This volume is different from the other volumes concerning the Sixth Congress of the All-China Federation of Labor in that it contains no resolutions or regulations of the Congress but has texts of more speeches than any other volumes listed in this section. Among the speeches are some by Li Li-san, Ch'en Yün, Liu Ning-i, and Chu Hsüeh-fan. The appendix includes a brief account of the first five congresses of the Federation.

790. Liu Chang-sheng 劉長勝 and others. Chung-kuo kung-ch'an tang yü Shang-hai kung-jen 中國共產黨與上海工人 (The Chinese Communist Party and the Shanghai Workers). Shanghai, Lao-tung, 1951. 88 pp. (4460.28/7277)

A collection of eight articles presenting fragmentary stories of labor strikes and activities of the Communist cells in several Shanghai companies. The events described took place between the 1920's and the 1940's.

791. Shang-hai tsung kung-hui. Mi-shu ch'u 上海總工會秘書處 (ed.). Chieh-fang hou ti Shang-hai kung-yün tzu-liao 解放後的上海工運資料 (Source Materials on the Labor Movement in Shanghai After the Liberation). Shanghai, Lao-tung, 1950. 254 pp. (4460.28/2321)

A source book on the labor movement in China in general, and in Shanghai in particular, for the period from May to December 1949. The materials are classified into four sections. The first two deal with the activities of Shanghai workers shortly before and after the Communist capture of the city at the end of May 1949. Section III is a chronology of important events in the labor movement in China for the period of May to December 1949, and the last section consists of important related documents of the same period.

792. _____. Wen-chiao pu 文教部 (ed.). San-shih nien lai ti Shang-hai kung-yün 三十年的上海工運 (Thirty Years of the Labor Movement in Shanghai). Shanghai, Lao-tung, 1951. 27 pp. (4460.14/2321.14)

A fragmentary account of the Shanghai labor movement from 1921 to 1949, edited by the Cultural and Educational Department of the General Labor Union of Shanghai.

793. Shan-tung sheng tsung kung-hui 山東省總工會 (ed.). Kung-yün wen-chi 工運文集 (Selected Documents on the Labor Movement). Shantung, Hsin-hua, 1946. 85 pp. microfilm. (4474/2592)

Materials concerned with the labor movement are selected editorials of the Liberation Daily, excerpts from Mao Tse-tung's writings, speeches by Li Yü and Chou En-lai, and various directives. Published for cadre reference in the postwar labor movement.

794. Tung-pei shu-tien 東北書店 (ed.). Chih-kung yün-tung ts'an-k'ao tzu-liao 職工運動參考資料 (Reference Materials on the Labor Movement). Harbin, same, 1948. 55 pp. (4474/5150.1)

The bulk of the materials are eleven articles on labor problems selected from the Tung-pei jih-pao and the Ha-erh-pin jih-pao. The remaining documents are (1) a directive of the Northeast Bureau of the CC of the CCP, June 10, 1948, on the protection of captured cities; (2) regulations of the General Labor Union of Harbin; and (3) a declaration of the Second Congress of Worker's Representatives of Harbin.

795. _____. Chih-kung yün-tung wen-hsien 職工運動文獻 (Documents on the Labor Movement). Vols. III and IV. Harbin, same, 1949. 50 and 54 pp. (4474/5150)

Volume III includes a number of documents relating to the Sixth Congress of the All-China Federation of Labor. In addition, there is a short article on the first five congresses of the Federation. All documents contained in Volume IV were issued by the Northeast Bureau of the CC of the CCP.

XX. THE WOMEN'S MOVEMENT

Works pertaining to the women's movement in this period are scant. Most of the works included here are related to the First All-China Women's Congress held in Peiping in March 1949.

796. Chung-hua ch'üan-kuo min-chu fu-nü lien-ho hui hsüan-ch'uan chiao-yü pu 中華全國民主婦女聯合會宣傳教育部 (ed.). Chung-kuo fu-nü ti-i tz'u ch'üan-kuo tai-piao ta-hui chung-yao wen-hsien 中國婦女第一次全國代表大會重要文獻 (Important Documents Relating to the First All-China Women's Congress). Peking, same, 1949. 86 pp. (4176/5486.56)

Edited and published by the Propaganda and Educational Department of the All-China Association of Democratic Women, this volume contains reports and resolutions of the First All-China Women's Congress as well as regulations and the names of officers of the Association.

797. Chung-kuo fu-nü ti-i tz'u ch'üan-kuo tai-piao ta-hui 中國婦女第一次全國代表大會 (The First All-China Women's Congress). Hong Kong, Hsin-min-chu, 1949. 108 pp. (4176/0702)

Documents relating to the First All-China Women's Congress held in Peiping in March 1949, including reports from Ts'ai Ch'ang, Teng Ying-ch'ao (Mme. Chou En-lai), K'ang K'o-ch'ing (Mme. Chu Teh), and Li Te-ch'üan.

798. Lo Ch'iung 羅瓊 (ed.). Fu-nü yün-tung wen-hsien 婦女運動文獻 (Documents on the Women's Movement). 2nd ed. Harbin, Tung-pei shu-tien, 1948. 114 pp. (4176/6114)

A collection of documents relating to the women's movement, including CCP resolutions, two editorials from the Liberation Daily, and writings by Liu Shao-ch'i, Chu Teh, Kao Kang, Ts'ai Ch'ang, Wu Yü-chang, Ch'en Po-ta, Marx, Engels, and Stalin. The preface is dated 1946. Several other editions of the book are also available. The one that was published (by the Hsin min-chu ch'u-pan she) in Hong Kong in 1949 has an additional article by Teng Ying-ch'ao and the resolution of the CCP in September 1948 concerning the women's movement in Communist areas.

799. Shih-tai fu-nü 時代婦女 (Modern Women). Nos. 1-3. Kalgan, July 7 - September 7, 1946. (4176.1/6244.13)

There had been a number of women's periodicals in the Communist border regions during the war (for example, Chin-Ch'a-Chi fu-nü, Pei-yüeh fu-nü, and Chi-chung fu-nü), but they were either poorly printed or mimeographed. This monthly was published to meet the postwar need for a better magazine for women. It covers various topics concerning women in the Communist regions and the "newly liberated areas." Among the members of the editorial board were Ting Ling and Ch'eng Fang-wu.

XXI. INDUSTRIAL AND TRADE POLICIES

As more and more cities were captured by the Communist forces after World War II, it had become an important task for the CCP to take control of the economy of the captured cities and to develop their industry, commerce, and finance. Almost all of the following works were published in 1949, including the collections of documents concerning industrial and trade policies in Communist-controlled cities.

800. Chung-kuo ching-chi ti kai-tsao 中國經濟的改造 (Economic Reconstruction of China). 2 vols. Hong Kong, Hsin min-chu, 1949. 117 and 168 pp. (4355/7923)

Volume I is arranged under these subject headings: (1) increase of agricultural production; (2) development of industries; (3) improvement of communications; and (4) market management and government commercial enterprises. Volume II follows the same arrangement with an additional chapter on cooperatives. Among the materials included are writings by Ch'en Po-ta, speeches of Ch'en Yün and Lü cheng-ts'ao, decisions of the Northeast Bureau of the CC of the CCP, government regulations, comments from the Tung-pei jih-pao, Jen-min jih-pao, and of the New China News Agency.

801. [Chung-kuo jen-min chieh-fang chün. P'ing-Ching ch'ien-hsien ssu-ling pu. T'ien-ching shih] chün-[shih] kuan-[chih wei-yüan] hui. Mi-shu ch'u 中國人民解放軍平津前線司令部天津市軍事管制委員會秘書處 (comp.). T'ien-ching shih chün-shih kuan-chih shih-ch'i cheng-ts'e fa-ling hui-pien 天津市軍事管制時期政策法令彙編 (A Collection of Laws, Ordinances, and Policies of Tientsin Under Military Control). Vol. I. Tientsin, Hsin-hua, 1949. 51 pp. (4292.25/5687)

Compiled by the Secretariat of the Tientsin Military Control Committee, these documents, dated December 1948 to February 1949, cover the following subjects: military discipline, public safety, communication, finance, trade, and taxes.

802. Chung-kuo kung-ch'an tang. Chung-yang chung-yüan chü. Hsüan-ch'uan pu 中國共產黨中央中原局宣傳部 (ed.). Lun kung-shang yeh cheng-ts'e 論工商業政策 (On Industrial and Commercial Policies). Honan, Hsin-hua, 1949. 80 pp. (4540/5640)

Edited by the Propaganda Department of the Chungyuan Bureau of the CC of the CCP, these twelve articles by Jen Pi-shih, Mao Tse-tung, Ch'en Po-ta, the Tung-pei jih-pao, and the New China Daily discuss the Communist industrial and commercial policy in general, in Manchuria, and in the Hopeh-Shantung-Honan Border Region.

803. Hsin min-chu chu-i kung-shang cheng-ts'e 新民主主義工商政策 (The New Democratic Industrial and Commercial Policies). 2nd and enlarged ed. Hong Kong, Hsin min-chu, 1949. 189 pp. (4540/2135a)

The regulations and documents contained in this book are arranged under seven subject headings: (1) basic economic programs, including some of Mao Tse-tung's speeches on the subject; (2) protection of city industrial and commercial policies, as seen in editorials and comments from the New China News Agency and the Tung-pei jih-pao, as well as orders issued by Lin Piao and Lo Jung-huan; (3) trade and tax regulations in Shantung and North China; (4) unified currency in Shantung, North China, and the other Communist regions in the Northwest; (5) resolutions of various industrial and commercial conferences in North China; (6) the labor movement and labor-capitalist relations; and (7) a decision of the Northeast Bureau of the CC of the CCP on former employees of government enterprises, etc.

804. Hua-shang pao 華商報 (ed.). Chieh-fang ch'ü mao-i hsü-chih 解放區貿易須知 (Trade Information from the Liberated Areas). Hong Kong, same, 1949. 43 pp. (4540/4043)

A selection of texts previously published in the Hua-shang pao in February and March of 1949, about business and trade regulations in Communist-controlled Shantung Province.

805. Hua-tung ch'ü kuo-wai mao-i kuan-li chü 華東區國外貿易管理局 (ed.). Hua-tung ch'ü kuo-wai mao-i kuan-li chan-hsing pan-fa chi fu-piao 華東區國外貿易管理暫行辦法及附表 (Provisional Regulations of International Trade in East China). n.p., same, 1949. (4546/5687)

Edited and published by the Bureau of International Trade in East China, this pamphlet consists of ten regulations and documents relating to the import and export business in East China.

806. Kuan-yü kung-shang yeh ti cheng-ts'e 關於工商業的政策 (Concerning Industrial and Commercial Policies). Hong Kong, Chung-kuo ch'u-pan, 1949. 94 pp. (4540/7923a)

    This book includes (1) an excerpt from Mao Tse-tung's speech at a cadre meeting in Shansi-Suiyuan, April 1, 1948; (2) an article by Ch'en Po-ta on labor and tax policies; (3) the New China News Agency's editorial on labor movement; (4) Liu Ning-i's article discussing the industrial policy in the liberated areas; and (5) directives of various Border Regions concerning import and export business as well as other trade regulations.

807. Yang Po 楊波 . Shan-tung chieh-fang ch'ü ti kung-shang yeh 山東解放區的工商業 (The Industry and Commerce of the Shantung Liberated Area). Shantung, Hsin-hua, 1946. 61 pp. (4432.15/4234)

    With the exception of Li Yü's report to the Shantung Industrial and Commercial Conference (June 1945) on the economic conditions of the province, the remaining eight articles (by Yang Po, Hsüeh Mu-ch'iao, and others) were written in 1946 on the textile, salt, and chemical industries, the cooperatives, and various other aspects of industry and commerce in the province.

XXII. THE COMMUNIST RULE

    Most of the works listed in this section were written by refugees in Hong Kong who had lived in or visited various Chinese cities under Communist control after 1947. With a few exceptions, they are generally written in a bitter and angry tone.

808. Chang Kuo-hsing 張國興 . Chu-mu pa-yüeh chi 竹幕八月記 (Eight Months Behind the Bamboo Curtain). [Singapore], Ta kuang-ming, [1950]. 115 pp. (4292.261/1367)

    Reports on the Communist rule for the period of April 23, 1949 (when Nanking fell to the Communists), through December 23 of the same year (when the author, a Chinese correspondent for the United Press, arrived in Hong Kong from Nanking). The first part of the book deals with the fall of Nanking and its first month under the Communist rule; the latter part is devoted to the general condition of the nation and the people's attitude toward the new regime. Part of the material was taken from articles written for the UP shortly after the author's arrival in Hong Kong.

809. Chang Ping-yen 章炳炎. Kung-ch'an tang tsen-yang chih-li P'ing Ching 共產黨怎樣治理平津 (How Did the Chinese Communists Rule Peiping and Tientsin). Taipei, Tzu-yu Chung-kuo, 1950. 65 pp. (4292.261/0419)

    First published in Hong Kong in 1949, this pamphlet reports on the first few months of Communist rule in Tientsin and Peiping. Among the subjects described are cultural and education institutions, industry and trade, courts, general living conditions, and the condition of the liberals.

810. Chang Shou-ch'u 張守初. Ch'ih-se ta-lu chen-hsiang 赤色大陸真相 (The Real Picture of the Red Mainland). Taipei, Hua-kuo, 1951. 82 pp. (4292.261/1333)

    A critical report of the early Communist rule by an eyewitness who lived for ten months under the new regime. The book describes the unhappy situation of (1) the workers, peasants, urban petty bourgeoisie, and national bourgeoisie; (2) landlords, KMT secret agents, and missionaries; and (3) KMT military and political figures who went over to the Communists. A chapter is devoted to each of the above items. The last chapter of the book deals with the Communist army.

811. Chu Ch'ang-ch'ing 朱長清. Pei-kuo ts'ang-sang chi 北國滄桑記 (Violent Changes in North China). n.p., Hsin Chung-kuo, 1949. 24 pp. (2992/2973)

    The author recounts his bitter experiences in Peiping during the first few months of the Communist rule in 1949.

812. Ch'u-san-hu 楚三戶 (pseud.). T'ien-liang chien-hou 天亮前後 (Before and After Dawn). Kowloon, Tzu-yu, 1950. 83 pp. (4292.261/4813)

   Written by a Hunanese whose father was a member of the prominent local gentry and of the National Assembly, this personal account describes the author's life in Hunan and Kwangsi before and after the regions fell into Communist hands. Politically, the author was apparently associated with the Hunanese faction whose power had been waning since the rise of Chiang Kai-shek in the 1920's. The book provides an interesting glimpse of the attitudes and activities of Ch'eng Ch'ien (Governor of Hunan) and T'ang Sheng-chih.

813. Chung-pao she 忠報社 (ed.). Huo-min p'an-kuo chi 禍民叛國記 (A Record of Rebellion and Calamity). Hong Kong, Hai-wai, 1947. 112 pp. (4292.2/5343)

   The bulk of the book consists of reports of Communist rule in northern Kiangsu, Dairen, and Yenan as written by defected Communists, and reports by KMT journalists on Yenan after the city was captured by the Government army in 1947. It also contains two Communist documents: "An Outline of the General Plan for Underground Struggles," supposedly issued on March 12 [1947] by the Central Political Bureau after its enlarged meeting at Wayaopao; and "Present Program for the Liberated Areas," which concerns land reforms and the civil war.

814. Huang Chüeh 黃覺. Hsüeh-hsing ssu-i 血腥四邑 (The Four Bloody Districts). Hong Kong, Ya-chou, 1953. 215 pp. (4292.261/4871)

   A personal account of a defected Communist who was Chief of the Salt Bureau of Wuchou, Kwangsi, after the Communist victory. The story begins with his joining a Communist study group as a student in Canton in 1947. The narration of his underground and infiltration work in Canton before the Communist capture of the city is interesting. The book gives a rather lengthy account of Communist economic and financial policies affecting the author's own duties in Kwangtung and Kwangsi.

The author came from one of the four districts in Kwangtung to which many overseas Chinese belong. Although the book includes a brief account of life in his native district, the misleading title was probably used to attract attention in Hong Kong and abroad.

815. Huang Ming 黃明. "Chieh-fang" chung ti Chiang-nan chen-hsiang "解放"中的江南真相 (The Real Picture of the Country South of the Yangtze Under "Liberation"). Taipei, Tzu-yu Chung-kuo, 1950. 68 pp. (4292.261/4862)

A bitter personal account of life after the Communist capture of Nanchang, Kiangsi, in May 1949, to the author's escape to Canton in August of the same year, with interesting information on Communist and Nationalist political figures.

816. Huang Tao-ming 黃道明. Chieh-fang ch'ü hui-lai 解放區回來 (Return from the Liberated Area). Hong Kong, Ch'en Hsüan-hsing, 1949. 52 pp. (4292.25/4836)

A favorable report of a trip (March-May, 1949) from Canton to Peiping through the Communist area.

817. Liu Shao-t'ang 劉紹唐. Hung-se Chung-kuo ti p'an-t'u 紅色中國的叛徒 (Red China's Rebel). Taipei, Chung-hua jih-pao, 1951. 234 pp. (4292.26/7220)

The personal account of a Peking University student who participated in Communist study programs after the fall of Peiping and later worked for the Communists as a newspaperman and government functionary. His experience reveals the problems and difficulties of a non-Communist intellectual working with Party members as well as the conflict between the old and the new cadres in the Communist regime.

818. Lo Pin-sheng 羅賓蓀. Su-pei chen-hsiang 蘇北真相 (The Real Picture of North Kiangsu). n.p., Li-hsiang, 1947. 282 pp. (4292.24/6134)

A glorified picture of the Kiangsu area under Communist control, but with useful references to the New Fourth Army, land reform, journalism, culture, and the workers' and peasants' movements.

819. Nieh Keng-sheng 聶更生. Hsi-tzu hu-pien hua Chung-kung 西子湖邊話中共 (On the Chinese Communists at West Lake). Kowloon, Tzu-yu, 1951. 38 pp. (4292.261/1412)

A fragmentary account of Hangchou, Chekiang, under Communist rule by a writer who remained there for twenty months after the city had fallen into Communist hands.

820. P'ei Yu-p'eng 裴有朋. Wo Lai tzu Tung-pei nu-kung ying 我來自東北奴工營 (I Came from a Slave Labor Camp in Manchuria). Hong Kong, Ya-chou, 1954. 203 pp. (4292.25/1346)

Reminiscences of the secretary-general of the KMT at Yingkou, who became a prisoner when the port fell to the Chinese Communists in February 1948. The story begins with his arrest by Chinese Communists, and about one-third of the book is devoted to his subjection to "labor reform" before his escape from the mainland.

821. Hsiao-hsiao 蕭蕭 (pseud.). Ts'ung t'ieh-mu li ch'u-lai 從鐵幕裡出來 (Escape from the Iron Curtain). Kowloon, Tzu-lu, 1953. 60 pp. (4292.26/4242)

An account of a KMT army officer from the time he was subjected to Communist indoctrination after the fall of Foochow, Fukien, in August 1949 to his escape to Hong Kong via Hunan and Canton.

822. Tai-wan sheng hsin-wen ch'u 台灣省新聞處 (comp.). T'ieh-mu hou ti Chung-kuo 鐵幕後的中國 (China Behind the Iron Curtain). Taipei, same, 1950. 167 pp. (4292.261/4391)

Compiled and published by the Information Office of the Taiwan Provincial Government, this is a collection of newspaper articles of uneven quality, falling into five categories: (1) eyewitness accounts; (2) the real picture of Communist rule; (3) victims; (4) analyses of the CCP; and (5) the disillusionment of the people with the new regime. Many of the writings are from KMT sources.

823. Ting Tso-shao 丁作韶. Chieh-ch'uan kung-ch'an tang ti nei-mu 揭穿共產黨的內幕 (Uncover the Black Screen of the Chinese Communist Party). [Taipei?], Hsin Chung-kuo wen-hua, 1949. 18 pp. (4292.25/1220)

A glossary of terms often used by the Chinese Communists -- such as people, liberation, turnover, democracy, freedom, anti-imperialism--showing that the Chinese Communists do not use these terms as they are generally understood. The author, a lawyer, was a member of Tientsin Assembly and one of the representatives who negotiated for the "peaceful surrender" of Tientsin when the city was being besieged by Communist forces.

824. _____. Kung-ch'an tang ti pa-hsi 共產黨的把戲 (The Communist Party Juggle). Taipei, Hsin Chung-kuo wen-hua, 1949. 20 pp. (4292.26/1220)

A keen observation of the military, financial, economic, educational, and cultural policies of the CCP.

825. _____. T'ieh-mu hou ti Hua-pei 鐵幕後的華北 (North China Behind the Iron Curtain). [Taipei?], Hsin Chung-kuo wen-hua, 1949. 22 pp. (4292.261/1220)

A critical report of Communist rule in Peiping and Tientsin.

826. Tung Shih-chin 董時進. Kung-ch'ü hui-i 共區回憶 (Reminiscences of Communist Rule). Kowloon, Tzu-yu, 1951. 143 pp. (4292.261/4163)

Known as Shih-tsin Tung in this country, the author was one of the many educated Chinese who thought they could get along under the new Communist regime in 1949. After 18 months, during which time he was able to travel quite widely, he was disillusioned and fled to Hong Kong. This book includes firsthand information and the author's observation of life in many parts of the country. Among the subjects discussed are freedom, taxes, propaganda, land reform, the economic situation, and the intelligentsia under Communist rule.

827. _____. Kung-ch'ü hui-i hsü-p'ien 共區回憶續篇 (Reminiscences of Communist Rule: A Supplement). Kowloon, Tzu-yu, 1952. 58 pp. (4292.261/4163.1)

This pamphlet consists of three articles on the following subjects: the anti-American campaign, the causes of the CCP victory, and how to understand the real nature of the CCP.

828. Wang Ching-yüan 王靜遠. Nan-pen chi 南奔記 (Flight to the South). 2nd ed. Taipei, Tzu-yu Chung-kuo, 1950. 28 pp. (4292.261/1153)

Random notes on Peiping before and after the fall of the city to the Communists. The author left Peiping for Nanking and Shanghai on March 17, 1949. His impressions of Nanking and Shanghai during the turbulent times are vividly recorded.

829. Yang Chih 楊志. Chieh-fang ch'ü yin-hsiang chi 解放區印象記 (Impression of the Liberated Area). n.p., Lien-ho, [1949]. 44 pp. (4292.25/4243)

Eight articles by Chinese and foreign writers giving their impressions of Manchuria, Peiping, the Honan-Anhwei Border Region, and other Communist-controlled areas.

830. Yang Tun-san 楊敦三. Hua-chung t'ieh-mu 華中鐵幕 (Central China Behind the Iron Curtain). Taipei, Min-chu, 1950. 109 pp. (4292.26/4201)

Written by a middle school principal who was also the President of the Wuchang Assembly, this is an account of the author's life under Communist rule between May 1949, when Wuhan fell to Communists, and July of the same year, when he escaped from Wuchang.

XXIII. THE YEAR OF TRIUMPH

By January 1949 the Communist military victory had become a certainty as a result of three major campaigns. After the Liaohsi-Shenyang (Mukden) Campaign (September 12 - November 2, 1948), the whole of the Northeast Provinces (Manchuria) fell into Communist hands. With the conclusion of the Huai-Hai Campaign near Hsuchow in Kiangsu from November 7, 1948 to January 10, 1949, Nanking and Shanghai were exposed to Communist attack. At about the same time (December 5, 1948 - January 31, 1949), the Tientsin and Peiping Campaign resulted in the fall of Tientsin on January 15 and the "peaceful liberation" of Peiping on January 31. Just before the fall of Peiping, Chiang Kai-shek announced his "retirement." Acting President Li Tsung-jen came out with an appeal for peace, but was unable to accept the Communist terms. On April 23, Nanking fell, followed by Shanghai on May 27. In the course of the year, the major cities were captured one by one by the Communist forces. On October 1 the Central People's Government of the People's Republic of China was founded, with Peiping (renamed Peking) as the capital.

The Central People's Government was elected by the People's Political Consultative Conference, which convened on September 21-30, 1949 and adopted a number of organic laws for the new regime. Because they are actually more relevant to the post-1949 period, no works on the Conference are listed here. Included in this section are periodicals, most of them published in 1949, containing articles reflecting the chaotic and shifting political situation in China in that year of triumph for the Chinese Communist Party.

831. Chang Han-sai 張寒塞 (ed.). Kuang-ming chao-yao cho jen-min ti ch'eng-shih 光明照耀着人民的城市 (People's Cities Shining Brightly). n.p., Pei-fang ch'u-pan, 1949. 32 pp. (4292.9/133.96)

Among the newspaper dispatches collected in this book are reports of the occupation of Mukden, Tsinan, and Kaifeng by the Communist armies.

832. Cheng-chih hsin-wen 政治新聞 (Political News). Vol. I, Nos. 4 and 6. [Shanghai?], February 21 - March 12, 1949. (2992/1307)

This magazine carries articles mainly concerned with the current activities of KMT military and political figures. Full of rumors and gossip.

833. Cheng-i 正義 (Righteousness). No. 11. Shanghai, March 25, 1949. (2992/1185)

Contains pro-KMT articles on the current political and military situation.

834. Chin-jih hsin-wen 今日新聞 (Today's News). Vol. I, No. 3. Nanking, March 10, 1949. (2992/8607)

Political gossip about the peace negotiations and the activities of the leaders in the National Government.

835. Ch'üan-wei 權威 (The Authority). Nos. 1-9. Canton, March 4 - May 5, 1949. (9200/4150)

A weekly of political gossip about the National Government and its leaders during the turbulent times of 1949.

836. Chün-jen hun 軍人魂 (The Souls of the Soldiers). Nos. 1, 3, and 4. Canton, June 1 - August 25, 1949. (2992/3581)

A comprehensive periodical covering politics, economics, culture, military affairs, etc., with special emphasis on KMT political thought and military education. Among the contributors are Chiang Kai-shek, Li Tsung-jen, Ho Ying-ch'in, and Yen Hsi-shan.

837. Ch'ün-li ch'u-pan she 羣力出版社 (ed.). Cheng-ch'ü chen-cheng ti min-chu ti ho-p'ing 爭取真正的民主的和平 (Strife for Genuine and Democratic Peace). n.p., same, 1949. 35 pp. (2992/1422)

　　This pamphlet contains: (1) Mao Tse-tung's statement of January 14, 1949, making eight demands as conditions for peace; (2) the statement made by Li Chi-shen and 55 other "liberal and democratic persons" (January 22) on the current situation; and (3) several articles discussing the peace talks between Communist authorities and the National Government, the latter being led by Li Tsung-jen.

838. Ch'ün-yen 羣言 (Mass Opinion). No. 34. n.p., March 12, 1949. (2992/1506)

　　Most of the articles in this weekly deal with peace talks and the policies of the National Government.

839. Chung-kung nei-mu 中共內幕 (Inside the Chinese Communist Party). No. 2. n.p., April 1, 1949.

　　An Anti-Communist semi-monthly with articles on current Communist activities and factions analysis.

840. Chung-kuo cheng-chih nei-mu 中國政治內幕 (Inside Stories of Chinese Politics). Vol. I, No. 6. Tientsin, November 10, 1948. (2992/5613)

　　Almost all the articles in this issue are political gossip about the National Government and its high officials.

841. Chung-kuo hsin-wen 中國新聞 ("The Chinese News"). Vol. I, No. 1 - Vol. VI, No. 12. Nanking and Canton, July 7, 1947 - December 26, 1949. (9200/5607)

A non-partisan magazine carrying "inside information" (gossip) on the National Government and its high officials. Each volume consists of twelve issues. It was published in Canton after issue Volume IV, No. 7; the Hoover Library has an incomplete file of the post-1949 issues published in Hong Kong and Taiwan.

842. Chung-liu 中流 (Midstream). No. 101/102. Chengtu, October 20, 1949. (2992/5300)

A non-Communist magazine devoted to political gossip. This issue contains a story on Ch'en Shao-yü's leadership in the CCP.

843. Feng-hsing 風行 (Wide Circulation). Nos. 12-13. Canton, October 2 - October 9, 1949. (2992/7122)

The articles in this magazine deal almost exclusively with the political situation in Canton at the time of the Communist victory.

844. Hai-ch'ao chou-pao 海潮週報 (The Tide). Nos. 1 and 8. [Shanghai], January 21 - March 18, 1949. (9200/3334.23)

These two issues of this weekly carry political gossip, articles on the KMT-CCP negotiations, and articles on the activities of high officials of the National Government at the time.

845. Hsin hsi-wang 新希望 ("The New Hope Weekly"). Nos. 5-7, 17, 28, and 46. Taipei, March 14, 1949 - January 7, 1950. (9200/0403)

Edited by I Chün-tso, this weekly carries articles mainly on current domestic politics and the activities of high National Government officials. Issue No. 5 contains an article by the magazine's own special correspondent on Yang Sen's visit to Yang Fu-ch'eng. It is one of the very few reports on the life of Yang Fu-ch'eng, who had been placed under house arrest after the "Sian Incident."

846. Hsin shih-tai 新時代 (The New Times). Vol. I, No. 2. Shanghai, March 15, 1949. (2992/0262)

A semimonthly with articles on the KMT-CCP peace negotiations, this magazine is hostile to the CCP and the "Third Force." This issue includes an article attacking Liang Sou-ming.

847. Hsin-wen shih-chieh 新聞世界 (The News World). Nos. 11, 13-37, 39-52/53, 55, 58, 60, and 63-71. Canton and Hong Kong, February 20, 1949 - September 22, 1951. (4200/0746)

A semimonthly full of current political gossip. First published in August 1948.

848. Hsin-wen t'ien-hsia 新聞天下 (The News World). Nos. 7-8. Chengtu, October 9-23, 1949. (2992/0711)

A bimonthly first published in July 1949. These two issues carry articles on political figures and events of the last days of the Kuomintang regime on the mainland.

849. Hsin-wen tsa-chih 新聞雜誌 (The News Magazine). New Vol. I, Nos. 10-12; Vol. II, Nos. 1, 5, 6, and 12. Nanking and Shanghai, September 25, 1948 - March 20, 1949. (9200/0700)

First published in December 1945, most of the articles published in this semimonthly are political gossip, describing the moves and activities of the National Government as well as its leaders. It has Hong Kong and Peiping editions.

850. Hua-chung wen-hui 華中文匯 (A Collection of Writings from the Central China Press). Nos. 2, 7, and 8. [Hankow], June 15 - November 15, 1949. (4292.01/4507)

A collection of writings reprinted from the Tung-pei jih-pao, the Nanking New China Daily, the Peiping Chieh-fang pao (to be distinguished from the Liberation Daily), and many others. The reprints, however, do not appear to be very useful or valuable, with perhaps the exception of an editorial from the Tung-pei jih-pao on the shift of party work from villages to cities, and of Liu Po-ch'eng's talk at a symposium of workers' representatives in Nanking.

851. Jen-min jih-pao hao-wai 人民日報號外 (The People's Daily: Extra). Peiping, April 21, 1949. (2992/8764)

On the grounds that the delegation of the National Government refused to sign the peace agreement, Mao Tse-tung, in his capacity as the Chairman of the Chinese People's Revolutionary Military Council, and Chu Teh, in the name of the Commander-in-Chief of the Chinese People's Liberation Army, jointly ordered the Communist commanders and forces to pursue the goal of "liberating" the whole nation. This special issue of the People's Daily contains the text of this order.

852. Kung-p'ing pao 公平報 (Justice). New Nos. 1-12, 39, 40, and 47. Hong Kong, March 1947 - May 10, 1949. (2992/8314)

This magazine was first published in April 1941. The first 12 issues were published every ten days; the remaining available issues are monthly publications. Its articles are primarily political gossip about the policies of the National Government, KMT-CCP relations, current events, and the Democratic League.

853. Li-ming ti hao-chio 黎明的號角 (A Trumpet at Dawn). n.p., n. pub., n.d. 21 pp. (2992/2626)

These writings appear to be collected from Communist publications written in the spring of 1949. They attacked the

KMT government, analyzed the current political situation, and discussed the eight-point peace conditions demanded by Mao Tse-tung.

854. Liang Sheng-chün 梁升俊. Chiang-Li tou-cheng nei-mu 蔣李鬥爭內幕 (The Inside Story of the Struggle Between Chiang Kai-shek and Li Tsung-jen). Hong Kong, Ya-lien, 1954. (2970/3922)

    Published originally serialized in the Hong Kong Chen-pao, this book was written by Li Tsung-jen's confidential secretary, who was a journalist in World War II. It is one of the few excellent Chinese books in recent years that reveal politics in the highest political circles. It gives an interesting account of internal friction in the National Government from January 1949 (when Chiang Kai-shek stepped down from power and Li Tsung-jen became the Acting President) through the end of the year when Li came to the United States. It includes an interesting account of Li's call on President Truman at the White House early in 1950. It furnishes valuable information about peace negotiations with the Communists conducted by Li Tsung-jen. As could be expected, the author was critical of Chiang's leadership and sympathetic toward Li's efforts.

855. Shang-hai t'e-hsieh 上海特寫 (The Shanghai Special). No. 2. Shanghai, March 19, 1949. (9200/3223)

    This magazine carries articles on current political events and figures, especially those of the National Government.

856. Shih-shih hsin-wen 時事新聞 (The News). Nos. 19 and 37. Canton and Hong Kong, June 1, 1949 - January 16, 1950. (9200/6507)

    A ten-day periodical containing mainly articles of political gossip.

857. Shih-tai ch'u-pan she 時代出版社 (ed.). Ho-t'an hui ch'eng kung ma 和談會成功嗎 (Will the Peace Negotiations Succeed?). n.p., same, 1949. 48 pp. (2992/6222)

   An excellent discussion of the forthcoming KMT-CCP peace talks to be held in Peiping in April 1949 and an examination of previous peace negotiations. The articles are well written, but their authorship is not given.

858. Ta-chung hsin-wen 大眾新聞 (Mass News). Vol. II, No. 4. Nanking, March 18, 1949. (2992/4607.40)

   This semimonthly issue carries articles on the KMT-CCP peace talks, the CCP propaganda and newspapers, and the New Democratic Youth League. This is not a Communist magazine.

859. Ta-ti hsin-wen 大地新聞 (The World News). Vol. I, No. 11. Hanchung, October 25, 1949. (2992/4407)

   The articles published in this semimonthly issue are mainly concerned with the current political and military situation; included are writings about the famous Ma families of the Northwest during the Communist advance to that part of the country.

860. Yeh Ch'ing 葉青 [pseud. of Jen Cho-hsüan 任卓宣]. Kung-ch'an tang wen-t'i 共產黨問題 (The Communist Problem). Nanking, Hsin Chung-kuo, 1949. 28 pp. (2992/2123.40)

   In discussing the Communist problem posed for the National Government, the author, a noted KMT theorist, here maintains that the problem can only be solved by force.

861. Yin-shih 隱士 (pseud.). Li-Chiang kuan-hsi yü Chung-kuo 李蔣關係與中國 (Li Tsung-jen, Chiang Kai-shek, and China). Kowloon, Tzu-yu, 1954. 139 pp. (2970/7341)

A sympathetic account of Li Tsung-jen's career, with special emphasis on his relations with Chiang Kai-shek. The last four chapters deal with the 1937-49 period.

862. Yü-chou hsin-wen 宇宙新聞 (World News). No. 5. Chengtu, October 30, 1949. (2992/3307)

This anti-Communist magazine contains articles dealing with the last struggles of the National Government in southwestern China and the current activities of various minor political parties in Peiping.

863. Yü-lun 輿論 (Public Opinion). Vol. II, No. 6. Shanghai, March 16, 1949. (2992/7802)

This semimonthly is not a Communist publication, nor does it appear to be a KMT organ. The articles contained in this issue touch upon such topics as current politics in the National Government, peace negotiations, and trade in the "liberated areas."

APPENDIX I

A List of Personal, Corporate, and Geographical Names Appearing in the Annotations

This list provides Chinese characters for the personal, geographical, and institutional names occurring in the annotations, as well as for newspaper and periodical titles therein. Different names of one person are also listed alphabetically.

Also included here are obscure place names, including the new geographical names of the publishers' locations mentioned in the entries. As a rule, all diacritical marks and hyphens are omitted in geographical names. Throughout the text I have frequently used the English names of some organizations and newspapers; in some cases their Chinese characters are given here without romanizations.

Ai Ch'ing 艾青
Ai Ssu-ch'i 艾思奇
All-China Students' Association 中華全國學生聯合會
Association for Promoting Constitutional Government 中國民主促進會
Association for Promoting Democracy 憲政促進會
Association for the Anti-Japanese War Studies 抗日戰爭研究會
Association for the Study of Anarchism 安那其主義學會

Central Cadre Committee of the Third Party of China 中國第三黨中央幹部會
Central Cadre Educational Department 中央幹部教育部
Central News Agency 中央通訊社
Chang Chih-jang 張志讓
Chang Chün-mai (Carsun Chang) 張君勱
Chang Han-fu 章漢夫
Chang Hao 張浩
Chang Hsi-jo 張奚若
Chang Hsin-fu 張莘夫
Chang Ju-hsin 張如心
Chang Hsüeh-liang 張學良
Chang Hsüeh-shih 張學詩
Chang Kia-ngau (Chang Chia-ao) 張嘉璈
Chang Kuo-ch'üan 張國權
Chang Kuo-t'ao 張國燾
Chang Lan 張瀾
Chang Mu-t'ao 張慕陶

Chang Nai-ch'i 章乃器
Chang Po-chün 章伯鈞
Chang Shen-fu 張申府
Chang Tan 張膽
Chang Ting-ch'eng 張鼎承
Chang Tung-sun 張東蓀
Chang Wen-t'ien 張聞天
Changchun 長春
Chaoan (in Kwangtung) 潮安
Chaoyang College of Law (Chaoyang University) 朝陽學院 (朝陽大學)
Chen-li 真理
Chen-pao 真報
Ch'en Ch'ang-hao 陳昌浩
Ch'en Chia-k'ang 陳家康
Ch'en Chin-k'un 陳瑾昆
Ch'en I. See Ch'en Yi.
Ch'en Po-ta 陳伯達
Ch'en Shao-yü 陳紹禹
Ch'en Tu-hsiu 陳獨秀
Ch'en Yi (Ch'en I) 陳毅
Ch'en Yün 陳雲
Cheng Chen-to 鄭振鐸
Ch'eng Ch'ien 程潛
Ch'eng Fang-wu 成仿吾
Chengteh 承德
Chi-chung fu-nü 冀中婦女
Chi Yün-lung 紀雲龍
Chiamussu 佳木斯
Chiang Nan-hsiang 蔣南翔
Ch'iao Kuan-hua 喬冠華
Ch'iao Mu 喬木
Ch'iao-sheng pao 僑聲報
Chiaochangkou Incident 較場口事件
Chiaotung (in Shantung) 膠東
Chiaotung Cultural Association 膠東文協
Chieh-fang pao 解放報
Chieh-fang she 解放社
Ch'ien-feng pao 前鋒報
Ch'ien-wei pao 前衛報
Chih Kung Tang 致公黨
Chin-Ch'a-Chi fu-nü 晉察冀婦女
Chin-Ch'a-Chi jih-pao 晉察冀日報
Chin Chün-chih 金君致
Chin Chung-hua 金仲華
Chin-Sui jih-pao 晉綏日報

Ch'in Pang-hsien 秦邦憲
Chinese Association for Civil Rights 中國國際人權保障會
Chinese Liberation Action Committee (Known as the Third Party) 中華民族解放行動委員會
Chinese Revolutionary League 中華民族革命同盟
Ch'ing-chih 青之
Ch'ing-nien wen-hua 青年文化
Chinghsien (in Anhwei) 涇縣
Chinhua (in Chekiang) 金華
Chitung 冀東
Chou Chien-jen 周建人
Chou En-lai 周恩來
Chou Hsin-min 周新民
Chou Li-po 周立波
Chou Pao-chung 周保中
Chow Ching-wen (Chou Ch'ing-wen) 周鯨文
Chu Hsüeh-fan 朱學範
Chu Teh (Chu Te) 朱德
Ch'u An-p'ing 儲安平
Chuchiang (in Kwangtung) 曲江
Chün-cheng chou-pao 軍政週報
Ch'ün-sheng pao 群聲報
Chung Ho Tang 中和黨
Chung-hua jih-pao 中華日報
Chung-hua min-tsu tzu-yu lien-meng 中華民族自由聯盟
Chung-kuo ch'ing-nien 中國青年
Chung-kuo jen-min chieh-fang chan-cheng ho hsin Chung-kuo wu-nien chien-shih 中國人民解放戰爭和新中國五年簡史
Chung-kuo lao-tung nien-chien 中國勞動年鑑
Chungyuan 中原

Democratic Constitutionalist Party 中國民主憲政黨
Democratic League 中國民主同盟
Democratic National Reconstruction Association 民主建國會
Democratic Reconstruction Army 民主建國軍
Democratic-Socialist Party 民社黨 (中國民主社會黨)

Fan Ch'ang-chiang 范長江
Fan Wen-lan 范文瀾
Fang Fang 方方
Fei Hsiao-t'ung 費孝通
Feng Chung-yün 馮仲雲
Feng Pai-chü 馮白駒
Feng Wen-pin 馮文彬

Feng Yü-hsiang 馮玉祥
Fuyu 扶餘

Hangchou 杭州
Hantan (in Shantung) 邯鄲
Hengyang 衡陽
Ho Lung 賀龍
Ho-p'ing jih-pao 和平日報
Ho Sung 何松
Ho Ying-ch'in 何應欽
Ho Yung-chi 何永佶
Hsi-pei k'ang-Jih chün-cheng ta-hsüeh 西北抗日軍政大學
Hsi-tung 希東
Hsia Yen 夏衍
Hsiang Ying 項英
Hsiao Ching-kuang 蕭勁光
Hsiao Hsiang-jung 蕭向榮
Hsiao Hua 蕭華
Hsiao K'o 蕭克
Hsiao San 蕭三
Hsin chung-hua pao 新中華報
Hsin-min pao 新民報
Hsinghsien (in Shansi) 興縣
Hsipei (Northwest China) 西北
Hsü Te-yen 許德衍
Hsü T'e-li 徐特立
Hsuanhuatien 宣化店
Hsüeh Mu-ch'iao 薛暮橋
Hu Ch'iao-mu 胡喬木
Hu Sheng 胡繩
Hu Shou-yü 胡守愚
Hu Yü-chih 胡愈之
Hua Kang 華崗
Huachung (Central China) 華中
Huaipei 淮北
Huan Hsiang 宦鄉
Huang-chia-ts'un 黃家村
Huang Wen-chieh 黃文杰
Huang Yen-p'ei 黃炎培
Huapei (North China) 華北
Huatung (East China) 華東

I Chün-tso 易君左
I-meng tao-pao 沂蒙導報

Jao Sou-shih 饒漱石
Jen Pi-shih 任弼時
Joint Office of the Chinese Youth National Salvation Organizations
中華青年救國團體聯合辦事處
Jukao (in Kiangsu) 如皋

K'ai Feng 凱豐
Kalgan (Changchiakou) 張家口
K'ang-chan chou-pao 抗戰週報
K'ang-chan jih-pao 抗戰日報
K'ang K'o-ch'ing 康克清
K'ang Sheng 康生
K'ang-ti pao 抗敵報
Kao Chi 高集
Kao Kang 高崗
Kao Tzu-li 高自立
Kuan Hsiang-ying 關向應
Kuang-ming jih-pao 光明日報
Kung-ch'an tang jen 共產黨人
Kung-ch'an tang-yüan 共產黨員
Kung-p'ing pao 公評報
Kuo Hua-jo 郭化若
Kuo-min jih-pao 國民日報
Kuo Mo-jo 郭沫若
Kuohsien (in Shansi) 崞縣

Lei-feng 雷風
Li Chao-lin 李兆麟
Li Fu-ch'un 李富春
Li Fu-jen 李敷仁
Li Hsien-nien 李先念
Li Kung-p'u 李公樸
Li Li-san 李立三
Li Lin 李林
Li-lun yü hsien-shih ts'ung-k'an 理論與現實叢刊
Li Ta-ming 李大明
Li Te-ch'üan 李德全
Li Tsung-jen 李宗仁
Li Wei-han 李維漢
Li Yü 黎玉

Liang Jo-ch'en 梁若塵
Liang-p'ing 亮平
Liang Sou-ming 梁漱溟
Liao Ch'en-yün 廖陳雲（廖程雲）
Liao Ch'eng-chih 廖承志
Liaopei 遼北
Liao Yao-hsiang 廖耀湘
Liaotung 遼東
Liberation Daily (Chieh-fang jih-pao) 解放日報
Licheng (in Shansi) 黎城
Lin-i (in Shantung) 臨沂
Lin Piao 林彪
Lin Po-ch'ü 林伯渠
Lin Tsu-han 林祖涵
Lin Yü-ying 林毓英
Lishan 禮山
Liu I 劉逸
Liu Ning-i 劉寧一
Liu Po-ch'eng 劉伯承
Liu Shao-ch'i 劉少奇
Liu Shih 柳湜
Liu Ssu-mu 劉思慕
Liu Ya-lou 劉亞樓
Liu Ya-tzu 柳亞子
Lo Fu 洛甫
Lo Jui-ch'ing 羅瑞卿
Lo Jung-huan 羅榮桓
Lo Lung-chi 羅隆基
Lo Mai 羅邁
Lo Ping-hui 羅炳輝
Lo Teng-hsien 羅登賢
Lu I 陸詒
Lu Ting-i 陸定一
Lü Cheng-ts'ao 呂正操
Lunan 莒南

Ma Hsü-lun 馬叙倫
Ma Yin-ch'u 馬寅初
Mai-chin pao 邁進報
Mao Tse-tung 毛澤東
Mao Tun 茅盾
Min-pen she 民本社
Min-tsu ch'u-pan she 民族出版社

Nan-fang jih-pao 南方日報
National Salvation Association 救國會
National Social Party 國社黨（中國國家社會黨）
New China Daily (Hsin-hua jih-pao) 新華日報
New China News Agency (Hsin-hua she) 新華社
Nieh Jung-chen 聶榮臻
North University 北方大學
Nosaka Sanzo 野板參三
Nung-min shih i-chia 農民是一家

Okano Susuma 岡野進

Pa-lu chün chün-cheng tsa-chih 八路軍軍政雜誌
Pai Ch'ung-hsi 白崇禧
P'an Kuang-tan 潘光旦
P'an Tzu-nien 潘梓年
Peasants' and Workers' Democratic Party 農工民主黨
Pei-yüeh fu-nü 北嶽婦女
P'eng Chen 彭真
P'eng Te-huai 彭德懷
P'eng Tse-min 彭澤民
People's Political Council 國民參政會
Pinhai 濱海
Pingshan 平山
Po Ku 博古
Pohai 渤海
Political Study Clique 政學系
Production Campaign Series 生產運動小叢書

Research School of Revolutionary Practice 革命實踐研究院
Revolutionary Committee of the Kuomintang 中國國民黨革命委員會
Rural Reconstruction Group 鄉村建設派

Sa Ch'ien-li 沙千里
Sa K'ung-liao 薩空了
Sao-tang pao 掃蕩報
September 3 Society 九三學社
Shang-wu jih-pao 商務日報
Shanghai Vocational Association for National Salvation 上海市職業界救亡協會
She-hui k'o-hsüeh chi-ch'u chiao-ch'eng 社會科學基礎教程
Shehsien 涉縣

Shen Chih-yüan 沈志遠
Shen Chün-ju 沈鈞儒
Shen-Kan-Ning pien-ch'ü ti-erh chieh ts'an-i hui ti-erh tzu ta-hui ts'o-lu 陝甘寧邊區第二屆參議會第二次大會撮錄
Shen-Kan-Ning pien-ch'ü ti-san chieh ts'an-i hui ti-i tzu ta-hui hui-k'an 陝甘寧邊區第三屆參議會第一次大會彙刊
Shen Yün-lun 沈雲龍
Sheng-huo chih-shih 生活知識
Sheng-huo pao 生活報
Sheng-huo shu-tien 生活書店
Shih-chieh jih-pao 世界日報
Shih Fu-liang 施復亮
Shih Liang 史良
Shih-tai chou-pao 時代週報
Shihchiachuang 石家莊
Suchung 蘇中
Suiteh 綏德
Sun Pao-i 孫寶毅
Sunan 蘇南
Sung Yün-pin 宋雲彬

Ta-chung jih-pao 大眾日報
Ta-kang pao 大剛報
Ta Kung Pao 大公報
Ta-p'ing 達平
Taihang Area 太行區
Taiwan Democratic Self-Government League 台灣自治同盟
Tan Kah Kee (Ch'en Chia-keng) 陳嘉庚
T'an Cheng 譚政
T'ang Sheng-chih 唐生智
T'ao Hsing-chih 陶行知
T'ao Shang-hsing 陶尚行
Teng Ch'u-min 鄧初民
Teng Fa 鄧發
Teng Hsiao-p'ing 鄧小平
Teng Ying-ch'ao 鄧穎超
Third Party 第三黨
Ti Chao-pai 狄超白
Ti-ssu yeh-chan chün 第四野戰軍
T'ien Han 田漢
Tienshui Field Headquarters 天水行營
Ting Ling 丁玲
Tou-cheng sheng-huo 鬥爭生活
Ts'ai Ch'ang 蔡暢
Ts'ai Ho-sen 蔡和森

Tseng Chao-lun 曾昭掄
Tseng Ch'i 曾琦
Tsitsihar 齊齊哈爾
Tso Ch'üan 左權
Tso Shun-sheng 左舜生
Tsou T'ao-fen 鄒韜奮
Tung-pei ch'ing-nien 東北青年
"Tung-pei feng-yün" 東北風雲
Tung-pei jih-pao 東北日報
Tung Pi-wu 董必武
Tzu-wei pao 自衛報

United Kwantung Democratic Youth Association 關東民主青年聯合會總會
United North China University 華北聯合大學
United Northwest Youth National Salvation Association 西北青年救國聯合會

Vocational Education Group 中華職業教育社(派)

Wang Chen 王震
Wang Chia-hsiang 王稼祥
Wang Ching-wei 汪精衛
Wang Han-min 王漢民
Wang Jo-fei 王若飛
Wang Kung-tu 王公度
Wang Ming 王明
Wang Shao-t'ung 王少桐
Wang Shih-wei 王實味
Wang Shou-tao 王首道
Wang Tsao-shih 王造時
Wang Yün-sheng 王芸生
Wayaopao 瓦窰堡
Weihsien 威縣
Wen-hui pao 文匯報
Wen I-to 聞一多
Wenteng (in Shantung) 文登
Wu Hsien-tzu 伍憲子
Wu Tsao-ch'ih 伍藻池
Wu Yü-chang 吳玉章
Wuan 武安
Wuchou 梧州

Yang Ching-yü 楊靖宇
Yang Fu-ch'eng 楊虎城
Yang Kang 楊剛
Yang Shang-k'un 楊尚昆
Yang Sung 楊松
Yang Tsao (pseud. of Yang Ch'ao) 羊棗 (楊潮)
Yang Wei-yü 楊衛玉
Yeh Chien-ying 葉劍英
Yeh Hsi-shan 閻錫山
Yeh pai-ho-hua 野百合花
Yeh T'ing 葉挺
Yen Pao-han 閻寶航
Yingkou 營口
Youth Party 中國青年黨
Yü-hsi jih-pao 豫西日報
Yü Huai 于懷
Yü Ta-fu 郁達夫

APPENDIX II

List of Publishers

The following is a list of publishers referred to in this volume. It is alphabetically arranged by the abbreviations used in the text; the abbreviations are followed by full names in romanization and in Chinese characters. When the publisher and the editor (or author) are the same, the word "same" is given for the publisher in the text. Chinese characters for obscure or newly named places of publication are given in Appendix I.

Chahar Chiao-yü t'ing ---- Ch'a-ha-erh sheng-cheng-fu chiao-yü t'ing 察哈爾省政府教育廳
Chan-shih ---- Chan-shih ch'u-pan she 戰時出版社
Chan-tou ---- Chan-tou ch'ing-nien she 戰鬥青年社
Chen-hua ---- Chen-hua ch'u-pan she 鎮華出版社
Chen-li ---- Chen-li she 真理社
Cheng-i ---- Cheng-i pien-i she 正義編譯社
Cheng-kung ---- Cheng-kung kan-pu hsüeh-hsiao 政工幹部學校
Cheng-lun ---- Cheng-lun ch'u-pan she 正論出版社
Cheng-pao ---- Cheng-pao she 正報社
Chi-Lu-Yü ---- Chi-Lu-Yü shu-tien 冀魯豫書店
Chi-na ---- Chi-na ch'u-pan she 集納出版社
Chi-nan ---- Chi-nan shu-tien 冀南書店
Chieh-fang ---- Chieh-fang she 解放社
Chien-kuo ---- Chien-kuo shu-she 建國書社
Chien-kuo shu-tien 建國書店
Chih-yüan ---- Chih-yüan shu-chü 智源書局
Chin-Ch'a-Chi ---- Chin-Ch'a-Chi jih-pao she 晉察冀日報社
Chin-jih ---- Chin-jih ch'u-pan she 今日出版社
Chin-pu ---- Chin-pu ch'u-pan she 進步出版社
Chin-Sui ---- Chung-kung Chin-Sui fen-chü 中共晉綏分局
Ch'ing-nien ---- Ch'ing-nien ch'u-pan she 青年出版社
Ch'iu-chih ---- Ch'iu-chih ch'u-pan she 求智出版社
Ch'iu-shih ---- Ch'iu-shih ch'u-pan she 求是出版社
Ch'uang-k'en ---- Ch'uang-k'en ch'u-pan she 創墾出版社
Ch'un-ch'iu ---- Ch'un-ch'iu shu-tien 春秋書店
Ch'ün-chung ---- Ch'ün-chung lien-ho ch'u-pan she 群眾聯合出版社
Ch'ün-chung ch'u-pan ---- Ch'ün-chung ch'u-pan she 群眾出版社
Ch'ün-chung jih-pao ---- Ch'ün-chung jih-pao she 群眾日報社
Ch'ün-li ---- Ch'ün-li shu-tien 群力書店
Chung-chih ---- Chung-chih shu-chü 眾志書局
Chung-chung ---- Chung-chung ch'u-pan she 中中出版社

Chung-hsin ---- Chung-hsin ch'u-pan she 中心出版社
Chung-hua jih-pao ---- Chung-hua jih-pao ts'ung-shu ch'u-pan wei-yüan hui 中華日報叢書出版委員會
Chung-kuo ch'ing-nien ---- Chung-kuo ch'ing-nien ch'u-pan she 中國青年出版社
Chung-kuo ch'u-pan ---- Chung-kuo ch'u-pan she 中國出版社
Chung-kuo fu-nü ---- Chung-kuo fu-nü she 中國婦女社
Chung-kuo jen-min ---- Chung-kuo jen-min chieh-fang chün tung-pei chün-ch'ü cheng-chih pu hsüan-ch'uan pu 中國人民解放軍東北軍區政治部宣傳部
Chung-kuo kuo-min tang ti liu tsu ---- Chung-kuo kuo-min tang chung-yang wei-yüan hui ti-liu tsu 中國國民黨中央委員會第六組
Chung-kuo yao-lan ---- Chung-kuo yao-lan pien-yin she 中國要覽編印社
Chung-kuo wen-t'i ---- Chung-kuo wen-t'i yen-chiu so 中國問題研究所
Chung-pao ---- Chung-pao she 忠報社
Chung-wai ---- Chung-wai wen-hua she 中外文化社
Chung-wai ch'u-pan ---- Chung-wai ch'u-pan she 中外出版社
Chung-yang wen-wu ---- Chung-yang wen-wu kung-ying she 中央文物供應社
Chung-yüan ---- Chung-yüan ch'u-pan she 中原出版社

Fan-kung ---- Fan-kung ch'u-pan she 反攻出版社

Hai-hung ---- Hai-hung ch'u-pan she 海虹出版社
Hai-wai ---- Hai-wai shu-tien 海外書店
Hai-yen ---- Hai-yen shu-tien 海燕書店
Ho-p'ing ---- Ho-p'ing ch'u-pan she 和平出版社
Ho-chung ---- Ho-chung ch'u-pan she 合眾出版社
Ho-tso ---- Ho-tso ch'u-pan she 合作出版社
Hsien-shih ---- Hsien-shih ch'u-pan she 現實出版社
Hsien-tai ---- Hsien-tai shih-liao she 現代史料社
Hsin-chung ---- Hsin-chung ch'u-pan she 新中出版社
Hsin Chung-kuo ---- Hsin Chung-kuo ch'u-pan she 新中國出版社
Hsin Chung-kuo wen-hua ---- Hsin Chung-kuo wen-hua kung-ssu 新中國文化公司
Hsin Chung-kuo pao-she 新中國報社
Hsin-hua ---- Hsin-hua shu-tien 新華書店
Hsin-hua jih-pao 新華日報華北分館
Hsin-min ---- Hsin-min pao 新民報
Hsin min-chu ---- Hsin min-chu ch'u-pan she 新民主出版社
Hsin min-chu pao ---- Hsin min-chu pao-she 新民主報社
Hsin-sheng ---- Hsin-sheng ch'u-pan she 新生出版社

Hsin-wen tsa-chih ---- Hsin-wen tsa-chih ch'u-pan she 新聞雜誌出版社
Hu-pin ---- Hu-pin shu-tien 滬濱書店
Hua-ch'iang ---- Hua-ch'iang ch'u-pan she 華強出版社
Hua-kuo ---- Hua-kuo ch'u-pan she 華國出版社
Hua-pei ---- Hua-pei shu-tien 華北書店
Hua-ts'ui ---- Hua-ts'ui ch'u-pan she 華萃出版社
Hua-yen ---- Hua-yen ch'u-pan she 華延出版社

I-chih ---- I-chih shu-tien 益智書店
I-hsing ---- I-hsing shu-tien 一星書店

Jen-min ---- Jen-min ch'u-pan she 人民出版社

K'ang-chan ch'u-pan ---- K'ang-chan ch'u-pan pu 抗戰出版部
K'ang-chan shu-tien 抗戰書店
K'ang-Jih ---- K'ang-Jih chan-shu yen-chiu she 抗日戰術研究社
Ko-ming shih-chien ---- Ko-ming shih-chien yen-chiu yüan 革命實踐研究院
K'o-hsüeh ---- K'o-hsüeh ch'u-pan she 科學出版社
Kuang-hua shu-tien 光華書店
Kung-jen ---- Kung-jen ch'u-pan she 工人出版社
Kung-jen wen-hua ---- Kung-jen wen-hua she 工人文化社
Kuo-hsün ---- Kuo-hsün shu-tien 國訊書店
Kuo-hun ---- Kuo-hun shu-tien 國魂書店
Kuo-min ---- Kuo-min t'u-shu ch'u-pan she 國民圖書出版社
Kuo-nan ---- Kuo-nan yen-chiu so 國難研究所

Lao-tung ---- Lao-tung ch'u-pan she 勞動出版社
Li-hsiang ---- Li-hsiang ch'u-pan she 理想出版社
Li-lun ---- Li-lun yü shih-chien she 理論與實踐社
Li-shih ---- Li-shih tzu-liao kung-ying she 歷史資料供應社
Lien-ho ---- Lien-ho pien-i she 聯合編譯社

Min-chih ---- Min-chih ch'u-pan she 民治出版社
Min-chu ---- Min-chu ch'u-pan she 民主出版社

Nan-hai ---- Nan-hai ch'u-pan she 南海出版社
Nan-hua ---- Nan-hua ch'u-pan she 南華出版社

Pa-lu chün ---- Pa-lu chün chün-cheng tsa-chih she
八路軍軍政雜誌社
Pa-lu chün lien-fang ---- Pa-lu chün lien-fang cheng-chih pu
八路軍聯防政治部
Pa-t'i ---- Pa-t'i shu-tien 拔提書店
Pai-hsing ---- Pai-hsing ch'u-pan she 百姓出版社
Pei-chi hsing ---- Pei-chi hsing ch'u-pan she 北極星出版社
Pei-fang tsa-chih ---- Pei-fang tsa-chih she 北方雜誌社
Po-chung ---- Po-chung she 播種社

San-lien ---- San-lien shu-tien 三聯書店
Shang-hai shu-pao ---- Shang-hai shu-pao tsa-chih lien-ho fa-hsing so
上海書報雜誌聯合發行所
Shang-hai tsa-chih ---- Shang-hai tsa-chih kung-ssu 上海雜誌公司
She-hui ---- She-hui ch'u-pan she 社會出版社
Sheng-huo ---- Sheng-huo shu-tien 生活書店
Sheng-li ---- Sheng-li ch'u-pan she 勝利出版社
Sheng-lu ---- Sheng-lu ch'u-pan she 生路出版社
Shih-nien ---- Shih-nien ch'u-pan she 十年出版社
Shih-shih ---- Shih-shih hsin-wen she 時事新聞社
Shuo-wen ---- Shuo-wen she ch'u-pan pu 說文社出版部

Ta-chung ---- Ta-chung jih-pao she 大眾日報社
Ta-chung sheng-lu ---- Ta-chung sheng-lu she 大眾生路社
Ta-chung shu-tien 大眾書店
Ta-chung wen-hua ---- Ta-chung wen-hua ho-tso she 大眾文化合作社
Ta-kuang-ming ---- Ta kuang-ming ch'u-pan she 大光明出版社
Ta shih-tai ---- Ta shih-tai shu-tien 大時代書店
Ta-kung ---- Ta-kung ch'u-pan she 大公出版社
T'ao-fen ---- T'ao-fen shu-tien 韜奮書店
Tsai-sheng ---- Tsai-sheng she 再生社
Ts'ao-yüan ---- Ts'ao-yüan ch'u-pan she 草原出版社
Tsung-heng ---- Tsung-heng wen-hua shih-yeh kung-ssu
縱橫文化事業公司
Tu-li ---- Tu-li ch'u-pan she 獨立出版社
Tu-shu sheng-huo ---- Tu-shu sheng-huo ch'u-pan she 讀書生活出版社
T'uan-chieh ---- T'uan-chieh ch'u-pan she 團結出版社
Tung-pei jih-pao ---- Tung-pei jih-pao she 東北日報社
Tung-pei min-chu ---- Tung-pei min-chu lien-chün tsung cheng-chih pu
東北民主聯軍總政治部
Tung-pei shu-tien 東北書店
T'ung-i ---- T'ung-i ch'u-pan she 統一出版社
T'ung-su ---- T'ung-su t'u-wu ch'u-pan she 通俗讀物出版社
Tzu-yu ---- Tzu-yu ch'u-pan she 自由出版社

Tzu-yu Chung-kuo ---- Tzu-yu Chung-kuo she 自由中國社
Tzu-yu shih-chieh ---- Tzu-yu shih-chieh ch'u-pan she 自由世界出版社
Tzu-yu wen-ts'ung ---- Tzu-yu wen-ts'ung she 自由文叢社

Wen-hua ---- Wen-hua kung-ying she 文化供應社
Wen-ts'ung ---- Wen-ts'ung ch'u-pan she 文叢出版社

Ya-chou ---- Ya-chou ch'u-pan she 亞洲出版社
Ya-lien ---- Ya-lien ch'u-pan she 亞聯出版社
Ya-tung ---- Ya-tung t'u-shu kuan 亞東圖書館
Yang-ming ---- Yang-ming shan-chuang 陽明山莊
Yu-lien ---- Yu-lien ch'u-pan she 友聯出版社

ADDENDUM

During the last two years, the Hoover Institution has acquired a number of rare Chinese periodicals concerning the Chinese Communist movement in the 1920's and the 1930's. Some of these are issues which bridge gaps in the periodical holdings included in the first volume of the present work; others are entirely new titles. The Addendum is designed to up-date and supplement the information previously given concerning the periodical holdings in the Hoover Institution.

Part I of this Addendum up-dates and supersedes holdings information for fourteen of the periodicals included in the earlier volume of this bibliography. The original item numbers accompany the entries. Part II is an alphabetical list of nineteen new titles with brief annotations.

PART I

67. Hsin ch'ing-nien 新青年 (La Jeunesse). Vol. I, No. 1 - Vol. IX, No. 6. Shanghai and Canton, September 15, 1915 - July 1, 1922. (Vol. IX, Nos. 3-6 on microfilm). Hsin ch'ing-nien chi-k'an 新青年季刊 (La Jeunesse Quarterly). Nos. 1-4. Canton, June 15, 1923 - December 20, 1924. Microfilm. Nos. 1-2, 4. April 22, 1925 - May 25, 1926. Microfilm. (9200/0258)

100. Hsiang-tao chou-pao 響導周報 (The Guide Weekly). Nos. 1-110, 112-175, 177-183, 187-191, 193, 201. September, 1922 - July, 1927. Microfilm. (4292.01/2374)

102. Jen-min chou-k'an 人民週刊 (People's Weekly). Nos. 1-2, 10-19. February - August, 1926. Microfilm (except No. 10). (4292.01/8731)

107. Chung-kuo ch'ing-nien 中國青年 (Chinese Youth). Nos. 26-50, 76-100, 134, and 138. Shanghai, April, 1924 - October, 1926. Also Nos. 1-137 (October, 1923 - October, 1926) on microfilm. (4292.01/5658)

154. Hsing-shih 醒獅 (Awakened Lion). Nos. 53-103/104, 114, 126, 137-169, 172/173. Shanghai, October, 1925 - February, 1928. (4737.2/1142f)

172. Hung-ch'i 紅旗 (Red Flag). Nos. 1-23, 48-49, 51-55, 57-65, 68-70, 76, 79, 82-88, 90-118, 120-121, 123-124. Shanghai, November 20, 1928 - July 26, 1930. Nos. 1-23 on microfilm. (4292.01/2108)

223. Hung-se Chung-hua 紅色中華 (Red China). Nos. 1-4, 7-8, 10, 12-16, 18, 20-21, 23-25, 27, 30, 34-90, 92-111, 114-129, 132, 135-136, 139-140, 142-145, Special Supplements 1-7 (January 22, 1934 - February 3, 1934), 146-166, 168-185, 188-191, 193, 204-205, 207-240, 243. Juichin, December, 1931 - October, 1934. Microfilm. (4292.23/2254)

241. Hung-ch'i chou-pao 紅旗週報 (The Red Flag Weekly). Nos. 3-6 (Supplement to No. 6), 10, 12, 16, 21, 25, 27, 29-31, 33, 49, 50, 52, 59-62. March, 1931 - November, 1933. (4292.01/2108.2)

245. Tang ti chien-she 黨的建設 (The Party's Reconstruction). Nos. 1-6 (microfilm), 11. June, 1932 - January, 1933. (4292.01/9210)

246. Tou-cheng 鬥爭 (Struggle). Nos. 1-31, 34-35, 38, 40-73, 96, 104-105, 107-110. February, 1933 - September, 1934. Microfilm (except Nos. 96, 104-105, 107-110). (4292.01/7225)

264. Ch'ing-nien shih-hua 青年實話 (The True Words of Youth). Vol. Nos. 3, 11, 13-23, 30 (December, 1931 - November, 1932); Vol. II, Nos. 1-26, 30-31 (January-October, 1933); Vol. III, Nos. 1-2 5-6, 8, 10-11, 13-18, 21-24, 89-106, 108-109, 111-113 (Novemb 1933 - September, 1934). Microfilm. (4292.53/5830)

288.   Ch'an-kung pan-yüeh k'an 剷共半月刊 (Root Out the Communists Semi-Monthly). Nos. 1-10/11, 17/18, 21, 28. Shanghai, September, 1930 - October, 1932. (Nos. 1-9, and 21 on microfilm). (2987/0497)

301.   Chung-yang chou-pao 中央週報 (Central Weekly). Nos. 91, 143, 226, 238, 242, 247, 284-294, 300-311, 313-315. Nanking, March, 1930 - June, 1934. (4738.01/5534)

349.   Kung-li pao 公理報 (Justice Journal). Nos. 918-919, 921-922, 926-927. Peiping, December, 1936 - February, 1937. Mimeographed. (2990/8314f)

PART II

Ch'ien-feng 前鋒 (The Vanguard). Nos. 1-3. Canton, July 1, 1923 - February 1, 1924. Microfilm. (4738.01/8285)

Edited by Ch'ü Ch'iu-pai and published about the same time as the <u>Hsin ch'ing-nien chi-k'an</u> 新青年季刊, this official Chinese Communist publication carries articles by Ch'en Tu-hsiu, Yün Tai-ying, Hsiang Ching-yü, Chang Tai-lei, Ts'ai Ho-sen, Liu Jen-ching, in addition to those by Ch'ü Ch'iu-pai.

Ch'un lei 春雷 (Spring Thunder). Nos. 1-3. Canton, October, 1923 - May, 1924. Microfilm. (4296/5616)

An official organ of the Chinese anarchists. It contains a number of articles refuting Communism.

Chung-kuo hai-yüan 中國海員 (Chinese Seamen). Nos. 4, 5, 7. Canton, February-October, 1926. Microfilm. (4510/5636)

    The official organ of the Chinese Seamen's Union. No. 4 contains reports to and proceedings of the National Congress of the Chinese Seamen's Union held from January 5-9 in Canton, including a report by Su Chao-cheng 蘇兆徵 on the history and activities of the Union. No. 5 is a special issue devoted to discussions of the resolutions of the Congress.

Chung-kuo hsüeh-sheng 中國學生 (Chinese Student). No. 1. May 26, 1925. Nos. 18, 22/23-31, 35, 37, 42-45. Shanghai, February-December, 1926. Microfilm (except Nos. 18, 42-45). (4180.1/5672.32)

    The official organ of the Students Federation of China 中華民國學生聯合會總會, reports weekly on student activities in various parts of China, and provides a commentary on current political affairs. No. 25 is a special issue on the May 4th Movement; No. 29 is devoted to the commemoration of the May 30th Incident. The resolutions passed by the Eighth National Congress of the Federation are discussed in No. 35.

Chung-kuo kuo-min tang chou-k'an 中國國民黨週刊 (The Kuomintang Weekly). Vol. II, Nos. 2-3, with two supplements. Shanghai, October 24-31, 1926. Microfilm. (4738.01/5667)

    An official publication of the Kuomintang right-wing, criticizing the Kuomintang-Communist entente then in effect and advocating the purge of Communists from the Kuomintang. Contributors include Tsou Lu 鄒魯, Chang Chi 張繼, and Chü Cheng 居正. Two supplements: one issued on October 10, 1926 in commemoration of the founding of the Republic, and the other on the sixtieth birthday anniversary of Dr. Sun Yat-sen on November 12, 1926.

Chung-shan chu-i chou-k'an 中山主義周刊 (The Sun Yat-senism Weekly). Nos. 1-3. Shanghai, December 20, 1925 - January 3, 1926. Microfilm. (4738.01/5208)

    Published by the Sun Yat-sen Study Group of the Shanghai University, with Kao Erh-po 高爾柏 as editor. No. 1 carries a speech by Ch'ü Ch'iu-pai on "The National Revolution and Class Struggle"; No. 2

provides the text of a speech by Yün Tai-ying on "Sun Yat-senism and Tai Chi-t'aoism." Notes on both of these speeches were taken by Ch'in Pang-hsien.

Chung-yang cheng-chih hui-i Wu-Han fen-hui yueh-pao 中央政治會議武漢分會月報 (Monthly Report of the Wuhan Branch of the Central Political Conference). Vol. I, Nos. 1, 3-4; Vol. II, No. 1. Wuhan, July-November, 1928. Microfilm. (2984/5513)

  The Wuhan Branch of the Central Political Conference was established on May 18, 1928 by the Central Executive Committee of the Kuomintang to direct the political affairs of Hupeh and Hunan. Li Tsung-jen was appointed chairman, and its members consisted of Pai Ch'ung-hsi, Chang Chih-pen 張知本, Chang Hua-fu 張華輔, Lu Ti-p'ing 魯滌平, and others. Among various official reports which appear regularly in this monthly publication are those concerning Communist activities in Hupeh and Hunan, and measures taken against them.

Chung-yang pan-yüeh k'an 中央半月刊 (The Central Semi-Monthly). Vol. I, Nos. 1-24; Vol. II, Nos. 1-4. Nanking, October, 1927 - November, 1928. Microfilm (except Vol. II, Nos. 1-4). (4738.30/5597)

  The official organ of the Propaganda Section of the Kuomintang published after the April, 1927 purge. Frequent contributors to this anti-Communist publication were Wu Chih-hui, Tai Chi-t'ao, Li Shih-tseng, Sun K'o, Hu Han-min, Chiang Kai-shek, and Liu Lu-yin.

Fang kung yüeh-k'an 防共月刊 (Defense Against Communism Monthly). Nos. 1, 3-4. Nanking, December, 1936 - March, 1937. Microfilm. (4292.23/7471)

  A Kuomintang anti-Communist publication. No. 1 contains a review of military campaigns against the Communist forces in 1935, and an article by Chang Shu-sheng 張書紳 on Ch'en Tu-hsiu and the Chinese Communist Party, including the text of a joint statement on Kuomintang-CCP relations issued by Ch'en Tu-hsiu and Wang Ching-wei in which they urged forebearance and continued cooperation (issued on April 5, 1927, just prior to Chiang Kai-shek's coup against the Communists in Shanghai). Also included in No. 1 is a reprint of a Chinese Communist pamphlet for the guidance of the cadres on how to organize labor. No. 3 contains articles on the Sian Incident and on the history of communism in Northern Shensi. No. 4 surveys Communist activities in North China, and also carries an account of the police raid on the Tsinghwa University dormitories on December 1, 1935 resulting in the arrest of some of the leaders of the Northern Bureau of the CCP and the capture of a number of Communist documents. Both Nos. 3 and 4 carry reports on student activities in the Peiping area, and a special section on Communist activities in China and abroad. Each issue reports on Chinese government anti-Communist measures during the preceding month.

Hsien-ch'ü 先驅 (The Vanguard). No. 7. Shanghai, May 1, 1922. (4292.01/5638)

Official organ of the Socialist Youth League of China, and predecessor to the Chung-kuo ch'ing-nien 中國青年 (Chinese Youth). Twenty-five issues were published from January 15, 1922 to August 15, 1923 at which time publication ceased. Issue No. 7 includes a message to labor from Ch'en Tu-hsiu, and an article by Ts'ai Ho-sen on the direction of the Chinese labor movement. For an essay on this publication see Wu-ssu shih-ch'i ch'i-k'an chieh-shao 五四時期期刊介紹, Vol. II, pp. 12-31. A cumulative table of contents covering all twenty-five issues is provided in the same book, pp. 620-626.

Hsin chien-she 新建設 (New Construction). Vol. I, Nos. 1-6; Vol. II, Nos. 1-2. Shanghai, November 20, 1923 - August 20, 1924. Microfilm. (4738.01/0210)

An important Communist publication during the Kuomintang reorganization period (1923-1924). The most frequent contributors to this publication were Yün Tai-ying and Han Chüeh-min 韓覺民. Among Yün's articles are: "On the Three People's Principles" (Vol. I, No. 1); "On the Theory of Tutelage," "Revolution and Party" (Vol. I, No. 2); "The Question of Education in the Revolutionary Movement" (Vol. I, No. 3); "The Principle of Nationalism" (Vol. I, No. 4); "The Basic Force of the Chinese Revolution" (Vol. I, No. 5); and "A Survey and Critique of Current Financial Situation in China" (Vol. I, No. 6). Han Chüeh-min's contributions are: "The Characteristics of the Kuomintang" (Vol. I, No. 1); "Revolutionary Steps of the Kuomintang" (Vol. I, No. 3); and "The Principle of Livelihood and the Question of Communist Penetration of the Kuomintang" (Vol. I, No. 5). Documents relating to the reorganization of the Kuomintang appear in Vol. I, No. 1 (The January 1, 1923 manifesto); Vol. I, No. 2

(Manifesto on the reorganization); Vol. I, No. 4 (Manifesto of the First National Congress of the Kuomintang and an account of the Congress including namelists of delegates, proceedings, etc.). A draft land law for the city of Canton by Liao Chung-k'ai, and an article on Chinese peasants by Hsiao Chu-nü 蕭楚女 are available in Vol. II, No. 1. Vol. II, No. 2 provides the manifesto of the Sixth National Congress of the Students Federation of China.

Hsin kuo-chia 新國家 (New Nation). Vol. I, Nos. 1-12; Vol. II, Nos. 1-3. Peking, January, 1927 - March, 1928. Microfilm. (4618/0263)

An official publication of the "Nationalists" 國家主義者. Starting more or less concurrently with the Kuomintang purge of the Communists in April 1927, a number of anti-Communist articles began to appear in its pages. The most notable among these are the following articles written by Chu Chen-hsin 朱枕新: "History of the Chinese Communist Movement," "Communist Plundering in Hunan" (Vol. I, No. 8); "From the Socialist Youth League of China to the Communist Youth Corps of China," "A Glimpse of the Red Terror in China" (Vol. I, No. 9); "Reminiscences of Terrified Shanghai" (Vol. I, No. 10); "The Development of the Communist Youth Corps of China," "Reminiscences of the Nanchang Revolt," and "Chinese Communist Party and the Women of China" (Vol. I, No. 11).

Hsin min-kuo 新民國 (New Republic). Vol. I, Nos. 1-6; Vol. II, No. 1. Peking, November 15, 1923 - February 1, 1925. Microfilm. (4738.01/0276)

Edited and published by some of the faculty members of Peking University, including Li Ta-chao who contributed two articles: "The Nation's Difficult Times and Energetic Citizens" (Vol. I, No. 2), and "Eugenics" (Vol. I, No. 6). A number of Sun Yat-sen's speeches and writings on the reorganization of the Kuomintang are published in Vol. I, Nos. 1, 2, 4. His first four lectures on the Principle of Nationalism are available in Vol. I, Nos. 5-6; and an article on Pan-Asianism is printed in Vol. II, No. 1.

The following are some of the other important articles in this publication:

Vol. I, No. 1, "The World Character of the China Question" by Liu Jen-ching 劉仁靜 ;

Vol. I, No. 2, "National Revolution Is Prerequisite to the Reconstruction of China" by Kuo Ch'un-t'ao 郭春濤;

Vol. I, No. 3, "An Account of the Struggle Between Democratic Rule and Anti-Democratic Rule" by Ho Meng-hsiung 何孟雄;

Vol. I, No. 4, an account of the First National Congress of the Kuomintang including speeches, reports, proceedings, a list of delegates, the manifesto of the Congress, the Constitution of the Kuomintang, and also the Constitution of the All-China Railroad Union;

Vol. I, No. 5, "Kwangtung After the Kuomintang Reorganization";

Vol. I, No. 6, "Progressives and the Kuomintang" by Wu Chih-hui;

Vol. II, No. 1, "Politics and the Masses" by Wang Ching-wei.

Kai-tsao 改造 (Reconstruction). Vol. I, No. 1/2 - Vol. IV, No. 10. Peking, September 1, 1919 - September 15, 1922. Microfilm. (4001/1433)

An important publication during the May Fourth Period, edited by Chang Tung-sun 張東蓀, Yü Sung-hua 俞頌華, and Liang Ch'i-ch'ao 梁啓超, with frequent contributions by Chang Chün-mai 張君勱 (Carsun Chang), devoted to the discussion of socialism but with an anti-Marxist orientation. Volumes I and II were published under the title Chieh-fang yü kai-tsao 解放與改造 (Emancipation and Reconstruction) from September 1 1919 to August 15, 1920. An essay on this publication as well as its cumulative table of contents is available in Wu-ssu shih-ch'i ch'i-k'an chieh-shao 五四時期期刊介紹 (Introduction to Periodical Literature of the Era of the May Fourth Movement), Vol. I, pp. 352-379 and pp. 825-833 respectively.

Ko-ming ch'ing-nien 革命青年 (The Young Revolutionist). Vol. I, Nos. 5-7. Canton, October, 1926. Microfilm. (4738.01/4858)

An official publication of the Department of Youth of the Kuomintang carrying articles on party work with youth, etc. No. 5 provides a report on the activities of the Students Federation of China. A pre-purge publication.

Kung yü 工餘 (La Laboro). Third Year, No. 2. Shanghai and Paris, September 31, 1924. Microfilm. (4296/1189)

An anarchist publication sponsored by the Chinese labor group and the Work-and-Study Group in France. Strongly anti-Communist, this publication is devoted primarily to the writings and thought of Kropotkin and other leading anarchists. An essay on this publication and a cumulative table of contents of issue numbers 13, 14, 16, 17 and 19 are in Wu-ssu shih-ch'i ch'i-k'an chieh-shao 五四時期期刊介紹 (Introduction to Periodical Literature of the Era of the May Fourth Movement), Vol. III, p. 264 and pp. 728-729 respectively.

Meng ya 萌芽 (Sprout). Vol. I, Nos. 1-2. Shanghai, January-February, 1930. No. 1 on microfilm. (5202/4471)

An official organ of the Left-Wing Writers' League of China, this publication carries articles by Feng Hsüeh-feng 馮雪峯, Lu Hsün, and others. Five issues were published; issue number 6 was published under the title Hsin lu 新路 (New Path). Starting with number 7 the title Wen-hsüeh yüeh-pao 文學月報 (Literary Monthly) was adopted.

T'o-huang che 拓荒者 (Reclaimer). Vol. I, Nos. 1-3. Shanghai, January-March, 1930. Microfilm (except No. 1). (5202/5641)

Another organ of the Left-Wing Writers' League of China, superseding the Hsin-liu yüeh-pao 新流月報 (New Current Monthly) edited by Chiang Kuang-tz'u 蔣光慈. Yin Fu 殷夫, Ch'ien Hsing-ts'un 錢杏邨, Shen Tuan-hsien 沈端先, and Chang T'ien-i 張天翼 were frequent contributors. No. 3 includes an article by Pan Han-nien 潘漢年 on the "Meaning of the Left-Wing Writers' League of China" and an article signed by a "Correspondent" describing the founding of the League.

Wu-ch'an ch'ing-nien 無產青年 (Young Proletarian). Nos. 2, 4. November-December, 1927. Microfilm. (4292.01/8058)

An official organ of the Communist Youth of China. No. 4 contains an unsigned article and an article by Jen Pi-shih 任彌時 on the 1927 Canton Uprising, as well as an open letter issued by the Communist Youth of China and addressed to the members of the workers and peasants army and to the Chinese labor on the occasion of the uprising.

INDEX

This index lists names of authors and titles appearing in this bibliography as well as subject entries. The numbers refer to entries, not to pages.

Ai Ch'ing, 82
Ai Ssu-ch'i, 108
All China Democratic Federation of Women, 785
All-China Labor Federation, 781, 782, 786, 787, 789, 795
All-China Land Conference, 763, 766
All-China Students' Association, 736, 738
All-China Youth Congress, 755
Amerasia Magazine, 616
Anti-Japanese Military and Political Academy, 241, 256, 262, 314, 321, 328
"April 8th Accident," 18, 19, 23
Association for Anti-Japanese War Studies, 222
Association for Cultural and Educational Studies, 146
Association for Promoting Constitutional Government, 43, 164, 324
Association for Promoting Democracy, 657, 695
Association for the Study of Anarchism, 696
Association for the Study of Current Affairs, 208
Atkinson, Brooks, 622

Barrett, Col. David D. (USA), 180
Bisson, T. A., 622

Border Regions: general (see also CCP: attitudes toward), 14, 33, 43, 48-50, 52, 54, 55, 57, 60, 131, 233, 417, 420, 421, 424, 507, 863; Chiaotung (Shantung), 376-391; Hainan Island, 398, 399, 401, 402; Hunan-Hupeh-Kiangsi, 192; Kiangsi, 279, 761, 781; Kiangsu-Anhwei, 60, 180, 181, 185, 411, 413, 415, 818; Kwangtung, 398-402, 435, 633; Luchung (Shantung), 393, 394; Lunan (Shantung), 367; Pinhai (Shantung), 395-396; Pohai (Shantung), 392, 397; Shansi-Chahar-Hopeh, 2, 43, 60, 138, 158, 196, 197, 207, 213, 221, 232, 236, 237, 332-344, 581, 758, 771; Shansi-Hopeh-Honan, 2, 406, 466; Shansi-Hopeh-Shantung-Honan, 345-364, 771, 773; Shansi-Suiyuan, 300, 403, 404, 411, 412; Shantung, 60, 365-397, 408, 411, 804, 807; Shensi-Kansu-Ningsia, 2, 43, 54, 58-60, 106, 118, 163, 241-331, 741, 771; Suchung Military Region, 407; Yenan, 241, 246-262, 526, 596
Browder, Earl, 128
Byrnes, James, 617, 618

CCP. See Chinese Communist Party.
Central News Agency, 57, 224

Chan-ch'ang, 332
Chan-chü tsai k'ai-shih pien-tung, 650
Chan-hsien, 108
Chan-k'ai fan-sheng yü tzu-wo p'i-p'ing, 65
Chan-k'ai fan-tui wu-shen ti tou-cheng, 280
Chan-shih p'eng-yu, 376
Chan-tou chung ti chieh-fang ch'ü min-ping, 236
Chan-tou tsai T'ai-hang-shan shang, 358
Chan-tsai k'ang-chan ti li-ch'ang shang tui-yü hsin-ssu-chün shih-chien chiang chi-chü kung-tao hua, 177
Ch'an-ti t'ung-hsün, 212
Chang, Carsun, 681, 684, 686, 700
Chang Chan, 510
Chang Cheng-ming, 159
Chang Chia-ao, 510
Chang Chih-chung, 159
Chang Chih-i, 109
Chang Chih-jang, 696
Chang Chih-kuo, 310
Chang Chih-p'ing, 330
Chang Chün-mai. See Chang, Carsun.
Chang Han-fu, 2, 3, 108
Chang Han-sai, 627, 831
Chang Hao. See Lin Yü-ying.
Chang Hsi-jo, 678
Chang Hsin-fu, 525
Chang Hsin-ju, 82, 84
Chang Hsüeh-liang, 721
Chang Hsüeh-shih, 515
Chang Ju-hsin, 29, 30
Chang Kia-ngau. See Chang Chia-ao.
Chang Kuo-ch'üan, 717
Chang Kuo-hsing, 808
Chang Kuo-t'ao, 43, 110, 134, 262
Chang Lan, 661
Chang Li-hsing, 611
Chang Mu-t'ao, 149
Chang Nai-ch'i, 108, 140, 668

Chang Ping-yen, 809
Chang Po-chün, 668, 698, 725
Chang Shen-fu, 677, 702
Chang-shih kung-jen shou-chieh tai-piao ta-hui hui-k'an, 780
Chang Shou-ch'u, 810
Chang Ta-chün, 16
Chang Tan. See Chang Chan.
Chang Ti-fei, 31
Chang T'ieh-chün, 160
Chang Ting-ch'eng, 229, 592
Chang Tung-sung, 696, 710, 724
Chang Wen-t'ien, 131, 133, 257
Chang Yu-ch'ih ho san-lien ti wen-hua hsüeh-hsi, 302
Ch'ang-ch'un jih-pao, 429
Chao Ch'ao-kou, 246
Chao I-po, 781
Chao Kuan-i, 17
Ch'e-ti kai-pien wo-men ti ling-tao tso-feng, 538
Chen-li. See also Tou-cheng, 374
Ch'en Ch'ang-hao, 222
Ch'en Chia-k'ang, 2, 753
Ch'en Chia-keng, 182
Ch'en Chien-hua, 314
Ch'en Chin-k'un, 717
Ch'en Chün, 178
Ch'en Chün-yen, 691
Ch'en I. See Ch'en Yi.
Ch'en Kuo-hsin, 241
Ch'en Lei, 733
Ch'en Po-ta, 2, 3, 32, 43, 96, 135, 149, 557, 584, 755, 774, 798, 800, 802, 806
Ch'en Shao-yü. See Wang Ming.
Ch'en Shao-yü (Wang Ming) chiu-kuo yen-lun hsüan-chi, 110
Ch'en Ts'ung-i, 179
Ch'en Tu-hsiu, 149, 150-156, 157, 158
Ch'en Yen, 242
Ch'en Yi, 2, 26, 73, 180, 194, 543
Ch'en Yün, 43, 66, 218, 789, 800
Cheng Chen-to, 673

Cheng-chih hsieh-shang hui-i, 605
Cheng-chih hsieh-shang hui-i chih chien-t'ao, 606
Cheng-chih hsieh-shang hui-i shih-mo chi, 609
Cheng-chih hsieh-shang hui-i ts'e-hsieh, 610
Cheng-chih hsieh-shang hui-i wen-hsien, 607
Cheng-chih hsieh-shang hui-i wen-hui, 604
Cheng-chih hsin-wen, 832
Cheng-chih kang-ling ts'an-k'ao tzu-liao, 48
Cheng-chih kung-tso lun-ts'ung, 232
Cheng-chih lu-hsien, 686
Cheng-chih min-chu hua yü chün-tui kuo-chia hua, 601
Cheng-chih pao-t'u p'ing-lun, 576
Cheng-chih yüeh-k'an, 161
Cheng-ch'ü chen-cheng ti min-chu ti ho-p'ing, 837
Cheng-ch'ü ch'üan-mien ti-k'ang ti sheng-li, 556
Cheng-chün fu-yüan wen-hsien, 581
Cheng-feng wen-hsien, 67
Cheng-hsieh wen-hsien, 608
Cheng-hsüeh hsi. See Political Study Clique.
Cheng-i, 833
Cheng-i pao, 430
Cheng-lun, 628
Cheng min-chu ti Chung-kuo cheng-tang, 661
Cheng-pao, 417
Cheng-pao ch'u-pan she, 535
Cheng-pao she t'u-shu pu, 629
Cheng Wei, 61
Ch'eng Ch'ien, 812
Ch'eng Chin-wu, 315
Ch'eng Fang-wu, 342, 543, 585, 799
Ch'eng-hsiang kuan-hsi wen-t'i, 555
Ch'eng Shih, 194
Chi-Chin jih-pao she, 557

Chi-Jo-Liao jih-pao, 431
Chi-nai, 692
Chi-nan hsing-shu, 345
Chi-nan hsing-shu ti-i tz'u ts'ai lien hui pao-kao yü tsung-chieh, 345
Chi-nan yin-hang T'ai-hang ch'ü hang. Kung-shang kuan-li tsung-chü yen-chiu shih, 346
Chi-tung hsing, 365
Chi Yün-lung, 511, 513
Ch'i-ch'i hsüan-yen chi ch'i yen-chiu, 536
Ch'i-ch'i jih-pao, 432
Ch'i-ch'i-ling t'uan ti-erh lien, 309
Ch'i-lai chih-chih nei-chan wan-chiu wei-wang, 171
Ch'i Li, 243
Ch'i-p'ien pi-hsü chieh-ch'uan, 693
Ch'i Sheng, 281
Ch'i Shih-chieh, 247
Ch'i Wu, 347
Chia-chin chun-pei chin tung chü-hsing ti san-ko ta-hui, 265
Chiang Chieh-shih ti no-yen yü tzu-pai, 45
Chiang Chieh-shih yüan-tan yen-shuo yü cheng-chih hsieh-shang hui-i, 600
Chiang Chih-chien, 181
Chiang-chün pi-pai, 612
Chiang Chung-cheng. See Chiang Kai-shek.
Chiang Kai-shek, 1, 32, 39, 45, 127, 159, 165, 171, 183, 557, 560, 574, 576, 581, 584, 590, 600, 605, 608, 612, 614, 615, 621, 652, 661, 686, 690, 836, 854, 861
Chiang Kai-shek, Mme., 510
Chiang ko-ming chin-hsing tao-ti, 630
Chiang-Li tou-cheng nei-mu, 854
Chiang Nan-hsiang, 752

284

Chiao-tung chün-ch'ü. Cheng-chih pu, 377
───. Ch'ien-hsien pao-she, 378
───. Tsu-chih pu, 379
Chiao-tung hsin-hua shu-tien, 366, 558
Chiao-tung hua-pao, 380
Chiao-tung ta-chung, 381
Chiao-yü chen-ti, 333
Chiao-yü chen-ti she, 316, 317, 318, 334, 335
Chiao-yü chieh ti ying-hsiung mu-fan, 316
Ch'iao Kuan-hua. See Ch'iao Mu.
Ch'iao Mu, 3, 141, 613, 692, 713, 730
Ch'iao-mu. See also Hu Ch'iao-mu.
Chiaochangkou Incident, 660
Chieh-ch'uan kung-ch'an tang ti hei-mu, 823
Chieh-fang (Peiping), 434
Chieh-fang (Yenan), 43
Chieh-fang chan-cheng hui-i lu, 641
Chieh-fang ch'ü Chin-Ch'a-Chi hsing, 340
Chieh-fang ch'ü ch'ün-chung chiao-yü chien she ti tao-lu, 320
Chieh-fang ch'ü hui-lai, 816
Chieh-fang ch'ü mao-i hsü-chih, 804
Chieh-fang ch'ü ti kung-ch'ang ching-ying yü kuan-li, 281
Chieh-fang ch'ü ti sheng-chian yün-tung, 285
Chieh-fang ch'ü ti t'u-ti cheng-ts'e yü shih-shih, 770
Chieh-fang ch'ü yin-hsiang chi, 829
Chieh-fang chün sheng huo, 639
"Chieh-fang" chung ti Chiang-nan chen-hsiang, 815
Chieh-fang hou ti Shang-hai kung-yün tzu-liao, 791
Chieh-fang jih-pao (Shanghai), 433
Chieh-fang jih-pao (Yenan), 44
Chieh-fang jih-pao. See also Liberation Daily, 44, 45, 559, 560, 600

Chieh-fang she, 68, 162, 537, 630, 757, 782
Chieh-shao nan-ch'ü ho-tso she, 282
Chien-fei hua-chung ti-wei yü min san-shih-ch'i nien shih-erh yüeh san-shih jih chih-shih tang cheng chün wu ta jen-wu, 631
Chien-k'u fen-tou ying-chieh kuang-ming, 397
Chien-kuo chou-pao, 561
Chien-kuo ch'u-pan she, 182
Chien-kuo jih-pao, 435
Chien-ming ho-li fu-tan chan-hsing pan-fa, 351
Chien-ping, 512
Chien-tsu chien-hsi i-wen chieh-ta, 760
Ch'ien-hsien, 213
Ch'ien-hsien yüeh-k'an, 195
Ch'ien-wei pao, 237
Chih-hsing chung-yang wu-ssu chih-shih ti chi-pen tsung-chieh chi chin-hou jen-wu, 773
Chih Kung Tang, 657, 699
Chih-kung yün-tung ts'an-k'ao tzu-liao, 794
Chih-kung yün-tung wen-hsien, 795
Chih-shih, 513
Chih-shih fen-tzu yü chiao-yü wen-t'i, 537
Chih-yeh chiao-yü she (p'ai). See Vocational Education Group (of China).
Ch'ih-se ta-lu chen-hsiang, 810
Chin-Ch'a-Chi chün-ch'ü cheng-chih pu, 196, 197, 198
Chin-Ch'a-Chi hua-pao, 336
Chin-Ch'a-Chi hsin-hua shu-tien, 758
Chin-Ch'a-Chi jih-pao, 334
Chin-Ch'a-Chi jih-pao, 436
Chin-Ch'a-Chi jih-pao she, 562, 614, 632, 759

Chin-Ch'a-Chi pien-ch'ü chi Chang-shih ko-chieh chui-tao "ssu-pa" yü-nan lieh-shih ch'ou-wei-hui, 18
Chin-Ch'a-Chi pien-ch'ü hsing-cheng wei-yüan hui, 337
Chin-Ch'a-Chi pien-ch'ü hsing-cheng wei-yüan hui. Shih-yeh ch'u, 338
Chin-Ch'a-Chi pien-ch'ü hsing-cheng wei-yüan hui. Shih-yeh ch'u. Nung-hui, 339
Chin-Ch'a-Chi pien-ch'ü kung-jen wu-i chi-nien hua-ts'e, 784
Chin-Ch'a-Chi pien-ch'ü ti lao-tung hu-chu, 339
Chin-Ch'a-Chi pien-ch'ü tsung kung-hui, 783
———. Kung-jen pao-she, 784
Chin-Ch'a-Chi pien-ch'ü yin-hsiang chi, 341
Chin-Chi-Lu-Yü chün-ch'ü cheng-chi pu, 348, 601
Chin-Chi-Lu-Yü pien-ch'ü cheng-fu, 349, 350
Chin-Chi-Lu-Yü pien-ch'ü cheng-fu. Mi-shu ch'u, 602
Chin-Chi-Lu-Yü pien-ch'ü cheng-fu. Ti-i t'ing, 760
Chin-Chi-Lu-Yü pien-ch'ü Chi-Lu-Yü ti-shih hsing-cheng tu-ch'a chuan-yüan kung-shu, 351
Chin-Chi-Lu-Yü pien-ch'ü ko-chieh chui-tao ta-hui ch'ou-wei-hui, 19
Chin-Chi-Lu-Yü pien-ch'ü tiao-ch'a yen-chiu shih, 352
Chin-Chi-Lu-Yü Yüan-ch'ü tzu-chüeh t'uan-chieh yün-tung ti ching-yen, 353
Chin Chün-chih, 161
Chin Chung-hua, 126, 141, 143
Chin I-hung, 761
Chin-jih chih mo-ts'a wen-t'i, 163
Chin-jih chung-kung, 596
Chin-jih hsin-wen (n. p.; 1939), 214
Chin-jih hsin-wen (Nanking), 834
Chin-jih ti Yen-an, 251
Chin-pu jih-pao, 437
Chin san-shih nien chien-wen tsa-chi, 257
Chin-Sui pien-ch'ü hsing-cheng kung-shu. Min-chiao ch'u, 403
Chin-Sui pien-ch'ü kang-chan yü chien-she kai-k'uang, 404
Chin-Sui pien-ch'ü sheng-ch'an wei-yüan hui, 762
Chin Tung-p'ing, 248
Ch'in Pang-hsien. See Po Ku.
China Publishing House (Hong Kong), 43
Chinese Association for Civil Rights, 712
Chinese Communist Party (CCP) (as subject): see also People's Republic of China; and KMT (see also United Front; civil war), 1-3, 8, 9, 33, 36, 58, 72, 116, 124, 127, 130, 143, 144, 146, 148, 154, 155, 159-176, 213, 228, 230, 257, 262, 418, 422, 426, 519, 524, 556-626, 632, 658, 671, 682, 695, 697, 713, 730, 833, 837, 838, 844, 846, 851-853, 856-858, 860, 863; and peasantry (see also land laws and reform), 136, 269, 298, 415; and Sino-Japanese War (see also CCP, Army), 2, 8, 9, 14, 36, 39, 43, 45, 50, 52, 54, 58, 59, 64, 71, 73, 85, 86, 106, 108, 117, 127, 128, 137, 149, 150, 154, 158, 199, 203, 207, 208, 211, 215, 218, 219, 222, 226, 241, 336, 358, 387, 402, 428, 536; and the intelligentsia, 535, 543, 549, 696, 722, 728, 826; and USSR, 1, 520, 554, 623; army (see also CCP: militia and the headings under specific military groups), 194-240, 312, 424, 435, 522, 533, 542, 550, 572, 597,

636, 639, 641, 644-646, 800, 810; Army-civilian relations, 303, 306, 307, 309, 310, 311, 369, 377; attitudes toward, 808-830; bibliography of publications, 423; biographies of elite, 16-28, 40, 127, 513, 609; civil war, 6, 9, 36, 234, 385, 398, 417, 419-421, 425-427, 507, 516, 519, 531, 549, 568, 613, 623, 627-654, 660, 713, 716, 719, 722, 723, 726, 731, 733, 736, 808, 831, 833, 837, 843, 844, 851, 857-860, 862; Constitution of, 75, 94, 98, 540, 543; cooperative labor farms, 282, 294, 295, 297, 338, 339, 807; defection of members, 99, 110, 247, 256, 814; foreign policy of, 408, 548, 551; general, 535-555, 658; government-Party relations, 81; history of, 4, 8, 9, 13, 40, 45-47, 78, 80, 81, 109, 127, 242, 244, 399, 401, 428, 539; industrial policy, 800-807; inner-Party struggle, 27, 93, 95, 98, 102, 839; land laws and reform, 3, 38, 276, 277, 279, 337, 347, 350, 353, 355, 367, 374, 375, 383, 388, 389, 392, 395, 402, 407, 411, 416, 552, 554, 595, 757-779, 813, 818, 826; mass line (see also Mass Movements), 80, 96, 98, 102, 104, 313, 353, 546, 552, 554; membership, 66, 74, 79, 88, 91, 102, 107, 270, 517; military strategy (see also CCP: army; and Guerrilla Warfare), 204-206; militia (see also CCP: army), 201, 211, 235-240, 337, 368, 385, 395; organization, 70, 79-81, 83, 91, 102, 105, 145, 216, 243, 269, 384, 385, 402, 542, 553, 554, 596; policy and resolutions, 2, 3, 38, 43, 48, 56, 63, 68-72, 76, 77, 85, 101, 109, 127, 129, 130, 136, 156, 163, 213, 263-269, 272-275, 318, 337, 343, 350, 387, 402, 413, 417, 418, 421, 521, 523, 535, 536, 542, 548, 562, 569, 594, 621, 626, 630, 745; recruitment and expansion, 38, 74, 88, 517, 543; rectification movements, 2, 65, 67, 80, 89, 93, 100, 535; theory and practice, 7, 10, 11, 15, 48, 56, 70, 79, 83, 84, 87, 90, 92, 93, 97, 102-104, 129, 132, 151, 155, 160, 205, 356, 379, 573, 823; urban policy of, 542, 549, 555, 631, 800-807, 850; war effort, 212-234, 281, 283, 285, 287-290, 292, 293, 300, 303, 383, 631

Chinese League for Freedom, 691
Chinese Liberation Action Committee, 109, 146, 418, 655, 6 660, 661, 698
Chinese Revolutionary League, 109
Ching-chi wen-t'i yü ts'ai-cheng wen-t'i, 287
Ching-ch'i t'uan ti ti-ch'i lien, 310
Ching san-lü pa-t'uan erh-lien ti wen-hua huo-tung, 304
Ch'ing-chiao tao-pao, 633
Ch'ing-chih. See P'ing-hsin.
Ch'ing-chiu wen-hsien, 740
Ch'ing-nien Chung-kuo, 438
Ch'ing-nien p'ing-lun, 563
Ch'ing-nien sheng-huo, 734
Ch'ing-nien shou-ts'e, 750
Ch'ing-nien t'uan wen-ta, 749
Ch'ing-nien tang. See Youth Party (of China).
Ch'ing-suan tang-nei ti Meng-sai-wei chu-i ssu-hsiang, 89
Chiu-ching shui tsai fa-tung nei-chan, 638
Chiu-i pa i-lai, 46

Chiu-kuo pi-hsü mieh Chiang, 574
Chiu-kuo shih-jen t'uan tsu-chih kang-yao, 147
Chiu-kuo wu-tsui, 140
Chiu-san hsüeh-she. See September 3 Society.
Chiu-wang, 112
Chiu-wang chou-k'an, 113
Ch'iu-kuo hui. See National Salvation Association.
Ch'iung-yai ku-tao shang ti tou-cheng, 402
Chou Chien-jen, 731
Chou Ch'ing-wen. See Chow Ching-wen.
Chou En-lai, 2, 43, 68, 106, 110, 118, 120, 128, 137, 163, 164, 226, 521, 581, 590, 592, 617, 620, 621, 625, 701, 721, 793
Chou En-lai, Mme. See Teng Ying-ch'ao.
Chou En-lai yü Teng Ying-ch'ao, 137
Chou Erh-fu, 322, 340, 514, 515
Chou Hsin-min, 671
Chou Li-po, 218, 341, 405
Chou-lun, 694
Chou-mo pao-she, 20
Chou-pao, 695
Chou Pao-chung, 515
Chow Ching-wen, 532, 721
Chronologies (various), 8, 40, 45, 46, 167, 202, 418, 419, 428, 537, 615, 642, 658, 747, 791
Chu Ch'ang-ch'ing, 811
Chu Hsüeh-fan, 787-789
Chu-mu pa-yüeh chi, 808
Chu Teh, 2, 29, 30, 43, 68, 73, 106, 120, 127, 128, 171, 183, 184, 187, 199, 212, 213, 217, 220, 223, 225, 246, 257, 303, 397, 521, 534, 547, 572, 590, 592, 614, 617, 630, 732, 748, 798, 851
Chu Teh, Mme. See K'ang K'o-Ch'ing.

Ch'u An-p'ing, 707
Ch'u-san-hu, 812
Ch'u-tung chung ti hsin-ssu-chün, 192
Ch'ü-chi pi-hsiung chi, 647
Ch'ü-chu Jih-pen ch'iang-tao ch'u Chung-kuo, 226
Ch'üan chieh-fang ch'ü jen-min tung-yüan ch'i-lai fen-sui Chiang Chieh-shih ti chin-kung, 615
Ch'üan-kuo ch'i-lai chih-chih tang-ch'ien yen-chung wei-chi, 187
Ch'üan-kuo min-chu fu-nü lien-ho hui ch'ou-pei wei-yüan hui, 785
Ch'üan-li chun-pei ta fan-kung, 634
Ch'üan-min chou-k'an, 114
Ch'üan-min k'ang-chan, 115
Ch'üan-t'i nung-min ch'i-lai p'ing-fen t'u-ti, 759
Ch'üan-wei, 835
Chüeh-wu ch'i-lai hsiang kuo-min tang fan-tung p'ai k'ung-su fu-ch'ou, 635
Chui-tao "ssu-pa" yü-nan lieh-shih chi-nien ts'e, 18
Chün-cheng chou-pao, 588
Chün-jen hun, 836
Chün-min chih-chien, 305
Chün-min kuan-hsi, 311
Chün-ta tsung hsiao cheng chih pu, 47
Ch'ün-chung, 564
Ch'ün-chung (Hankow, Chungking, and Shanghai), 2
Ch'ün-chung (Hong Kong), 3
Ch'ün-chung jih-pao she, 538
Ch'ün-chung kung-tso shou-ts'e, 777
Ch'ün-chung tsa-chih she, 564
Ch'ün-li ch'u-pan she, 837
Ch'ün-li pao, 382
Ch'ün-yen, 838

Ch'ün-yün chih-shih hui-pien, 354
Chung-cheng jih-pao, 439
Chung-chi kuo-wen tu-pen, 210
Chung-chien, 696
Chung Ho Tang, 659
Chung-hsin ch'u-pan she, 33, 183
Chung-hua chih-yeh chiao-yü she (p'ai). See Vocational Education Group (of China).
Chung-hua ch'üan-kuo min-chu fu-nü lien-ho hui hsüan-ch'uan chiao-yü pu, 796
Chung-hua ch'üan-kuo tsung kung-hui, 786
Chung-hua jih-pao, 168
Chung-hua lun-t'an, 698
Chung-hua min-tsu chieh-fang hsing-tung wei-yüan hui. See Chinese Liberation Action Committee.
Chung-hua min-tsu ko-ming t'ung-meng. See Chinese Revolutionary League.
Chung-hua shih-pao, 440
Chung-Jih chan-cheng yü kuo-chi, 120
Chung Kung, 116
Chung-kung chih mi-mi chün-shih kung-tso, 205
Chung-kung chün-shih, 200
Chung-kung chung-yang k'ang-ch'an hsüan-yen chi, 69
Chung-kung chung-yang kuan-yü k'ang-Jih ken-chü ti t'u-ti cheng-ts'e ti chüeh-ting, 276
Chung-kung fan shou-hsiang hsing-tung chih p'i-p'an, 597
Chung-kung ho-i hsing-ch'i yü pi-K'ua, 10
Chung-kung jen-ming tien, 16
Chung-kung jen-wu, 21
Chung-kung jen-wu su-miao, 17
Chung-kung k'ang-chan i-pan ch'ing-k'uang ti chieh-shao, 211
Chung-kung ko-chü hsia chih cheng-chih, 55
Chung-kung nei-mu, 28

Chung-kung nei-mu, 839
Chung-kung mi-mi, 70
Chung-kung pu-fa hsing-wei chi p'o-huai k'ang-chan shih-shih chi-yao, 184
Chung-kung tang-ti tsu-chih yü k'ung-chih, 79
Chung-kung ti min-chu tang-p'ai, 657
Chung-kung ti min-ping chih-tu, 239
Chung-kung ti t'u-ti kai-ko cheng-ts'e, 766
Chung-kung t'u-kai yü Chung-kuo t'u-ti wen-t'i, 761
Chung-kung wang ho-ch'u ch'ü, 578
Chung-kung wen-t'i p'ing-i, 160
Chung-kung wen-t'i t'i-yao, 176
Chung-kung yü erh-chieh ts'an-cheng hui, 165
Chung-kuo cheng-chih nei-mu, 840
Chung-kuo cheng-chih wen-t'i chiang-hua, 12
Chung-kuo chieh-fang ch'ü jen-min tai-piao hui-i ch'ou-pei wei-yüan hui mi-shu ch'u, 48
Chung-kuo chieh-fang ch'ü shih-lu, 63
Chung-kuo chih-kung tang tang-chang, 699
Chung-kuo chih-kung yün-tung ti tang-ch'ien jen-wu, 782
Chung-kuo chih-kung yün-tung wen-hsien (by Chao I-po), 781
Chung-kuo chih-kung yün-tung wen-hsien, (by Chung-hua ch'üan-kuo tsung kung-hui), 786
"Chung-kuo chih ming-yün" p'i-p'an, 32
Chung-kuo chih pei-chi, 6
Chung-kuo chin-tai cheng-chih chien-shih, 47

Chung-kuo ching-chi ti kai-tsao, 800
Chung-kuo ch'ing-nien, 745
Chung-kuo ch'ing-nien (Yenan), 741
Chung-kuo ch'ing-nien she, 742-746
Chung-kuo ch'ing-nien tang. See Youth Party.
Chung-kuo ch'ing-nien tang cheng-kang, 687
Chung-kuo ch'ing-nien tang tang-shih tzu-liao, 688
Chung-kuo ch'ing-nien t'ung-hsin, 747
Chung-kuo chü-ta pien-hua ti i-nien, 594
Chung-kuo fu-nü ti-i tz'u ch'üan-kuo tai-piao ta-hui, 797
Chung-kuo fu-nü ti-i tz'u ch'üan-kuo tai-piao ta-hui chung-yao wen-hsien, 796
Chung-kuo ho-p'ing chih-lu, 618
Chung-kuo hsin min-chu chu-i ch'ing-nien t'uan, 748
Chung-kuo hsin min-chu chu-i ch'ing-nien t'uan ti-i tz'u ch'üan-kuo tai-piao ta-hui wen-hsien, 752
Chung-kuo hsin min-chu chu-i ch'ing-nien t'uan t'uan-chang chiang-hua, 742
Chung-kuo hsin min-chu chu-i ch'ing-nien t'uan. Chung-yang tsu-chih pu, 749
Chung-kuo hsin min-chu chu-i ch'ing-nien t'uan. Ho-pei sheng T'ang-shan shih kung-tso wei-yüan hui, 750, 751
Chung-kuo hsin min-chu chu-i ch'ing-nien t'uan. Hua-nan kung-tso wei-yüan hui. Hsüan-ch'uan pu, 398
Chung-kuo hsin min-chu yün-tung chung ti tang-p'ai, 658
Chung-kuo hsin-wen, 841
Chung-kuo hung-huo ssu-shih nien, 13

Chung-kuo jen-min cheng-chih hsieh-shang hui-i ti-i chieh ch'üan-ti hui-i tai-piao fang-wen chi, 25
Chung-kuo jen-min chieh-fang chan-cheng, 654
Chung-kuo jen-min chieh-fang chan-cheng san nien chan-chi tsung-chieh, 636
Chung-kuo jen-min chieh-fang chün. Hua-pei chün-ch'ü. Cheng-chih pu, 235, 516
Chung-kuo jen-min chieh-fang chün. Hua-tung yeh-chan chün. Cheng chih-pu, 539
Chung-kuo jen-min chieh-fang chün. P'ing-ching ch'ien-hsien ssu-ling pu. T'ien-ching shih chün-shih kuan-chih wei-yüan hui. Mi-shu ch'u, 801
Chung-kuo jen-min chieh-fang chün ti san-shih nien, 202
Chung-kuo k'ang-chan liang-nien pi-sheng, 117
Chung-kuo ko hsiao tang-p'ai hsien-k'uang, 655
Chung-kuo ko-ming chi-pen wen-t'i (Hsüeh Mu-ch'iao), 5
Chung-kuo ko-tang ko-p'ai hsien-chuang, 663
Chung-kuo k'o-hsüeh yüan. Li-shih yen-chiu so. Ti-san so, 263
Chung-kuo kung-ch'an tang chi ch'i yü kuo-chi chih kuan-hsi kang-yao, 4
Chung-kuo kung-ch'an tang. Chi-Lu-Yü ch'ü tang-wei. Hsüan-ch'uan pu, 356
Chung-kuo kung-ch'an tang. Chi-Lu-Yü ch'ü tang-wei. She-hui pu, 637
Chung-kuo kung-ch'an tang. Chi-Lu-Yü ch'ü tang wei-yüan hui, 354, 355

Chung-kuo kung-ch'an tang. Chin-Ch'a-Chi chung-yang chü. Hsüan-ch'uan pu, 277
Chung-kuo kung-ch'an tang. Chung-yang chung-yüan chü. Hsüan-ch'uan pu, 802
Chung-kuo kung-ch'an tang. Chung-yang Hua-pei chü. Tang-hsiao chiao-wu ch'u, 540
Chung-kuo kung-ch'an tang. Chung-yang shu-chi ch'u, 71
Chung-kuo kung-ch'an tang. Chung-yang wei-yüan hui, 72, 73, 763
Chung-kuo kung-ch'an tang. Hsi-pei chung-yang chü. Tiao-ch'a yen-chiu shih, 278, 282, 283, 284
Chung-kuo kung-ch'an tang hsüan-ch'uan kung-tso tsung chien-t'ao, 145
Chung-kuo kung-ch'an tang. Hu-nan sheng wei-yüan hui. Hsüan-ch'uan pu, 22
Chung-kuo kung-ch'an tang. Hua-tung chü. Min-yün pu, 764
Chung-kuo kung-ch'an tang. Hua-tung chun-yang chü, 541
Chung-kuo kung-ch'an tang k'ang-chan wen-hsien, 85
[Chung-kuo kung-ch'an tang.] Liao-pei sheng wei-yüan hui. Hsüan-ch'uan pu, 74
Chung-kuo kung-ch'an tang lieh-shih chuan, 26
Chung-kuo kung-ch'an tang nei-mu, 124
Chung-kuo kung-ch'an tang. Nen-chiang sheng wei-yüan hui, 765
Chung-kuo kung-ch'an tang. Shan-tung fen-chü. Hsüan-ch'uan pu, 367
Chung [-kuo] kung[-ch'an tang] tai-piao t'uan, 23
Chung-kuo kung-ch'an tang tang-chang, 75

Chung-kuo kung-ch'an tang tang-chang chiao-ts'ai, 540
Chung-kuo kung-ch'an tang ti-ch'i tz'u tai-piao ta-hui yüan-shih ts'ai-liao hui-pien, 76
Chung-kuo kung-ch'an tang ti kuang-hui chao-yao tsai Hai-nan tao-shang, 399
Chung-kuo kung-ch'an tang ti liu-chung ch'üan-hui wen-chien, 77
Chung-kuo kung-ch'an tang tui chung-hua min-tsu ti kung-h hsien, 49
[Chung-kuo kung-ch'an tang. Tung-pei chü], 517
Chung-kuo kung-ch'an tang yü chung-hua min-tsu, 78
Chung-kuo kung-ch'an tang yü Shang-hai kung-jen, 790
Chung-kuo kung-ch'an tang yü t'u-ti ko-ming, 279
Chung-kuo kuo-chia she-hui tang. See National Social Party (of China).
[Chung-kuo kuo-min tang.] Chung-yang kai-tsao wei-yüan hui. Ti-liu tsu, 79, 80, 81, 200, 201
Chung-kuo kuo-ming tang ko-ming wei-yuan hui. See Revolutionary Committee of the Kuomintang.
Chung-kuo min-chu chih-lu, 568
Chung-kuo min-chu hsien-cheng tang tang-shih, 685
Chung-kuo min-chu hsien-cheng tang ti li-ch'ang, 683
Chung-kuo min-chu she-hui tang. See Democratic-Socialist Party (of China).
Chung-kuo min-chu she-hui tang chuan-chi, 681
Chung-kuo min-chu ts'u-chin hui. See Association for Promoting Democracy (of China).
Chung-kuo min-chu t'ung-meng. See Democratic League (of China).

Chung-kuo min-chu t'ung-meng erh-chung ch'üan-hui cheng-chih pao-kao, 665
Chung-kuo min-chu t'ung-meng san-chung ch'üan-hui, 666
Chung-kuo min-chu t'ung-meng ti hsing-chih yü jen-wu, 670
Chung-kuo min-chu t'ung-meng tsung-pu, 665, 666, 667
Chung-kuo nei-chan chung ti liang-t'iao lu-hsien, 565
Chung-kuo nei-mu, 711
Chung-kuo nü-tzu ta-hsüeh chao-sheng chien-chang, 319
Chung-kuo ssu ta chia-tsu ti wei-chi, 425
Chung-kuo tang-tai cheng-tang lun, 664
Chung-kuo ti-hou k'ang-Jih min-chu ken-chü ti kai-k'uang, 50
Chung-kuo ti-san shih-li ch'u-hsien, 691
Chung-kuo t'u-ti fa ta-kang, 763
Chung-kuo t'u-ti wen-t'i yü t'u-ti kai-ko, 774
Chung-kuo t'ung-i wen-t'i, 591
Chung-kuo wang ho-ch'u ch'ü, 722
Chung-kuo wen-t'i wen-hsien, 418
Chung-liu, 842
Chung-mei p'ing-lun, 700
Chung-pao she, 813
Chung-shan jih-pao, 441
Chung-Su jih-pao, 442
Chung-teng kuo-wen, 324
Chung-yang chih-hsing wei-yüan hui ti-ssu tz'u ch'üan-t'i hui-i tso-chan pao-kao, 645
Chung-yang jih-pao (Chengteh), 443
_____. (Chungking), 444
_____. (Shanghai), 445
_____. (Nanking), 446
Chung-yang jih-pao (Canton), 447
Civil War. See CCP: civil war; also CCP and KMT.
Common Program (see also Political Consultative Conference), 670

Communist legal system, 56, 61, 243, 337, 363, 404, 406

Democratic Constitutionalist Party (see also Democratic-Socialist Party), 683, 685
Democratic League, 418, 426, 475, 568, 582, 626, 651, 655, 657, 660, 661, 665-680, 702, 707, 710-712, 753, 852
Democratic-Liberal Groups (see also under names of specific groups), 2, 3, 20, 25, 48, 420, 425, 428, 582, 587, 655-732, 862
Democratic National Reconstruction Association, 418, 655, 657, 658, 661
Democratic Reconstruction Army, 640
Democratic-Socialist Party, 659, 664, 681-685, 729
Domei (Japanese News Agency), 231

East China Field Army, 539
Education (see also under specific educational institutions), 29, 59, 63, 102, 107, 114, 134, 213, 243, 269, 302, 304, 308, 314-331, 333, 335, 337, 342, 349, 360, 363, 366, 384, 390, 403, 513, 528, 529, 537, 596, 694, 709, 753, 754
Eighteenth Group Army, 169, 209, 210, 213, 220, 224, 225, 227, 232, 332, 373, 643
Eighth Route Army, 127, 131, 207, 209, 213, 215, 216, 219, 220, 223, 229, 230, 243, 288-291, 303, 304, 315, 341, 344, 635
Engels, Friedrich, 798
Epstein, Israel, 406

"Fa-chan sheng-ch'an" "yung-cheng ai-min" wen-hsien chi, 303
Fa-ling hui-pien (1942), 349
Fa-ling hui-pien (1946), 350
Fan Ch'ang-chiang, 118, 143
Fan Feng-lin, 165
Fan-kung, 51
Fan-shen, 411
Fan-tui nei-chan pao-wei ho-p'ing pao-wei chieh-fang ch'ü, 588
Fan Wen-lan, 32, 82, 361
Fang Fang, 3, 279
Federation of Labor Unions, 477
Fei Hsiao-t'ung, 675, 684, 696, 700
Fei-tang ti tou-cheng ts'e-lüeh, 11
Fei-tang ti tsu-chih yü ts'e-lüeh lu-hsien, 80
Fei-tang tsu-chih hsi-t'ung t'u-piao hui-pien, 81
Fen-chan erh-shih-san nien ti Hai-nan tao, 401
Fen-sui ti-chu fan-pa yin-mou, 767
Feng Chung-yün, 2, 26, 518
Feng-hsing, 843
Feng-huo tung-pei, 519
Feng Pai-chü, 399, 400, 401
Feng Wen-pin, 528, 745, 748
Feng Yü-hsiang, 613
Feng-yün, 689
First All-China Youth Conference, 548
Fu-hsiao ch'u-pan she, 638
Fu-nü yün-tung wen-hsien, 798
Fushih. See Border Regions: Yenan.

Guerrilla warfare, 71, 106, 152, 204, 207, 208, 211, 213, 222, 227, 232, 336, 341, 357, 380, 398, 400, 511, 518, 641

Hai-ch'ao chou-pao, 844
Hai-yün, 24
Hall, Kathleen, 138
Hao-jan, 215
Ho Ch'ang-kung, 216
Ho-erh-li ta-shih ti "kung-hsien," 616
Ho Lung, 43, 213, 225, 246, 303
Ho-p'ing chien-she hsin Chung-kuo, 558
Ho-p'ing jih-pao (see also Sao-tang pao), 57, 669
Ho-p'ing jih-pao (Chungking), 448
_____. (Shanghai), 449
_____. (Hankow), 450
_____. (Mukden), 451
Ho-p'ing min-chu ti tao-lu, 603
Ho-p'ing min-chu t'ung-i chien-kuo chih-lu, 679
Ho-p'ing she, 701
Ho Sung, 255
Ho-t'an hui ch'eng-kung ma, 857
Ho Ying-ch'in, 183, 187, 836
Ho Yung-chi, 702
Hou Wai-lu, 119
Hsi-tung, 279
Hsi-tzu hu-pien hua Chung-kung, 819
Hsia-kuan hsüeh an, 701
Hsia Yang, 185
Hsia Yen, 120, 535
Hsiang-ch'ün, 418
Hsiang p'o-k'ou yao-fan ch'ih, 733
Hsiang-ts'un chien-she p'ai. See Rural Reconstruction Group.
Hsiang Ying, 68, 178, 186, 187
Hsiang Ying chiang-chün yen-lun chi, 186
Hsiao Chien-ying, 121
Hsiao Ching-kuang, 222
Hsiao-hsi, 566
Hsiao Hsiang-jung, 232
Hsiao-hsiao, 821
Hsiao Hua, 65
Hsiao K'o, 43, 213

Hsiao Min-sung, 567
Hsiao San, 26, 754, 756
Hsiao Tsung, 568
Hsiao Wen-che, 656
Hsiao Yeh-na, 657
Hsien-hsing fa-ling hui-chi, 337
Hsien-tai Chung-kuo cheng-tang yü cheng-chih, 656
Hsien-tai hsin-wen, 668
Hsin chan-hsien, 122
Hsin chan-shih k'o-pen, 196
Hsin ch'ang-ch'eng she, 52
Hsin cheng-lun, 520
Hsin chiao-yü hui, 320
Hsin chiao-yü lun-wen hsüan-chi, 334
Hsin chieh-fang ch'ü ti ch'ün-chung sheng-ch'an, 762
Hsin ch'ün-chung, 406
Hsin Chung-hua pao, 452
Hsin chung-hua pao (Yenan), 172, 187
Hsin Chung-kuo ch'u-pan she, 217
Hsin Chung-kuo jen-wu chih, 20
Hsin Chung-kuo pao-she, 166
Hsin Chung-kuo p'ing-lun chi, 166
Hsin Chung-kuo shih tsen-yang tan-sheng ti, 9
Hsin Chung-kuo ti shu-kuang, 617
Hsin Chung-kuo tsai chin-chan chung, 217
Hsin Chung-kuo wen-hsien ch'u-pan she, 658
Hsin hsi-wang, 845
Hsin-hsin hsin-wen, 453
Hsin hsüeh-shih, 218
Hsin-hua jih-pao, 53
Hsin-hua jih-pao, 53, 521, 569, 617
Hsin-hua jih-pao Hua-pei fen-kuan, 187
Hsin-hua jih-pao tzu-liao shih, 543
Hsin-hua she, 419
Hsin-hua shih-shih ts'ung-k'an she, 25
Hsin-hua wen-chai, 570
Hsin kuo-min jih-pao, 454

Hsin min-chu chu-i ch'eng-shih cheng-ts'e, 542
Hsin min-chu chu-i kung-shang cheng-ts'e, 803
Hsin min-chu chu-i wen-hua chiao-yü, 317
Hsin min-chu shou-ts'e, 422
Hsin-min pao, 246
Hsin-min pao (Chungking), 455
_____. (Nanking), 456
_____. (Peiping), 457
Hsin-min shu-tien, 249, 639
Hsin-nien hsien-tz'u, 592
Hsin-pao, 458
Hsin-ping chün-shih chiao-ts'ai, 368
Hsin she-hui ti hsin nü-kung, 785
Hsin sheng-ming pao, 459
Hsin-sheng pao, 460
Hsin-sheng tsa-chih, 571
Hsin shih-ch'i ti lu-hsien, 572
Hsin shih-tai, 846
Hsin-ssu-chün chien Shan-tung chün-ch'ü tang-wu wei-yüan hui, 544
Hsin-ssu-chün man-chi, 178
Hsin-ssu-chün Shan-tung chün-ch'ü ssu-ling pu, 368
Hsin-ssu-chün shih-chien chen-hsiang, 183
Hsin-ssu-chün Su-chung chün-ch'ü ti-ssu ti-fang wei-yüan hui, 407
Hsin-Su pao, 461
Hsin-ti jen-wu yü hsin-ti li-liang, 545
Hsin wen-hua, 573
Hsin wen-hua fu-wu she, 574
Hsin-wen pao, 462
Hsin-wen p'ing-lun, 702
Hsin-wen shih-chieh, 847
Hsin-wen t'ien-hsia, 848
Hsin-wen tsa-chih, 849
Hsiu-yang chih-nan, 84
Hsiung Ch'i, 123
Hsü Shu-huai, 321

Hsü Te-yen, 696
Hsü T'e-li, 149, 323, 570
Hsü Yu-lai, 124
Hsüan-chu wen-chien, 274
Hsüeh-chan pa-nien ti Chiao-tung tzu-ti ping, 386
Hsüeh-ch'ang, 712
Hsüeh-hsi chih-shih she, 604
Hsüeh-hsi sheng-huo, 107
Hsüeh-hsing ssu-i, 814
Hsüeh Mu-ch'iao, 5, 807
Hsüeh-shih sheng-huo, 125
Hu Ch'iu-yüan, 6
Hu-ch'ün kou-tang hsien-hsing chi, 659
Hu En-tse, 735
Hu Lin, 736
Hu-nan ko-ming lieh-shih chuan, 22
Hu Shou-yü, 680
Hu Yü-chih, 143, 692
Hua-chung jih-pao, 463
Hua-chung t'ieh-mu, 830
Hua-chung wen-hui, 850
Hua Kang, 2, 135, 570, 692
Hua-pei cheng-wu wei-yüan hui. Cheng-wu t'ing. Ch'ing-pao chü, 167
Hua-pei hsin-hua shu-tien pien-chi pu, 618, 640, 660
Hua-pei jih-pao, 464
Hua-pei tsung kung-hui ch'ou-pei wei-yüan hui, 787
Hua-shang pao, 420, 421, 804
Hua-tung ch'ü kuo-wai mao-i kuan-li chan-hsing pan-fa chi fu-piao, 805
Hua-tung ch'ü kuo-wai mao-i kuan-li chü, 805
Hua Ying-shen, 26
Huai-an O-ch'ien hsiang t'u-ti kai-ko ching-yen chieh-shao, 764
Huan Hsiang, 723
Huan-nan shih-pien ch'ien-hou, 179
Huan-nan shih-pien ti chen-hsiang Su-pei shih-pien ti chen-hsiang, 180

Huan-nan t'u-wei chi, 193
Huang-ch'iao chan-tou, 185
Huang chüeh, 814
Huang Feng, 219
Huang Kan-yin, 669
Huang Ming, 815
Huang Tao-ming, 816
Huang T'ao, 202
Huang Wen-chieh, 2
Huang Yen-p'ei, 250, 662, 706, 709, 710
Hui-i ti-san-tzu kuo-nei ko-ming chan-cheng shih-chi ti Shang-hai hsüeh-sheng yün-tung, 735
"Hundred Regiment Offensive," 225
Hung-ch'i p'iao-p'iao pien-chi pu, 641
Hung-ch'ü shih-lun t'e-chi, 215
Hung-chün ti-pa chün tang ti sheng-huo, 216
Hung Huang, 522
Hung-mien ch'u-pan she, 85
Hung-se Chung-kuo ti p'an-t'u, 817
Hung Yen-lin, 546
Huo-kuo ts'an-min ti kung-fei chün-shih, 201
Huo-min p'an-kuo chi, 813
Huo-yüeh ti Fu-shih, 252
Hurley, Patrick J., 616

I-chiu-ssu-ch'i Chung-kuo yao-lan, 428
I-chiu-ssu-ch'i nien shang-pan nien lai ch'ü tang-wei kuan-yü t'u-kai yün-tung ti chung-yao wen-chien, 355
I-chiu-ssu-ch'i nien shou-ts'e, 420
I-chiu-ssu-ch'i nien tou-cheng jen-wu yü ch'ien-t'u, 547
I-chiu-ssu-chiu nien shou-ts'e, 421

I chiu ssu san nien liu-shou ping-
    t'uan sheng-ch'an chien-she,
    289
I-chiu-ssu-san nien sheng-ch'an
    yün-tung chung ti ching-yen,
    283
I-chiu-ssu-ssu nien tung-hsüeh yün-
    tung tsung-chieh, 403
I-chiu-ssu-wu nien pien-ch'ü ti chu-
    yao jen-wu ho tso-feng wen-t'i,
    270
I Chün-tso, 845
I-erh-chiu shih yü Chin-Chi-Lu-Yü
    pien-ch'ü, 364
I-erh-i min-chu yün-tung chi-nien
    chi, 739
I-erh-i ti hui-i, 736
I-ko cheng-fu i-ko tang, 175
I-ko huo-cho liu-shih ko, 398
I-ko ko-ming ken-chü ti ti ch'eng-
    ch'ang, 347
I-meng tao-pao, 237
I-nien-lai Chung-Jih cheng-chü ti
    yen-pien, 577
I-nien lai ti yung-cheng ai-min
    kung-tso, 306
I-shih pao, 465
"Incident of the Seven Gentlemen,"
    140
International Communist movement,
    1, 4, 43

Jao Sou-shih, 26, 191
Japan. See Sino-Japanese War and
    CCP: Sino-Japanese War.
Japanese Collaborators (see also
    Wang Ching-wei), 230-232
Japanese Communist Party, 2, 151
Jehol Province, 523
Jen Cho-hsüan, 34, 41, 148, 860
Jen-min chan-cheng, 197
Jen-min chiang-ling ch'ün-hsiang,
    24
Jen-min chieh-fang chan-cheng
    liang-chou nien tsung-chieh ho
    ti-san nien ti jen-wu, 629
Jen-min chou-pao, 619
Jen-min ch'u-pan she, 54, 203,
    251, 642
Jen-min jih-pao, 800
Jen-min jih-pao (Dairen), 469
———. (Hantan), 466
———. (Hantan and Shihchiachuang),
    468
———. (Peiping), 470
———. (Peiping) (Peking), 471
———. (Wuhan), 467
Jen-min jih-pao hao-wai, 851
Jen-min min-chu chuan-cheng ti
    li-lun yü shih-chien, 35
Jen-min pao, 703
Jen-min shih-chi, 704
Jen-min shih-tai, 575
Jen-min ti chün-tui (newspaper),
    643
Jen-min ti chün-tui (by Wang
    Hsiang-li), 233
Jen-min ti sheng-li, 14
Jen-min ti ta-hsüeh, 342
Jen-min ti yung-shih men, 627
Jen Pi-shih, 26, 43, 68, 213, 215,
    223, 535, 542, 543, 748, 765,
    771, 802
Jen-tao, 682
Jen ti chieh-chi hsing, 90
Jen T'ien-ma, 252
Jen-yen chou-k'an, 705
Jih-pen t'ou-hsiang hou ti Chung-
    kuo kung-ch'an tang, 554
Jo-ho sheng jen-min tai-piao hui-i
    ching-kuo chi chüeh-i an, 523

K. N. , 86
K'ai-chan ta kuei-mu ti ch'ün-
    chung wen-chiao yün-tung, 322
K'ai Feng, 2, 43, 68, 86
K'ai-ming jih-pao (Hengyang), 172
Kalgan (capture of), 197
Kan-pu hsüeh-hsi, 548
Kan Yu-lan, 27

K'ang-chan, 126
K'ang-chan chien-kuo chung chih Chung-kuo ch'ing-nien tang, 690
K'ang-chan ch'ien-hou, 121
K'ang-chan chou-pao. See Chien-kuo chou-pao.
K'ang-chan ch'u-pan she, 127
K'ang-chan chung ti cheng-tang ho p'ai-pieh, 109
K'ang-chan chung ti Chung-kuo cheng-chih, 58
K'ang-chan chung ti Chung-kuo chiao-yü yü wen-hua, 59
K'ang-chan chung ti Chung-kuo ching-chi, 60
K'ang-chan chung ti Chung-kuo chün-shih, 208
K'ang-chan chung ti pa-lu chün, 220
K'ang-chan i-lai chung-yao wen-chien hui-chi, 71
K'ang-chan jih-pao, 299
K'ang-chan jih-pao, 472
K'ang-chan ming-lun chi, 128
K'ang-chan pa-nien lai ti pa-lu chün yü hsin-ssu-chün, 209
K'ang-chan pao, 473
K'ang-chan shih-ch'i pien-ch'ü chiao-yü chien-she, 335
K'ang-chan ta-hsüeh, 221
K'ang-chan wu chou-nien t'e-chi, 39
K'ang-chan yü wen-hua, 408
K'ang chien kuo-ts'e hsia chih Chung-kuo kung-ch'an tang, 190
K'ang-han li-kung, 409
K'ang-Jih chan-cheng chih i-i, 150
K'ang-Jih chan-cheng shih-ch'i chieh-fang ch'ü kai-k'uang, 54
K'ang-Jih chan-cheng shih-ch'i Chung-kuo jen-min chieh-fang chün, 203
K'ang-Jih chiu-kuo chih-nan, 86
K'ang-Jih ken-chü-ti cheng-ts'e t'iao-li hui-chi: Chin-Ch'a-Chi chih-pu, 343

K'ang-Jih ken-chü-ti cheng-ts'e t'iao-li hui-chi: Shen-Kan-Ning chih-pu, 269
K'ang-Jih min-tsu t'ung-i chan-hsien chih-nan, 68
K'ang-Jih min-tsu t'ung-i chan-hsien lun, 119
K'ang-Jih yu-chi chan-cheng ti i-pan wen-t'i, 222
K'ang K'o-ch'ing, 732, 797
K'ang Sheng, 26, 43, 68, 149
K'ang-ta i fen-hsiao. Cheng-chih ch'u, 129
K'ang-ta kuei-lai, 321
K'ang-ta tung-t'ai, 328
K'ang-ta yü ch'ing-nien, 314
K'ang-ti, 188
K'ang Yu-wei, 685
Kao Chi, 610
Kao Hsi-ping, 524
Kao Jih-pen she-hui chu-i che, 151
Kao Kang, 3, 43, 65, 87, 104, 244, 263, 270, 293, 299, 301, 322, 327, 769, 798
Kao K'o-fu, 223
Kao Shu-hsün, 640
Kao Shu-hsün chiang-chün Han-tan ch'i-i t'e-chi, 640
Kao Wei-sung, 304
Ken-chü ti p'u-t'ung chiao-yü ti kai-ko wen-t'i, 318
Keng-yün, 422
KMT. See Kuomintang.
Ko k'ang-Jih tang-p'ai ti hsüan-ch'uan huo-tung, 146
Ko-ming chen-li ch'u-pan she, 576
K'o-kuan, 706
Korean Communist Party, 423, 511
Korean War, 427
Koreans in United Northeast Anti-Japanese Army, 108
Kuan-ch'a, 707
Kuan-chung pao, 410

297

Kuan Hsiang-ying, 26
Kuan Lin-cheng, 644
Kuan-ping kuan-hsi, 312
Kuan-tung jih-pao, 474
Kuan-yü cheng-shih cheng-ts'e ti chi-ko wen-hsien, 549
Kuan-yü ch'ien tung-pei ti-hsia tang tsu-chih chih tang-yüan yü k'ang lien kan-pu ti chüeh-ting, 517
Kuan-yü chih-shih fen-tzu ti kai-tsao, 535
Kuan-yü ch'üeh-ting chieh-chi ch'u-shen wen-t'i, 379
Kuan-yü hsien-cheng yü t'uan-chieh wen-t'i, 164
Kuan-yü hsin chieh-fang ch'ü ta-liang fa-chan tang ti wen-t'i, 541
Kuan-yü hsin-ssu-chün shih-chien hua-ch'iao yü-lun i-pan, 182
Kuan-yü hsin ti chih-shih fen-tzu kan-pu ti i-hsieh wen-t'i, 88
Kuan-yü hsüeh-hsi wen-t'i chi Huai-pei ch'ü tang-wei ti hsin, 97
Kuan-yü kung-ch'an tang-yüan ch'i-chieh wen-t'i, 99
Kuan-yü kung-shang yeh ti cheng-ts'e, 806
Kuan-yü kung-tang wen-t'i chih chien-t'ao yü wu-jen ying-ch'ü chih fang-chin, 130
Kuan-yü pu-tui chih-hsing hsin tang-chang nei chi-ko wen-t'i ti chieh-shih yü ch'u-pu kuei-ting ts'ao-an, 544
Kuan-yü pu-tui chung chien-li hsin min-chu chu-i ch'ing-nien t'uan, 743
Kuan-yü shih-pa chi-t'uan chün hsing-tung cheng-hsiang, 224
Kuang-fu ch'u-pan she, 577
Kuang-hua chou-pao, 708
Kuang-jung kuei-yü min-chu, 424
Kuang-ming chao-yao cho jen-min ti ch'eng-shih, 831
Kuang-ming ch'u-pan she, 670
Kuang-ming jih-pao, 475
Kuang-ming pao (edited by Liang Sou-ming), 671
Kuang-ming pao (edited by Lu I), 672
Kuang-ming pao, 476
Kuang-tung jen-min k'ang-Jih yu-chi chan-cheng hui-i, 400
Kung-ch'an tang chih tsui-o, 168
Kung-ch'an tang jen, 379
Kung-ch'an tang p'o-huai k'ang-chien chih ching-kuo, 170
Kung-ch'an tang p'ou-hsi, 15
Kung-ch'an tang ti chieh-p'ou, 7
Kung-ch'an tang ti pa-hsi, 824
Kung-ch'an tang tsen-yang chih-li Ping Ching, 809
Kung-ch'an tang wen-t'i, 860
Kung-ch'an tang-yüan, 379
Kung-ch'ü hui-i, 826
Kung-ch'ü hui-i hsü-p'ien, 827
Kung-chün nei-mo chieh-p'ou, 194
Kung-fei chan-lüeh chan-shu chih yen-chiu, 204
Kung-fei chün-shih chih p'ou-hsi, 206
Kung-fei t'u-ti cheng-ts'e chih yen-chiu, 768
Kung-fei t'ung-chan kung-tso ti ts's-lüeh yü yün-yung, 132
Kung-jen jih-pao, 477
Kung-jen ti hsin t'ien-ti, 788
Kung-lun ch'u-pan she, 205
Kung-p'ing pao, 669
Kung-p'ing pao, 852
Kung-tang p'o-huai k'ang-chan yin-mou ti tsung pao-lu, 189
Kung-tso t'ung-hsün (Hopeh-Shantung-Honan), 357
Kung-tso t'ung-hsün (Northwest), 550
Kung-tso t'ung-hsün (Puhai), 392
Kung-yün wen-chi, 793
Kunming Student Incident, 660
Kuo Chi-chiao, 206

Kuo-chi ch'u-pan she, 605
Kuo-chi shih-shih yen-chiu hui, 131
Kuo-fang pu, 645
Kuo-fang pu shih-cheng chü tzu-liao mu-lu: Kung-fei shih tzu-liao chih-pu, 423
Kuo-hsün (Chungking), 709
Kuo-hsün (Hong Kong), 710
Kuo Hua-jo, 222
Kuo-kung chih-chien, 173
Kuo-kung ho-tso ti wei-lai, 174
Kuo-kung hsiang-k'o, 167
Kuo-kung liang-tang k'ang-chan ch'eng-chi pi-chiao, 230
Kuo-min cheng-fu chu-hsi kuang-chou hsing-yüan. Cheng-chih pu, 578
Kuo-min cheng-fu. Kuo-fang pu. Shih-cheng chü, 423
[Kuo-min cheng-fu]. Nei-cheng pu. Tiao-ch'a chü, 7
[Kuo-min cheng-fu]. Ssu-fa hsing-cheng pu. Tiao-ch'a chü, 132
Kuo-min ching-chi tiao-ch'a ch'u-pu yen-chiu, 352
Kuo-min hsin-pao, 478
Kuo-min jih-pao, 669
Kuo-min jih-pao, 479
Kuo-min ko-ming chün. Ti pa-lu chün. Lien-fang chün. Cheng-chih pu. Hsüan-ch'uan pu, 411, 579
Kuo-min ko-ming chün. Ti shih-pa chi-t'uan chün. Cheng-chih pu, 169, 225
Kuo-min tang ko-ming wei-yüan hui. See The Revolutionary Committee of the Kuomintang.
Kuo-min tang ti sui-ching cheng-ts'e, 637
Kuo-ming, 580
Kuo Mo-jo, 3, 123, 125, 126, 660, 677, 695, 700
Kuo Mo-jo hsien-sheng tsui-chin yen-lun chi, 123
Kuo nei-wai hsing-shih, 623

Kuo-she tang. See National Social Party (of China).
Kuo-shih t'ung, 598
K'uo-ch'ing ssu-hsiang chieh ti mi-wu, 133
Kuomintang (KMT) (see also United Front; Chiang Kai-shek), 1, 6, 8, 10, 20, 25, 45, 48, 59, 109, 146, 163, 418, 425, 426, 428, 522, 556-626, 637, 647, 655, 660, 676, 732, 768, 832, 834-836, 838, 840, 841, 844, 845, 847-849, 854, 855, 862, 863
Kuomintang, The (author). See Chung-kuo kuo-min tang.

Labor Heroes' Conference, 291, 299
Labor Movement, 3, 780-795
Lai-tung hsien cheng-fu i-chiu-ssu-liu nien shang pan-nien min-cheng kung-tso tsung-chieh, 383
Lai-tung hsien cheng-fu min-chu yün-tung tsung-chieh pao-kao, 384
Lai-yang hsien cheng-fu kuan-yü pa chiu shih yüeh-fen chi-ko wen-t'i ti pao-kao, 385
Land Reform (see also CCP: land laws and reform), 361, 552, 722, 757-779
Lao-tung cheng-ts'e yü t'u-ti cheng-ts'e ch'u-pu chien-ch'a, 407
Lao-tung hu-chu ti tien-hsing li-tzu ho ching-yen, 338
Lenin, 88, 545, 769
Li-chan, 236
Li Chao-lin, 26, 513, 525
Li-ch'eng hsiao-pao, 412
Li Chi-shen, 837
Li-Chiang kuan-hsi yü Chung-kuo, 861

Li Fu-ch'un, 2, 43, 68, 86, 301, 329
Li Fu-jen, 717
Li Hsien-nien, 405
Li Hsü, 606
Li-hua, 607
Li I-shan, 55
Li I-sheng, 401
Li-keng, 285, 770
Li Kuang, 789
Li Kung-p'u, 114, 125, 140, 671, 712
Li Li-ch'u, 253
Li Li-san, 3, 542, 787, 789
Li Lin, 541
Li Mien, 35
Li-ming ti hao-chio, 853
Li-po. See Chou Li-po.
Li Pu, 424
Li Shih-han, 8
Li-shih wen-hsien she, 581, 582, 608
Li Ssu-mu, 143
Li Ta-ming, 683, 685
Li Te-ch'üan, 797
Li Tsung-jen, 630, 836, 837, 854, 861
Li Tu, 525
Li Wei-han, 2, 3
Li Yü, 301, 373, 374, 769, 793, 807
Liang-chung tso-feng, 377
Liang Jo-ch'en, 680
Liang-nien i-lai t'o-p'ai tsui-hsing ti tsung-chieh, 158
Liang P'ing, 136
Liang Sheng-chün, 854
Liang Sou-ming, 671, 732, 846
Liao Ch'eng-chih, 26, 43, 221, 226, 452
Liao Kai-lung, 9
Liao-ning jih-pao, 480
Liao Yao-hsiang, 527
Liberated areas (see also Border Regions), 2, 3, 863

Liberation Daily, 39, 76, 78, 102, 162, 187, 228, 230, 237, 299, 318, 322, 325, 327, 329, 372, 397, 417, 521, 534, 547, 556-558, 562, 564, 569, 572, 574, 576, 586, 588, 590, 592, 594, 601, 608, 612, 614-616, 619, 621, 622, 624-626, 632, 648, 650, 652, 793, 798. See also Chieh-fang jih-pao.
Lien-ho jih-pao, 481
Lin Chen, 711
Lin Chung-kuo, 170
Lin Feng, 528
Lin Piao, 2, 37, 43, 68, 106, 226, 246, 252, 515, 521, 803
Lin Po-ch'ü, 39, 43, 106, 128, 164, 252, 264, 318, 323, 570, 755
Lin Tsu-han, 2, 68, 131
Lin Ying, 402
Lin Yü-ying, 130
Ling-tao tso-feng, 313
Liu Ch'ang-sheng, 790
Liu I, 658
Liu Ning-i, 2, 3, 789, 806
Liu Pai-yü, 254, 526
Liu Po-ch'eng, 2, 73, 207, 364, 527, 643, 850
Liu Shao-ch'i, 2, 3, 29, 30, 43, 65, 68, 71, 84, 89-96, 103, 277, 293, 542, 771, 798
Liu Shao-t'ang, 817
Liu Shih, 115, 143
Liu-shou ping-t'uan ti ying-hsiung men ho mu-fan che, 290
Liu Tzu-chiu, 97
Liu Wang Li-ming, 712
Liu Ya-lou, 222
Liu Ya-tzu, 125, 532, 710, 724
Liu-yüeh i-lai kuo-kung t'an-p'an chung-yao wen-hsien, 620
Lo Ch'iung, 286, 798
Lo Fu, 2, 43, 68, 86, 127, 128, 221

Lo Jui-ch'ing, 43, 195, 207, 232
Lo Jung-huan, 370, 373, 803
Lo Lung-chi, 668, 675, 711, 717, 720
Lo Mai, 2, 43, 82, 317, 322, 327, 584
Lo Pin-sheng, 818
Lo Ping-hui, 26, 570
Lo Teng-hsien, 2
Long March, 127, 234
Lu Chieh, 226
Lu chih-yu i-t'iao, 713
Lu-chung ch'ü k'ang-Jih min-chu cheng-ch'üan chien-she ch'i-nien lai ti chi-pen tsung-chieh chi chin-hou chi-pen jen-wu, 393
Lu-chung hsing-cheng kung-shu, 393
Lu-chung wen-hsieh, 394
Lu Hsün, 111, 153
Lu Hsün School of Arts, 256
Lu P'ing, 255
Lu Ting-i, 2, 3, 213, 232, 551
Lü Cheng-ts'ao, 2, 207, 800
Lun chan-chü, 621
Lun cheng-chih min-chu hua yü chün-tui kuo-chia hua, 567
Lun chieh-fang ch'ü chan-ch'ang, 199
Lun chih-shih fen-tzu, 543
Lun ch'ün-chung kuan-tien, 769
Lun ch'ün-chung lu-hsien, 96
Lun Chung-kuo cheng-chih yü Chung-kuo wen-hua ti tung-hsiang, 42
Lun hsin chieh-fang ch'ü t'u-ti cheng-ts'e (by Chieh-fang she), 757
Lun hsin chieh-fang ch'ü t'u-ti cheng-ts'e (by Hsin min-chu ch'u-pan she), 772
Lun hsin chieh-tuan
Lun hsin Chung-kuo, 139
Lun kung-ch'an tang, 98
Lun kung-ch'an tang yüan ti hsiu-yang, 91
Lun kung-shang yeh cheng-ts'e, 802
Lun kuo-chi chu-i yü min-tsu chu-i, 92
Lun ling-tao fang-fa, 104
Lun Ma Lieh chu-i chüeh-ting ts'e-lüeh ti chi-ko chi-pen yüan-tse, 129
Lun shih-chieh mao-tun, 613
Lun so-wei chieh-fang ch'ü cheng-ch'üan wen-t'i, 57
Lun tang (1946), 93
Lun tang (1950), 94
Lun tang-nei tou-cheng, 95
Lun tung-pei chiao-yü ti kao-ko, 528
Lun Wang Shih-wei ti ssu-hsiang i-shih, 82

Ma Chi-ling, 256
Ma families, 859
Ma Han-ping, 227
Ma-hsieh-erh shih-hua chi-shih, 611
Ma Hsü-lun, 673, 692, 695, 700, 701, 710, 731
Ma Yin-ch'u, 668, 677, 696, 700
Manchuria, 3, 51, 59, 510-534, 579, 581, 590, 613, 650, 651, 660, 678, 702, 704, 767, 777, 787, 788, 829
Mao Tse-tung, 2, 3, 27, 29-34, 35, 36, 37-42, 43, 58, 67, 68, 71, 73, 77, 84, 86, 88, 106, 118, 120, 127, 128, 131, 133, 136, 207, 212, 222, 223, 226, 246, 250, 252, 257, 259, 262, 266, 277, 279, 287, 299, 301, 303, 317, 322, 324, 327, 329, 397, 406, 535, 542, 543, 547, 556, 568, 569, 570, 572, 581, 583, 592, 614, 624, 626, 630,

661, 754, 756, 771, 772, 793, 802, 803, 806, 837, 851, 853
Mao Tse-tung chi-ch'i chi-t'uan, 27
Mao Tse-tung hsüan-chi, 36
Mao Tse-tung lun, 29
Mao Tse-tung p'i-p'an, 34
Mao Tse-tung ssu-hsiang shih Chung-kuo jen-min ta ko-ming sheng-li ti ch'i-chih, 37
Mao Tse-tung t'an-hua ti chien-t'ao, 33
Mao Tse-tung ti chün-shih lu-hsien chi chung-kung ti wu ta cheng-ts'e, 38
Mao Tse-tung ti ssu-hsiang chi tso-feng, 30
Mao Tse-tung tsai Chung-ch'ing, 583
Mao Tse-tung yü hung-huo, 40
Mao Tun, 126, 677, 700
Marshall Mediation, 568, 594, 611-626, 648
Marx, Karl, 798
Mass Movements (see also CCP: Mass Line), 43, 58, 134, 208, 243, 269, 337, 353, 354, 383, 392, 735, 818
Mei-yu kung-ch'an tang chiu mei-yu Chung-kuo, 228
Meng-pang jen-shih ti cheng-yen, 622
Military Council (KMT), 183
Min-chu (Shanghai), 673
Min-chu (Kweilin), 674
Min-chu cheng-ch'üan, 56
Min-chu chien-kuo hui. See Democratic National Reconstruction Association.
Min-chu chien-she, 413
Min-chu chien-she chiang-hua, 61
Min-chu ch'ing-nien (Dairen), 755
Min-chu ch'ing-nien (Kalgan), 754
Min-chu ch'ing-nien (Peiping), 753
Min-chu chou-k'an (Kunming), 675
Min-chu chou-k'an (Peiping), 676

Min-chu hsien-cheng tang. See Democratic Constitutionalist Party (of China).
Min-chu hsing-ch'i k'an, 677
Min-chu pan-yüeh k'an (Peiping), 678
Min-chu pao, 482
Min-chu sheng-huo, 714
Min-chu shih-tai (Canton), 715
Min-chu shih-tai (Hong Kong), 716
Min-chu ts'u-chin hui. See Association for Promoting Democracy (in China).
Min-chu t'ung-meng. See Democratic League.
Min-chu t'ung-meng wen-hsien, 667
Min-chu wen-ts'ung ch'u-pan she, 661
Min-chu yü t'uan-chieh, 159
Min-hsien yüeh-k'an she, 679
Min-i, 134
Min-meng p'i-p'an, 669
Min-ping, 395
Min-ping kung-tso shou-ts'e, 237
Min-ping tai-piao ta-hui shou-ts'e, 240
Min-ping ying-hsiung, 235
Min-she tang. See Democratic-Socialist Party (of China).
Min-tsu kung-lun, 135
Min-tsu yeh-hsin, 152
Min-yen, 718
Min-yen pao, 483
Ming-hsin chi, 717
Minority parties. See Democratic-Liberal Groups.
Mo-ts'a ts'ung-ho erh lai, 169
Mobilization Society of Wuhan, 328
Mongolia, 136
Mu-ch'ien hsing-shih, 559
Mu-ch'ien hsing-shih ti fen-hsi, 136

Mu-ch'ien kuo-nei-wai hsing-shih yü ts'an-cheng, 111
Mu-ch'ien shih-chü chih-nan, 557
Mu-fan chih-tao yüan Sun Yung-chang, 533
Mu Hsin, 646
Mutual labor assistance. See CCP: Cooperative labor farms.

Nan-cheng pei-chan erh-shih-wu nien, 234
Nan-ching wan-pao, 484
Nan-fang jih-pao, 400
Nan-hsia chi, 405
Nan-hsien hsün-hui, 646
Nan-pen chi, 828
National Salvation Association, 109, 140, 655, 714
National Salvation Program, 86, 112-114, 147
National Social Party (see also Democratic-Socialist Party), 109, 146, 655, 661
Nei-wu t'iao-ling chi-lü t'iao-ling ts'ao-an, 373
New China Daily, 57, 172, 187, 207, 560, 583, 602, 608, 612, 802
New China News Agency, 164, 214, 525, 564, 594, 595, 612, 615, 616, 621, 623, 629, 634, 638, 647, 648, 652, 659, 660, 748, 782, 785, 786, 800, 803, 806
New Democracy, 5, 12, 29-31, 34, 42, 317
New Democratic Youth League, 3, 80, 740-756, 858
New Fourth Army (see also New Fourth Army Incident), 106, 163, 186, 188, 209, 221, 229, 405, 407, 418
New Fourth Army Incident, 163, 165, 177-193
New Sixth Army (KMT), 527

Nieh Jung-chen, 2, 336, 340, 778
Nieh Keng-sheng, 819
Ning-sheng, 57
Niu Shan, 229
North Shensi Public Academy, 241, 256
Northeast Anti-Japanese Allied Army. See United Northeast Anti-Japanese Army.
Northern University, 360, 361
Nung-min shih i-chia, 379

Ou Chiang-tung, 190

Pa-lu chün chün-cheng tsa-chih, 207
Pa-lu chün ho lao-pai-hsing, 198
Pa-lu chün. Lien-fang chün. Cheng-chih pu. Hsüan-ch'uan pu, 288, 305, 358
Pa-lu chün. Liu-shou ping-t'uan. Cheng-chih pu, 230, 289-292, 306, 307
Pa-lu chün pai-t'uan ta-chan t'e-chi, 225
Pa-lu chün. Shan-tung Chiao-tung chün-ch'ü. Cheng-chih pu, 386
Pa lu-chün ti ch'ing-nien chan-shih, 229
Pa-lu chün ti ying-hsiung yü mu-fan, 344
Pa tsu-kuo t'ui-hsiang tu-li tzu-yu chieh-fang, 737
Pai Ch'ung-hsi, 183
Pai Shui, 137
P'an Kuang-tan, 684
P'an Tzu-nien, 2, 658
Pao-wei Chung-kuo t'ung-meng, 138
Peasants' and Workers' Democratic Party, 657
Pei-fang tsa-chih, 359

Pei-fang t'ung-hsün, 360
———, 361
Pei-fang wen-hua, 585
Pei-kuo ts'ang-sang chi, 811
P'ei Yu-p'eng, 820
P'eng Chen, 3, 43, 158, 778
P'eng Te-huai, 2, 43, 68, 73, 106, 127, 128, 183, 184, 187, 195, 212, 215, 217, 218, 223, 225, 226
P'eng Tse-min, 725
People's Democratic Dictatorship, 35, 41
People's Liberation Army. See CCP: Army.
People's Political Council, 111, 159, 165, 172, 250, 257, 560
People's Republic of China, attitudes toward, 808-830; founding of, 3, 9, 831-863
Philippines Communist Party, 2
Pien-ch'ü chiao-yü t'ung-hsün, 323
Pien-ch'ü ch'ün-chung pao, 485
Pien-ch'ü tang ti li-shih wen-t'i chien-t'ao, 244
Pien-ch'ü ti lao-tung hu-chu, 284
Pin-hai nung-ts'un, 396
P'ing-hsin, 139
P'ing kung-ch'an tang ti tsu-chih, 105
P'ing-lun pao, 587
Po Chiang Chieh-shih, 560
Po I-po, 773
Po Ku, 2, 18, 26, 43, 68, 110, 246
Po Mao Tse-tung ti "lun jen-min min-chu chuan-cheng," 41
P'o-ch'an ti cheng-chih li-lun, 586
P'o-hai jih-pao, 486
Political Consultative Conference, 2, 12, 25, 35, 61, 418, 420, 548, 558, 567, 568, 579, 584, 590, 600-610, 617, 626, 657, 660, 661, 670, 702, 721, 724, 753
Political Study Clique, 659

Propaganda activities, 64, 102, 145, 146, 341, 384, 414, 542, 826, 858
Pu-tui lao-tung ying-hsiung, 291
Pu-tui lao-tung ying-hsiung ti tai-piao, 288
Pu-tui sheng-huo, 308

Rectification movements. See CCP: rectification movements.
Red Army Academy, 136
Republican Revolution (1911), 5, 150
Revolutionary Committee of the Kuomintang, 657
Rosinger, L. K., 622
Rural Reconstruction Group, 655, 663
Russo-German Non-Aggression Pact, 741

Sa Ch'ien-li, 140
Sa K'ung-liao, 671, 710
Sa Meng-wu, 715
Sa Ying, 425
Sai-shang hsing, 118
San-shih nien-lai ti Shang-hai kung-yün, 792
Sao-tang pao (see also Ho-p'ing jih-pao), 262
September 3 Society, 657
Shan-tung chiao-tung chün-ch'ü chi chiao-tung ch'ü hsing-cheng kung-shu lien-ho kung-pu ling, 390
Shan-tung chieh-fang ch'ü ti kung-shang yeh, 807
Shan-tung chün-ch'ü. Chieh-chih pu. Hsüan-ch'uan pu, 369
Shan-tung chün-ch'ü. P'o-hai ch'ü cheng-chih pu, 397
Shan-tung hsin-hua shu-tien, 623
Shan-tung hua-pao, 370

Shan-tung jen-min ti hsin-sheng, 371
Shan-tung sheng cheng-fu Shan-tung chün-ch'ü kung-pu chih ko-chung t'iao-li kang-yao pan-fa hui-pien, 387
Shan-tung sheng Chiao-tung ch'ü cheng-li t'u-ti teng-chi ch'en-pao teng-chi chan-hsing pan-fa, 388
Shan-tung sheng. Chiao-tung ch'ü. Hsing-cheng kung-shu, 387, 388
——— . Tang-wei hsüan-ch'uan pu, 99, 588
Shan-tung sheng Chiao-tung ch'ü min-kuo sa wu nien tu cheng-liang pan-fa, 389
Shan-tung sheng tsung kung-hui, 793
Shang-hai hsin-hsüeh yen-chiu yüan, 647
Shang-hai t'e-hsieh, 855
Shang-hai tsung kung-hui mi-shu ch'u, 791
Shang-hai tsung kung-hui wen-chiao pu, 792
Shang-jao chi-chung ying, 191
Shang-wu jih-pao, 487
Shang-wu jih-pao, 248
Shangjao (Kiangsi) KMT concentration camp, 191
Shen Chih-yüan, 727, 774
Shen Chün-ju, 114, 125, 140, 714
Shen-Kan-Ning pien-ch'ü cheng-fu, 264
Shen-Kan-Ning pien-ch'ü cheng-fu. Chiao-yü t'ing, 324
Shen-Kan-Ning pien-ch'ü cheng-fu. Min-cheng ting, 271
Shen-Kan-Ning pien-ch'ü cheng-fu, Pan-kung t'ing, 265, 272, 280, 293, 325, 326
Shen-Kan-Ning pien-ch'ü cheng-ts'e t'iao-li hui-chi hsü-pien, 272
Shen-Kan-Ning pien-ch'ü chiao-yü fang-chen, 325
Shen-Kan-Ning pien-ch'ü chien-cheng shih-shih kang-yao, 273
Shen-Kan-Ning pien-ch'ü erh-liu-tzu ti kai-tsao, 278
Shen-Kan-Ning pien-ch'ü fu-yüan ti shuo-ming, 245
Shen-Kan-Ning pien-ch'ü ho-tso she ko-pu yeh-wu kuei-tse, 294
Shen-Kan-Ning pien-ch'ü ho-tso shih-yeh shih-cheng yüan-tse, 295
Shen-Kan-Ning pien-ch'ü hsiang-hsüan tsung-chieh, 271
Shen-Kan-Ning pien-ch'ü, hsüan-chü wei-yüan hui, 274
Shen-Kan-Ning pien-ch'ü mao-i kung-ssu yeh-wu hsü-chih, 296
Shen-Kan-Ning pien-ch'ü min-chien fang-chih yeh, 286
Shen-Kan-Ning pien-ch'ü shih-cheng kang-ling, 275
Shen-Kan-Ning pien-ch'ü shih-lu, 243
Shen-Kan-Ning pien-ch'ü ti-erh chieh ts'an-i hui ch'ang-chu wei-yüan hui, 268
Shen-Kan-Ning pien-ch'ü ti-erh chieh ts'an-i hui chung-yao wen-hsien, 266
Shen-Kan-Ning pien-ch'ü ti-erh chieh ts'an-i hui hui-k'an, 268
Shen-Kan-Ning pien-ch'ü ti-i chieh ts'an-i hui shih-lu, 264
Shen-Kan-Ning pien-ch'ü ts'an-i hui ch'ang-chu hui ti shih-i tz'u cheng-fu wei-yüan hui ti-wu tz'u lien-hsi hui-i chih chüeh-ting chi yu-kuan ching-chi wen-hua chien-she ti chung-yao t'i-an, 267
Shen-Kan-Ning pien-ch'ü ts'an-i hui wen-hsien hui-chi, 263
Shen-Kan-Ning pien-ch'ü tsu-chih lao-tung hu-chu ti ching-yen, 297

Shen-Kan-Ning pien-ch'ü wen-chiao ta-hui hsüan-chi, 327
Shen Kan tiao-ch'a chi, 242
Shen-pao, 488
Shen-pei chien-ying, 262
Shen-pei chih hsing, 259
Shen-pei lun-kuo hua, 258
Shen-pei niao-k'an, 256
Shen-pei yin-hsiang chi, 253
Shen Yün-lun, 689
Sheng-ch'an wen-hsien, 301
Sheng-huo pao, 527
Sheng-huo shu-t'ien, 172
Sheng-huo tsai Yen-an, 255
Sheng-li ch'u-pan she wen-hua tzu-liao shih, 28
Shih-chi p'ing-lun, 719
Shih-chia-chuang jih-pao, 489
Shih-chieh hsin-ch'ao, 589
Shih-chieh jih-pao, 57
Shih-chieh jih-pao (Chungking), 490
Shih-chieh jih-pao (Peiping), 491
Shih-chieh wan-pao, 492
Shih Fu-liang, 695
Shih-hsien ho-p'ing min-chu ti wen-hsien, 590
Shih-hua pao, 493
Shih Liang, 140
Shih-lun, 624
Shih-lun hsüan-chi, 551
Shih-lun hsüan-chi, 562
Shih-lun hsüan-chi, 595
Shih-mo jen ying-fu chan-cheng tse-jen, 419
Shih-mo shih kung-ch'an tang, 74
Shih-shih hsin-wen, 856
Shih-shih hsüeh-hsi ts'ai-liao, 648
Shih-shih jih-pao tzu-liao shih, 591
Shih-shih k'o-k'o wei lao pai-sheng hsing-li ch'u-pi, 87
Shih-shih wen-hsien hsüan-chi, 579
Shih-shih wen-t'i yen-chiu hui, 58-60, 208
Shih-tai ch'ing-nien, 756
Shih-tai chou-k'an, 720
Shih-tai ch'u-pan she, 857
Shih-tai fu-nü, 799
Shih-tai jih-pao, 494
Shih-tai p'i-p'ing, 721
Shih-tai ti yin-hsiang, 526
Shih-tai wen-hsien she, 140
Shih-tai wen-hua ch'u-pan she, 722
Shih-tsin Tung. See Tung Shih-chin.
Shih yü wen, 723
Shui tsai t'o, 584
Sian Incident, 118, 127, 845
Sino-American Association, 700
Sino-Japanese War (see also CCP: Army, and CCP: Sino-Japanese War), 2, 8, 9, 14, 36, 39, 43, 45, 50, 52, 54, 58, 59, 64, 71, 73, 86, 106, 108, 114, 115, 117, 123, 126-128, 149, 150, 154, 158, 199, 203, 207, 208, 211, 215, 218, 219, 222, 226, 241, 336, 358, 387, 402, 428, 536, 568, 709
Sino-Soviet relations (see also CCP and USSR), 1, 520
Smedley, Agnes, 127
Snow, Edgar, 220, 223
So-wei pien-ch'ü, 241
Soong, T. V., 138
Soviet areas. See Border Regions.
Ssu-hsiang fan-sheng hsüan-chi, 100
Ssu-ko min-pan hsiao-hsüeh, 326
"Ssu-pa" hsün-kuo chu lieh-shih chi-nien ts'e, 19
"Ssu-pa" pei-nan lieh-shih chi-nien ts'e, 23
Stalin, 88, 798
Stilwell, Gen. Joseph, 616
Stuart, J. Leighton, 614, 625
Students, 3, 30, 425, 660, 678, 694, 702, 733-739, 741, 753, 754, 814
Su-Huan erh fen-ch'ü Jen-min pao she, 592
Su-O tsai Chung-kuo, 1
Su-pei chen-hsiang, 818

Su-pei kuei-hung, 181
Su Shih-p'ing, 371
Sui-te fen-ch'ü wen-chiao ta-hui mi-shu ch'u, 414
Sun Pao-i, 10, 684
Sun Wei-min, 61
Sun Yat-sen, 6, 135
Sun Yat-sen, Mme., 2, 127, 138, 143
Sung-hua chiang shang ti feng-yün, 515
Sung Jen-ch'iung, 348
Sung Jen-ch'iung kuan-yü cheng-chih kung-tso ti pao-kao, 348
Sung Yün-pin, 714

Ta-chih, 101
Ta-chung hei-pan pao, 414
Ta-chung hsin-wen, 858
Ta-chung jih-pao, 65, 372, 588, 649
Ta-chung jih-pao, 495
_____. (Lin-i), 496
_____. (Shantung Liberated Area), 497
Ta-chung jih-pao she, 39, 171, 237
Ta-chung pao, 498
Ta-chung sheng-huo, 141
Ta hou-fang ti min-chu yün-tung, 660
Ta Kah-kee. See Ch'en Chia-keng.
Ta-kang pao, 510
Ta-kang pao, 499
Ta-kuang pao, 500
Ta Kung Pao, 215, 223, 583, 619
Ta Kung Pao (Chungking), 62
_____. (Shanghai), 501
_____. (Tientsin), 502
Ta-lien jih-pao, 503
Ta-lu, 157
Ta-p'ing. See Lo Teng-hsien.
Ta-tao, 593
Ta-tao Chiang Chieh-shih chien-li hsin Chung-kuo, 651
Ta-ti chou-pao, 724

Ta-ti hsin-wen, 859
Ta-tien ch'a-chien tou-cheng tsung-chieh, 367
T'ai-hang ch'ü hsing-cheng kung-shu, 362
T'ai-hang ch'ü i-chiu-ssu-liu nien chung-yao wen-chien hui-chi, 363
T'ai-hang ch'ü shui-wu kung-shang kung-tso li-nien lai chung-yao chüeh-ting chih-shih ming-ling, 346
T'ai-hang ch'ü ssu-fa kung-tso kai-k'uang, 362
T'ai-wan sheng hsin-wen ch'u, 822
Taiwan, Communist movement on, 80
Taiwan Democratic Self-Government League, 657
T'an Cheng, 2, 232, 313, 329
Tang-ch'ien chih-kung yün-tung ti chi-ko wen-hsien, 783
Tang-ch'ien shih-chü chung-yao wen-t'i, 625
Tang-ch'ien ti chin-chi jen-wu, 372
Tang-nei huo-yeh wen-chien, 552
Tang-p'ai wen-t'i, 148
Tang ti chien-she, 102
Tang-yüan chi-pen chih-shih, 356
Tang-yüan chiao-ts'ai (1946), 103
Tang-yüan chiao-ts'ai (1947), 539
Tang-yüan chiao-ts'ai (1949), 553
T'ang Sheng-chih, 812
T'ang Tsung, 11
T'ao-fen wen-chi, 142
T'ao Hsing-chih, 677, 709
T'ao Shang-hsing (pseud.). See Liu Shao-ch'i.
Ten-Point National Salvation Program. See National Salvation Program.
Teng Ch'u-min, 12, 658, 677, 692, 713
Teng Fa, 2, 18, 26, 43, 293

307

Teng Hsiao-p'ing, 2, 43, 73, 213
Teng-ta, 738
Teng Tzu-li, 293
Teng Yen-ta hsien-sheng hsün-nan shih-wu chou-nien chi-nien hui, 725
Teng Yen-ta ti tao-lu, 725
Teng Ying-ch'ao, 2, 51, 137, 257, 778, 797, 798
"Third Force," (see also Democratic-Liberal Groups), 587, 671, 677, 693, 722, 723, 725, 727, 846
Third Party. See Chinese Liberation Action Committee
Ti Chao-pai, 774
Ti-ch'i ping-t'uan cheng-chih pu, 553
Ti-hou chan-ch'ang shang ti min-ping, 238
Ti-hou k'ang-Jih min-chu ken-chü ti chieh-shao, 52
Ti-jen k'ou-chung ti pa-lu chün hsin-ssu-chün yü Chung-kuo kung-ch'an tang, 231
Ti-k'ang, 143
Ti-liu tz'u ch'üan-kuo lao-ta chüeh-i, 787
Ti-liu tz'u ch'üan-kuo lao-tung ta-hui, 789
Ti pa-lu chün, 127
Ti pa-lu chün hsing-chün chi: K'ang-chan shih-tai, 219
Ti pa-lu chün tsai Shan-hsi, 223
Ti-san tz'u kuo-nei ko-ming chan-cheng kai-k'uang, 642
Ti shih-pa chi-t'uan chün. Shan-tung chün-ch'ü ssu-ling pu. Chün-shih chiao-ts'ai pien-shen wei-yüan hui, 373
Ti shih-pa chi-t'uan chün. Tsung-cheng chih pu, 309-313
Ti shih-pa chi-t'uan chün. Tsung cheng-chih pu. Hsüan-ch'uan pu, 209, 210, 238, 311, 344

Ti-wo tsai hsüan-ch'uan chan-hsien shang, 64
T'ieh-mu hou ti Chung-kuo, 822
T'ieh-mu hou ti Hua-pei, 825
Tien-ching shih chün-shih kuan-chih shih-ch'i cheng-ts'e fa-ling hui-pien, 801
T'ien Han, 700
T'ien-liang chien-hou, 812
Ting Li, 239
Ting Ling, 252, 364, 799
Ting Tso-shao, 823, 824, 825
T'ing-chan wen-hsien, 582
T'o-p'ai tsai Chung-kuo, 149
Tou-cheng, 374
Tou-cheng sheng-huo, 367, 379, 541
Trotskyites (see also Ch'en Tu-hsiu), 109, 149, 157, 158, 218
Truman, President Harry S., 590, 617, 618, 854
Tsai fan feng-so tou-cheng chung chien-li yü chuang-ta ch'ing-nien t'uan, 744
Tsai min-chu yü t'uan-chieh ti chi-ch'u shang chia-ch'iang k'ang-chan cheng-ch'ü tsui-hou sheng-li, 162
Tsai-sheng, 684
Tsai-sheng, 658
Ts'ai Ch'ang, 26, 797, 798
Ts'ai-fang erh-chi, 426
Ts'ai-fang san-chi, 427
Ts'ai Ho-sen, 131
Ts'an-cheng hui yü yen-lun tzu-yu, 172
Ts'ang-hai hsing, 726
Ts'ao Chü-jen, 426, 427
Tsen-yang chien-li hsin min-chu chu-i ch'ing-nien t'uan, 745
Tsen-yang shih yu-ch'ien che ch'u-ch'ien yu-li che ch'u-li, 153
Tsen-yang tso kung-tso tsung-chieh, 546

308

Tsen-yang tso i-ko kung-ch'an tang-yüan, 66
Tsen-yang tsu-chih ch'i-lai, 300
Tseng Chao-lun, 675, 702
Tseng Ch'i, 690
Tseng Sheng, 400
Tso Ch'üan, 2, 26, 213
Tso Hung-yü, 690
Tso Shun-sheng, 257, 677, 686, 690
Tsou T'ao-fen, 115, 126, 140, 141, 142, 143, 566
Tsou Yang, 173
Tsu-chih ch'i-lai, 299
Tsu-chih ch'i-lai, 298
Tsui-hou ti cha-tzu, 522
Ts'ui Kao-chün, 13
Ts'ui Yün-ch'ang, 258
Tsung-heng t'ien-hsia, 662
Tsung tung-yüan yu tsung p'eng-k'uei, 649
Ts'ung ch'i-ch'i tao pa-i-wu, 8
Ts'ung kuo-chi hsing-shih kuang-ch'a Chung-kuo k'ang-chan ch'ien-t'u, 154
Ts'ung t'ieh-mu li ch'u-lai, 821
Tu-li min-chu ho-p'ing, 626
Tu Yüan, 174
T'u-kai cheng-tang tien-hsing ching-yen, 771
T'u-ti cheng-ts'e chung-yao wen-chien hui-chi, 277
T'u-ti cheng-ts'e fa-ling hui-pien, 776
T'u-ti kai-ko chung ti chi-ko wen-t'i ho san-ko tien-hsing ching-yen, 765
T'u-ti kai-ko hou ti cheng-ts'e, 775
T'u-ti kai-ko yü cheng-tang, 758
T'u-ti tsung-chieh pao-kao, 375
T'uan-chieh k'ang-chan yü chung-kung, 116
T'uan-chieh ti ta-hui sheng-li ti ta-hui, 101
T'uan-yüan chiao-ts'ai, 751

Tung-hai ch'ü i-nien lai cheng-ch'üan kung-tso tsung-chieh pao-kao, 391
Tung-hsüeh tsung-ho chiao-ts'ai, 394
Tung-pei chiao-yü she, 528, 529
Tung-pei ch'ien-feng, 530
"Tung-pei feng-yün." See Sung-hua chiang-shang ti feng-yün.
Tung-pei heng-tuan mien, 514
Tung-pei hsing-cheng wei-yüan hui. Pan-kung t'ing, 300
Tung-pei hua-pao, 531
Tung-pei jen-min cheng-fu. Nung-lin pu, 776
Tung-pei jih-pao, 425, 529, 538, 545, 548, 615, 619, 794, 800, 802, 850
Tung-pei jih-pao, 504
Tung-pei jih-pao she, 594, 595, 650, 651, 777
Tung-pei k'ang-Jih lien-chün shih-ssu nien k'u-tou chien-shih, 518
Tung-pei san-yüeh chi, 510
Tung-pei shih-pao, 505
Tung-pei shu-tien, 104, 794, 795
Tung-pei ssu-nien lai chiao-yü wen-chien hui-pien, 529
Tung-pei ti hei-an yü kuang-ming, 525
Tung-pei wan-ch'üan chieh-fang, 516
Tung-pei wen-hua, 532
Tung-pei wen-t'i, 521
Tung Pi-wu, 2, 63, 574
Tung Shih-chin, 826, 827
Tung Shun-ts'ai, 528
Tung-yüan ch'i-lai nu-li fen-tou feng-sui Chiang Chieh-shih ti chin-kung, 652
Tung-yüan she, 328
T'ung-i chan-hsien chu wen-t'i, 727
T'ung-i chan-hsien hsia ti Chung-kuo kung-ch'an tang, 131

T'ung-i ch'u-pan she, 554
Tzu-ch'in, 192
Tzu-wei pao, 650
Tzu-yu p'i-p'an, 728
Tz'u-cheng, 609

United Democratic Army, 514, 526
United Front, 43, 68, 72, 86, 108-176, 207, 243, 727
United League for Defending China, 138
United Nations, 2, 624
United Nations Day (1944), 162
United North China University, 342, 513
United Northeast Anti-Japanese Army, 108, 513, 514, 518, 521, 525, 526, 534
United States, China policy of (see also Marshall mediation), 2, 590, 603, 612, 614, 615, 617-620, 624, 626, 630, 676, 678
United States, Communist Party of, 2, 120, 128
United States, Japan policy of, 722
USSR, 1, 43

Vocational Education Group, 146, 655, 662, 663

W. R. B., 596
Wai-chiao pu ch'ing-pao, 144
Wan-hsiang, 729
Wang Chen, 207, 227, 405
Wang Chen nan-cheng chi, 227
Wang Chia-hsiang, 43, 68, 78, 131, 207, 232
Wang Chien-ch'u, 533
Wang Ching-wei (see also Japanese collaborators), 106, 161, 166-168, 228
Wang Ching-yüan, 828
Wang Chung-ming, 259

Wang Erh-te, 657
Wang Han-min, 159
Wang Hou-sheng, 105
Wang Hsiang-li, 233
Wang Jo-fei, 18, 26, 43
Wang Kung-tu, 149, 157
Wang Ming, 2, 43, 68, 86, 106, 110, 111, 129, 131, 133, 149, 255, 256, 257, 319, 842
Wang Ping, 301
Wang Shao-t'ung, 217
Wang Shih-wei, 82, 84
Wang Shou-tao, 43, 131, 232, 405
Wang Ssu-ch'eng, 40
Wang ssu-ling-yüan tsai hou-ch'in hui-i shang ti tsung-chieh pao-kao, 653
Wang Ta-chung, 145
Wang Tsao-shih, 140
Wang Yün-sheng, 710, 720
War Criminals (see also Japanese collaborators), 2, 630, 651
Wei chih-chih nei-chan erh tou-cheng, 632
Wei Chü-hsien, 663
Wei feng-i tsu-shih erh tou-cheng, 292
Wei ho-p'ing erh fen-tou, 569
Wei k'ang-chan liu chou-nien chi-nien hsüan-yen, 73
Wei k'ang-chan ssu-chou nien chi-nien hsüan-yen, 72
Wei kung-yeh p'in ti ch'üan-mien tzu-chi erh fen-tou, 293
Wei-mo, 158
Wei shih mo yao chiao-fei yü chiao-fei tsung t'i chan yao-i, 644
Wei shun-chieh tang ti tsu-chih erh tou-cheng, 778
Wei-ta-fa-shih (pseud.). See Wei Chü-hsien.
Wei Tan-po, 17
Wei Tien-hsiang pan ho Chang Hsü-yu p'ai, 378

Wei tu-li ho-p'ing min-chu erh tou-cheng, 614
Wei t'uan-chieh chiao-yü ch'ing-nien i-tai erh tou-cheng, 746
Wei Tung-pei ti ho-p'ing min-chu erh tou-cheng, 534
Wen-chiao kung-tso hsin fang-hsiang, 329
Wen-hsien, 106
Wen-hua chiao-yü cheng-ts'e, 366
Wen-hua chiao-yü yen-chiu hui, 64, 107, 146
Wen-hui ch'u-pan she, 610
Wen-hui pao, 577
Wen-hui pao, 508
Wen I-to, 671, 675, 712, 726
Wen Ku-yin, 597
Wen-ts'ui, 730
Wen-tsung, 415
Wo lai tzu Tung-pei nu-kung ying, 820
Wo-men fan-tui nei-chan, 731
Wo-men ti chu-chang, 564
Wo-men tuan-jan yu-chiu, 155
Wo tui-yü k'ang-chan ti i-chien, 156
Women's Movement, 43, 137, 796-799
Women's University (Yenan), 256, 319
World Youth Congress, 753
Wu Han-chang, 330
Wu Han-chen, 147
Wu-han jih-pao, 509
Wu Hsien-tzu, 682, 685
Wu Jui, 234
Wu-lung hsien cheng-fu t'u-ti kai-kao tsung-chieh, 779
Wu Man-chün, 175
Wu Tsao-ch'ih, 684
Wu Wen, 260
Wu Yü-chang, 2, 43, 164, 574, 798
Wu-yüeh ti Yen-an, 261
Wu-yüeh ti Yen-an pien-chi wei-yüan hui, 261

Yalta Agreement, 524
Yang Chi, 428
Yang Chih, 829
Yang Ching-yü, 26, 513, 755
Yang Ching-yü ho k'ang-lien ti-i-lu chün, 511
Yang Erh, 598
Yeh-feng, 732
Yang Fu-ch'eng, 845
Yang Kang, 705
Yang K'uei-chang, 555
Yang Ping-an, 654
Yang Po, 807
Yang Sen, 845
Yang Shang-k'un, 195
Yang Sung, 741
Yang Tsao, 705
Yang Tun-san, 830
Yang Wei-yü, 709
Yao Ch'uan-k'eng, 664
Yeh Chien-ying, 2, 106, 211
Yeh Ch'ing. See Jen Cho-hsüan.
Yeh Hu-sheng, 14
Yeh pai-ho hua (see also Wang Shih-wei), 82
Yeh T'ing, 18, 26, 178, 187, 570
Yen-an chien-wen lu, 248
Yen-an feng-kuang, 249
Yen-an i hsüeh-hsiao, 315
Yen-an i-yüeh, 246
Yen-an jih-pao, 506
Yen-an kuei-lai, 250
Yen-an nei-mu, 247
Yen-an nei-mu, 260
Yen-an sheng-huo, 254
Yen-an shih-li ti-i wan-ch'üan hsiao-hsüeh-hsiao, 330
Yen-an ta-hsüeh kai-k'uang, 331
Yen-fou she, 240
Yen Hsi-shan, 836
Yen Pao-han, 717
Yen-t'ai jih-pao, 507
Yenan. See Border Regions: Yenan.
Yenan University, 325, 331
Yin Keng-nan, 42

Yin-shih, 861
Yin Yang, 193
Ying-ming, 609
Young China Party. See Youth Party or Ch'ing-nien tang.
Youth Party, 109, 146, 257, 655, 659, 686-690
Youth problems, 29, 51, 114
Yu-kuan cheng-chih hsieh-shang hui-i wen-chien hui-chi, 602
Yü Chen-pang, 15
Yü-chou hsin-wen, 862
Yü Chung-hua, 176
Yü-hsi jih-pao, 757
Yü Huai, 2, 727
Yü Jun-t'ang, 664
Yü-lun, 863
Yü-lun chou-pao, 599
Yü Mao Tse-tung lun Chung-kuo ko-ming, 31
Yü O pien-ch'ü shih-cheng kang-ling, 416
Yü Ta-fu, 692
Yü Tsai hsien-sheng chi-nien wei-yüan hui, 739
Yüan Ching-hsin, 262
Yüan-tung hung-huo ti chien-yin hou-ko, 524
Yüan-wang, 680
Yung-ai mu-fan, 369
Yung-cheng ai-min, 307

HOOVER INSTITUTION BIBLIOGRAPHICAL SERIES

I. *A Catalogue of Paris Peace Conference Delegation Propaganda in the Hoover Library.* 1926. 96 pp. Out of print.

II. *An Introduction to a Bibliography of the Paris Peace Conference,* by Nina Almond and Ralph H. Lutz. 1935. 32 pp. $1.00.

III. *Japanese-Sponsored Governments in China, 1937–1945. An Annotated Bibliography Compiled from the Materials in the Chinese Collection of the Hoover Library,* by Frederick W. Mote. 1954. viii, 68 pp. Out of print.

IV. *Leaders of Twentieth-Century China. An Annotated Bibliography of Selected Chinese Biographical Works in the Hoover Library,* by Eugene Wu. 1956. vii, 106 pp. $2.50.

V. *Japanese Penetration of Korea, 1894–1910; A Checklist of Japanese Archives in the Hoover Institution,* by Andrew C. Nahm. 1959. 103 pp. Out of print.

VI. *The Chinese Student Movement, 1927–1937; A Bibliographical Essay Based on the Resources of the Hoover Institution,* by John Israel. 1959. 22 pp. Out of print.

VII. *The Overseas Chinese; A Bibliographical Essay Based on the Resources of the Hoover Institution,* by Naosaku Uchida. 1959 (second printing, 1960). 134 pp. $2.50.

VIII. *The Chinese Communist Movement, 1921–1937; An Annotated Bibliography,* by Chün-tu Hsüeh. 1960. vii, 131 pp. $2.50.

IX. *Madagascar (the Malagasy Republic); A List of Materials in the African Collections of Stanford University and the Hoover Institution on War, Revolution, and Peace,* by Peter Duignan. 1962. vii, 25 pp. $1.00.

X. *Guide to Russian Reference Books. Volume I: General Bibliographies and Reference Books,* by Karol Maichel. 1962. 92 pp. $5.00.

XI. *The Chinese Communist Movement, 1937–1949; An Annotated Bibliography,* by Chün-tu Hsüeh. 1962. 312 pp. $5.00.

All orders should be directed to:
PUBLICATIONS DEPARTMENT
HOOVER INSTITUTION
STANFORD UNIVERSITY
STANFORD, CALIFORNIA